Nineteenth-Century Jewish Literature

STANFORD STUDIES IN JEWISH HISTORY AND CULTURE

EDITED BY *Aron Rodrigue and Steven J. Zipperstein*

Nineteenth-Century Jewish Literature
A Reader

Edited by Jonathan M. Hess, Maurice Samuels,
and Nadia Valman

STANFORD UNIVERSITY PRESS
STANFORD, CALIFORNIA

Stanford University Press
Stanford, California

©2013 by the Board of Trustees of the Leland Stanford Junior University.
All rights reserved.

This book has been published with the assistance of the Moses M. and Hannah L. Malkin Distinguished Professorship in Jewish History and Culture, College of Arts and Sciences, University of North Carolina at Chapel Hill, as well as the Judaic Studies Program at Yale University.

No part of this book may be reproduced or transmitted in any form or by any means, electronic or mechanical, including photocopying and recording, or in any information storage or retrieval system without the prior written permission of Stanford University Press.

Printed in the United States of America on acid-free, archival-quality paper

Library of Congress Cataloging-in-Publication Data

Nineteenth-century Jewish literature : a reader / edited by Jonathan M. Hess, Maurice Samuels, and Nadia Valman.
    pages cm. – (Stanford studies in Jewish history and culture)
"The texts collected in this volume were all written originally in English, French, or German."
Includes bibliographical references.
  ISBN 978-0-8047-7546-5 (cloth : alk. paper) –
ISBN 978-0-8047-7547-2 (pbk. : alk. paper)
   1. Jewish fiction–19th century–Translations into English. 2. English fiction–Jewish authors. 3. Jews–Fiction. I. Hess, Jonathan M., 1965- editor of compilation.
II. Samuels, Maurice, editor of compilation. III. Valman, Nadia, editor of compilation. IV. Series: Stanford studies in Jewish history and culture.
  PN6120.95.J6N56 2013
  808.83'98924–dc23
                              2012041291

ISBN 978-0-8047-8619-5 (electronic)

Typeset by Bruce Lundquist in 10.5/14 Galliard

Table of Contents

Introduction ... 1

1. *Literature and the Invention of the Ghetto*

   Leopold Kompert, "The Peddler" (1849) ... 25

   Alexandre Weill, "Braendel" (1860) ... 64

   David Schornstein, "The Tithe" (1864) ... 94

   Samuel Gordon, "Daughters of Shem: A Study in Sisters" (1898) ... 123

2. *Historical Fiction and the Sephardic Experience*

   Grace Aguilar, "The Escape: A Tale of 1755" (1844) ... 185

   Ludwig Philippson, "The Three Brothers" (1854) ... 210

   David Schornstein, "The Marranos: A Spanish Chronicle" (1861) ... 248

3. *Experiments in Jewish Realism*

   Eugénie Foa, "Rachel; or, The Inheritance" (1833) ... 293

   Ben-Lévi, "The March 17th Decree" (1841) ... 303

   Salomon Formstecher, "The Stolen Son: A Contemporary Tale" (1859) ... 312

   Amy Levy, "Cohen of Trinity" (1889) ... 346

   Israel Zangwill, "Anglicization" (1902) ... 356

4. *Fictions of Religious Renewal*

Ben Baruch, "The Preacher and the Bellows" (1844) — 387

Ben-Lévi, "The Fish and the Breadcrumbs" (1846) — 398

Sara Hirsch Guggenheim, "Aurelie Werner" (1863–64) — 407

Israel Zangwill, "Transitional" (1899) — 440

Sources — 465
Suggestions for Further Reading — 467

Nineteenth-Century Jewish Literature

Introduction

The beginnings of modern Jewish literature are rarely said to have been much before the 1880s, when eastern European authors such as S. Y. Abramovitsh (1835–1917), writing under the pen name Mendele Mocher Sforim, began to put Hebrew and Yiddish literature on the map in new ways. Indeed, both Hebrew and Yiddish literature came to achieve international prominence over the course of the twentieth century, boasting Nobel Prize laureates such as Isaac Bashevis Singer (1978) and S. Y. Agnon (1966). Singer, a Polish Jew who spent much of his adult life in the United States writing in Yiddish, and Agnon, a native of Poland who settled in Mandate Palestine as a young man and who wrote in Hebrew, are but two examples among many. In the aftermath of the Holocaust and the creation of the State of Israel, the postwar period witnessed a dramatic expansion of modern Hebrew literature. It also saw an explosion of Jewish literature written in English, with writers such as Philip Roth, Cynthia Ozick, Michael Chabon, and Jonathan Safran Foer enjoying—like Singer and Agnon before them—a wide readership of Jews and non-Jews alike.

As the literature collected in this volume makes clear, envisioning the history of modern Jewish literature as a development that begins in eastern Europe in Hebrew and Yiddish and develops to fruition in Israel and North America in Hebrew and English runs the risk of obscuring as much as it illuminates. Modern Jewish literature had a long and complex history before the 1880s, and not just among those figureheads of the Jewish Enlightenment who, starting in the late eighteenth century, inaugurated the auspicious project of reviving Hebrew as a viable literary language. In central and eastern Europe—the areas where the vast majority of European Jews lived—Jews typically used

Hebrew for ritual, prayer, and study while speaking Yiddish as their daily vernacular. With its understanding of Torah and Talmud study as a commandment and ritual to be performed publicly, premodern Jewish culture knew no equivalent to either the notion of reading as a private act of contemplation that gained ascendancy in the Christian Middle Ages or the concept of "reading for pleasure."[1] From the sixteenth century on, nevertheless, central and eastern European Jewish culture favored Torah and Talmud study and privileged Hebrew literacy at the same time as it developed a rich tradition of epics, romances, legends, fables, and chapbooks written in Yiddish, many of which survived well into the nineteenth century.[2] Indeed, in the early modern period, Yiddish literature became a fixture in the central and eastern European Jewish world, sanctioned reading material for women that was doubtlessly enjoyed by men as well, if only as a guilty pleasure acknowledged to occupy a lower cultural plane than the sacred texts men were enjoined to study.

Starting in the era of the French Revolution, large numbers of Jews across central and western Europe began to experience dramatic social, economic, and political change. Both internal Jewish reform efforts and government initiatives promoting greater integration brought about a radical restructuring of Jewish life, and Jews began to engage with, and feel part of, the non-Jewish world in ways their medieval ancestors could not have fathomed. Historians have typically described this process of integration with both the ideologically fraught term *assimilation* and the more neutral *acculturation*. During the nineteenth century, Jews experienced modernity in a variety of ways. They migrated to urban centers and took advantage of new economic opportunities, increasingly abandoning what had been traditional Jewish

---

1. See Daniel Boyarin, "Placing Reading: Ancient Israel and Medieval Europe," in *The Ethnography of Reading*, ed. Jonathan Boyarin (Berkeley: University of California Press, 1993), 10–37; also see Jeffrey Veidlinger, "Reading: From Sacred Duty to Leisure Time," in *Jewish Public Culture in the Late Russian Empire* (Bloomington: Indiana University Press, 2009), 67–113. [Unless otherwise noted, all footnotes to texts are the editors'.]

2. Jean Baumgarten, *Introduction to Old Yiddish Literature*, ed. and trans. Jerold C. Frakes (Oxford: Oxford University Press, 2005), 38–71; also Dan Miron, *A Traveler Disguised: The Rise of Modern Yiddish Fiction in the Nineteenth Century* (Syracuse, NY: Syracuse University Press, 1996), 1–3; and Stephen Lowenstein, "The Yiddish Written Word in Nineteenth-Century Germany," *Leo Baeck Institute Year Book* 24 (1979): 179–92.

professions of peddling and small-scale trading. In keeping with the ethos of nineteenth-century liberalism, they often came to privilege the individual over more communal forms of social organization. As they did so, they—like others in the nineteenth century—faced the challenge of reconciling rational and scientific worldviews with traditional religious beliefs. For Yiddish-speaking Jews in regions such as Alsace in eastern France, acculturation inevitably meant adopting a new vernacular. And just as French Jews in the nineteenth century came to speak French as their mother tongue, Jews in the German-speaking world adopted German as the language of everyday life, often identifying strongly with German language, literature, and culture. In eastern Europe, the pace of social transformation was different; clearly defined nation-states with national languages often did not emerge until after World War I; and the sheer numbers of Jews enabled Yiddish to survive well into the twentieth century. An analogous dynamic is apparent in the case of Ladino, the form of Judeo-Spanish spoken by many Jews in the Ottoman empire.[3] For Jews in central and western Europe, however, acculturation typically meant linguistic assimilation, and by the mid-nineteenth century Jews in these countries tended no longer to be versant in Jewish vernaculars.

As this anthology demonstrates, when it came to literature, Jews who grew up speaking French, German, or English in the nineteenth century hardly sought complete assimilation. To be sure, there were some prominent Jews who left Judaism behind, such as the celebrated Berlin salonière Rahel Levin Varnhagen or the writer Heinrich Heine, who famously described baptism as the "entry ticket to European civilization." The most famous English "Jew" of the era—Benjamin Disraeli, writer and prime minister—was baptized as a teenager. For the vast majority of Jews during the nineteenth century, nevertheless, modernity meant not abandoning Judaism but finding new ways of connecting with and grappling with Jewish tradition, and it is here that Jewish literature came to play such a crucial role. Recent scholarship has brought to light the existence of a dynamic world of specifically Jewish forms of

---

3. See Sarah Abrevaya Stein, *Making Jews Modern: The Yiddish and Ladino Press in the Russian and Ottoman Empires* (Bloomington: Indiana University Press, 2004); and Olga Borovaya, *Modern Ladino Culture: Press, Belles Lettres, and Theater in the Late Ottoman Empire* (Bloomington: Indiana University Press, 2011).

literature in the nineteenth century—fiction by Jews, about Jews, and in some cases designed largely for Jews. This literature contains fascinating insights into the process of Jewish acculturation and provides a vital framework for understanding developments in Jewish belles lettres during the twentieth century in central and western Europe and beyond. By offering a strategic selection of texts written in French, English, and German mostly between the 1830s and 1900, this volume gives students of Jewish literature access to an understudied chapter in modern Jewish literature.

Based on what we know about both early modern Jewish culture and nineteenth-century literature, it should come as no surprise that many of the authors whose work we present in this volume were women. Traditionally, Jewish women were much closer to vernacular literary culture than Jewish men, and the popular genre of the novel that achieved such preeminence in eighteenth- and nineteenth-century Europe was often seen in gendered terms as well, as a literary form consumed largely by women. Much of the literature presented here was first published in serialized form, in new periodicals targeting Jews, and much of it bears the markers of the other tear-jerking romances, witty social satires, sentimental melodramas, and colorful adventure tales we have inherited from the nineteenth century. Within the Jewish world of the nineteenth century, however, this literature was not seen merely as a legitimate activity for women's leisure time or as a subordinate current in Jewish life. Indeed, many of the authors whose work appears here were themselves respected rabbis and leaders of the Jewish community. The literature they wrote, like the novels by pioneering women writers such as Grace Aguilar, was typically recommended as suitable reading for men, women, and adolescents alike. In Germany, the Modern Orthodox rabbi Marcus Lehmann, who launched *Der Israelit* (1860–1938), the most significant German-Jewish orthodox newspaper of its era, regularly marketed his own collection of tales as an ideal bar mitzvah present, the perfect choice of reading material to mark Jewish boys' entry into adulthood. By the late nineteenth century, secular literature had clearly become a fixture in modern Jewish life, achieving a prominence and respectability that would have been unthinkable just a century before in a culture that had traditionally privileged men's study of sacred texts.

The texts collected in this volume were all written originally in English, French, or German, and the volume is organized according to topic and genre rather than national context in order to underscore some of the common ways in which Jewish literature grappled with the challenges of modernity. In France, England, and the German lands, the production of Jewish literature began in earnest in the 1830s and 1840s, and many of the works collected here enjoyed a particularly long shelf life. Many were translated into any number of languages and thus were consumed by a wide, international readership. The German translation of Aguilar's historical novel *The Vale of Cedars* (1850), to cite one example, went through multiple editions in the nineteenth and twentieth centuries. Like so much German Jewish literature, Aguilar's novel was translated into Hebrew, Yiddish, and numerous other languages. Eugénie Foa's novel *La Juive* (The Jewess) appeared in a German translation in 1835 just months after its French publication. Leopold Kompert's popular German-language ghetto tales were also translated into many languages, including Czech, Dutch, English, French, Hebrew, Italian, Romanian, and Yiddish. The Jewish literature presented in this volume is important, in other words, because it was a transnational phenomenon, one that both accompanied the process of integrating the Jews into the system of nineteenth-century nation-states and also transcended national boundaries.

Of course, no selection can be comprehensive. Indeed, Jewish literature was produced in many other centers of Jewish life as well. Even before the late nineteenth century, there were Russian Jews who wrote literature in Russian.[4] In the Ottoman empire, by the 1840s Ladino-language newspapers were already dominated by novellas and novels, many of which were creative adaptations of foreign material, particularly French and Hebrew sources.[5] The Danish-Jewish writer Meir Aron Goldschmidt earned international recognition for his 1846 novel *En Jøde* (A Jew), which was translated into any number of European languages in the nineteenth century. In the Netherlands there were writers

---

4. Maxim D. Shrayer, *An Anthology of Jewish-Russian Literature: Two Centuries of Dual Identity in Prose and Poetry*, 2 vols. (Armonk, NY: Sharpe, 2007).

5. See Stein, *Making Jews Modern*, 60; and Olga Borovaya, "The Role of Translation in Shaping the Ladino Novel at the Time of Westernization in the Ottoman Empire," *Jewish History* 16 (2002): 263–82.

such as Estella Hijmans-Hertzveld (1837–81), known for her poems on biblical themes. And even before mass immigration from eastern Europe brought large numbers of Jews to America, starting in the 1880s, periodicals such as Isaac Mayer Wise's *The Israelite* (launched in 1854 and called *The American Israelite* after 1874) began to publish fiction, particularly Wise's own novels. Journals like *The Occident* (1843–69) and the *American Jewish Advocate* (1843–68) also published a great deal of literature, especially by women such as Grace Aguilar, and were read widely on both sides of the Atlantic.[6] Particularly before the rise of Hebrew and Yiddish literature toward the end of the nineteenth century, however, it was in France, England, and the German lands where Jews had the most developed literary spheres. Our decision to limit this volume to texts produced in French, English, and German reflects the fact that for so many modernizing Jews in the nineteenth century, French, English, and German served as the dominant languages.

By means of the themes they invoke and the forms they take, the texts collected in this volume offer a window into the rich diversity of nineteenth-century Jewish literature. Jews during this period, of course, did not confine their reading to Jewish literature, and historians and literary critics alike have long since pointed out the importance that reading played in Jewish encounters with the non-Jewish world. For German Jews in particular there was a long tradition of claiming an elective affinity with European high culture. Part of what this volume aspires to do is to make it easier for students, scholars, and lay readers alike to enter the complex landscape of nineteenth-century literary culture to gain an understanding of the workings of popular Jewish literary forms. By focusing our attention on popular literature, much of which was originally published in Jewish newspapers and monthly journals, we gain a fresh perspective on the ways Jews used fiction to grapple with the challenges of the modern world. This volume seeks to open our eyes to the ways in which literature served Jews in the nineteenth century less as a path away from Judaism than as a new way to revisit and reinvent Jewish tradition and history,

6. See Diane Lichtenstein, *Writing Their Nations: The Tradition of Nineteenth-Century American Jewish Women Writers* (Bloomington: Indiana University Press, 1992); also Lance J. Sussman, *Isaac Leeser and the Making of American Judaism* (Detroit: Wayne State University Press, 1996).

a crucial venue for reflecting on the nature of Jewish modernity. The texts in this volume hardly represent a singular birthplace of modern Jewish literature; like any complex cultural phenomenon, Jewish literature boasts multiple birthplaces. But as we continue to think about the forms and functions of Jewish literature today, it can be instructive to dwell on the unique role that fell to literature in the nineteenth century as a site for reflecting on Jewish identities. The texts collected here should offer scholars, students, and lay readers alike an excellent place to start.

The conditions under which the texts in this volume were produced differed considerably from place to place: from Aguilar's native London, to the small town in Moravia (modern-day Czech Republic) where Sara Hirsch Guggenheim penned her novellas, to the cosmopolitan world of Paris to which Alexandre Créhange (Ben Baruch) emigrated from the French province of Lorraine. Moreover, the pace and form of modernization with which writers engaged differed across national contexts. In France, Jews gained equal rights in 1790 and 1791, during the revolution. Napoleon spread emancipation to the lands he conquered, but whereas most German states withdrew citizenship from the Jews after Napoleon's defeat in 1815, French Jews never lost their civil rights. Indeed, in 1831, the French state assumed financial responsibility for Jewish religious expenses, as it already had for the Catholic and Protestant churches. In England, Jews were free to organize worship as they wished, but were restricted from some professions and ineligible for election to Parliament until the mid-nineteenth century. Jews in the German lands, meanwhile, saw their political status improve more gradually, in fits and starts over the course of the nineteenth century. Within Jewish communities change was also registered differently. The impact of the German reform movement was felt much more lightly in both France and Britain. Among Jews in France and Britain, conversion to Christianity was negligible as a social phenomenon. In the German lands, baptism could promise greater social advantages, and conversion rates were slightly higher, although Jews there never converted in large numbers in the nineteenth century.

These various circumstances naturally produced different contexts for the production and consumption of print culture among European

Jews. While the earliest works of French-Jewish fiction were produced in the 1830s and 1840s by the first generation of Jews to be born as French citizens, German-Jewish literature emerged against the background of an ongoing public debate about the question of Jewish emancipation. Attracted by the ideology of *Bildung*, German Jews used literary culture as a means of balancing their multiple identities and allegiances, and to sustain a sense of their successful integration into the bourgeoisie.[7] In France, Jewish writers used fiction to reconcile Jewish tradition with the legacy of the French Revolution.[8] In England, Jewish literature emulated bourgeois cultural values. Writers sought to combat the perceived threat of conversion, to provide cultural uplift to the poorer classes, and to inspire sympathy and understanding in gentile readers; later in the century they came to articulate the complexities of social mobility.[9] In order to clarify the specific circumstances in which the stories in this volume were published, each is prefaced by an introduction that helps situate the text and its author locally and nationally, in terms of both literary and social history.

What is immediately apparent, however, is that the different motives and concerns that generated Jewish literature in different national contexts frequently overlapped. All the writers included here, in fact, grapple with global issues of Jewish modernization, and they often do so in strikingly similar ways. Nowhere is this more apparent than on the level of language choice. The very act of writing fiction in German, French, or English represented a major sign of acculturation. Most of the authors in this collection were writing in their native language when they wrote in German, French, or English, even if they also spoke Yiddish and used Hebrew as a liturgical language. In some instances, they belonged to the first generation of their families to speak a non-Jewish language as their daily vernacular. Writing fiction in these languages not only implied linguistic proficiency; it indicated a deep

---

7. Jonathan M. Hess, *Middlebrow Literature and the Making of German-Jewish Identity* (Stanford, CA: Stanford University Press, 2010).

8. Maurice Samuels, *Inventing the Israelite: Jewish Literature in Nineteenth-Century France* (Stanford, CA: Stanford University Press, 2010).

9. Bryan Cheyette, "'From Apology to Revolt': Benjamin Farjeon, Amy Levy and the Post-Emancipation Anglo-Jewish Novel, 1880–1900," *Transactions of the Jewish Historical Society of England* 24 (1982–86): 253–65.

familiarity with the national literary traditions to which the authors were contributing.

These authors did not simply write "Jewish" literature in German, French, or English. They produced literature that reflected the literary codes and styles of these majority cultures. The French writer Ben-Lévi, for example, displayed a confident knowledge of the French literary tradition and explicitly borrowed plot structures from his fashionable contemporary, the realist writer Honoré de Balzac. Even his orthodox counterpart, Ben Baruch, would cite the seventeenth-century French Catholic theologian Jean-Baptiste Massillon in order to make his case for a return to the Jewish religious tradition. In the Austrian empire, the Bohemian-Jewish writer Kompert did not just produce tales from the ghetto; he drew on the work of a whole host of gentile contemporaries interested in crafting new forms of German national literature with regional content. Guggenheim, writing for a modern orthodox readership in the German-speaking world, was no less entrenched in eighteenth- and nineteenth-century literature than her Jewish and non-Jewish peers; those familiar with Gotthold Ephraim Lessing's bourgeois tragedies will find numerous echoes of dramas like *Miss Sara Sampson* or *Emilia Galotti* in Guggenheim's "Aurelie Werner." And Aguilar in England, like David Schornstein in France and Ludwig Philippson in Germany, composed historical fiction that owed much to Sir Walter Scott, whose historical novels caught Europe by storm in the early nineteenth century.

The texts collected here thus illustrate just how well a certain segment of European Jewry had adopted European culture as its own in the nineteenth century. Yet these texts do not merely epitomize the modernization process; they also thematize it. Like their real-life counterparts, the Jewish characters in these texts are on the move, migrating from rural villages to urban centers. Daniel Peyser in Israel Zangwill's "Transitional" moves from Germany to Portsmouth to London, while his counterpart Solomon Cohen in "Anglicization" migrates from Russian Poland to London via the provincial English town of "Sudminster." When David Blum in Ben-Lévi's "The March 17th Decree" returns from the Napoleonic Wars, he finds his Alsatian village so transformed by industrialization as to be unrecognizable, so he makes his way to Paris. The great tragedy of a tale like Kompert's "The Peddler" is that its protagonist finds himself painfully caught between two worlds, torn between the lures of bourgeois life in Vienna and the family ties to traditional Jewish life in his native Bohemia. Some of the characters in these texts engage in traditionally Jewish forms of economic activity, such as peddling and small-scale money lending, or devote themselves to traditional religious pursuits (rabbi, cantor, scribe). Others, however, take up more modern occupations, becoming lawyers, writers, soldiers, bankers, or department store owners.

Even as they illustrate the social and demographic changes that were transforming the Jewish communities of central and western Europe, these writers explore the controversies such changes ignited. Many of these texts show how a family's rapid assimilation produces generational conflict. The father in "Anglicization" cannot countenance his son's decision to join the British army and risk his life in the Boer War. The parents of the Yeshiva students in Weill's "Braendel" fear that their children will convert to Catholicism. Other stories describe the struggle over religious reform that divided the German-Jewish community in this period. While France and England largely avoided the kind of religious schism that took place in Germany, they also experienced pressures from the reform movement as well as a rising tide of religious indifference. In these texts, we discover how nineteenth-century Jews experienced these controversies as well as the various strategies they proposed for dealing with them.

The question of intermarriage recurs frequently. Many of the characters, particularly the female characters, find themselves caught between conflicting duties, between parents who want them to marry a Jew and a desire to assert their independence through romantic self-determination. Though increased interaction between Jews and gentiles in the nineteenth century certainly made intermarriage an issue of genuine concern, the recurrence of the theme suggests that it also provided a symbolic means of exploring a more general struggle between the desire for individual freedom and the pull of religious and cultural tradition. Significantly, the authors included in this collection do not all fall on the same side of the debate. While Guggenheim and Samuel Gordon depict the negative consequences that intermarriage entails for the Jewish spouse, Foa proves much more amenable to the proposition of marrying a non-Jew, even if she stops short of depicting an actual interfaith union. For some of the women authors collected here, rebelling against

Jewish law was bound up with a larger feminist challenge to a tradition seen as patriarchal and repressive.[10]

These texts provide interesting insights into the ways that nineteenth-century Jews defined Jewishness at a time when increasing numbers were leaving traditional Jewish religious practice behind. While the pseudo-scientific racial theorizing we associate with the Nazi era did not really appear until the late nineteenth century, some Jews in the early to mid-nineteenth century were already beginning to employ what appears to be a biological or racial definition of Jewishness to express a notion of difference that was not purely religious. Jewish writers in Germany, France, and Britain often borrowed representational conventions from non-Jewish writers (such as Walter Scott) and painters (such as Eugène Delacroix) to endow their Jewish characters with a distinct physiognomy. The narrator of Foa's story "Rachel," for example, guesses at the Jewish identity of the eponymous heroine because of her long, curly black hair and pale, oval face. Similarly, the narrator in Sara Guggenheim's "Aurelie Werner" introduces this novella's Jewish protagonist by stressing her dark black hair and rich locks, which are cause for notice in the case of a woman who is otherwise a perfect example of classical beauty.

When Jewish writers in the mid-nineteenth century employed stock physical tropes to describe their Jewish characters it was often to express a sense of Jewish solidarity and to argue for Jewish political equality. As Lisa Moses Leff explains, Jewish writers in 1830s and 1840s France, particularly those associated with the Saint-Simonian movement, argued that Jews constituted one of several races found in France, each with its own distinctive physical and moral qualities, and hence deserved inclusion in the national body along with the Gauls and the Franks.[11] In Britain, at a time in which most Jews were striving to define themselves as a purely religious minority, the novelist and statesman Benjamin Disraeli used the rhetoric of race as a marker of positive Jewish traits and argued that Jews should be especially welcomed into the nation because of their noble lineage. By the late nineteenth century, in contrast, some Jewish writers re-

---

10. On Germany, see also Marion A. Kaplan, *The Making of the Jewish Middle Class: Women, Family, and Identity in Imperial Germany* (New York: Oxford University Press, 1991).

11. Lisa Moses Leff, *Sacred Bonds of Solidarity: The Rise of Jewish Internationalism in Nineteenth-Century France* (Stanford, CA: Stanford University Press, 2006), 98–99.

sorted to racial descriptions to underline their critique of contemporary Jewish urban life. In Amy Levy's fiction, for example, awkward Jewish bodies inhabit a world of social unease and crass materialism.[12]

While many of these texts are set in an identifiably modern present, others take place either in a remote historical period or in a rural space that seems almost outside of history altogether. And yet even these unmodern settings offer important insights into the process of Jewish modernization. While the Jewish tradition had always venerated its history, returning through ritualized forms of remembrance to events such as the exodus from Egypt, only in the nineteenth century did Jews begin to show an interest in their recent, diasporic past.[13] The sudden outpouring of historical fiction in the nineteenth century was part of a larger undertaking by the historians associated with the Wissenschaft des Judentums movement in Germany to write the modern history of the Jewish people. These Jewish historians sought out a useable past, one that would help solidify a sense of communal affiliation in the present, at a time when traditional forms of communal identification were waning. The great advantage of fiction in this context was the tremendous liberty it enjoyed in imagining the past, whether this was the noble legacy of Spanish Jewry before the tragedy of the Inquisition or the world of traditional Jewish village life that was quickly receding from view in the nineteenth century. Very much like Moritz Daniel Oppenheim's mass-produced prints of traditional Jewish family life that circulated widely in nineteenth-century Europe and North America, Jewish literature also manufactured a Jewish past that helped serve present-day interests. In this context, literature took on new roles as an agent and medium of historical memory.

These texts tell us about the politics of Jewish modernity, but their messages are different and not always transparent. Crucial here is the way that plot and narrative commentary are either aligned or brought into counterpoint. Many of the writers collected here, for example, use

---

12. See Nadia Valman, "The Shadow of the Harem: *Fin-de-siècle* Racial Romance," in *The Jewess in Nineteenth-Century British Literary Culture* (Cambridge: Cambridge University Press, 2007), 173–205.

13. Yosef Hayim Yerushalmi, *Zakhor: Jewish History and Jewish Memory* (Seattle: University of Washington Press, 1982), 86.

stories of the particularity of Jewish life as an opportunity, paradoxically, to affirm their patriotism as citizens of their respective nation-states. Thus Schornstein follows his model Aguilar in ending his tale of escape from the persecutions of the Spanish Inquisition with a paean to France, the land of "justice" that has granted asylum to the crypto-Jewish refugees. In "The Stolen Son," even more dramatically, Salomon Formstecher attributes the resolution of the plot and the restoration of order to a single individual, the brave Prussian consul, the "representative of the court of tolerance and intelligence" amid czarist barbarism and corruption. (The Damascus blood libel of 1840, which Formstecher's plot recalls, was in fact refuted through the intervention of an international consortium of Western notables.) But plot and narrative commentary are not always so neatly aligned. Ben-Levi's searing chronicle of the cruelties endured by one Jewish family following the Napoleonic decree of 1808, for example, ends with an extraordinary and unexpected affirmation by the suffering survivor of republican patriotism, whose values, in his view, endure despite this momentary flaw. In contrast, Zangwill's "Anglicization" ends on a note of despairing cynicism, with the Anglo-Jewish hero mourning his patriotism as an unrequited love affair. These last two examples suggest a relationship between Jews and state authority that is contradictory, unmutual, even mysterious.

These works of fiction thus shed light on many of the ideological and historical divisions that characterized the transition to modernity for Jews in central and western Europe. In doing so, they also tell us something about how nineteenth-century Jews used popular literature as a means of shoring up identities that modernity had made newly problematic. Seen together, they helped create forms of Jewish culture that were both national and transnational, a distinctly Jewish literary sphere that allowed modernizing Jews to debate the meaning of their Jewishness but in so doing bound them all the more closely to it.

With their various insights into the modernization of central and western European Jews in the nineteenth century, these texts are clearly of great historical value. But what do they offer students of literature? And what do they offer general readers? In other words, how good are they? In many ways, these writings fit squarely within the dominant generic conventions of the time—the sentimental romance, the historical novel, the adventure tale, the study of manners, and so on. By and large, they do not seek to innovate on an aesthetic level but rather affirm their adherence to the conventions of the genre in question. This makes them often predictable and occasionally trite. And yet, when we read these texts within their generic horizon—which is to say, with and against the other forms of genre fiction they resemble—we begin to appreciate the often quite witty or subtle ways in which they vary conventional structures. We also begin to appreciate the radical nature of their appropriation of the literary forms of the dominant culture for specifically Jewish ends.

These are not great writers in the way that Proust or Kafka or Bellow or Roth are great writers. For the most part, they are not very linguistically inventive. Their use of German, French, or English is with some exceptions quite standard. Aside from the occasional interjection of a Yiddish or Hebrew word or phrase, they generally write just as most of their non-Jewish contemporaries did—in a language that may strike twenty-first century readers as quaint or outdated. (The translations of French and German texts presented here strive to preserve the feeling of the original through the use of a nineteenth-century vocabulary, syntax, and cadence.) Indeed, one often has the feeling that these writers are performing their sense of belonging to the linguistic community in question through the very conventionality of their language.

Beneath these surface similarities, however, lies a highly innovative project of adapting European literary forms to fit new Jewish needs. These texts have important lessons to teach us about German, French, and English literature precisely because of their knowing, responsive, and imaginative use of elements of contemporary style and genre. This volume is structured, accordingly, to foreground the creative ways in which Jewish writers recast contemporary fashions in literature to address issues of specific interest to a rapidly changing Jewish community. Despite significantly varying local contexts, a number of key themes and forms preoccupied Jewish writers across England, France, and the German-speaking world. Each of the four sections of this volume focuses thus on a different mode of Jewish literary engagement with contemporary European literature.

The first two sections bring together Jewish versions of two extremely popular fictional genres of the period: the village tale and the historical novel. In different ways, both are the literary stepchildren of Sir Walter Scott, the dominant influence on fictional attempts to grapple with the upheavals of modernity in the nineteenth century. Scott's novels, set in the British past but widely read throughout Europe, depicted the difficult struggle toward national unity through the reconciliation of ethnic or religious differences. In continental Europe, however, these texts tended to be read for their detailed representations of local or regional folklore, custom, and dialect facing the threat of state-imposed modernity—and it was in these terms that Scott's influence was most strongly felt.[14]

The genre of the village tale, which was later to be used to such famous effect by George Sand and George Eliot, was in fact pioneered in German by the Jewish writers Berthold Auerbach and Alexandre Weill in the 1840s. Auerbach and Weill did not focus exclusively on Jewish life, however, but on the tolerant environment of the villages of the Black Forest and Alsace respectively, where Christians and Jews lived and worked together amicably, both equally resisting the encroachment of metropolitan regulations and attitudes. While subsequent writers in this genre were more explicitly antimodern, Jewish writers in the village story and "ghetto story" tradition, observes Josephine Donovan, "notably Auerbach, Weill, Kompert, and Franzos . . . evinced a desire to preserve local ethnic particularity while embracing the emancipatory ideals of modernity."[15] Several of the texts in our selection embody the particularly Jewish adaptation of the village tale that became known already in the 1850s as the ghetto tale. These texts encompass precisely such contradictory impulses, including themes like the appeal of secular education in "Braendel" and "Daughters of Shem," the small-mindedness of village gossip in "The Tithe," and the complex representation of "The Peddler" who is both narrow in his theology and boldly generous in his dealings with his gentile peasant clients. Formally, the narratives shift between recording the detail of Jewish familial and communal life and imaginatively evoking the ghetto as an otherworldly, fantastical place. While Kompert's educated protagonist observes his traditional

---

14. Josephine Donovan, *European Local-Color Literature: National Tales, Dorfgeschichten, Romans Champêtres* (New York: Continuum, 2010), 97–137.
15. Ibid., 104.

family with ethnographic detachment, other stories move their readers through more mystical plot devices (such as the miraculous lottery win that restores social harmony in "The Tithe" or Braendel's self-identification as biblical prophetess).

Ghetto nostalgia would go on to become a major theme in modern Jewish literature, and it served a complex function for Jews in the throes of acculturation. It is not a coincidence that Sholem Aleichem's stories about life in the eastern European shtetl, which were adapted as the 1964 Broadway musical *Fiddler on the Roof*, would have such an appeal for American audiences in the middle of the twentieth century, at just the moment that the children of eastern European immigrants had finally begun to feel fully American. These sanitized and idealized visions of the Jewish past helped assimilating Jews to mourn for a lost world as well as to ensure that that this world was safely dead and buried. The Jewish writers in France, Germany, and the Austrian empire who pioneered this modern form of Jewish nostalgia—such as Kompert, Weill, and Schornstein—faced the same paradoxical longing for a past they hoped to leave behind but did so several generations before their eastern European and American counterparts.[16]

While the invention of the ghetto created a Jewish space seemingly outside of time, the stories in the second section of this book seek to place Jews at the center of historical change. In these tales, crypto-Jews escape the oppressions of an archaic regime—Inquisition Spain—for modern liberal states or modernizing projects. Grace Aguilar, the English progenitor of Sephardic historical fiction, drew from late eighteenth-century Gothic fiction the titillating tropes of the persecuted heroine, jealous suitor, torture dungeon, and corrupt clergy, and her Jewish versions of the genre were well placed to appeal to popular anti-Catholicism as well as Jewish readers in early Victorian England.[17] In writing historical novels, Aguilar, Philippson, and Schornstein drew heavily on popular forms of sentimental melodrama typical of the his-

---

16. On the phenomenon of "ghetto nostalgia," see Richard I. Cohen, "Nostalgia and 'Return to the Ghetto': A Cultural Phenomenon in Western and Central Europe," in *Assimilation and Community: The Jews in Nineteenth-Century Europe*, ed. Jonathan Frankel and Steven J. Zipperstein (Cambridge: Cambridge University Press, 1992), 147–50.

17. Nadia Valman, "Women of Israel: Femininity, Politics and Anglo-Jewish Fiction," in *The Jewess in Nineteenth-Century British Literary Culture* (Cambridge: Cambridge University Press, 2007), 85–129.

torical romance. But they were also participating in one of the key forms of philosophical fiction of their age. Inspired, like the village tale, by the example of Walter Scott, the historical novel resonated with the impulse in Romantic nationalism to look to the past to provide narratives of struggle, triumph, or martyrdom that could authorize newly emerging identities. In Scott's novels, as Murray Pittock argues, "writers across Europe could find analogues for the historic struggles of their own societies, and . . . develop a fictional articulation of the anteriority of the national self for the first time in their history."[18]

For Jews too, this genre represented a popular, accessible form of the new historical consciousness that proposed Jewish history, rather than revelation, as the basis for modern Jewish identity. Jews creatively adapted the forms of historical fiction—a genre often linked to nineteenth-century projects of nation-building—to the needs of a minority within the nation-state and beyond it. Indeed, in each of these stories, Jewish destiny following the flight from Spain entails not just finding a new home but embracing a world-historical mission—whether as emissaries of tolerance, in the case of Aguilar and Schornstein, or, much more strikingly in the case of Philippson, as agents of religious, economic, and military progress both among and beyond Jewish communities. Just as importantly, Scott's pan-European bestseller *Ivanhoe* (1819) had helped establish a set of conventions for depicting Jews—and especially for depicting Jewish women—that we find repeated in many of the texts collected here. But these Jewish writers also responded to Scott by reversing some of his key assumptions about the place of Jews within the modern European nation-state. Whereas Scott's novel has its Jewish characters leave England for Muslim Spain, where in the twelfth century Jews still enjoyed greater freedom, all of the literary texts here show Jews escaping from Spain to find new adoptive homelands. If Scott's historical novel attempted to forge a sense of national identity through the exclusion of the Jew, the Jewish writers who imitated him argued that Jews belonged in their European homelands.[19]

18. Murray Pittock, "Scott and the European Nationalities Question," introduction to *The Reception of Sir Walter Scott in Europe*, ed. Murray Pittock (London: Continuum: 2006), 6.
19. On Scott's female Jewish imitators in England, see Michael Galchinsky, *The Origin of the Modern Jewish Woman Writer: Romance and Reform in Victorian England* (Detroit: Wayne State University Press, 1996).

The usable past that Jewish historical fiction created by focusing on the Jewish experience in Spain was also a traumatic past. With their fixation on the bloody period of the Spanish Inquisition and on the horrible suffering it inflicted on Jews for being Jews, Jewish writers of historical fiction adapted dominant tropes in contemporary European literature and used them to underscore Jewish suffering. In doing so, they created a type of Jewish fiction that is in many ways still with us, a literature that channels past trauma into justification for modern affiliation—a role played by much Holocaust fiction today.

The third section, "Experiments in Jewish Realism," showcases the variety of fictional forms deployed by nineteenth-century Jewish writers. Formstecher's "The Stolen Son" recasts recent events in European Jewish history, the Mortara kidnapping case of 1858 and the Damascus blood libel of 1840, within the plot structure of a Dickensian melodrama, involving concealed identities, coincidence, and dramatic reversals of fortune. In "Anglicization," Zangwill likewise adapts the form of social satire used by Charles Dickens and Anthony Trollope to reflect on the social ambition of Anglo-Jews and the confusions of identity it produces. But Jewish subjects also push some of these writers to the limits of narrative form. In 1886 the Anglo-Jewish writer Amy Levy claimed that the Jew was an unduly neglected but especially interesting subject for the novel because of "his surprising virtues and no less surprising vices; leading his eager, intricate life; living, moving, and having his being both within and without the tribal limits."[20] The complex double consciousness of the Jew that Levy identifies here is evident in the fiction collected in this volume. Kompert's "The Peddler," for example, is structured through a dual narrative, in which the third-person narration recounting Emanuel's observations of the ghetto household to which he returns incognito is repeatedly intercut with an epistolary narrative where he documents his inner turmoil. By contrast, Foa's and Levy's stories, with their unreliable narrators, suggest the enigmatic and ultimately unknowable nature of the unhappy Jewish protagonists.

The texts in the final section, "Fictions of Religious Renewal," indicate that, alongside their new explorations of Jewish pasts and places, nineteenth-century Jewish writers continued to foreground questions of

---

20. Amy Levy, "The Jew in Fiction," *Jewish Chronicle*, 4 June 1886, 13.

religion. Religious controversy remained a vibrant resource for literary fiction, whether in the form of Ben Baruch's parable, Ben-Lévi's philosophical dialogue, or Guggenheim's and Zangwill's sentimental romances. These stories engage directly with the spiritual challenges facing Jews across Europe in the nineteenth century from both inside and outside Jewish communities: how or whether to reconcile religion and rationality, Christianity and Judaism, individual desire and kinship loyalty. In using literature as a forum for theological debate, these writers gave ordinary readers access to the arguments articulated more abstractly by religious leaders and pamphleteers. In turn these texts, read together, give us a sense of European Judaism in the nineteenth century, not as moribund, but as a continually evolving, living tradition in which literature was beginning to take on roles that would have been inconceivable a century earlier.

The texts collected in this volume all attest to the vibrant and seminal nature of the Jewish literature that was produced by nineteenth-century Jews writing in English, French, and German. In its intense and dynamic engagement with general European culture, this literature opens our eyes to the complexity of an understudied chapter in modern Jewish literature. It arguably also constitutes an early example of minority or ethnic fiction in the European tradition, analogous to the Scottish and Irish "national tale" genre of the early nineteenth century that was widely read beyond the British Isles. Writing in major European languages but from the perspective of a minority group, these writers show how dominant languages and cultural registers could be used to express the needs, desires, and longings of the marginalized. Moreover, the themes that we find repeated in this nineteenth-century Jewish literature—the conflict between generations, the struggle of women against patriarchal tradition, the attractions and dangers of assimilation—clearly foreshadow many of the concerns of postcolonial or immigrant writers from a wide variety of cultural traditions today. While we are not arguing that these Jewish writers offer an example to follow, or that the solutions they propose to the problems facing minority groups are still valid, they do represent an important historical precedent for minority writers seeking to express themselves within a dominant, hegemonic literary tradition.

What did reading Jewish literature mean for Jews in the nineteenth century? Like so much of the literature we have inherited from the period, many of the texts collected here reflect on this issue explicitly. The young impressionable minds of Weill's Joël and Gordon's Zillah are opened up to possibilities outside their traditional Jewish worlds by their secular reading, generating a fear that was often expressed in eastern European Jewish literature as well.[21] Foa's tragic heroine Rachel, forced to fend for herself after her husband abandons her, is, as if in self-punishment, gradually killing herself through writing.

Perhaps the most haunting story of reading, however, is that recounted in Kompert's "The Peddler." As an inset narrative, offered by Channe, the mother, as a reward for her young son's diligent Talmud study, the story holds an ambiguous aura of pleasure and threat, and it is tantalizingly withheld from the reader until the very end of the text. In the event, however, it is related by the narrator himself, Emanuel, who uses it to reveal his own identity as the prodigal son, a new incarnation of the boy in the story. In the story, a boy who loves reading is led away to a distant city and to conversion to Christianity by the lure of finding the ending to a book (presumably a New Testament) that he has been given. As a result, his mother dies, but at the moment of her death he sees a vision of her, in which she demands: "Do you think that if you had stayed with me you wouldn't have found out the end of that book? Stand up and repent!"

With its combination of reason and high emotion, this parable holds within its cryptic form the same paradoxes that produce the moving dramas in this volume. It powerfully suggests the danger, seduction, and pain associated with reading and the new horizons to which it leads. And yet, in her chastisement of her apostate son, the ghostly mother does not advocate the prohibition of reading. On the contrary; what she challenges is his assumption that Judaism is inadequate—incapable of providing spiritual closure. Her words also recall him to his youthful days spent illicitly reading fragments from the community *genizah* (the repository for sacred texts that have been damaged but cannot be destroyed). However partial the text, the boy's brilliance always enabled him to reconstruct the whole narrative. The mother's

---

21. See, for example, Iris Parush, *Reading Jewish Women: Marginality and Modernization in Nineteenth-Cenury Eastern European Jewish Society* (Waltham, MA: Brandeis University Press, 2004), esp. chap. 7, "'A Hebrew Maiden, Yet Acting Alien': Women Who Read European Languages," pp. 207–26.

words thus call him back to Judaism and to her, but crucially they also remind him of the powers of his own analytic mind, which can figure out endings for himself without needing to be given them. The texts collected in this volume offered acculturating nineteenth-century Jews the chance to experience the thrill of fiction—the encounter of other minds, the exploration of other destinies, the experience of other worlds—but without leaving Jewish culture behind. Like a *genizah*, these texts emerge from the archive of the nineteenth century to provide modern readers with the equal thrill of reconstructing a crucial moment in the Jewish past.

Section 1 *Literature and the Invention of the Ghetto*

Leopold Kompert, "The Peddler" (1849)
Translated from the German by Jonathan M. Hess

Leopold Kompert (1822–86) hailed from the Jewish district of a small town in Bohemia, a region of the Austrian empire that is part of the Czech Republic today. Kompert was part of a generation of Bohemian Jewish intellectuals who left behind the relatively insular worlds inhabited by their ancestors and took advantage of new possibilities open to Jews in the Austrian empire. Like many of his peers, Kompert attended German-language schools and universities, eventually coming to identify wholeheartedly with both democratic politics and the liberating force of secular culture. After stints as a private tutor, he became a journalist and eventually established himself as a writer in Vienna, where he held offices in the Jewish community and served on the city council.

Kompert's literary career began in earnest with his breakout volume *Aus dem Ghetto* (From the Ghetto, 1848), a collection of tales that built on the interest in regionalism and local color that dominated much German prose fiction in the aftermath of Berthold Auerbach's best-selling *Schwarzwälder Dorfgeschichten* (Black Forest Villages Tales, 1843). The ghetto tale eventually came to be one of the dominant genres of German-Jewish literature in the nineteenth century. Kompert was not the first bard of the Jewish ghetto, but following the publication of *Aus dem Ghetto* and its sequel volumes—*Böhmische Juden* (Bohemian Jews, 1851), *Neue Geschichten aus dem Ghetto* (New Stories from the Ghetto, 1860), and *Geschichten einer Gasse* (Stories from the Jew's Street, 1864)—he became one of the most popular. His works went through numerous editions in the nineteenth century, enjoyed a wide readership among Jews and non-Jews alike, and were translated into many languages, including Czech, Dutch, English, French, Hebrew, Italian, Romanian, and Yiddish.

"Der Dorfgeher" (The Peddler) first appeared in 1849 in Julius Fürst's weekly newspaper *Der Orient*, a periodical that targeted both Jews and non-Jews interested in Jewish scholarship and current events. It was subsequently republished in Kompert's second major anthology of ghetto tales, *Böhmische Juden*, and republished yet again in Kompert's complete works. In its explicit concern with the tensions between tradition and modernity, its treatment of assimilation and intermarriage, and its sympathetic portrayal of traditional Jewish life, it exemplifies Kompert's efforts to create prose narratives for the general public celebrating the noble sufferings of the Jewish past.

※

One Friday afternoon, a hurried boy carrying a heavy folio volume under his left arm came leaping out of the rabbi's house, which stood right next to the synagogue. The child seemed to be around eleven, and his face was glowing. Perhaps this was due to the passion of inner excitement, or simply to the weight of the book he was carrying. In this moment, at any rate, he had a wonderfully beautiful expression on his face! Lots of people were either standing around or walking through the street, but no one thought to ask this boy about his rosy cheeks or the drops of dew glistening on his forehead! To do so one would have had to have been God himself, but also without compassion. Disturbing children when they are running with joy is like throwing stones into the path of the blind, and the Bible forbids this!

But when the boy went by the "Schlafstube," the place where itinerant beggars sleep on the Sabbath, one of these guests did not want to let him go by without asking him a question.

"Young boy," the beggar exclaimed, "can you tell me something?"

Like someone running down a steep mountain, the child could only make himself stop with considerable effort.

"What?" he asked while turning himself around, with quiet frustration visible at the corners of his mouth.

"Can you tell me where Schimme Prager lives? I have a 'plett'[1] for him, I'm supposed to eat at his home for the Sabbath."

"And why shouldn't I know that?" the boy exclaimed, astonished. "He's my father."

The beggar hurriedly took several steps toward the boy.

"Is that really true, what you're saying?" he asked, eagerly grabbing him by the hand. His voice was marked by inexpressible trembling.

"Who else should be my father?" the child asked.

---

1. An assignment, given out by the clerk of the community, to dine at a Jewish home on the Sabbath. [Author's note.]

It was clear that he was put off, the way spirited children often are when people ask uncomfortable questions about their parents.

"I'm sorry, I'm sorry," the beggar continued with the same level of hurried excitement. "Isn't your name Benjamin, my child, and don't you have a sister named Rösele? Doesn't she have beautiful black hair? And is she still so full of such infectious, heartfelt happiness? Does she still sing such magnificent songs, particularly on Friday evenings, when father comes home from the synagogue? You know, 'Salem Alechem, Alechem Salem.'[2] And your mother, of course! Her name is Channe. Praised be God, is she still doing well and healthy? Does she still wear the black velvet hair covering and the gold ducat around her neck?"

Suddenly the beggar stopped, putting his hand over his mouth as if he had betrayed too much. He then said quietly, with a smile, "If you know, my child, where Reb Schimme Prager lives, take me there—so long as you're willing."

Benjamin—and this was in fact his name—was so astonished and agitated that he did not know what to make of the strange appearance of the beggar. Never had anyone inquired into his family circumstances in such an intimate and penetrating way. The boy could not respond.

Strangely, the beggar did not seem to be waiting for a response. Looking downward, but with a marvelous smile on his lips that became more beautiful and victorious the further they went, he walked alongside the boy through all the meanderings of the street, even through the dark passageways that were difficult to navigate without a guide. All of a sudden they stood before Reb Prager's home, and the boy seemed to recall the enthusiasm with which he had left the rabbi's house. He tore himself away from his companion with a powerful leap and went into the house. The beggar remained outside at the door. He did not dare enter.

"Didn't I tell you," he heard the boy call out, "that I would be able to read my first page of Talmud on Friday? I kept my word, mother, now it's your turn."

"Yes, yes, my child," a female voice agreed, and hearing this voice turned the beggar pale. "Yes, yes, but not before father has had the

---

2. "Shalom Aleichem" in Hebrew, "Sholem Aleychem" in standard Yiddish, or "Salem Alechem" in the Yiddish dialect used by Kompert were standard forms of greeting among central and eastern European Jews. The song referred to here is a traditional Jewish song for welcoming the Sabbath.

chance to examine you on the page of Talmud. Nowadays, Benjamin, one has to be careful. But he'll have pleasure enough when he gets home. Do you want an advance?"

To the beggar, who was eavesdropping, it seemed as if the mother had planted two tender kisses on the cheeks of her child before Benjamin could even answer. For several minutes this sweet exchange of giving and taking seemed to continue. The beggar felt powerful tremors raging through his veins and had to hold onto the door. He heard Benjamin telling his mother about meeting a "peculiar" beggar whom he had left outside.

At that point both mother and child stepped outside, and the beggar barely had time to jump to the side.

"God welcome you, guest," the mother said. "Do you have a plett for me?"

Unable to speak, the beggar handed her his written assignment for the Sabbath meal. He was dumbfounded when, with a hand gesture, the mother refused the piece of paper and said, "How am I supposed to get by? I'm sorry. I have to send you back. I can't keep you here. My Shabbes is already made, and I wasn't counting on you."[3]

"So I have to leave?" the beggar asked, trembling, his eyes fixed on the ground. "You don't want to keep me here for the Sabbath?"

The mother, taken aback and overcome by the peculiar, painful tone of this exclamation, looked carefully at the beggar. She did not know what to make of his concern. But then she said, speaking from her magnificent heart, "Nu, nu, if you're so interested in poor people's food, then stay, my guest.[4] On Shabbes you shouldn't go hungry. God knows that Channe Prager doesn't run a household where she feeds five mouths but can't manage to feed a sixth."

"Do you know what?" Benjamin said suddenly, "I'll give our guest my portion of the fish!"

"Nu, do you see, guest?" the mother continued, smiling at the boy triumphantly. "Nu, do you see that you'll have plenty to eat? Benjamin will give you his fish, and there will be a piece of *barches* for you as well.[5]

---

3. *Shabbes* is Yiddish for "Sabbath."
4. The Yiddish interjection *nu*, meaning "so" or "well," appears in the original.
5. White bread for the Sabbath. [Note in the original; *Barches* was the term generally used in German and western Yiddish for challah, the ceremonial bread used for the Sabbath.]

Come, you must stay. My son Elijah is far away from home. Do I know whether he'll have a Shabbes dinner tonight? How could I have forgotten that? So please come, you won't go hungry, I'll make sure of it."

Fortunately, at this very moment Reb Schimme Prager, the master of the house, came home, making it unnecessary for the beggar to respond or express his gratitude. The heavy pack on his back clearly identified him as a peddler. Benjamin flew over to him and exclaimed, "Welcome, father, welcome, father! Do you know that I can read my first page of Talmud?"

Before responding, Reb Schimme placed his hand on the holy place on the doorpost where "Shaddai," the secret name of God, peered out through a little shining glass window. He then brought his hand reverently up to his lips. This made the entire figure of the peddler appear higher and mightier than it had seemed at first sight. It was as if proximity to God were elevating him above the load of his pack and above himself. His face was easier to make out, it was one of those countenances that only the ghetto knows: a furrowed brow marked by grief, trouble, and the difficulties of life. The beggar was startled deeply at this sight.

Walking on into the room, the peddler tossed off his pack like a giant caterpillar and finally said, "That's what you say, Benjamin, my dear, but what does the world say about this? Nowadays it's hard to put one over on people, and a page of Talmud isn't easy."

"So why don't you test me?" Benjamin said with a pride that was easy to comprehend.

"Now that's the way to talk," the peddler said while nodding his head. "Since you're so eager and ready, why don't we go see our cousin Reb Jaikew tomorrow? What do you say? Let's go to our pious cousin Reb Jaikew, and you'll tell him, 'Cousin, you must examine me. My father doesn't believe that I can already read my first page of Talmud.' And Benjamin dear, let me tell you, if you pass his test like a good boy should, then I'll have a new jacket made for you, one befitting a nobleman. We'll go to Reb Maier the cloth merchant, and you can pick out the fabric yourself."

At this point, Channe came forward. The good mother that she was, she wanted her child to have the pleasure of greeting his father first. "Schimme," she said with a trace of anger, "so what's this? You don't even greet your wife?"

The peddler smiled at her and reached out his hand. She was appeased. "What kind of a week did you have, Schimme?" she asked.

"I had a week like never before, Channe dear. I made some money, but the best thing was the pretty peasant woman, yes, the pretty peasant woman." While saying this, the peddler smiled enigmatically.

"What's with this peasant woman?" Channe spoke up, and the mother's otherwise pale and dear face turned a beautiful red. But laughing, she continued, "Maybe you're in love, Reb Schimme? That's just what I need!"

"Maybe, maybe," the peddler smiled, even more enigmatically.

"Your days are past, my dear Reb Schimme," Channe said, shaking her shoulders. "You're an old little apple, and a sour one too."

"But I should live and be happy," the father called back, laughing. "She's giving me grief, but the peasant woman, my pretty peasant woman, I can't stop thinking about her."

The beggar kept his eyes fixed on husband and wife while this peculiar scene was going on. Now that it was over, he didn't know where to look. But when Reb Schimme turned away from the mother and went on about his enigmatic "peasant woman," he noticed the beggar standing at the door. "Salem Alechem," he said, shaking his hand.

"Alechem Salem," the beggar responded.

"Where do you come from?" the examination began.

"I—I come from Hungary."

"What are you really? To me you don't really look like a beggar. There's something else about you."

"Me?—I'm a teacher."

"And you're going begging like this? Don't you have a father and a mother?

"Yes, they should both live to a hundred."

"Let me ask you something foolish. What's your father's name?"

"My father's name is . . . Reb Schimme. My mother's name is . . . Channe!"

Husband and wife looked at each other with surprise. It seemed that the mother now had a whole series of questions for the beggar, yet at that moment, much to their horror, they heard the happy voice of the caretaker of the synagogue calling out that the Sabbath was about to begin. Channe remembered that she still had work to do in the kitchen and in the house; the lamp had not yet been filled, and Benjamin had not even twisted the wicks yet; the white tablecloths had not been set out either. And what about Reb Schimme? He was still wearing the peddler's attire he wore during the rest of the week and he had not even shaved yet. The beggar excused himself. He had to tear himself away forcefully from the ground on which he, like Moses, was supposed to have stood with bare feet.[6] As he passed by the mother working outside in the kitchen, she called after him that he should not have hard feelings, and that he should not forget to come later that day. She had grown to like him, this foreign and strange guest! Walking quickly, he left the house and went back to the "Schlafstube."

An excerpt from a letter from Emanuel to Clara

Your teacher's lessons have yielded far too little fruit, my dear Clara! Two hours in the ghetto have convinced me that you do not know Jews and Judaism at all! Why is this? I have never told you what it is all really about, the unfathomable, intangible perfume of the wine—I mean the spirit. There's one thing you should think about, Clara. The *world spirit* that died on the cross with the blond Rabbi of Nazareth started off in a ghetto like this one. Indeed, I tell you, glimmers and buds are still alive today among its inhabitants! Two hours have convinced me of this . . .

I have already seen my parents, and neither of them recognized me. My little brother Benjamin is one of those late flowers of marital love that God sends those people whom he wants to ensure will smile at each other for a long time. I met him by chance in the street! This boy's face is intelligent and alive and marked by a wonderful beauty. Then I went to my mother and stood across from her! I flirted with the danger of being recognized much as one might play with a sharp tool that could easily draw blood. But no one recognized me. I could have been a great actor.

Do not fear for me, my beloved girl! I know how necessary it is for my peace of mind to remain in this situation! My longing is now satisfied. I have seen them all before the waves of an old faith

---

6. In Exodus 3:5, Moses is asked to take off his sandals before approaching the holy ground where the burning bush is located.

engulf me and I rise up again at the shore of a new faith, where God's love awaits me in human form. Do not fear!

You cannot imagine what strange company I am keeping as I write you this letter. I am in a "Schlafstube," the place where heaps of Jewish beggars sleep when Sabbath brings them to the ghetto. I am one of these! Tattered figures from all parts of the earth—Polish, German, and Hungarian beggars—are loafing around me. I am writing this letter in their company. Two steps away from me is a Polish woman nursing her sick child. The once beautiful features of her face are weathered and destroyed by grief, but her eyes—they have often reminded me of yours.

The Sabbath is entering the ghetto, and to hold onto my quill any longer begins to be a sin. Let me close. I shall see you soon, dear Clara!

Emanuel returned from the synagogue to his parents' brilliantly lit Sabbath room to find his father singing the ancient melody of the song of peace, "Salem Alechem, Alechem Salem." Reb Schimme walked back and forth in the room as he sang, and Benjamin sat at the table looking at his prayer book. The boy had a delicate voice that was high-pitched and welcoming, ringing out like a small silver bell over the father's bass, which was also not unpleasant to the ear. Benjamin often sang alone while the father was silent, the bright sounds of the boy's voice resonating upward into the room like a whirling lark. Occasionally, when Benjamin "slipped over" a word by accident, his father would correct him, and the song would then burst forth from the boy's lips even more triumphantly and marvelously. This lasted for about a quarter of an hour, during which time Emanuel sat in a corner of the room, as would seem appropriate for a guest, strangely moved by his father and brother's duet.

At times it was as if he heard deep, heartfelt sobbing in the room. He turned around and peered into the shadow of the oven, where his bed had once stood, where he had had his first dreams. He saw there, in this same bed, a female figure burying her head in the pillows. This must be his sister Rösele! So she was no longer singing the beautiful Sabbath song which Benjamin was now chanting with his magical voice? Was there no more peace in her breast? Was she no longer as happy and joyful as in those distant times in the past?

At that moment, Reb Schimme interrupted his song to let Benjamin's voice continue on alone, and he too noticed the girl's suppressed cries. With his hands crossed over his back he stopped in front of the mother who was staring into the lamp light deep in thought.

"What's with *her* again?" he asked, pointing toward Rösele with an almost angry shrug of the shoulders. "Why does she have to ruin my Shabbes?"

"Do I know?" Channe responded with a series of silent and lively gestures as is so typical in the ghetto. "Do I know what's wrong with her? She's probably distraught."

"If you're distraught, then sit at the table," Reb Schimme called out to Rösele. "But don't ruin the holy Shabbes for me."

But the girl did not even hear these words. The sobbing grew stronger. Benjamin was now singing a jubilant song accompanied by the father's rumbling bass, but even this could not cover up Rösele's crying, which poured forth from her heart more and more forcefully. Now that it had finally been noticed, the crying became loud weeping, like a hidden roaring stream that had broken through a dam.

Reb Schimme stood in front of Channe once again. With both his voice and gestures he asked her again, but much more gently and quietly than before, "Why? What's wrong with her again? I'm a poor, tormented man, and why does the one day in the week which I can enjoy with my wife and child need to be ruined like this? This is like screaming up at God. Do I have such pleasure from my peddling that she can't leave me alone just for today?"

"Try to convince her with such wisdom, if you can," Channe said, with concern. "Do you have eight hundred gulden in your sack?[7] Can you make her a wedding? Once you can do that, she'll change. But let her cry now. Sometimes a girl needs to cry simply because she was born."

"Shema Yisroel!"[8] exclaimed Reb Schimme, smacking his hands together. "So my own wife and my own child don't want to believe that I'm a poor, tormented man? Wouldn't I already have brought Rösele under the canopy six times if I had been able to afford it?"

---

7. The gulden was the official currency of the Austrian empire during the period in which this novella is set.

8. "Shema Yisroel" or "Shema Yisrael" (Hear O Israel) (Deut. 6:4) is the beginning of one of the most important Jewish prayers.

"Have you ever heard me say this?" Channe spoke back. "Do you think I don't know where God lives? Just one thing I'll say. Our children give us nothing. If you have daughters, they make you gray before you manage to marry them off. And a boy? He'll move away from home and act as if he has neither father nor mother. What do we get from Elijah, for instance? Do you even know where he is?"

"Now she's starting with *that*," Reb Schimme said with a defensive hand gesture, as if he wanted to stifle not just his wife's words but the whole train of painful thoughts they threatened to bring forth. "I beg you, Channe, don't ruin my Shabbes."

At precisely that moment Benjamin finished singing King Solomon's "A Woman of Valor."[9] He was such an excellent singer that he saved the most beautiful trills for the end, and the final notes of the song jumped, swirled, and hissed like the last sparks hopping up and down from the cinders of a burning piece of paper. The contrast between Rösele's tearful heartache and the all-consuming joy of Benjamin's childlike spirit cut to the heart of Emanuel's soul. Benjamin brought the prayer book to his lips, kissed the pages he had just finished singing, and closed it. He then looked around the room, bright-eyed, as if to ask whether anyone could still be distressed after a song like this.

And in fact, Rösele's crying had subsided. She stood up, and Emanuel was able to peer into the pale face of a lost beauty, seeing the distraught traits of an old maid. He did not recognize the Rösele of his childhood.

"Should I set the table?" she asked peacefully, as if she had never known a care in the world.

"Why are you asking?" Reb Schimme responded, seeming angry, but then he quickly added, "Have I already given you my blessing today, Rösele? It seems to me that I haven't."

Without answering, Rösele bowed down her head, and her father placed his hands on her head, getting ready to bless her. Emanuel only saw his lips move; he didn't hear the blessing.

"Your mother went with me for six years before we could make a wedding," he said, as if trying to console her. "With God's help you'll get your Shmuel this year yet. Is there more that you want?"

Emanuel was deeply disturbed, for he recognized that the family

---

9. Proverbs 31. [Note in the original; the full citation is Prov. 31:10–31.]

scene he had just witnessed was likely nothing new. His sister's composure was almost mechanistic now. Clearly, she had had more than her share of suffering in the past. The accusations that the father hurled at her of forcefully disturbing the Sabbath seemed to be part of the family routine.

Emanuel found his place at the table next to his little brother Benjamin. As soon as the washing of the hands and the prayers over the Sabbath bread were over, the father seemed to regain his original cheerful spirit.

"Channe, my dear," he exclaimed happily during the meal. "Do you want I should tell you about my pretty peasant woman?"

"I have other things on my mind," she responded, annoyed. "Where is our Elijah now? I'd much rather speak about *him*."

"You think I carry him around with me in my sack?" the peddler cried out in laughter. "What would I know about him?"

"God, God!" the mother cried out, driven by a sudden burst of emotion that she could not suppress. "I'd give half my life to see my Elijah again, if only for just one minute, just enough time to say, 'Why don't you come back to me, my son?'"

What a peculiar mystery of the soul! This mother spent the entire evening thinking about nothing but her son. This was not caused by a certain resemblance to Emanuel, or by a gesture only recognizable to a mother's eye. It was as a thirteen-year-old boy that Emanuel had left his father's house; he was returning as a grown man. Was it the appearance of the strange "guest"? We cannot solve this riddle, just as we have no words to describe the anguish of the son sitting there listening to his mother. We would not wish this situation on anyone. Emanuel managed as best he could by focusing on his little brother Benjamin. Emanuel's blood was throbbing and raging through his veins.

He was a dear and friendly brother, this Benjamin, a rare find! When the fish came to the table he insisted vehemently on giving the guest his portion. Emanuel protested loudly, in vain.

"But what are you going to eat?" the mother said to Benjamin, although she seemed to agree with his decision.

"I," Benjamin said with glowing eyes, "I won't eat anything."

"But fish is your favorite dish," Rösele pleaded with him.

"So I'll leave the table," the boy said, already standing up.

"What are you going to tell the boy?" his mother whispered to Reb Schimme, with a blessed smile. "Isn't God supposed to keep him healthy and strong? The way he walks and stands, he's Elijah all over again. Elijah was just like this as a child."

As he watched the guest eat his portion of fish, Benjamin displayed the same strength of character that motivated him to offer it to him. It was a peculiar sight to see the fine boy with his hands pressed on the table, his face glowing with the joy of his decision—or was it the seeds of regret?—as his eyes moved back and forth between the bowl where his property was disappearing piece by piece and the guest who was eating his food. If Emanuel had permitted himself to follow his instincts, he would have taken the child into his arms and kissed and hugged him as long as he could. But he had to be satisfied with consuming Benjamin's fish in silence, his cheeks blushing brightly.

When the meal was done it was time to pray again, and Emanuel was ashamed to admit that he no longer knew the blessing over the meal as he once did. After the prayer, Benjamin fetched his song book, and he and his father began to sing the traditional Sabbath songs. Soon enough, the father's voice became weaker and weaker and sleepier and sleepier. Benjamin still had a long way to go when he heard the loud snoring of the peddler. He had sunken into a chair; apparently he no longer needed to praise the God of his forefathers. Rösele too, drunk with sleep, had wobbled into the other room.

The only ones left were Benjamin, who was still singing, the mother, and Emanuel. Emanuel felt the precariousness of his situation and sought to take moves to cut short his visit. Without raising his eyes he stood up, quietly said good night, and quickly stepped toward the door.

"Guest, guest!" the mother called after him, "why are you going already? Stay a bit longer, I've not yet had the chance to talk with you at all."

Emanuel turned around. "What do you want?" he asked in a barely perceptible voice.

"Tell me, guest," the mother began, "how did you come to wander about in the world? You certainly don't look like you were born a . . . "

"Born a beggar, you mean? I wasn't."

"So why? I'm happy to feed you, as God knows, but I'll bet that your mother isn't pleased at what you're making of your life. Is she still alive?"

"Yes, she should live to one hundred."

"And?"

"What?"

"Why didn't you stay with her?"

"It was too confining for me at home."

"Peculiar, peculiar! This is the way every boy talks when he wants to go into the world. None of them wants to stay home, and where does that come from? It's because human beings are never satisfied. People always go out looking for better food, as if someone's standing behind them with a whip, hunting them and driving them out. If a boy's mother makes his bed with nice pillows so that he's comfortable at night, he'd prefer that a woman whom he doesn't even know would put stones under his head. It's like that small child that never wanted to be blessed by its father. Only after the child died did it understand, bitterly, that the father's blessing meant something. Every Friday night it had to get out of its cold grave and place its head under its father's hands. It never found peace. And this is true for every boy. A boy always comes back to father and mother, and often when it's too late. I tell you, guest, a boy that doesn't need the blessings of its parents because he's far away from them, this boy won't do well. You mark my words. A mother should only want daughters. They stay true to her. She can keep them at home, but a boy is like a swallow, flying away as soon as it gets its first feathers."

"So you wish you hadn't given birth to Elijah?" Emanuel asked quietly. His heart was beating louder than the sound of his voice.

"Shema Yisroel," the mother exclaimed, with horror. "Did I say something like that? I can't imagine what I'd be in the world without my Elijah. He was the one whom I had to give birth to. And don't think, my guest, that a mother doesn't derive any pleasure from her child even if he's gone far away from her! God almighty takes care of us! When such a mother is distressed and sad, without an idea how her son is doing in the big world out there, she still has something. I take down my big prayer book, and read a few chapters of my psalms, and guest, you won't believe how much that does for me. I can see my Elijah standing before me, healthy, handsome, and cheerful, brimming with good fortune. He laughs with and at me for being so concerned over him. 'Shema Yisroel,' I call out, 'how should I know that you're doing so well?' Now guest, do you believe I take pleasure in my Elijah?"

"Mother, splendid mother," Emanuel muttered.

"What are you saying, guest?" Channe asked, trying to make out his words.

"I just meant," Emanuel responded, "that I'd give anything to be blessed by my mother just one more time!"

For several minutes Channe stared at the guest. "If you're such a good Jew," she began, "and if that's what you want, then you're deserving of what I'd like to do for you. Come here, my son," she said, deeply moved, "I want to call you that for a moment and will imagine that you're my Elijah. God can't have anything against giving a stranger one's blessing. Come here, I want to bless you."

With his head bowed down, covered by his mother's hands, Emanuel received her blessing. Benjamin's song was still echoing through the Sabbath ghetto when the prodigal son stood in front of his father's house muttering an evening prayer the likes of which had never before risen up to the stars in heaven.

Postscript to the letter above

Let me remain here just this one night, Clara. After this I will belong to you, your faith, and your heaven for eternity! Just this one night!

I have now accomplished everything I intended to in withdrawing from the light of your eyes for such a long time. I have seen my parents, my siblings, and my native region, and I have received my mother's blessing. I could be leaving now but I am not. Just this one night! It is as if ties that I thought I had cut off long ago are pulling me to remain here. There is something that I still have to do here, but I do not know what it is.

I am eager to give you a portrait of my parents, but I cannot do so in this letter. Condensing an entire world of poetry into two or three pieces of paper would make the letter blush, no doubt! I shall need time for this.

Farewell. Not a shadow of doubt or fear should pass over the countenance of my guardian angel. I know only all too well how much I owe you and your father.

By writing this letter I am undertaking a great risk worthy of a medieval knight, and the lady of my heart should drape a tender prize around my neck. It is an adventure fitting of a serpent or a dragon. For I am writing amid a group of sleeping beggars here. All that needs to happen is for a boisterous fly to bump into someone's nose, and then the serpent will wake up and spew his venom on me. Am I not desecrating the Sabbath?

And yet I should not profane it, if only because of the eighteen houses that separate me from my parents. I have become an entirely different person.

Our "guest" was in no position to leave the ghetto on the next day either, given that it was the actual Sabbath. How was Emanuel going to engineer this? Was he supposed to escape from the threatening tangle of beggars in the "Schlafstube" without a scratch, his pack on his back and his walking stick in his hand? And Benjamin's examination was today; he had to find out whether the boy would earn the "nobleman's jacket."

Early in the morning, Emanuel looked out through the dirty window panes of the "Schlafstube" to see his father walking to the synagogue, with Benjamin following close behind. In one hand Benjamin was holding the Bible, in the other he was carrying the white robe that men wrapped themselves up with during prayer. With a son's eye, he was pleased to see how magnificent his father looked. What a different sight he was from the man bearing the burden of his pack of wares yesterday. He recognized his father's thirty-year-old wedding suit, which had become his attire for the Sabbath.

The sight of Benjamin filled him with greater melancholy. He saw his second youth, the living reflection of his own childhood. Just like Benjamin, he too used to carry the Bible for his father on the way to synagogue. His face used to glow with the same sort of righteous pride as he slaved away carrying the heavy book that had served as a pillar for millennia. Years will come and go, he thought to himself, and this iron fortress of faith will be reduced to a heap of rubble, reminding you that not even thoughts are immortal. This boy Benjamin will meet the same fate as his brother Emanuel. May heaven protect him from this!

Almost as if he were seeking to unload the rising storms of his soul, Emanuel stepped into the street and followed the pair all the way to the synagogue.

Inside the synagogue Emanuel chose the most humble seat possible, near the entrance. From there he could look into the dense crowd of men gathered to pray and catch a glimpse of his father and brother. How strange! Emanuel's soul and spirit were open to being stirred up, and his memory was acting as the bell ringer for his feelings, seeking to sound all the bells of his childhood. Yet we need to confess that the Sabbath prayer service made no impression on him at all. Indeed, his soul was offended by its disorderliness, by the complete independence with which those assembled were crying out their prayers. Nevertheless, there was one thought that occupied him, and that he intended to tell Clara about upon his return. For Emanuel's sake, we must pass this on to the reader.

"Do you want to know, Clara," he planned to say to her, "why Jews usually appear so independent in life? It is not the natural spirit of speculation, nor it is a higher talent, nor is it a resilient form of intelligence gained from persecution. Walk into a synagogue, and you'll find breathless, unmelodious bawling and pagoda-like bending and bowing down. Your people often ridicule this, with justification. But this is the key to the matter. You'll notice tremendous independence in the way those praying express their feelings. Each individual cries out, moves and stirs about as if he were having a personal audience with God. You have saints who help you climb the ladders you build up to heaven, while you all watch below in wretched humility as they present your sacrificial offerings. The Jew, however, has the advantage of the immediacy of his prayer. Should someone who has such an open relationship with his God be timid around other human beings? You have too many intermediaries who pray, plead, and act for you."

Upon his return, he wanted to tell Clara about this, along with many further things she could not learn from others and certainly not from books. In the meantime, he was a desolate beggar being taken in for the Sabbath, and he had to suffer everyone leaving the synagogue greeting him with a cozy "Salem Alechem" and a brotherly handshake. He even saw the rich Joseph Brandeis coming toward him; the mere thought of his wealth had made him dizzy as a child. His father and Benjamin came over, and the latter's sweet face was full of fear and anxious excitement. The child put out his hand toward him and said breathlessly, "Are you coming along to the examination? You have to be there!"

"May I?" Emanuel asked, looking at his father.

"If it were up to Benjamin, he'd summon the entire congregation," the father responded, his voice betraying a trace of concern over how well his child would perform. "Do I know whether he'll pass the test? A page of Talmud isn't easy, Benjamin, and four eyes are enough if one's headed for disgrace."

"Just come along," Benjamin pleaded.

It was not a long walk to cousin Reb Jaikew's house; he lived on the same street as the synagogue. Emanuel recalled how he used to tremble with fear when he had to ascend the dark, narrow flight of stairs to get examined by his cousin Reb Jaikew on the Sabbaths of his childhood. He remembered the dark figure of this relative, who was universally revered. The cousin was still young then, but people still were scared to look at him. Emanuel could only imagine what a terrifying impression the cousin would make today, with his pale countenance marked by the furrows of deep knowledge and the bushy brows over the gray eyes! But he also remembered the bliss he felt when his cousin was satisfied with him. He would call to his wife to keep ready a piece of Sabbath fruit for Elijah, which he would be permitted to go pick up in the afternoon.

"Aren't you scared, my dear Benjamin?" he asked the boy as they walked up the steps.

"Not a bit," the child responded. His shaking hands indicated that he was lying.

When they came in, the cousin was sitting in front of a thick book, which he was studying. During Emanuel's absence his appearance had hardly improved.

"Good Shabbes, cousin," the father greeted him timidly.

"May he who has arrived be greeted!" a muffled tone responded. The cousin hardly looked up from his book.

"Nu, tell him," the father whispered to Benjamin. "Go and ask him."

Mortal agony enveloped the boy's sweet face. Timidly, his soul had receded into its furthest reaches. Benjamin's body was consumed with fear.

"I'd like to get examined, Cousin Reb Jaikew," the boy stuttered almost imperceptibly.

"Examined? On what?" the cousin asked, in a dry monotone.

"On my first page of Talmud" was Benjamin's answer.

A mirthless smile came over the cousin's face, but it disappeared immediately, as if it had remained there too long. "You little fool," he said slowly, "there in the corner I have a shelf that is full of books. Can I know which one you've been studying from?"

"The first page of Baba Mezia."[10] Benjamin blushed as he corrected his mistake.

A new smile, even more ice-cold than the first, came over the cousin's face like a quick flash of lighting. "How old are you?" he asked after a pause.

"I'll be eleven at the New Year."

"And you're learning your first page of Talmud?" He asked this question in such a muffled monotone that it was difficult to determine whether he was mocking or admiring Benjamin. He pointed toward a place in the bookcase where Benjamin could find the appropriate folio.

"Now begin," he spoke, after Benjamin had opened up the first page of the book. At this point the father, who had been standing back with respectful timidity, stepped forward and put on his glasses, leaning over Benjamin's shoulders so that he would not miss any of the examination. Benjamin began with hesitation but then became more sure of himself. Words can hardly express what a strange feeling it was for the peddler to hear his child explicating the difficult meaning of the Talmud in the vernacular. Benjamin spoke in the chanting tone typical of Talmud study, with all accompanying gestures and movements. He would twiddle his thumbs and then rise up to make a triumphant conclusion.

No, good Reb Schimme, we want to pass by the pleasures of this moment in silence, without a word. From time to time, however, Reb Schimme's face showed concern and fear; this happened whenever the cousin would cross-examine the boy, asking him questions that were not in the book. The sweet boy would then furrow his brow and think hard. Eventually, his face would betray him, and a fleeting flash of his eyes would reveal he understood the cousin. The cousin would nod his head and stroke his beard, allowing Benjamin to continue since he had answered the question, and on the peddler's lips a mild paternal smile would blossom, like a spring flower.

Finally the examination came to a close. The boy's forehead was covered with sweat, his face was aglow, and a silence full of expectation

---

10. The title of a section from the Talmud. [Note in the original.]

filled the room. The cousin stared into the room but then turned to the father and said, "The boy has a head made of iron. If he pays attention, something great may become of him." He then turned his head back to the open door and exclaimed, "Zirl, Zirl, come out for a second."

His wife, Aunt Zirl, appeared at the door. "You should know, Zirl," he said to her, "that the boy Benjamin will come to you this afternoon at three. I want you should give him two little apples, no more and no less. Do you hear me? I'm not going to tell you what to do, as much as you might want this, you wrinkled old woman. That's enough."

The cousin then stood up, as if he wished his guests had already left, and walked the Talmud over to the bookcase from which Benjamin had taken it earlier. The peddler, however, took the boy by the hand and said, "Benjamin, my dear, you've given me such pleasure in my life. Tomorrow you'll go with your mother to Reb Maier the cloth merchant." He then wished cousin Jaikew a good Shabbes and all the best and started with Benjamin toward the door.

The cousin's voice called him back.

"Reb Schimme," he said, "you should watch out for this boy. He has intelligence, and I hope he doesn't end up like Elijah. What do you hear from Elijah?"

"Nothing, nothing at all," the father responded, becoming sad again after so much joy.

"Elijah had such a great mind," the cousin continued, "and what became of him? With his intelligence and shrewdness he could have become the district rabbi. And what became of him? You don't even know where he is! Do you think it's likely that he's remained a good Jew? What a shame it is for Elijah, a huge shame. He could have become something great—and now, perhaps he has . . ."

The peddler, who understood what the cousin was going to say, exclaimed, "God forbid," with shock. He reached for the door handle with a hurried "Good Shabbes."

When they left, Emanuel became severely agitated, wondering how he had been able to march on into his cousin's home accompanying his father and brother like that. Next to them he felt so guilty, as if he had just washed his hands in blood. Overwhelmed and confused, he took advantage of a curve in the street to tear himself away from Benjamin. He hurried off without saying good-bye.

Without thinking how far his feet would take him, Emanuel spent the Sabbath afternoon walking. His heart was restless, raging back and forth between extremes, and this agony drove him far away. It was not until the ghetto lay in the dusky distance behind him that, almost involuntarily, he realized that he had kept the promise he made to Clara: he had in fact spent just one night under the spell of his parents. He had escaped and he was happy that he had. He credited the spirit of love for his triumph; love was clearly more powerful than all other bonds, even those of parents or siblings. Frequently, he imagined Clara walking next to him, her arms draped around his neck. Blissfully, he imagined the closeness of her breath on his cheeks.

A moment later, though, he shuddered to think what his parents had said when he failed to show up for the midday meal. What did Benjamin think when he went by the "Schlafstube" only to be told that the beggar, whom he had loved so inexplicably, had disappeared on the holy Sabbath? If this boy becomes a disheartened misanthrope, Emanuel thought, it will be my own fault. His young soul was attracted to my soul like a flower seeking sunlight, and I gave it drops of poison. I stand before him not as a friend but as an enemy of religion who desecrates the Sabbath. The child will hate me his whole life long!

He was about to turn around and go back when he realized that he was already going toward home. Shocked, but also pleased, he returned to the "Schlafstube" late at night, as if he were sleepwalking. The other beggars told him that Benjamin had in fact been looking for him, concerned that he had missed lunch. The "guests," who could see from his dusty clothes that he had been desecrating the Sabbath, posed their share of mocking questions, making jokes at his expense.

"So where did you pray this evening?" one of the beggars asked him presumptuously, sizing him up from head to toe.

Even the Polish woman whose eyes had reminded him so strongly of Clara's did not hold back the mockery. Emanuel must have lost his way, since he certainly managed to lose the Sabbath.

Emanuel didn't dignify these remarks with a response. Exhausted, he threw himself down on one of the wooden benches. He felt that his soul was as pitiful as it could be. He had suffered so much since coming into the ghetto! And the suffering would not end if he left! He would be leaving Benjamin behind, having poisoned and defiled his magnificent spirit, as it were. Sooner or later people would discover the disingenuous circumstances under which he had visited his parents. And then there was the betrayal of his old faith, not to mention the dishonesty of his new faith. But nothing horrified him more than the betrayal of Benjamin's soul. He would love to have stood with a pure heart in front of the child; he felt he could not leave without apologizing to him. He even stood in front of his father's home several times and saw that the light was on. He saw his mother, Benjamin, and Rösele moving about. He blessed them, but every time he reached out to grab the door handle, he let go of it. This was his fate: to leave his native region as an enemy of religion, a desecrator of the Sabbath, and as someone who poisons souls.

On the next day, indeed, we find Emanuel really escaping, traveling down the road to a neighboring town where he was planning to catch a mail coach. Anxiety and sleeplessness were written legibly all over his pale face, and he was marching on in such deep thought that he failed to notice a fellow traveler on the road, a figure with a heavy pack on his back whom he would have been able to recognize as his father. It was not until his father was ten steps away that he heard the sounds of a Hebrew prayer. He looked up and cried out in horror.

His father turned around, gesturing at him with his hand not to interrupt him in prayer. He still had his phylacteries on, and he continued to walk on ahead, singing and praising the Lord under the open sky. This gave Emanuel time to prepare himself for the scene to come.

"Why didn't you come to eat with us, guest?" the peddler began. He had finished his morning prayers and was slowly putting away his phylacteries. "Didn't you like my wife's cooking?"

"I've never had better in my life," Emanuel responded timidly to his father's sarcasm.

"And yet you didn't come back? You took away all my Benjamin's joy. He refused to eat. In the afternoon, his mother wanted to tell him a little story because he had performed such miracles with the Talmud, and he didn't want to listen because *you* weren't there. What do you make of such a boy?"

"What story was that?" Emanuel thought he had found a wonderful means of steering the conversation away from the topic of his absence the day before.

"It's a story my wife makes a big deal of. She wouldn't sell it for gold. It recounts something that happened once in our own family, and when Channe wants to give one of her children pleasure, she tells this story. Benjamin was supposed to listen to it yesterday."

"Is there a baptized Jew in it?"

"How do you know that?"

"I've heard something about it."

Emanuel was not telling an untruth. His mother had told him this family tale when he was a child.

After starting off like this, father and son walked next to each other in silence. It was the father who began again, "Where are you actually headed, guest? Perhaps you don't know yourself?"

"You may be right, Reb Schimme," Emanuel said with a bleak smile.

"And that's fitting for a young man like yourself?" the peddler exclaimed. "Every person, and especially a Jewish child, has to have a plan in life."

"What if I were to tell you that I do have a plan?"

"That I don't need to know. I myself really don't know, by the way, why I'm even asking you such things. What do you concern me? I said that to my wife too, but she didn't agree."

"Why?"

"She can't forget you. She and Benjamin spent the whole day talking about you. I'm surprised she didn't cry when you didn't show up. She waited for you late into the night and refused to go to bed. Benjamin too. 'You fool,' I said, 'why do you care about this beggar? Is this the first time you've seen a beggar?' 'Schimme,' she said, 'you have no idea how it troubles me that the stranger hasn't come back. Did someone insult him?' Then Benjamin began to cry."

Despite his deep agitation, Emanuel understood well the difference between how his father and how his mother saw him. His father regarded him as a beggar. His mother saw him only as a stranger.

"No one insulted me," he spoke in a muted voice.

"Seriously, guest," the peddler continued, "where are you headed, really? I'd be happy to have you travel a part of the way with me. Why don't you accompany me to the first village?"

"I'll go as far as you like," Emanuel said, letting his guard down.

"I'll make it worth your while. In that village I'll show you a house, the likes of which you've never seen in the world. I'll take you to Reb Schmul the Randar,[11] where you can be sure you'll get a good piece of money and a snack for your journey. Splendid people live there. If one hundred beggars show up there, everyone gets something, and a thousand blessings stick to the house. That Jew, he has a heart, you'll never be treated that way by the peasants."

"But I've often heard that the peasants are hospitable," Emanuel said, then rephrasing his comment, "I mean, they're always happy to feed strangers."

"Why don't you try it out? Go to a peasant's home, and you'll see yourself. You'll hear the peasant and his wife say to you: 'We don't have anything. Go over there to the Jew. The Jew's richer than we are. The Jew has all our money!' If they don't tell you that, then my name isn't Schimme Prager. The Jew can give to everyone. He doesn't reflect when he gives, and that's because the Jew has a heart."

Hearing these strong words, Emanuel looked into his father's face. It was a beautiful red color, and he could not tell whether this was due to anger or mockery. He would have loved to show this face to his Clara.

Walking along with his father he heard all sorts of interesting things. Despite the narrow-mindedness and the prejudice which caused the son to smile from time to time, he was amazed at the peddler's intelligence and clarity of mind. He would not have expected to find this beneath the surface of this hunched over, wheezing figure. Emanuel had become so blinded by his own situation, so confused by the conflict in his soul, that he often forgot that this man was his father. Instead, he saw a stranger with a mysterious essence he had to examine and penetrate to prepare interesting comments for his Clara.

He was able to sustain this ill-fated delusion from time to time, but whenever he awoke from it he experienced a painful struggle. Emanuel took great pleasure in hearing the peddler's thoughts, and he enjoyed all his questions and answers. He experienced his anger and mockery, his faith and his superstition. But whenever he realized that this was his father, it was as if all his wounds were bleeding. It is difficult to depict

---

11. As Kompert explains at the beginning of his tale "The Randar's Children" (1848), *randar* is a term from "the jargon of the ghetto" for "arendator," designating the "leaseholder of a village pub or spirits distillery."

Emanuel's mood during his journey alongside his father. It changed like the weather, between rain and sunshine. Sometimes it was balmy and mild, and then in the next moment it would become wild and aggravated. This was inevitable. It was as if the very roots of Emanuel's soul were being threatened by the blows of an ax, with one major assault after another.

"Today, I know, I'm not going to do any business," the peddler said as they saw the houses of the village in front of them.

"How can you know that?"

"Because today is Sunday. I never earn anything on Sunday. How would the peasants have time to buy anything from me today? Just now they're ringing their church bells, then they'll eat, and in the afternoon the peasant will take his wife to the inn, where they'll dance and have a drink. How could I do business under these circumstances?"

"Why shouldn't the peasant be able to enjoy his Sunday?" Emanuel exclaimed, forgetting himself. "Don't you have your Sabbath?"

"You say the strangest things, my dear guest," the peddler said, visibly annoyed. "How can you compare our holy Shabbes to Sunday? And did I say that the peasant shouldn't have a day where he can rest and relax by the hearth? Who doesn't need Sunday? The peasant and the tradesman do, of course, and who understands this better than the Jew? That's why he has his Shabbes."

"This is all true, my dear Reb Schimme," Emanuel said, getting more and more irritated. "But if you know these things, why don't you choose to stay at home on Sunday? Why do you disturb the peasants' Sabbath?"

"What kind of talk is that?" the father cried out. "What kind of talk is that? I should lose two days of the week?"

"Oh," Emanuel exclaimed, overflowing with emotion, "the peasant should be disturbed on his Sunday just because you don't want to lose a day? The peasant shouldn't know that it's Sunday just because you don't want to leave your pack sitting idly in the corner with its old vests and handkerchiefs?"

"He can drink and dance and cry out with joy, can't he?" the peddler said with bitterness. "You think I'm disturbing his Sunday if I sell an old vest or a handkerchief from my pack? I have an old motto that's relevant here: 'The person who hurts himself the most is the Jew.'"

"What do you mean by that?" Emanuel asked, affected by the father's melancholy and bitter expression.

The peddler, however, remained stubbornly silent. Emanuel felt that he had cut through to the deepest fibers of his father's being.

"Are you still a Jew, guest?" he exclaimed suddenly, stopping right in front of Emanuel.

"What's that supposed to mean?" Emanuel asked in shock. "Why wouldn't I still be a Jew?"

"You don't seem like a Jew when you talk like that. What Jew would side with the peasant and blame himself? Alas, we are all God's creatures. Why don't you just say, 'What do I care about the Sabbath? Why don't I have my Shabbes at the same time as the peasants and tradesmen? Then I wouldn't have to go around with my old vests and handkerchiefs. I'd be able take off a day of the week and earn more money. Isn't this your point? You think, guest, that I have no idea what's going on in the world, that I don't know people talk about getting rid of Shabbes? Isn't this where you were going with your questions?"

"What if this were the case?" Emanuel responded with hesitation. He was happy, incidentally, to be able to discuss matters with his father in such general terms.

Speaking more mildly than one might have expected, the peddler said, "This is neither for you nor for me to decide. This is God's decision. But God said, 'On the seventh day you shall rest from your labors' (he quoted the Hebrew text from Genesis)—did God want that I should spend Shabbes hawking old vests and handkerchiefs? If so, wouldn't he have said, 'Schimme Prager, if you wish, you can make the seventh day of the week the first one. That's the day that Peter and Pawel will be sitting in the inn drinking and dancing and crying out with joy. You should go and sit down with them!' Or on the contrary, God could simply have said, 'Schimme Prager, I know you're a poor man in need of money. How about I give you fifty-two more days a year so that you can earn more?' Let me tell you, guest, if God wants me to make money, he'll manage to get it to me in just the five days of the week. Fifty-two days in the year should make such a huge difference? I can't believe that!"

At this point they reached the village. Whether because of lingering resentment or his excited state of mind, the peddler forgot to point out to his son how to get to the Randar, where he would get such noteworthy alms. But was that even still his father, the man burning with the passion of his life of faith, who was now creeping past the peasants' homes with his drawn-out call, "For sale, for sale, for sale!"? Emanuel watched what his father was doing with almost dreamlike wonder. But when his father reached out to tickle under her chin a peasant girl standing by the door, he felt all the blood rush to his head. Was that really the same person? Shaking his head, he left the village, unable to bear it there. He would wait for his father on the main road.

To Clara (written with a pencil on the main road)

I cannot even sketch for you the contours of my current position. Everything feels amorphous, bewildering, and never-ending. I am sitting on ruins, like that Roman.[12]

Music, music, where can I find the melody that will rid me of my disquietude and my lackadaisical indecisiveness? Like a thief I often sneak up on myself, forcing me to choose between my past and my current life. I am torn apart. I have lost my center of gravity since returning to my native region.

There's something I must confess to you. Bloody nails have come to remove your image from the frame of my soul. Father, mother, sister, and little brother have thrust their way in, covering up your image with veils so dense that I cannot see you. I can no longer see the light of your eyes. Oh, Lord in heaven, what will become of me?!

You should know my father, Clara, it would be worth your while. For several hours I've been, well, hawking with him, and it is only now that I am really getting to know him. This has truly been worth the effort. You would find the soul of such a Jew peculiar. Imagine a book that supplied you with the most beautiful things to read. You continue reading, on and on, amazed to hear the magnificent sound of powerful melodies. You do not know where they are coming from, or where they are headed. Everything tells you that you have discovered primal powers of humanity here, more beautiful and more splendid than you have ever seen before.

---

12. A reference to John Vanderlyn's celebrated portrait *Caius Marius Amidst the Ruins of Carthage* (1807), which won a gold medal in Paris in 1808.

But it is not simplicity or naïveté that you are finding here. It is a higher feeling, a sanctified biblical feeling, as it were. You read on—and suddenly you find the pages stuck together, and the melodies stop. You lose track of the wonderful living faith, and you cannot read further. The filth of life has bound the pages to each other, and the paste of vulgarity has cemented them together. It is a great misfortune for the inhabitants of the ghetto that you remain fixated on these passages. They jump out at you because initially they are an affront to your organs of touch and sight, and human beings never want to take the time to be thorough. You never read further in the book, and that is your loss. We are the ones who suffer from this.

Clara, can you do a favor for me, for your Emanuel? When you run into a peddler or hawker, think of my father! Do not be turned off in horror by the dirty, stuck together pages of the book.

It was right before the harvest. The crops were undulating lushly in the fields, and the quail and the larks were blissfully happy as they flew by. The peddler, however, was in a gloomy mood. He had earned very little this week, and Emanuel felt his father's worries. He looked with concern in his face whenever he saw him leaving a peasant's home without making a sale; the constant disappointment over misplaced hopes was readily apparent. Emanuel almost felt that he was responsible for his father's misfortune. But it was right before harvest time. The fields may have been full of golden crops, but the peasants had no money in their money chests, and the peddler's pack felt this!

"May God give us a good year this year," the peddler reverently said at one point when they walked by a field covered with grain. "There's a reason we pray every day in winter, 'Give dew and rain for a blessing on the face of the earth.' The peasant needs this."

"This prayer seems so strange to me," Emanuel said. "Does the Jew have fields? Is he a peasant?"

"Excuse me," the peddler laughed back at him. "Again you're saying the strangest things. How can a peddler live if the peasant doesn't have any money? And the other way around, who would lend the peasant money and wait to be repaid if the peddler weren't there? And who would buy the skin of the hare from the peasant if not the Jew? It would just rot away. Peasant and peddler, they belong together, and that's why we pray in winter, 'Give dew and rain for a blessing on the face of the earth.' I can't even imagine how the peasant would exist without the Jew."

"That sounds a bit odd," Emanuel smiled. "Normally people think those countries are the fortunate ones where peasants can exist without Jews."

"That means," the peddler said pensively, "that the peasant in these lands has more money? I'm not convinced that's entirely true. There's got to be more to it than that. Someone else would have to play the Jew. Who's going to bring the peasant what he needs, into his home? After all, he has to stay home. He can't run around! I tell you, guest, where there's no Jew, someone has to replace him."

"You may be right," Emanuel responded with a laugh, charmed by his father's intelligence. "It's nothing but envy, Reb Schimme!"

Emanuel's words here can serve us as a guiding star in analyzing the condition of his soul. Involuntarily, he first wished Clara were with him so that she too would be able to enjoy the pleasure of his father's company. But then he doubted whether, given their differences in upbringing and faith, she would see him with the same eyes as he did. Would her soul be able to pass through the same gates of poetry that his father, mother, and native region opened up for him? He had his doubts, and doubt is a knife that cuts both ways.

There were moments when Emanuel was pleased that his father had earned nothing in the course of the whole week. If this were the case, he might have a means of at least partially bridging the gulf that was now going to separate him from his father forever. He could throw gold into this gulf, so much and such lustrous gold that it would outshine his betrayal, the dark, burning stain of his life. He would be able to secure his parents' prosperity and well-being, surrounding them with riches. His father could sit in silent comfort at home, and his mother would not need to ask, "What kind of week did you have, Schimme?" He could make the most beautiful wedding for his sister Rösele, and Benjamin's future would be secure. The sweet boy would not have to become a peddler. He wanted to smooth everything out, appease everything, and put everything to rest. All they would have to do would be to let him keep his Clara.

"Why is it, guest," Reb Schimme said on one of the last days of the week, "that I'm so tired and worn out as if I had been battling with a giant? Maybe this is because I've earned no money?"

"Perhaps," Emanuel responded almost indifferently. "But I think there's another reason. Should I tell you about it?"

"Do tell," the peddler said, smiling.

"This will surely annoy you, but I can't help it. All week long you never eat any warm food. The only things you eat are onions and cheese and other foods that don't give your body energy. How would you not become tired and run down eating such things?"

"Good," the peddler said, "you may be right. But let me pose the same question a bit differently: where should I be getting warm food from?"

Emanuel felt he was ready to enter into risky terrain. Timidly, he began. "Yesterday, right at noon, you visited a peasant. I stood outside and distinctly heard the peasant woman invite you to join in their meal. But what did you say? You did everything you could to escape from the situation. Right afterward you and I were eating bread with moldy cheese. I ask you now, what should a person do when someone says to him, 'Come and eat and satisfy your hunger, it's my pleasure, and don't think of paying me.' Should a person flee, as if death were looking at him from the points of every fork, as if there were poison in every drop of soup? Or should he sit down and be merry and satisfy his hunger with God's bounty, even though it's prepared in pots that are not his own?"

"So you're saying," the peddler asked, furrowing his brow, "that I should have stayed and eaten with the peasant woman? I wouldn't do this for a million," he exclaimed passionately, "even if you were to pay me here on the spot in cash."

"I don't have so much with me," Emanuel said cautiously.

"Listen to me, "the peddler responded. "I can see that you don't believe me. Let me ask you just one question. Is life worth a million? For I'd give my life for this and not eat the peasant woman's food."

"Oh God," Emanuel thought to himself as he turned pale. "He speaks with such passion about these things! How will I ever bridge the gulf that is expanding exponentially in front of me? If he feels that a shadow of a small sin is already an attack on his life, then *my* betrayal will certainly cost him his life! And then there's my mother!"

His sadness now grew with every step that he took toward his father. He no longer had the courage to ask him questions. What else could he ask, and what kind of answers would he receive? Every word that his father spoke, everything that his father said, was a nail in the coffin of his happiness, a knife cutting right through the fabric that love and fondness had been weaving. Emanuel remained silent, his worried face bearing the shadows of a gloomy future.

The peddler had become fond of his companion during the week's journeys. He soon noticed Emanuel's change in mood and his silence, which he observed for a long stretch of the way.

"This is what you get, guest," he began, "from accompanying a poor peddler. If you had gone your own way, who knows what sort of good food you might have gotten? But now," he added with a stolen smile, "I'm going to visit my beautiful peasant woman. I want to speak with her, and she'll dish you up a plate of what she has in her house. You don't need to be embarrassed with me here. I know how to look the other way."

"Reb Schimme," Emanuel exclaimed from the depths of his soul. "*This* is the advice you're giving me?"

"And why not?" the peddler said with an indescribable tone. "Don't you want something warm to eat? Go and satisfy your hunger. It's no concern of mine what others do."

After a long pause Emanuel asked with a subdued voice, "Reb Schimme, would you give the same advice to your son if he found himself in the same situation?"

"Hush, hush," the peddler said, his mood gloomy all of a sudden. "Don't summon up the devil, he might come."

A cute little peasant girl with red cheeks approached the father when he entered the village. He smiled as he saw the little creature wobbling over to him.

"Baruschka," he called out to her. The child flew into his arms, and he gave her a warm kiss.

"What's your mother up to?" he asked him.

"She's at home," the child said, and she tore herself loose to run off to her mother.

"Whose child is that?" Emanuel asked with astonishment.

"The child's mother," the peddler explained, "was once the unhappiest woman on earth. The fact that she's doing better now, well, we have Schimme Prager to thank for that."

"Is this perhaps your pretty peasant woman?" Emanuel guessed forebodingly.

"She's the one," Reb Schimme said, "and since you said before that the peasant can't stand the Jew because the Jew refuses to eat from the same pot as he does, I want to tell you a story about my pretty peasant woman. The father of this woman lived two hours from here, where he was a village judge. I should only possess such a great fortune as her father."

"His name was Pawel, and he thought a great deal of me. I was like a child in his house, and I earned a lot of money there. The peasant had just one child. Normally Jews think they are the only ones who love their children, but peasants too will give up their life for their children. I was witness to this in my Pawel's case. For his daughter he would have snatched down the sun from the heavens. One day Pawel says to me, 'Schimme, next time you come out to us, bring me linen, fabric, needles, ribbons, and whatever else you have that's nice. I want to make a wedding for my daughter.' 'Who with?' I ask, 'You've not told me anything about this, Pawel!' He then names a young peasant's son from another village, whom I also knew well. 'You want to give her to *him*, Pawel?' I cry out, 'I won't bring you linen, I won't bring you ribbons, and you're not going to give your daughter to him.' 'Why not?' the peasant says. 'Because I won't stand for it. This Waczlaw is a gambler and a drunkard, and he'll make your daughter unhappy.' He then conceded to me that he knew about all this, but he had no power over his child. She wanted Waczlaw and would rather die than break off the engagement. 'Let me talk with her, Pawel,' I say. 'Talk to her,' the peasant says, and he has to turn away because his heart is wounded.

"I spoke with the daughter and told her what she was going to be doing to her father. With Christians, alas, it's different than with us Jews. A Jewish child knows that that it shouldn't even disturb its mother and father's sleep during the night. What else is there to say? She didn't want to listen to me, and four weeks later she became Waczlaw's wife. What happened? As if a prophet had predicted it, everything happened just as Schimme Prager said it would. Not two years had passed, and Waczlaw didn't have a penny of the money that he had gotten from his wife. He had drunk and gambled it all away. I didn't dare discuss this with Pawel's daughter, I was so sick over what had happened. She looked pale and emaciated, and once I saw bloody welts on her forehead—he must have been beating her. I didn't tell old Pawel anything about her, and God should give me as many thousand gulden as his daughter cost me. I lent her money, knowing she'd never be able to pay me back. This may have been wrong on my part, but . . . "

"Oh, no, no," Emanuel exclaimed, with great animation.

"I agree, but my wife knew nothing about it. What would I have told her about it? But keep listening! Whenever I visited old Pawel, he never wanted to let me get away. He always made me stay the night, giving me his best room, where he kept all his worldly possessions. Once Pawel and I stayed up late at night chatting. With all my speeches and stories I made the peasant happy like I hadn't seen for such a long time. When I noticed this, I decided to tell him about his daughter's situation. As soon as he saw I was about to speak her name, however, he jumped up madly and cried out, 'Listen, Schimme, if you want to stay on my good side, do not speak to me of her.' I would have been a fool not to keep quiet, for Pawel was important to me, and I earned lots of money from him. That very same night something happened that still makes my hair stand on end. I'm sleeping lightly, and I wake up around midnight to hear someone trying to open up the window from the outside. I'm terrified and can't speak a word, and my entire body is paralyzed, drenched in cold sweat. I just sit there and watch the window being opened and someone creeping into the room. All of a sudden, the moonlight enabled me to see better, and can you guess whom I recognized? Pawel's son-in-law Waczlaw. He was carrying an ax in his hand and was going to break open the chest where Pawel kept his money. At that point, God miraculously gave me back the power of speech and my strength. I jumped out of bed and screamed, 'What are you doing?' Waczlaw, responding quickly, grabs his ax and wants to strike me in the head. 'Strike me dead, Waczlaw,' I screamed, 'but you're not going to steal from your father-in-law.' God then performed a miracle. For as soon as I say that, Waczlaw collapses onto the floor and starts crying, making my heart tremble. I see this and start to say, 'So Waczlaw, you were planning to steal from your father-in-law and kill a man. This comes from the cursed life you lead, from your gambling and drinking.' He cried and begged me not to betray him. I promised him that I wouldn't, as long as he promised to change his ways. I sat next to him all night long, talking to him and giving him advice how he should start anew. Finally I gave him money so that he would not despair. Early in the morning I helped him escape through the window. What else should I tell you? Not a year passed, and Pawel's son-in-law had become the best and hardest-working peasant in the village. Pawel never knew about what had happened, and when he saw how much Waczlaw had changed, he helped him out. Now I can't go by this house without stopping; Pawel's daughter buys everything from me, even things she doesn't need. I helped make her happiness, I, Schimme Prager, the peddler!"

As if to confirm these words, in that moment a blossoming, vigorous young woman came through the doorway of a beautiful house.

"Welcome, my little father," she called out to him.

"Nu, what do you say to my peasant woman?" the peddler smiled, turning toward his companion. "If you want, you can go get something warm to eat. Do you want to?"

"No, no," cried out Emanuel, covering his eyes with his hands, in shame. He did not follow the father into the house.

To Clara

In the garret room of one of the most distinguished houses in Vienna there once lived a poor young man, a university student by vocation. His room was so high up that he could only commune with the smoke flying up the chimney or the tomcat walking on the roof on a silent summer night. Many days this student studied more than he ate, and as a result, his cheeks were pale and sorrowful. One day while downstairs, on the magnificent staircase of the third floor, he ran into a beautiful child, a girl around ten years old who looked at him with her wonderfully marvelous eyes. The student noticed the girl's angelic face quietly but unmistakably turn red. What a beautiful and wonderful child!

Several days later a servant called him down to meet with the merchant on the third floor. He came in trembling and heard a friendly, serious man ask him whether he would be willing to give his daughter lessons. "Clara," he heard the man utter, and all of a sudden his wonderful child appeared at the door, glowing in sweet red!

The student did his work well, I believe. He gave his rose all the perfume he could find, digging into the depths of his soul to do so. For many years, he raised his hands in blessing over the joyful development of her mind. He did not notice how she was growing physically. He had always looked down at her, she up at him. All of a sudden, however, he saw two eyes directly across from him, at his level. The eyes told him everything!

In their mythology lessons, he told her about Clytie, the beautiful nymph who constantly turned toward the rays of the sun. When going over this evocative myth, teacher and student alike blissfully followed Clytie's example. Looking up by chance, they saw that they were holding one another in each other's arms.

Alas, cold and uncanny hands are seeking to weave thorns and thistles into the beautiful fabric of our mythic love. Your noble father overcame so many deep-rooted prejudices. One day he said to me, "The state will only allow for your union under certain conditions. If you can figure out how to deal with that, then I have no objections."[13] Clara, life has beautiful moments!

I thought that this one inevitable step would be so easy that I undertook my journey back home with the jolliest possible disposition, like a comic actor wanting to see if he could get away with not being recognized by his parents. This act of deceit has come to take its revenge on me.

Forcibly, I'm reviewing the pages of my life and experiencing joy, consolation, and gratitude in doing so. I am still in control of the storm that is raging back and forth in these pages—but after one more day, perhaps after several more hours, it may catch hold of me. Can I know what will happen?

Friday had arrived, and Emanuel found himself on the path back to the ghetto. His foreboding had been correct. But it was not a storm that caught hold of him. A few words of his father were responsible for this decision—if a spontaneous reaction to enchantment can be called a decision. The peddler had noticed the growing sadness of his companion. He concluded that that the "guest" must be worried where he would eat on the Sabbath and thus extended to him a friendly invitation to come back with him and be his guest again if he had nothing else to do. He also knew that if he brought him back with him, Channe his wife and particularly Benjamin would be the happiest ones!

---

13. There was no legal provision for marriages between Jews and Christians in nineteenth-century Austria.

We cannot portray Emanuel's feelings during his retreat homeward, since we have no plummet to gauge the depths of this unfathomable ocean.

All day long Emanuel's gait was hurried, almost stormy. His father could not keep up with him. Often he would rest groaning under his burden while his companion marched on ahead, as if he could not arrive early enough.

"Guest, guest," the peddler had to call out to him. "You're hurrying as if someone were chasing you on with a whip. You must be scared that Shabbes is running away from you—I don't need to remind you how you ran away from *it* last week."

"If you knew what is driving me," Emanuel said, turning himself around, "all the horses in the world wouldn't be enough to take me away."

"You're that hungry?" the peddler asked, misunderstanding him. "And it's only been one week that you've not had any warm food! What am I supposed to do? I have fifty-two such weeks in the year. Just be patient, my wife will take care of you."

Despite his misery, Emanuel had to smile at his father's attempt to console him. Walking a more moderate pace, he went along with his father toward home, and soon the skies, towers, and houses greeted him. Seeing all this he felt no regret. But he was scared of how he was going to become the master of the scene awaiting him. He was full of firm resolve now. Fate itself had already made his decision for him.

When father and son came in, the mother was standing on top of the table, filling the seven-pronged lamp with oil from a little bottle, and Benjamin was twisting the cotton wicks between his fingers on top of the tabletop. The mother let out a loud cry when she saw the "stranger" and almost dropped the tiny jug of oil onto the floor. Benjamin stared at Emanuel as if he were horrified.

"Nu," the peddler said with a laugh, after warmly kissing the holy doorposts, "what's this? I don't get a 'Salem Alechem' from anyone?"

Channe responded with a deep sigh, "God welcome you, Schimme, God welcome you. On my life, you're giving me such a shock that I feel it all through my body."

The mother tried to descend from her high post carefully. Indeed, her entire being was shaking, like an instrument in which every string was vibrating.

"Why such a shock, Channe dear?" the peddler said. "Perhaps because I've brought back our 'guest' for you? Don't you have anything to eat on Shabbes? We'll throw something together for him. I thought, though, that I'd be giving you pleasure by bringing him back to you."

Channe, however, was not paying attention at all to what her husband was saying. All she saw was an almost lifeless Emanuel standing before her.

"You did well to come back, guest," she exclaimed passionately, with a radiant expression in her eyes. "This is God's doing. What am I talking about Shabbes? You can stay here the whole week, as long as you wish."

"If you have a wife and child, guest," the peddler said with a laugh, "just let us know. She'll feed them as well."

"Mother dear," Benjamin cried out, "you mustn't let him go back to the 'Schlafstube.'" He grabbed Emanuel's hand. "He'd just run away from us again."

"The child is right, as long as I live. You mustn't go there," the mother said at once.

"This time I shall not run away from you, dear Benjamin," Emanuel said. He bowed down to the boy with an excess of emotion and then hugged him for several minutes.

It would be impossible to portray the condition in which Emanuel spent the remaining hours leading up to the actual Sabbath. The "beloved bridegroom" (which is how the beautiful song describes the Sabbath) spread its perfume through the home.[14] The father was working hard to liberate himself from the dirt of being on the road all week by shaving and dressing up to receive the Sabbath as festively as possible. Emanuel was eavesdropping on the warm, intimate conversations of the child. Outside in the kitchen the mother was hard at work preparing the Sabbath meal, but she peeked inside frequently, her whispering lips and glowing eyes revealing that she was checking to make sure that her guest was still there. She did not want to lose him again.

In the evening, Emanuel came back from the synagogue with his father and little brother and stepped into the brilliantly lit Sabbath room. He heard both of them chant the greeting of peace, the "Salem

---

14. In the traditional Jewish Sabbath liturgy, the Sabbath figures as a bride to be welcomed.

Alechem," and he understood as never before the beautiful meaning of this sweet song.

Yes, peace, peace be with you! After such a week, after all the trials and tribulations that his father had to endure, he truly understood the necessity that a song like this should exist. "Peace, peace be with you!"

Rösele sat again in her usual corner and seemed to be absorbed in her sad dreams of a wedding. But she did not cry, and Emanuel interpreted this as a good sign. "Peace, peace be with you!" This was affecting her as well.

Emanuel sat down again next to his little brother at the table. Benjamin was so absorbed by the guest who had returned that he literally forgot to eat and drink. Emanuel too barely touched the generous portions of food which his mother had put on his plate, and as a result he had to suffer any number of mocking comments from Reb Schimme.

"So where did your hunger go?" he asked. "Why did you run like that? Don't be a fool: eat. You don't need to be embarrassed eating in front of *this* beautiful peasant."

After they had finished eating and praying, father and son began singing. This time, however, the peddler's voice descended into a mumble earlier than it had last week. Earning nothing all week had likely taken its toll on him. Rösele too had withdrawn to her room. Only Benjamin's little bell of a voice rang out into the Sabbath ghetto. Mother and son sat across from each other, and there were two angels fighting over this minute.

Channe began, "I'll tell you again, my dear guest. You did right in coming back to us. All week long my heart was full of sadness, and I didn't know why. I would have given my life to have you reappear for just a moment. I felt so unhappy whenever I realized, 'He left, and you'll never get to see him again.' My dear guest, I can't describe how I felt. I think I would have climbed the highest mountains just to have a look at you. I would have swum through the deepest waters if I had caught just a glimpse of the color of your clothes. I'm a fool, a big fool, but something must have happened to me. You'd have every right to laugh at me."

But Emanuel did not laugh. His face became pale. At this moment, Benjamin closed his prayer book and said "I don't want to sing anymore, I'll finish tomorrow. And now that the guest is here, I want you to tell me the little story that you promised me for learning Talmud. Now would be the best time."

Emanuel had a brilliant thought. "Benjamin," he exclaimed, barely able to catch his breath. "I want to tell you a different story, one I've thought about all week. I know you'll like it."

The boy gave him a strange look. He didn't understand why Emanuel seemed to be in such a feverish hurry. He looked up at his mother and said, "If we could do your story some other time, mother dear, I'd like . . . who knows when the guest will come back."

"Tell your story," the mother said. "My little story isn't going to run away from you."

"Imagine, Benjamin," Emanuel began, his voice uncertain. "A long time ago you had an aunt named Miriam, and she had an only child named Ruben. This child had always been a prodigy full of wisdom, and he could speak with the greatest rabbi about the Torah. People who heard him had their hair stand on end. But do you know what the boy's greatest pleasure was? You know, of course, that books containing the name of God can never be destroyed and that when such books are torn or damaged people throw them in that little wooden house? Well, after sundown, when he knew that the synagogue caretaker was visiting the rabbi, this boy would go remove a slat of wood from this little house.

"He would grab lots and lots of these books and take them home with him, staying up all night to try to figure out their meaning. Some of them were missing their beginnings, some of them their endings, and often there would be several pages missing all at once in the middle. But because of his brilliance he always knew what was in the missing sections.

"Listen to what happened. One evening when in the little house he has the feeling that a soft hand is placing a book in his hands. He wants to drop it, but it is as if it is riveted to him. He has to hold on to it. He carries the book home, and when he opens it up at night he sees that it is not in the sacred language. It is in a foreign language that he does not know. He is consumed by an intense desire to understand the book. He knows that the rabbi excommunicates those who read such books, and he loathes this.

"He finally comes to understand it. The final pages of this book are missing too, and he cannot figure out what the book means, as many times as he starts it over again from the beginning. One day he disappears, with the book in his hand. No one knows where he has gone. A beautiful woman appeared in his room. She took him away and promised to supply him with the end of the book. Shortly thereafter someone saw him in a distant city. He had 'converted,' and was riding on a horse next to a beautiful woman dressed in magnificent clothes. When Aunt Miriam heard about this, she dropped dead. In the night when her soul tore itself so suddenly from her body, the son dreamt that he was at the side of the beautiful woman when his mother stood before him and spoke: 'Do you think that if you had stayed with me you wouldn't have found out the end of that book? Stand up and repent!' She came to him three times like this.

"At the entrance to the synagogue in Amsterdam there once lay a *Baal Teshuva* [a repentant one] on the floor, whom the congregation was trampling on.[15] This man was . . . "

"*Elijah*, my Elijah," the mother cried out with such a shrill voice that it echoed throughout the house. She had fallen at his feet, pale and almost fainting. She had recognized this story all too well. The father, drunk with sleep, stood up quickly, and Rösele appeared at the door. "Elijah, my Elijah," one heard late into the night. And everything was as good as good can be.

(Written on Sunday)

The unfortunate one builds his hut close to the place where happiness resides. He strolls amid the happy ones, and his smile often seems as if it were borrowed from them. I shall smile, I shall be happy—but can I ever forget you, Clara?

---

15. The Hebrew term *Baal Teshuva* traditionally refers to a Jew who, after transgressing Jewish law, chooses to recommit to orthodox Judaism. The type of punishment that makes its way into this piece of Prager family lore is reminiscent of the way in which the Amsterdam community disciplined famous seventeenth-century heretics such as Uriel da Costa (1585–1740).

Alexandre Weill, "Braendel" (1860)
Translated from the French by Maurice Samuels

Alexandre Weill (1811–99) was born in the small Alsatian village of Schirhof, near Strasbourg. His maternal grandfather took an active role in revolutionary politics in the region and his father was a modestly successful livestock merchant. Destined for the rabbinate at a young age, he studied in Metz and Frankfurt, where he abandoned the Talmud for secular philosophy and literature, and nearly converted to Catholicism. After befriending the French writer Gérard de Nerval, he moved to Paris in the 1830s and rose to prominence in bohemian journalistic circles. Supported by his wife, Agathina Marx, who ran a successful dress shop on the Faubourg Saint-Honoré, he devoted himself to writing and politics, nearly winning a seat in the National Assembly after the revolution of 1848. Though initially a radical leftist, Weill briefly turned reactionary after 1848, before forsaking politics, like many of his disillusioned contemporaries, following Napoleon III's coup d'état in 1852. During the Second Empire (1852–70), Weill returned to Judaism, but increasingly subjected the religious tradition of his youth to scrutiny, rejecting the Talmud in favor of his own idiosyncratic brand of monotheism based on the five books of Moses.

Remembered today, if at all, as a friend of Heinrich Heine, Weill was an incredibly prolific and popular writer in a number of genres. He began writing fiction in his youth and would later claim to have invented the "village tale" in the 1830s, before Berthold Auerbach and George Sand had made it famous. Featuring humble characters in rustic settings, the "village tale" would become a major genre of Jewish belles lettres in the nineteenth century, just as large numbers of Jews were moving from small villages to urban centers. Many of Weill's village tales document a traditional Jewish life on the verge of extinction in mid-nineteenth-century France. Their lives governed by Jewish law and structured by the Jewish calendar, Weill's orthodox, Yiddish-speaking village characters perceive that change is in the air. The threat of modernity provides his plots with their principle motor.

Originally published in a volume entitled *Histoires de village* (Village Tales, 1860), "Braendel" describes the ill-fated love between an idealistic young woman and her materialistic fiancé, an erstwhile rabbinic student. Playing against the popular French stereotype of the passive, victimized "belle Juive" or beautiful Jewess, Weill's Braendel scorns external appearance and displays courage and a passion for learning that put the village boys to shame. The fact that Weill translates very common Hebrew and Yiddish words into French would indicate that he intended the story for a mainstream (i.e., non-Jewish) readership that was fascinated by this exotic Jewish world, but the story also serves as a platform for Weill's polemics with the Jewish religious authorities of his day as well as with his wealthy, secular coreligionists. Biting in its criticism of the Talmud, the story nevertheless praises the value that orthodox Jewish culture places on religious learning over worldly success. It is the conflict between religious tradition and modern materialism, a conflict that Weill saw as central to Jewish life in the nineteenth century, that divides the young lovers in the story. Ultimately, the values of traditional Judaism win out, but only to the extent that they emerge as the source of the universal democratic principles—liberty, equality, and fraternity—of the French revolutionary tradition that Weill prizes.

I.

Braendel was a young Jewess born and raised in an Alsatian village near Strasbourg. Her grandmother was the great-granddaughter of a rabbi from Mainz who was crushed in a wine press because he refused to worship an image of the Virgin. Her father was a sacred scribe. This is what the Jews call a man who knows how to copy the Pentateuch onto scrolls of parchment in block letters. For Israelites allow into their sanctuaries only Bibles that have been written by hand according to the ancient esoteric tradition. In addition to this, he copied and sold certain extracts of the five books of Moses that the Jews affix to the doors of their homes or that they encase in parchment and attach by means of tight straps both to their forehead and to their left arm, near the heart, during the morning prayer.

In 1793, Braendel's father went from being a sacred scribe to becoming the secretary to the famous commissioner Euloge Schneider, who was sent by Robespierre to Alsace before being denounced by Saint-Just and guillotined. The Jew was not honored with the guillotine; he died in prison. Braendel's mother, who used to be known as the beautiful Gudelle, died at the age of thirty.

All that Braendel had left was her grandmother, a pious woman who earned her keep by spinning *tzitzith*. The tzitzith is a fringe of wool that reminds Jews of the sacred tassels that used to be suspended from the banner of Zévaoth.¹ The wool should be taken from the back of a first-born ram. But in the absence of a first-born, it can be taken from a lamb belonging to a pious man. The Jews attach this fringe with a thousand mysterious and kabbalistic knots to a sort of double tunic, which they wear over the shirt, like a kind of flannel vest, and which they call *arbah kanfoth* (four corners).² They kiss it many times during the morning prayer. They also put tzitzith on the *taleth*, a white wool shawl that they don during prayer, and which became the surplice of the Catholic priest.

Selling tzitzith brought in about one franc and fifty centimes a week. For her part, Braendel went regularly into the forest to collect branches of dead trees and peat that she would sell in the village for twenty centimes a faggot. She made up to three trips a day, with the exception of Fridays and Saturdays. Friday is for Jews only a half day, since the Sabbath begins at sundown of the night preceding Saturday. Ordinarily the income of the two women did not exceed fifty centimes a day.

And yet, neither Braendel nor her grandmother ever asked for a handout. The granddaughter of the rabbi of Mainz would rather have starved to death. This is because, from the time of Moses to our own day, religious Jews only recognize one kind of nobility, that of sacred knowledge and of virtue. Braendel's grandmother, despite her poverty, looked down with a sovereign scorn on all the horse traders, shopkeepers, and rich industrialists. She considered them *am haarazim*, which is to say ignoramuses, common people.³ Their wives barely knew how to read and would all come to the synagogue to consult her on matters of religious ritual and on the innumerable prayers they had to say. When she was in a good mood, she would translate these prayers into German and recite some *thinoth* (improvised prayers) that nobody knew.⁴

She would be the first one summoned to the bedside of a sick or dying Israelite, because Jews confess before their death in front of a

---

1. I have elected to retain Weill's transcriptions of Yiddish and Hebrew words and to provide more standard transliterations in footnotes. A more standard transliteration here would be *Tzevaoth*.
2. Standard transliteration: *arbah kenafoth*.
3. The correct Hebrew plural would be *ammei ha-aretz*.
4. Standard transliteration: *tehinoth*.

dozen congregants, who recite aloud with the dying person a sacramental formula. Well versed in the details of all the ceremonies, she would give orders to the richest Jewish women whenever it came time to bathe and dress the dead or to take care of a sick person or a newborn baby. In her capacity as keeper of religious ceremonies (and for Talmudists, everything, from breakfast to dinner, is considered a religious act), she attended all the celebrations, all the parties for circumcisions or first communions,[5] engagements or weddings.

Thanks to these privileges, Braendel and her grandmother lacked for nothing. They claimed all the choicest morsels as their due, besides which the grandmother was a real cordon bleu of the art of Jewish cooking, which holds a fairly distinguished place in culinary circles. Braendel was just as learned as her grandmother and much more fanatical. She prayed three times a day, and every night made sure to read either a chapter of the Bible or one of the stories in Josephus. Alsatian Jews read the Bible and Josephus in German translation, printed in little Hebrew characters.[6]

Thanks to a translation of the Pentateuch and to her prayer books, Braendel had learned to read Hebrew and constantly regretted being a woman and thus excluded from the sacred study of the Talmud. She only derived consolation for these regrets by reading the heroic and marvelous stories of Miriam, Deborah, Esther, and the mother of the seven Maccabees. She burned with desire to resemble these noble women by sacrificing herself for the good of her people and devoting herself to the glory of the God of Israel.

Braendel was fifteen years old. Her pale face had a perfect oval shape and was shaded by crow-black hair that fell in thick tresses down to her waist and that she used instead of a cushion when she carried wood on her head. She wore a coarsely woven wool dress that came up to her neck and was fastened by two strings on the sides. Since the poor girl spent most of her days out walking, she was forced to hem her dresses above the ankle. Most often, she wore no stockings or shoes. Sometimes, she put on wooden clogs but she didn't hesitate to dangle them

---

5. Nineteenth-century French Jews often used the term *première communion* to refer to the bar mitzvah ceremony.
6. i.e., Yiddish.

from her bundle of wood in order to walk more easily. She moved with a lively and pleasant gait. No girl in the village could keep up with her. The bundles of wood stayed perfectly balanced atop her head raised up by her thickly braided black hair. Occasionally, in a naturally coquettish gesture, she would walk with her hand on her hip.

On Saturdays, which is to say on Friday nights, a bonnet hid her braids since Jewish women don't even do their hair on the Sabbath. On these occasions, the coarsely woven wool dress was replaced by one of Indian cotton that was almost new and that fell all the way to her ankles. Her little feet, enclosed in white stockings knitted by her grandmother, were hidden by black leather slippers, adorned with ribbons and a bow on the tops.

To be considered a beauty in the village, you had to have pink cheeks, a full bust, and a strong constitution. The pale Braendel was thus at first only known for her piety, and since she didn't take part in the games and pleasures of the other young girls her age, they called her the quiet one, the proud one, and sometimes even, in a malicious tone, the saint. Nor did Braendel ever unbutton the top of her dress like peasant girls do when it's hot. Winter and summer her dress was closed tightly about her neck and fell in pleats around her body. The village girls would bathe sometimes, after sundown, in the river that ran along the woods. Braendel would accompany them but never bathe. They would tease her and say that she must not have a good figure, to no avail. "What does it matter?" she would respond. "The important thing is to do good works." But, in reality, Braendel's body was white as marble and already, at fourteen, her bust rivaled that of Diana the Huntress. Her grandmother knew it. Thus, one night, she said before going to bed, "My daughter, we are poor, but no *am haaretz*, even a millionaire, is worthy of possessing you. You need a saint, a rabbi. Only a soul sanctified by the study of the law can appreciate the beauty of a virtuous woman. I would prefer, Braendel, to see you die young than to know you had married a horse trader, or a dealer in cattle, money, or dry goods."

"My mother," Braendel responded, "have you ever noticed young Joël, the son of Gidel?"

"Yes, my daughter. That young man is rich. Be on guard, especially against rich young men. Very often they lack faith."

"But grandmother, Joël studies the holy law. He's a *bachor* (student).[7] He is only seventeen and already he holds the title of rabbi."

"So, my child, is he in love with you?"

"No, mother, but I love him."

Braendel spoke these words in so calm a tone and you would have thought she was talking about some indifferent matter.

"Holy God, Lord in heaven!" cried the old woman. "What do I hear! My daughter is only fifteen and already she loves a man! Oh holy ancestor, martyr of the *Torah* (holy law), turn over in your grave, because shame is at the door of your family! This girl, whom I took for a saint, is going to dishonor us."

"Grandmother," responded Braendel, "those are big words. Know that Braendel will always remain an honest girl. But is it a crime to love a young student of the law? If Joël loves me back, I will become his wife. If not, I will stay the same Braendel."

"So you have spoken to him?"

"Yes, the other day. You know Grandjean, the goyish soldier (*goy* is a collective term for everything that isn't Jewish), who just came back from the army. He's a bad man, a drunk, who always wanders about in the forest. Well! The other day, Grandjean came up to me in the forest. He called me a wretched Jewess and was about to touch me with his impure hand when all of a sudden Joël appeared. He likes to go for a walks with a book in his hand in the middle of the woods."

"And what did Joël say to you? My daughter, Joël is much more dangerous for you than Grandjean."

"He said that I shouldn't go into the woods alone, that I'm too big and . . ."

"Too beautiful," interrupted the old lady. "So let him give you an income, then. Did he court you?"

"For heaven's sake! As if he were thinking of that! He has many other cares. Just think, grandmother, he is forced to abandon his studies and his books. His father is pulling him out of school for fear that he will abandon religion and succumb to the temptations of idolatrous and pernicious books. Apparently young Abram, who just converted to Catholicism in Metz, has terrified all the parents of young Jewish students.

---

7. Standard transliteration: *bachur*.

Starting tomorrow, they told me, Joël will no longer be a *bachor* and will have to become a horse trader. What a sacrilege! He who is so pious and scholarly! Oh how he chants the prayers, and how he recites the *Haftorahs* (chapters taken from the Prophets). Go on, grandmother, say what you like. If Joël continues on the holy path, Braendel will refuse him nothing. And if I have to sacrifice my youth and my beauty to keep him away from mundane commerce and bring him back to the Torah, I won't hesitate an instant. And if he wants my life, I am ready to give it to him."

"Woe is me!" cried the grandmother. "Is this the language of a daughter of Israel whom I thought was the worthy sister of Sarah and Rachel?"

"Rachel really loved Jacob. Jewish women show their virtue in the love that they feel for a worthy husband. Have no fear, dear grandmother. I really love Joël and I would be happy to become his wife. But Braendel will never give the enemies of our religion arms to use against us. I am a Jewess, grandmother, that is enough for me. Far from being ashamed of it, like so many young city girls, I am proud of it. They can kill me fifty times over before they can make me worship another God besides that of Abraham, Isaac, and Jacob!"

II.

Joël's father had made a fortune during the empire by selling horses to the army. He lost half of that fortune during the Hundred Days,[8] but despite that semiruin, he clung to his reputation as a rich man, especially vis-à-vis his coreligionists. Although he had frequent contact with army officers and daily relations with Catholic peasants from the village, he never slackened for an instant in the observance of the severe precepts of the Talmudic religion, which he performed with a scrupulous exactitude. You could even say he was fanatical in his piety. Now a fanatical Jew only poses a threat to other Jews. He would give his last penny to a Catholic friend, but not a crust of bread to a Jew who violated any of the 613 affirmative commandments, not to mention the innumerable prohibitions.

---

8. During the so-called Hundred Days (20 March–8 July 1815), Napoleon returned from exile on Elba and regained control of France before being definitively defeated at Waterloo.

He had destined his son for the rabbinate. From an early age, the young Joël showed intelligence and imagination. Moreover, he had a very loud voice and in these sorts of religious discussions he who screams the loudest is a saint in the eyes of the pious. At the age of ten, he learned French grammar, and soon, along with the Bible and the Talmud, they allowed him to read *Telemachus* and a *Summary in French of Jewish Ritual Duties* by Lambert.[9] At thirteen, the age of the first communion for Jewish boys (Jewish girls do not have a first communion), Joël himself performed the functions of the cantor and reader in the synagogue. Then, that evening at dinner, in front of all the invited dignitaries, the young bar-mitzvah (son of the law) gave a speech half in Hebrew and half in German, lasting two hours, on a subject taken from the Talmud, of which not a single person present understood a word. Thus was he greatly admired. After this speech, the rabbi of the village praised him and conferred on him the title of *haber* (colleague).[10]

That same evening, Joël was engaged to the daughter of a rich Israelite who had a twenty thousand franc dowry. The father of that young girl (she was only eleven) had the misfortune of having lost several sons and had destined his daughter, from birth, to a man of the law, which is to say a rabbi. The young Joël was more than a little proud of this title and wouldn't have traded it for that of king of France.

However, his reading of *Telemachus*, without shaking his faith, had made him think. Until then, the only beautiful women he knew were Sarah, Rebecca, Rachel, and Tamar. He had never looked at his young fiancée. She was Jewish and orthodox, that was enough. What good is it to admire the beautiful hair of a daughter of Israel, since it gets cut off on the day of her marriage and she is forced by the Talmud to cover her entire head winter and summer, day and night? A married Jewish woman must wear her blouse buttoned to the neck and only can dance with her husband. As for committing the crime of adultery, she might

---

9. *Les aventures de Télémaque* (1699), a didactic novel written by the Catholic theologian Fénelon for the crown prince, remained a bestseller into the nineteenth century. Lion Mayer Lambert (1787–1862) was the grand rabbi of Metz and author of a *Catéchisme du culte judaïque* (Catechism of the Jewish Religion, 1818) and an *Abrégé de la grammaire hébraïque* (Summary of Hebrew Grammar, 1843).

10. Standard transliteration: *haver*.

as well drown herself because no honest coreligionist would ever speak to her again.

Joël had thus never had an impure thought. But despite his firm desire to devote himself entirely to God, he couldn't help but admire Eucharis and to acknowledge to himself that Perle (which was the name of his fiancée) would never be a Eucharis.[11]

Then one day a shocking piece of news spread through the synagogues of Alsace. Several Jewish students from Saverne and Strasbourg had just converted to Catholicism in Metz. When this happens, their relatives go into mourning for the converts as if they had died. They sit on the ground, without shoes, for seven days, except for the Sabbath, rip a piece of their clothing, let their beards grow, eat eggs and lentils, and receive condolence visits from all the members of the community. The latter are commanded to go daily to the mourner's house without uttering a word. Joël's father was the uncle of one of the converts who had once seemed so likely to be a ray of light and glory for Israel. Thus he had to go into mourning for this *meshumet* (convert) of a nephew.

On that day, he had the following conversation with his wife: "Mother, I would rather that our son were struck down by apoplexy that to see him disavow our God."

"I agree with you," responded the mother. "God knows," she added, raising her eyes to the ceiling, "Like Hannah, I can say that I conceived my son in total purity. During my pregnancy, I never missed a prayer or offended another human being. Prostrate before the Creator, I prayed for Him to give his servant a son who would be a perpetual glory for Israel, even if he must die as a martyr to the faith. God heard my prayer. Joël is a chosen child. He is our son. Every day, I pray for him. When I see him singing with fervor in the synagogue and bowing down before God, my heart swells and wants to cry out with joy. But if Joël were ever to change, it would be the death of me."

"I was wrong to teach him French," the father responded. "I've heard it said that reading French is poison for a Jew."

"I've heard the rabbi say that German is even more dangerous," the mother added. "In Germany, the Jews live almost like the *goyim*. They no longer observe anything. They might as well just become Catholic."

---

11. Eucharis was one of Calypso's attendants in Fénelon's novel.

"Don't blaspheme, wife. Listen to what I have decided. Joël is our only son. I am getting old. I can no longer attend to my business like I used to do. Joël will replace me. Better a religious horse trader than a disloyal scholar and a traitor to the faith of his fathers. I believe I am pleasing God with this resolution. I don't want Joël to go to Metz or Frankfurt where the Catholics and Protestants will ambush him. Let him be a horse dealer and remain a Jew!"

The poor mother shook her head, saying, "And yet there isn't even a smidgeon of sin in my son's entire body. My heart tells me he will be one of the glories of the world!"

"The one thing that worries me is that Perle's father didn't want to give his daughter to a horse dealer. He will break his pledge."

"So let him. Perle is rich, but the grandfather of her mother seduced a young girl and didn't marry her. Those are the kinds of crimes that call down, sooner or later, vengeance from on high."

"I scoff at your seducer grandfather. But do you want to know what I really think? Perle is going to be ugly. Ah! If only she resembled Braendel! That girl doesn't have a penny, but she is a real pearl of beauty and virtue! It's true that Joël doesn't even know what a beautiful woman is. The poor child only thinks about his salvation."

"Just wait," said the mother. "Instead of making him leave now, let's keep him another year or two. Time will tell."

But a few months later, a new crop of *bachorim* having converted, both in Metz and in Germany, Joël's father, despite his wife's protestations, and at the risk of breaking his son's engagement, commanded Joël to follow him to the market, forbid him to attend the local Talmudic classes, and declared that he would no longer pay a penny for Joël's education.

Joël unhappily obeyed. He put on the trader's shirt and followed his father on horseback, cracking his whip like a real horse dealer. Through the horse trade, young Joël, who had never earned a penny, suddenly found himself in possession of some pocket change. He took up with the village ruffians and spent his money drinking with them.

His mother, however, never saw him on horseback without sighing, and for a month, she had been thinking about ways to get him to leave for Metz, even without his father knowing.

III.

It was the middle of summer. In that season, all the owners of horses in the village send them out to pasture, from midnight until five o'clock in the morning, in the royal forest, where the grass grows as sturdy and high as stalks of rye, because the park ranger refrains from cutting it in order to allow the soil to retain its natural fertilizer. From time to time, the ranger fines people, but these fines are paid by everyone collectively and if someone has to go to prison for a period, he accepts his martyrdom with good grace. Moreover, the horse herders are always minors, who are rarely convicted in court.

Young Joël had already passed more than one night in the forest, in the company of some other boys, who knew all the clearings, all the watering holes, and in case of trouble, all the back routes to escape at a gallop and return to the village without being recognized.

There is nothing so striking as the forest just before the break of day. It's almost as if nature is waking up, limb by limb, piece by piece. A few minutes before dawn, the owls let out piercing cries that resemble those of thieves. Those enemies of the light bawl and fuss as soon as they perceive a ray of sunshine falling on the shadows of their nests. Here and there a baby deer darts by at a gallop. Dead leaves do little somersaults on the ground. The lark, as soon as the owl grows silent, hazards some halting sounds. All of a sudden the trees start rustling in a continual whisper. A last veil of darkness covers everything for a second or two. In that interval, all life seems suspended. As if nature is holding her breath. But then the dawn appears on the other side of the horizon. Night is vanquished. The shadow of the peaks flees before the light of day, pale at first, then reddened by the dawn. All of nature seems to be singing a hymn in honor of the light. The birds chirp, the trees wave their branches, the shrubs sway with joy and happiness, the horses nay, the dog wags his tail and barks with satisfaction. And the man bows down, or else lifts his head toward the heavens and admires the Creator of all these marvels.

Joël was a poet. The Talmud had taught him that every plant sings with the glory of the Creator. From time to time, he would lend an ear to a marigold or a daisy, or a flowering bush, as if he had wanted, like a new Solomon, to learn their language. For according to the same Talmud, every plant sings its own particular hymn. Far from growing bored in the forest, he saw himself as fortunate for having obtained permission from his mother to spend the night there with the other adolescents, Jews and Catholics together, because when it came to cheating the government, religious differences ceased to matter.

It was during one of these summer nights that Joël, having attached the halter to the left foot of his animal, lay down on a flowery edge of a ditch that borders the woods and fell asleep. During his slumber, he saw a fiery figure, holding a scythe, who said to him: "Joël! Joël! Why have you left off studying the holy books for money and material possessions? Don't you know that you were chosen by God to combat the eternal Amalekites?[12] Get up, Joël, gird your loins and be on your way. Go to where the holy doctrine is studied night and day. Leave your parents and this village. The Lord has sent me to tell you to go! He will be with you. But wherever you go, don't forget to battle the Amalekites for all eternity!"

Joël, who during this dream thrashed in all directions and let out sighs like a man who wants to respond but can't, suddenly felt himself being pulled by the arm. He woke up, stumbled about, and found himself in front of a young girl holding a long rod with a hook at the end that was designed to cut off dead branches from trees.

"Who are you? And what do you want from me?" cried Joël.

"So you don't recognize Braendel?" responded the young girl. "I go to the woods to collect the branches that have fallen during the night. I met you there once before. It seems that you have had a bad dream. Your friends have left. Dawn is appearing at the tops of the trees."

"Yes, I had a dream. I saw an angel face to face." Then, looking at Braendel, whose hair blew wildly about her shoulders, Joël added: "By God's eternal life, Braendel, you resemble that angel. It had your forehead, your eyes, your mouth, and your figure. Your rod reminds me of the scythe it was carrying."

"And do you want me to repeat what it said?"

"How can you? Are you a prophetess, like Miriam or Deborah?"

"I am nothing of the kind. However I will repeat to you the words of your angel. What can a messenger of God tell you other than to go away, not to listen to your father, not to sacrifice the doctrine and the study of the sacred law for the pathetic calculations of the horse dealer?

---

12. *Amalekites* is a collective term designating idolatrous peoples. [Author's note.]

What is an animal merchant? An *am haaretz*, a coarse soul who feels nothing, who is nothing. How can you whom God destined to become a Hasid, a *zadig* (wise, just man), one of the first sons of Israel, how can you debase yourself and commit suicide in your mind and soul? Listen, Joël, I am only a poor girl. But if I were a boy like you, I would long ago have become famous in all of France."

Never had Joël heard such a language, especially from the mouth of a young girl. Braendel, still holding the pole in her left hand, truly had the look of a missionary angel. Her windblown hair appeared like wings, her flowing dress seemed copied from the image Joël had seen in the Bible. He couldn't help but look at her and admire her.

At this moment, a ray of dawn illuminated Braendel's face and Joël felt a holy shiver run down his body. Thinking he must still be dreaming, he fell at the young girl's knees and cried: "*Adonai Elohim*,[13] I shall obey your command, I shall bend to your will. I will leave here and all my life will be sacrificed to your glory."

Delighted by Joël's exaltation, Braendel threw down her pole and helped him rise up, saying, "But Joël, it is I. I am only the daughter of Gudelle, Braendel, who sells firewood. If I were an angel, I would devote myself to your happiness, for I love you, Joël. If I were a queen, you would be king."

"Oh Braendel," cried Joël, pressing himself against her like a frightened child. "You are my guardian angel. Only now, looking at you, listening to you, do I understand certain biblical stories. You are how the beautiful Esther must have seemed or like Rachel when Jacob saw her for the first time. Only now that I look at you, Braendel, do I feel that Perle is ugly. But have I seen you before?"

"You met me once before in the woods and you saved me from a miserable wretch who told me I was pretty even while calling me a cursed Jew. My grandmother, who is a wise woman, often tells me that my beauty will be the cause of my unhappiness. She would like to make me uglier. I have never looked in a mirror, but if it will make you leave the village, nothing in the world will stop me from being beautiful."

"Well, then, be beautiful, for God has sent you to me. I must love you. I love you and I will always love you."

---

13. "Lord God."

"But I am poor, Joël."

"I shall be poor like you."

"But you have Perle."

"I don't love her and I won't marry her. I only want to marry you."

"Listen, Joël. I love you too, but I love you as I love God. I want your soul to go toward Him and for you to think only of Him and His commandments. I don't love you because your father is rich, but because you have a great mind and a pious soul. Be a rabbi and I'm yours. Stay a horse dealer and I will snuff out my love along with my life."

"Braendel," Joël cried. "You are truly the angel that appeared to me last night. Through you I will return to God and to my studies. Come, receive my pledge!"

"No, Joël, that would be egotism on my part. Promise me only to leave, and you will see that if you are gone for fifty years, Braendel will wait for you for fifty years. But you will surely forget a poor girl."

"As for me, Braendel, when I have sworn on the Bible, they can burn me alive before I will break my oath."

"But you have to obey your parents, God commands it."

"God inclines souls toward good. Are you not from a truly noble family? Your grandfather was a martyr. Your father was a holy man. Braendel, you will be my wife, I swear it on the *schema*.[14] It is God's will."

"What joy!" the young girl cried. "We are engaged before God. I give you my soul and you give me yours in return. Now, if ever you betray me, my soul will torment you like a demon and you will have to exorcise it. You will go crazy. As for me, I will call myself Joël's wife. I will not fear the Sisras or the Goliaths. Any enemy of the Jews is my enemy. I will die of joy if I have to die for our faith. How great you are, my God, and how beautiful you are, my dear Joël, my rabbi, my master, my lord!" While speaking these words, she prostrated herself before him.

IV.

February was drawing to a close and Joël had not yet left. It wasn't his fault. First the mayor obstinately refused to give him a passport

---

14. Standard transliteration: *Shema*, the most holy Jewish prayer.

under the pretext that he didn't have his father's consent. Joël might have left without a passport but he at least needed a little money for the journey. He proposed to Braendel that she allow him to take fifty francs from his father if he promised to return it later, but Braendel wouldn't permit it.

"You are allowed to leave your father's house without his consent in order to serve God, but you are not allowed to steal from him," she said.

Everyone in the village was aware of Braendel's love for Joël, but since she was known to be very pious and since she didn't make the slightest scruple about proclaiming her love, nobody reproached her. Joël's mother would often say: "What a pity that holy child is so poor. She loves my son so much!"

The holiday of Purim was approaching. It is the anniversary of the day when Esther rescued the Jews from the clutches of Haman. The night before and the morning of that holiday, the story of Esther is read in synagogue, on parchment scrolls. All the children hold either a hammer or a rattle and every time the reader speaks the name of Haman, they bang loudly for ten minutes, every blow supposedly meant to blot out Haman, or at least his name. Attendance is mandatory and it is forbidden to eat anything before going to synagogue in the morning. They haven't eaten since the day before either, because Esther fasted before appearing in front of Ahasuerus. Around noon, the Jews give each other presents consisting of cakes, smoked meats, and candy, and in the evening, all the young people in the village go from one house to the next drinking, eating, singing, and dancing. On every food-laden table there is a piece of smoked meat and a big cake called a Haman, which everyone must eat. What is more, the Jews, who are normally so abstemious when it comes to alcohol, are required by the law to drink until they no longer know the difference between the names of Mordecai and Haman.

A month before the holiday of Purim, Joël had stepped on a bunch of thorns while out walking in a neighboring village. One of the thorns pierced the sole of his shoe and penetrated his foot. When he returned home, he stopped first at the home of Braendel, who was spinning tzitzith for her grandmother. The young girl, after having plucked out the thorn and dressed the foot, said to him:

"Joël, we are sinning all the time. Already six months have passed. You are still buying horses and you seem proud when you mount a fine, lively animal. And you even kiss me sometimes. Have you ever asked the rabbi if it's allowed to kiss a young girl if she is not your wife? Isn't it impure?"

"Dear Braendel," Joël responded. "Have no fears from that quarter. The Talmud, which I know well, does not forbid a man to kiss his fiancée. The law of Moses only requires a young man who has dishonored a young girl to marry her."

"So you still plan to marry me? Why, then, haven't you kept your pledge to God?"

"Do you want me to tell you everything I'm thinking, Braendel? I love you too much to leave you. It would be impossible for me to study without seeing you. I couldn't live without you."

"In that case, I am lost. I promised you to God and it was on that condition alone that I belong to you. Because I took an oath. I said to God in one of my prayers when I particularly felt His presence: 'Lord, if you turn Joël's heart toward me, if you make him love your servant, I will promise him to you and I will vow to tear him away from the material world in order to dedicate him to your glory and splendor.' So you see, I will have perjured myself. And what is more, if you stay, I won't marry you. But I cannot stop loving you. So go, even if you risk forgetting me, and consecrate yourself to God. What does my life matter, as long as we see each other again in *Gan Eden* (paradise), where my soul will wait for you."

"Leave?" cried Joël, clutching Braendel in his arms. "Leave and embrace old books instead of these fresh pink lips? Study treatises on women when I have God's most beautiful creature right here? Go in search of knowledge when I have happiness at home?"

"Joël, Joël! What am I hearing? What kind of language is this in the mouth of a rabbi? Do you love me because I am beautiful? Woe is me! The only part of myself I value is my soul. Remember Solomon's proverb: *Charm is deceptive and beauty is vain, but a woman who fears God shall be praised*. But if you love me for my beauty, you won't love me after my beauty has faded. As our sages have said: *Love that arises from a cause disappears along with that cause*. And I who love you with such a pure love, Joël. Joël, I beg you, leave me."

"Am I to blame?" cried the young man, while still clutching her to his heart. "Is it my fault if I love you more than God? See here, either you will be my wife or I will kill myself at your feet."

"Great God! What have I done? Is there not a single pious man who fears God on this earth? You know, Joël, that I love you more than my life. I am yours body and soul: but respect my grandmother who would die of sorrow. Wait until she is dead, even though I feel that in giving you my honor, I am also giving you my life."

Then, suddenly breaking free of Joël's arms and cocking her head, as if she were listening to a voice from on high, Braendel cried: "Do you hear? It's a *bath kol* (voice from heaven) that orders you to go. God be praised! God loves us." The young man, who also thought he had heard that voice, ran off like a criminal, and came back the next day to ask Braendel for forgiveness.

"Go," she said. "Beat your breast. Ask God to pardon you. Prepare yourself to leave."

"I will go after Passover, my treasure. God doesn't want me to die of homesickness."

"Your home is where God is."

"My home is where Braendel is."

V.

The day after that conversation, Braendel went to see the rabbi of the town.

"Rabbi," she said. "I have committed a great sin. I lit a flame on the Sabbath."

"My child, that is indeed a sin. And you, who know the Bible, know that Moses said: *You shall not light a fire in your dwelling on the Sabbath day*. But in light of your youth and your piety, I only command you to observe a half-day fast in expiation."

"And if I weren't young or pious?"

"You would fast from sunrise to sunset."

"Alas, my sin is much greater," Braendel replied. "I lit a flame that I cannot extinguish and the fire is threatening my honor and my life."

"You have a great reputation in the village," said Rabbi Lazarus. "They say you are the most learned, the most pious, and the most courageous girl. I thought of you for my son Aron who will soon be twenty."

"But your son is a shopkeeper. He doesn't study the law."

"In our family it is not necessarily the oldest or the youngest who gets to study. Someone has to work. My last son has the greater mind: he is the one I am sending off to study."

"Don't you fear, like the other fathers, that your son will be tempted by Christianity?"

"I only do my duty. The rest is up to God."

"You are wiser than Joël's father who prefers to have his son become a horse dealer."

"On that subject, my child, I have heard that you have lost your head for my former student. It is none of my business. But as a friend of your grandmother, it is my right to discuss it with you. Do you love Joël?"

Braendel lowered her eyes.

"And him? Could he marry you? His father is aiming higher without considering your beauty or your wisdom."

"Is it a crime to love?" asked Braendel, lifting her head.

"No, my daughter."

"And to love for the love of God, isn't that a good deed in the eyes of the one that judges us all?"

"I don't follow you."

"I have only loved Joël, and I have only attempted to make him love me, in order to tear him away from his lowly profession and bring him back to God. He promised me he would leave the village and go to a city where there is a great *beth hamedrasch* (house of study).[15] On that condition I pledged my faith. But alas! Joël has already succumbed to the sickness of the age. He forgets God because of my beauty. He pretends he cannot leave me and he has violent emotions that terrify me. Oh! I am unhappy because I am in love him. I thought he was better than the other young Jews, but he has read profane books, and I don't know if perhaps his father is right to keep him from continuing his study in a big city where, they say, there are many more dangerous books."

"Come, my daughter," said the rabbi. "Let me give you my blessing. You are a valiant daughter of Israel."

---

15. Standard transliteration: *beth ha-midrash*.

And Braendel placed her apron on her head in place of a veil, and leaned toward the rabbi. The latter placed his hand on her head and proclaimed:

"Let God, the God of Abraham, of Isaac, and of Jacob, the God of virtue and of strength, bless you, like he blessed Sarah, Rebecca, and Rachel. Let Him support you on the holy path, and cover you with his grace, from now to the thousandth generation, as he promised all his loyal servants through the mouth of our lord Moses, and through all his other holy prophets!"

Braendel wiped away her tears, which were streaming down her face, and said in a loud voice: "Amen." Then, as she took her leave, she added: "Alas! My dear rabbi, something tells me that this young man is not worthy of me and that I am sacrificing myself to a vain idol!"

VI.

For eight days Joël was forced to stay in bed. Instead of healing, his foot swelled up. All his friends came to visit him except for Braendel. Whenever someone dared to ask Joël why Braendel was snubbing him, another would respond: "Well now. Love thrives on snubbing. That's an Alsatian proverb." But Joël said nothing. Finally, after ten days, he learned that nobody had seen Braendel for forty-eight hours and that her grandmother seemed very sad. The young man, who reproached himself bitterly, resolved to go see her in spite of his foot. He found Braendel lying on her grandmother's bed, pale, disfigured, and hardly recognizable.

"What's wrong with you?" he cried. "Are you sick?"

"Take a good look at me," said the young girl, rising up with difficulty. "Am I still beautiful?"

"You are pale as a cadaver," responded Joël. "You frighten me."

"Well then, that's beauty for you: two days of fasting has put me in this state. You don't want to kiss me and I feel the tomb approaching."

"Good God! What an idea to fast for two days!"

"Wait, my penance is not yet complete. The rabbi imposed on me a fast for three days and three nights for having violated Divine modesty, for having allowed you to love me."

"That's impossible," Joël cried. "The rabbi doesn't have that right. It's murder."

"You are blaspheming, Joël. Your piety is stained by heresy. The rabbi is right. And moreover, I am the one who wanted to fast: it's to show you the vanity of beauty and of youth. I thought about cutting my hair."

"Your hair!" cried Joël rushing to touch her hair and measure it to make sure it was still long. "Your hair? Not for fifty rabbis! Not for the entire law!"

"Woe! Woe is me! Worldly love has destroyed you. But since I would have to cut my hair anyway on the day of our marriage . . . Look, I no longer know if I love you. You can plainly see that I am not a weak woman. Another word like that and you will be nothing to me."

"Pardon! Pardon!" cried Joël, kneeling before the bed. "It is true that I blasphemed. But what do you want? Loving you has made me crazy. I dream only of you. I think only of you!"

"And yet, you have to forget me as I will try to forget you. I was crazy to think that I could do a good deed in bringing you back to God. It seems that I myself am the obstacle to your conversion."

"But no, my dear Braendel. Once Passover has come, I will leave."

"But if you leave, not only will you forget me, which is nothing . . . I am resigned to it in advance and I have long known sorrow, poverty, and privation. But worse still you will forget God. You are too worldly. Do you want me to tell you everything I have been thinking? You are prouder of your handsome face than of your mind. Go away, you are lost for me. One or the other: either you will become a great rabbi in which case you will marry a rich Jewish girl from Strasbourg or Nancy, or you will deny your faith and fall into the arms of a profane woman. I have thought it over for eight days. Joël, allow me to finish my penance and forget me. Stay or go, Braendel is not destined to be your wife and you can be certain that Braendel will never be your mistress."

Scarcely had she uttered these last words than she collapsed on the side of the bed and lost consciousness. Joël tried at first to bring her back by kissing her. But when he saw that Braendel, even unconscious, refused him her lips, he called for help. They forced the young girl to take some food. She revived. Then they told Joël to go away and let her rest.

VII.

The holiday of Purim was on a Tuesday, the day of the animal market in Haguenau for the peasants and Jews of the region. On that day, since they had to listen to the story of Esther at dawn, the Jewish merchants from distant villages had to leave home at one in the morning in order to avoid missing synagogue and the market. Though still sick, Joël left with his father for Haguenau at two o'clock in the morning. They were on horseback and they had three full leagues to travel without counting the detours on account of flooding in the plain. From their village to Haguenau, you had to cross a thick pine forest. About a quarter of a league from the city, on the edge of the woods, there was madder-root growing and little sand deserts where the cavalry trained.

Joël had decided not to sell all his horses. But, because he knew that his father was in a hurry to return to the village, on account of the holiday, he hastened to make his purchases and leave the market. Besides almonds, pralines, and kosher meat—which is to say beef that has been slaughtered under a rabbi's supervision—he was determined to buy Braendel a new dress. Such a gift, which cannot be kept secret, is seen as an engagement present. He hoped this would bring Braendel back to him and secure her forgiveness, since she had not spoken to him since their last conversation. It was even said that she would become engaged to the rabbi's older son.

But while Joël was busy with his purchases, his father, having sold his last horse, decided to take advantage of a Catholic neighbor's cart to return to the village. Forgetting his son's injured foot, he left word to follow him home as soon as he could. The messenger charged with this commission was only able to find Joël, who had wandered off at around two o'clock in the afternoon in search of dresses. By this point, he couldn't find either a horse or a carriage to return to the village. The only other traveling companion he could find was Lemah the Redhead, a boy of twenty-five, a calf merchant, known for his brutal coarseness.

Joël had already tired his foot on the rough gravel-paved streets of the city and he had three long leagues to travel through a thick forest. Finally, making the best of a bad situation, he decided to set off on foot, giving Lemah a little money to carry his pack for him. But they had hardly entered the woods when he tripped and fell. He tried to get up but couldn't. His foot was more swollen than ever. He took off his shoe and couldn't get it back on.

"Lemah, I'll give you twenty francs if you can carry me to the village. You're strong. They say you can carry two calves on your back for four hours. I weigh less than a calf."

"Me, carry you?" cried the merchant. "Under one condition."

"Name it."

"But why don't you send for Braendel?" Lemah sneered. "She would certainly come to get you, and would have find the strength to carry you, since she loves you so much."

"So, are you jealous of my happiness?"

"Yes, if you want to know the truth. I like Braendel."

"Braendel for you? Pearls before swine, as they say."

"Well then, since I'm a pig, leave me alone and stay where you are." With that, he took off.

"Lemah! Lemah!" cried Joël, who squirmed on the ground. "Are you profane enough to leave a brother who has fallen? Remember that today is Purim!"

"Too bad. I'm in a hurry. Do you want to give Braendel to me? I'll carry you on my back in front of her."

"She would never like you. Braendel is from noble stock. She would scorn you."

"That's my business."

"Go on, then, and be damned! You know I'm a rabbi. Fear my curse: God listens to those He has chosen." This stopped Lemah.

"All that I can do for you is to point you toward Croix-Neuve, over there, and to tell your father to send a horse for you." With that, he set off at a fast pace.

VIII.

It was about three o'clock in the afternoon. Joël could not get up and was dragging himself on his knees toward Croix-Neuve, but he was so exhausted that he made little progress.

"Oh!" he said to himself, "This must be a punishment from heaven! Why did I give up sacred study for this lowly commerce? I was so well off, so content in front of my rabbi's stove! My hands were so white and my thoughts were so innocent! Now I think only of money and young girls. Yes, I have drunk from an intoxicating cup. They made me dance, those wretched people, they taught me to drink. They said I would be dishonored if Braendel didn't become my mistress. The saintly woman I love! Oh! I'm unworthy of her. I'm nothing but a vulgar sinner. But I will pull myself up! God is showing me the way. Yes, I will give up this horrible life. I will become again one of God's chosen. I will wash off my filth. I will resist their impious suggestions, just as, thank God, I have resisted them up to now. Let them all go to the devil. I will give myself body and soul to Braendel, that angel from on high. I will devote myself to God, who does not judge man on his fortune or on his mind, but only on his virtue and his deeds."

Then, returning to his present situation: "That miserable Lemah, that brute who dares to aspire to Braendel's love, he won't say a thing to my father. They won't send out help for a long time, because my family will think that I'm out with the young folk from the village who spend their evenings dancing and drinking. Without a miracle from up above, I'll have to spend the night in the forest. I'll be lucky if a wolf doesn't eat me. Let God's will be done!" he added, lying down on the grass of a ditch.

Joël was not afraid, but his foot was causing him terrible suffering. Every instant he was listening, but all he could hear was some far-off woodcutters returning home. He tried crying out but only his echo responded. Ordinarily, woodcutters do not stop in the evening on their way home, since they are committing a sort of crime in the forest. With that last hope gone, Joël, shivering with anxiety, mumbled a psalm and a prayer of distress that he knew by heart. But soon fever and delirium took hold of his mind and he couldn't distinguish any exterior sound. He rolled into the bottom of the ditch, fifty feet from Croix-Neuve.

Joël was not wrong in thinking Lemah wouldn't help him. Indeed, the latter had completely forgotten him, perhaps not out of wickedness but because he had barely arrived in the village when he joined up with a band of young boys and girls who were going from house to house, eating the Haman and drinking in honor of Mordecai. After an hour, Lemah and his companions were dead drunk and not one of them thought of poor Joël. His father and mother were also celebrating with their relatives and thought that their son must be out with his friends.

Only Braendel, who was following at a distance the noisy crowds and wandering past the houses where glasses were clinking and joyous sounds were echoing, was worried about Joël's absence. Even though she didn't want to meet him in the state in which she found most of the other young people, her heart, through some secret instinct, sensed danger. At first, she didn't dare ask the drunken hordes where Joël was. But around ten o'clock, not having seen him, she sent to his mother's house and asked her if her son was sick.

"Joël!" the latter cried. "But I don't know where he is. He didn't come home for dinner. I thought he was out with you. He loves you so!"

"I haven't seen him for eight days. How can he be nowhere? I made the round of all the houses where they are celebrating Purim and I didn't see him anywhere."

"Good God!" cried the mother. "And I wasn't even worried. Brave girl! You have more heart than his father who sold the last of his horses and forced him to make his way home on foot. Ah! If he thought like me, my angel, you would become the wife of my son. He will never find another woman equal to you."

"I'm not worried about me right now," responded Braendel. "I'm worried about your son. You said he had to come home on foot. Since his right foot is swollen and not yet healed, he must have stopped along the way. God only knows where he is! Come with me to the brasserie where all his friends are dancing, drinking, and singing, without even noticing the absence of one of their comrades. That's what such friends are good for!"

IX.

Braendel dragged the poor woman into the smoky room, which stank of sweat, beer, and wine, and cried out in a loud voice, "Aren't you ashamed, you children of honest Jews, to drink and dance when one of you, the best of you, is missing and nobody knows what has become of him?"

"Well then, here is the prophetess who is going to give us a sermon," exclaimed a lad with outstretched arms. "Let her marry her Joël and be done with it. I don't know if he's a good student, but he's certainly a poor horseman and as an infantryman he's not worth five hundred francs."

"For you, Dotter, who weigh men on scales," responded Braendel, "you certainly tell the truth, since you're the heaviest boy in the village." Then, turning to the others: "Who among you saw Joël in Haguenau?"

"Didn't Joël come back from the market?" they asked each other.

"Clearly nobody saw him," responded the distressed mother. "You have to go look for him, my children."

"I'm pretty sure," said a young girl, "that Lemah the Redhead gave me pralines and said that they came from Joël."

"You wretch!" Braendel cried out, dragging Lemah out of the corner. "You saw Joël in Haguenau?"

"Yes," groaned the drunkard.

"Where did you leave him?"

"In the forest."

"In the forest!" exclaimed several voices. "And you didn't help him?"

"Let Braendel go help him," mumbled the calf merchant. "He's lying near Croix-Neuve."

"Keep an eye on that man!" cried Braendel. "Eight days ago, when I saw him at the little fountain, he said he would play a nasty trick on Joël."

"What did you do to Joël?" exclaimed twenty voices! And twenty arms came down on Lemah's head.

"Is it any of your business?"

"Lemah," said the fat Dotter, gripping him by the throat. "Tell us right away where Joël is and what you did to him or five minutes from now you will be a dead man."

These words and gestures little by little sobered up the young man. "I didn't do anything to him," he mumbled. "Let me go, Dotter, I'm not a murderer. I'm not a goy."

"Swear on the name of the Lord that you did him no harm."

"Joël fell," responded Lemah. "He wanted me to carry him on my back. I was too tired. I left him near Croix-Neuve. Then I didn't give him another thought."

"Wretch! Pagan! Barbarian!" exclaimed twenty voices. "You abandoned your brother, a Jew, in distress." And within the blink of an eye, the back that Lemah hadn't wanted to lend to Joël was riddled with blows.

"Mercy! Have mercy!" exclaimed Braendel. "We don't need to punish him. We need to go find Joël. Arise, children of Israel, on your feet. There is a soul to save. Get on your horses and scour the forest."

"Scour the forest!" said Dotter. "It's thirty leagues around and it's black as night. It's midnight."

"If you're too cowardly to venture into the forest, and you should be, then give me a horse and I will go by myself," responded Braendel.

"What a girl! God save her!" said the mother. "With her, God will be on our side."

"She's capable of doing as she says," said a very young man. "However, Braendel, I haven't seen you on horseback for a long time."

"A horse, a horse! " she kept repeating. "Do I have to the stable myself and saddle one? Which one of you owns a horse?"

"Monsieur Heiser the mayor has two magnificent stallions," Dotter replied. "Go get them, Braendel."

"Alright then, I'm going. Monsieur the mayor, who is Catholic, has more heart than any of you craven drunkards!" With this, she was off as fast as her legs would carry her, leaving behind Joël's mother and all the young cowards who were still deliberating about what to do to save their friend.

"Bah!" Dotter said. "Joël is sleeping on the grass. Better to wait for day and to bring him home in a carriage."

"It's not very much fun," another said, "to wait at two o'clock in the morning near Croix-Neuve."

"Let's go to bed," said a third. "Joël is probably home by now. Braendel is making up stories. She likes people to talk about her."

"But we can't just go to bed as long as one of us is missing and in mortal danger," added Dotter. "Joël is delicate. Plus he's a *bachor*. If we abandon him, the rabbi will banish us and not one of us will be able to mount the *alménor* (the platform in the synagogue) when it his turn to be called to say the blessing for the reading of a chapter of the Bible.[16] If we're banned, the young girls will scorn us. Come on, brothers, we have to go look for Joël. But before leaving, let's say a prayer."

At this moment, Braendel passed by like lightning on the mayor's beautiful stallion. She was followed by the younger son of Monsieur Heiser who was mounted on the second stallion.

Braendel, like all the young village girls who work, rode a horse like a boy, which is to say straddling it.

---

16. Standard transliteration: *almenor*.

No sooner had he been told what brought Braendel to him than the mayor saddled the horse himself. But full of admiration for the young girl, he ordered one of his sons to follow her and watch out for her.

Ashamed to be surpassed in devotion by a young girl and by a Catholic, the most courageous young Jews also mounted on horseback and took off with lanterns and pine torches.

X.

In villages, the relation between man and beast is more intimate than in cities. When an animal distinguishes itself either through beauty or intelligence, the whole village adopts it and sees it as its property. The bay stallion of the mayor was one of these. He was as sweet tempered as he was proud. A child could guide him and ride him. Moreover, he seemed to know all the inhabitants of the village who never passed before him without giving him some friendly caress accompanied by flattering words. Like all intelligent animals, the stallion was an original. This is to say that a few oddities distinguished him from other examples of his species. For example, he hated spurs. A child could mount him easily and make him feed, but the instant a rider with spurs tried to jump on his back he would rear up and jump around until the weary rider got back down again, unless the horse preferred to throw him thirty feet away. The stallion had another tick. Even though his comrade was of the same breed, he made it a point of honor never to be overtaken by him. Harnessed together (which happened rarely), he was always, and no matter how he was attached, two steps ahead of him. Saddled separately, you could never make him walk behind his rival. In one leap, he would take the lead and obstinately keep it.

Braendel had stopped riding at the age of twelve, the time of life when the villagers no longer permit young girls this type of amusement. She therefore had to trust the goodness and the intelligence of the animal whose mane she stroked, saying: "My friend, go to Croix-Neuve." The horse, as if he understood the words of the young girl, took off at a gallop. But seeing himself followed by his rival, the gallop quickly turned into a furious race. In the blink of an eye, he was on the way to the forest. At first, Braendel cried with all her might: "Joël! Joël!" but soon the unbridled rapidity of her mount took her breath away. She dug in her heels, leaning her head over the neck of the stallion, who once on his way and feeling himself followed closely by his competition, didn't want to stop. The more Braendel's companion attempted to keep up with her, the more the stallion, fearing he was about to be overtaken, increased his pace.

They were followed, but distantly, by a few other young riders. All of a sudden, a black shadow passed in front of these latter horsemen. A second later, that shadow retraced its steps, stopped and whinnied. It was the bay stallion coming back to look for help.

"The stallion returns alone!" they cried. "Something bad has happened to Braendel!" And they all headed toward the spot from which the horse had come. To be safer, the young people dismounted and led their horses by the bridle, moving forward with caution by the light of their resin torches. They marched like that for a half hour, when fifty feet from Croix-Neuve, they found the unlucky young girl stretched out unconscious by a tree, all bloody. While some of them attempted to bring Braendel back to life, others found the unlucky Joël in the bottom of the ditch into which he had fallen, delirious and calling for Braendel. Alas! The poor girl was barely breathing. It was clear that some essential organ had been bruised. Blood was pouring in torrents out of her nose and mouth. Her chest was covered in blood. It seemed as if she had been thrown and broken in two by a tree.

"I told her," cried the mayor's son, "to let me go alone. She didn't want to. Poor girl!" And the young man burst into sobs.

Next to Joël, they found the package containing the new dress destined for his fiancée. They tore it to bandage Braendel. After this first aid, she was bundled in a coat and placed on a bed of grass and pine branches, next to Joël, whom they had to tie up to keep from thrashing about in his delirium. Then the sad cortège, preceded by funereal torches, set off toward the village.

It is said that bad news travels fast. Perhaps the unexpected return of the stallion had averted the townspeople that a tragedy had occurred, or perhaps some of the young people had alerted them by their cries, but before the lifeless body of Braendel had entered the village, all the inhabitants, men and women, old people and children, were standing in the street, crying in despair. Some thought that Joël had been devoured by a wolf, others talked of a broken leg. Nobody guessed the terrible truth. When it became known, there was a single cry of sadness.

"The crown of the village has fallen," exclaimed the rabbi. "Let all the Jews put on mourning!" And not only the Jews, but all the Catholics also cried over the premature end of that valiant girl. Only her grandmother was calm, saying: "Whatever God has done is good. Soon, dear soul, your grandmother will join you in paradise. I would have wanted to live to see you have a son who would have walked in the footsteps of our ancestor. But since the Lord above did not want it, let His will be done!"

As for Joël, nobody paid him any attention except his mother. The fever didn't leave him for two days. He was the last one in the village to learn of the death of Braendel.

XI.

The following day, all the Jewish women gathered in the house of the dead girl, to make her a wedding dress and to wash her with warm water and lay her out properly. For the Jews wash and dress their dead so that they can appear worthy in front of the King of kings.

The men assembled at the same time to make the coffin. The Jews always make their coffins themselves, the same for all regardless of fortune or birth. This coffin is composed of six unsanded boards. The next day, they placed the body in the bier without covering it. The Jews claim that the dead person hears everything that is said until the moment when the last nail is hammered into the cover of the coffin. That belief is a guarantee against premature burial. An hour before the body is taken away, all who know the dead person approach, touch the body's toes, and ask for forgiveness for all the offenses that they committed against the person.

Since the cemetery was located in the forest, not very far from Croix-Neuve, they needed a wagon. The mayor of the village offered his, and the stallion was harnessed to it. The poor animal was so sweet and sad that it seemed like he was stricken with regret. A child led him by the bridle. All the inhabitants, without distinction of age or sex, followed the coffin. The Jewish women, however, followed behind, their heads covered in veils as a sign of mourning. At the edge of the village, they stopped the wagon and everyone said a prayer, a sort of *De profundis*, mixed with cries and sobs. All the young people of the village followed Braendel's body all the way to the cemetery.

As for Joël, as soon as he was cured, he left for Metz in order to grant Braendel her final wish. Soon the study of profane subjects shook his Talmudic faith. He almost converted on a few occasions. But the image of Braendel would always appear between his heart and his head. Although he now enjoys a high social position, Joël never forgets, whenever he returns to Alsace, to place a little stone on the tomb of Braendel, his childhood friend. According to Jewish belief, when the soul comes down from on high to glide above the tomb of the body, that little stone announces that a friend has come to visit.

David Schornstein, "The Tithe" (1864)

Translated from the French by Maurice Samuels

David Schornstein (1826–79) was born in the Alsatian village of Brumath, the son of a cantor. From 1843 to 1846, he trained to be a teacher at the École normale of Strasbourg, before pursuing a literary career in Paris. Once in the capital, he wrote several plays and volumes of fiction while also working as a journalist, writing for both the reformist Jewish newspaper *Les Archives Israélites* and its orthodox rival, *L'Univers Israélite*, as well as for the mainstream publications *Le Charivari* and *L'Artiste*. He also served as an editor of *Le Petit Journal*, one of the first mass-market Parisian dailies, founded in 1863 by Moïse Polydor Millaud, a Jew from Bordeaux. A specialist in Jewish art and antiquities, Schornstein wrote a yearly review of Jewish artists in the Paris Salon for *Les Archives Israélites* in the 1860s. Under the pseudonym Georges Stenne, he published an introduction to the catalog to the Strauss collection of Jewish antiquities, which showed at the Universal Exposition of 1878.

Published serially in *Les Archives Israélites*, "La dîme" (The Tithe) describes the close bond between a cantor and a scribe in a small village in Eastern France, as well as the forces that threaten to tear their friendship apart. With its heavily idealized depiction of small-town Jewish life, the story epitomizes the brand of nostalgic "ghetto" fiction that became popular in France and Germany in the 1850s and 1860s, just as increasing numbers of Jews in these countries—like Schornstein himself— were leaving their villages behind for big-city life. Schornstein's story is even more idealizing than most: his village Jews bear little trace of the backwardness or superstition that Jewish reformers at the time criticized in their traditional coreligionists. The conflict between the cantor and the scribe stems from highly individualized character traits as well as from the stresses of small-town Jewish life. While the novella seems to take place in a kind of timeless present, signs of modernity lurk at the margins, threatening to render these kinds of characters—and the traditional Jewish values they represent—a thing of the past.

I.

Of all the character types created by Judaism's profound and unalterable respect for the sacred Law, the most curious and original is certainly the scribe, the sofer, charged with copying onto scrolls of parchment the 154 chapters or 5,844 verses of the books of Moses.

All the verses and words, even the very letters of the Pentateuch have been counted, such that a scroll written in Amsterdam or Paris resembles syllable for syllable, sometimes column for column, one executed in Livorno or Constantinople.

The work of the sofer is thus as meticulous as it is long and painstaking. The least little details are determined in advance, from the form of the characters to the manner in which they are drawn. Everything has been prescribed, from the blank spaces to the indentations and the variants in the spelling of the same words. The sofer even lends a hand in the making of his parchment and mixes his own ink. Every time he writes the venerated name of God the scribe must stop in order to ponder the holiness of the word he is about to trace with his freshly dipped pen. He also must carefully reread everything he has written up to that point to make sure that he has not made an error, for once he has written the holy tetragram he is not allowed to erase it.

This one little detail gives an idea of the work of the sofer, of the monotony and fastidiousness of his task that have such a fatal effect on his character. Rebb Auscher, the sofer of Wertheim, was no more an exception to that law than any of his colleagues. He was a phlegmatic man, meticulous, methodical, and thrifty with his words. The only one he overused was *am haaretz*, or ignorant person, which as a result of a habit acquired during the Talmudic discussions of his youth, he would throw in the face of anyone who contradicted him. Slow to make up his mind, he could not be shaken from a conviction. The quiet temperament of his wife and children had only reinforced the strength, or rather the inertia, of his will.

The sofer's work is poorly compensated. There is an old proverb about how the *soferim* never grow wealthy in the land of Israel. I don't know who gave birth to that pearl detached from the necklace of the world's wisdom, but in the case of Reb Auscher, the proverb's truth was amply confirmed: the sofer was not rich.

Nevertheless he was the happiest man in the community, next to the cantor of the synagogue that is, who was just as poor as the sofer but much more animated. Always occupied with his transcriptions of the divine word, Reb Auscher naturally possessed a great store of piety and submission to the will of God, the Talmud having long since taught him that the man who is content with his lot is truly rich. Moreover, if heaven had denied him a fortune, it had accorded him other favors. He had an excellent wife and two children, a boy and a girl, who were his joy and his consolation.

The boy was named Samuel. He was twenty-two years old and already a cantor in Berguen. Everyone agreed that he had talent and a remarkable way of officiating in the synagogue. Even if his situation was still modest, his parents could reasonably hope that he might one day aspire to one of the best cantorial positions in the Upper or Lower Rhine.

The girl was named Perle and she was indeed the pearl of all Wertheim. She was seventeen years old, her hair as blond as wheat, and her blue eyes lit up her fine face, which was expressive and full of candor.

Perle was kind and affectionate to a fault with her parents. It was she who prepared her father's work table each day and kept it in order. It was she who would bring him his pipe and tobacco after dinner, and would pour him his cup of coffee. It was also she who would interrupt him gently when he had been working too long and urge him to rest. The mother busied herself with making things, both the tools for her husband's work and religious objects whose sale supplemented the family's meager income. Perle alone took care of the household chores. The charming young girl devoted herself to her different occupations with such agility and so little noise that in her hands a task seemed to accomplish itself, as if by magic.

The hazan of Wertheim and the sofer were old friends. Together they had frequented the different Talmudic academies of Alsace and Germany, for in the old days these institutions where Jewish youth get a bit of learning still flourished. Endowed with totally opposite characters, the two young Talmudists were linked by a common trait; neither had ever had any fortune or success. The apathy of the one and the flightiness of the other hampered their studies. Thus when their fellow students were successively getting placed as rabbis or as tutors to wealthy families, neither of our two friends could obtain the Morenu or rabbinical diploma. It was even said that their title of Haber,[1] which gives them the right to the honorific Reb, was due to the extreme indulgence

---

1. A more standard transliteration would be *haver*.

of Rabbi Thias Weill of Karlsruhe. But such gossip can be considered slander, for Rabbi Thias Weill was not someone who would grant a Haber without it being merited. The descendents of that famous Talmudist, who today are living in Paris, can testify to that if necessary. Unable to arrive at the rabbinate, our two friends had to think of other careers: Reb Gerson sang well, Reb Auscher had fine penmanship. The latter therefore became a sofer, the former a hazan. Friendship had long kept them in the same schools; now chance brought them both to the same community of Wertheim, a few leagues from Strasbourg.

Nothing had ever troubled the friendly relations of the hazan and the sofer and of their families, who saw each other quite often. Reb Gerson had only one son: Gabriel. He was a vigorous lad, handsome, and well built. He was not the smartest boy, but he made up for it with a good heart and an honest character. He didn't like studying or singing in the synagogue. The precarious situation his father held in the little community hardly gave the young man a pronounced taste for the hazan's life, and he preferred instead to become a cloth merchant. Reb Gerson was sorry about this, but the mother was very proud to have a son who supported himself and wasn't dependent, like the father, first on the *parnass*,[2] then on the four assessors, and finally on each head of household.

Which is not to say that Gabriel's profession was so pleasing: far from it. His commerce took him for weeks at a time to villages spread throughout the valleys of the Vosges. He would leave on Sunday and stay in the mountains until Friday, peddling heavy bundles of cloth from hamlet to hamlet, from farm to farm, and living in an extremely sober manner. There are no Israelite establishments in these localities, and since Christian cooking is forbidden, traveling salesmen live like real anchorites in the mountains, eating only bread, eggs, salad, fruit, and potatoes cooked in hot coals. But neither pain nor privation hindered Gabriel, and after a long week of hiking and exertion, he would return to Wertheim, his heart beating joyously when he saw the first house of the village through the hawthorn bushes and the willows that bordered the stream. Not only because he was bringing home the small

---

2. Parnass (or parnas), literally "provider," is a title given to lay leaders of Jewish communities.

earnings of the week, not only because he was going to rest and enjoy Saturday, but because it was Friday, the night his family would go to Reb Auscher's house, and Gabriel would be near Perle, whom he had already greeted when passing by the modest house of the sofer.

How was the natural affection between the two young people born? They themselves didn't know. They had always loved each other without even a question.

One day Perle went to the wedding of one of her cousins. The wedding was held in Rosheim, a village situated a few leagues from Wertheim. Perle stayed over Saturday. When Gabriel arrived on Friday evening at the home of Reb Auscher and learned of the prolonged absence of the young lady, his face darkened. The evening seemed incredibly long to him and boredom gave way to vexation. He couldn't help but think that at that moment Perle was probably having fun, and anger overtook him when he thought that the young people of Rosheim had Perle all to themselves while he moped about in Wertheim. Gabriel was sullen all the next day and felt as if Saturday was dragging on forever.

Perle came back on Sunday.

The young man, who had promised himself to return to the Vosges without going to visit her, lay in wait for her return.

He stopped her on the threshold of her house at the very moment she came back.

"So did you have a good time in Rosheim?" he asked her in a reproachful tone.

"On the contrary, Gabriel," she responded. "Time moved ever so slowly."

"You love Wertheim that much?" he asked.

Perle didn't want to say anything more. Yes would have been a lie. No would have been a declaration of her love. To extricate herself from the situation, she began to pursue her own line of questioning.

"How did you spend Saturday?" she asked.

"Ah! Perle, I felt very sad and lonely."

"And now?"

"Now I am happy, Perle."

"So am I," replied the young girl. "But hush," she added. "Here is Zadoc the Redhead. Beware!"

She made a friendly gesture to the young man and disappeared rapidly.

Gabriel returned home, his spirit light and his heart brimming over with happiness.

From that day on he spent all his time making plans for the future, in which the daughter of the sofer played a starring role. Life seemed good to him despite all his business worries. His work even seemed easier, although the days he spent in the Vosges away from Wertheim felt doubly long.

Perle lent herself wholeheartedly to all of Gabriel's plans, only she asked him to keep quiet about them.

"I have no desire to be the favorite topic of conversation of all the gossips of Wertheim," he would say.

For the town had more than its share of gossips.

Gabriel tried as much as he could to hide his feelings and his happiness, but if Love is blind, lovers are hardly more farsighted. While the couple applauded each other for their little hypocrisy, the young people of Wertheim, who are no stupider than anywhere else, all saw that the pretty daughter of the sofer only had eyes for Gabriel.

He was not, however, the only one of the young men of Wertheim to cast his eyes in the direction of the charming girl. They swarmed around her. Even Zadoc the Redhead, the man who seemed the least susceptible to tender sentiments, was not blind to Perle's attractions.

This Zadoc the Redhead was a tall and thin boy, with an angular face, a pointy nose, and a shifty gaze. His hair was of such a strawberry blond that it earned him his nickname. People usually just called him the redhead for short. He was already thirty years old at the time, which in the village meant he was a confirmed bachelor. He earned a lot of money and if he hadn't gotten married already it was because he hadn't yet found a dowry to his liking, for he was above all stingy. There was only one thing that could be said in his favor: he was totally devoted to his old mother. What is more, the good woman was no less stingy than her son and had never allowed even a penny to go to waste.

Zadoc the Redhead was a wholesale hemp dealer. He was constantly on the road, traveling Alsace from top to bottom and even to Germany from time to time. During his frequent voyages he was often able to be of use to Reb Auscher, acting as his intermediary for clients in far-off places, sometimes finding him a new Pentateuch to copy, sometimes finding him an old one to restore. He rarely forgot to add something for himself in the bargain, such as a *mezuzah* or some *tephilim*, always true to the maxim that in this world you should never let an opportunity go by to turn a profit.

In between his trips, the redhead would thus often go to the sofer's house. He had watched Perle grow up and hadn't been slow to notice her budding grace and beauty. The simple and active young girl had turned his head and he had to remind himself constantly that she was poor and that her parents might well become his responsibility. Nevertheless he couldn't refrain from telling himself that she would make a charming housewife, that she was hardworking and thrifty, that she required nothing to look pretty and thus would be a true pearl of economy for her husband.

Often he would awaken from these daydreams and chide himself for getting carried away with such silliness. He was scared at the idea that an extravagance like that seemed so appealing to him. And when he learned that his rival Gabriel had found favor in Perle's eyes, he was almost grateful to the young man for being an obstacle to his senseless plans.

Rarely does even the least coquettish and least pretentious young girl mistake the nature of the feelings she inspires. Perle understood perfectly well the twin motives that made the redhead advance and retreat. She even was amused by it to the extent that she was persuaded that Zadoc would never ask for her hand in marriage. The hemp dealer's avarice protected her from what she knew would make her miserable, for Zadoc inspired in her a kind of fear and repulsion, as if she knew instinctively that that man would spread torment and hardship all along the path of his life.

II.

At this time, Reb Auscher was working harder than ever and was finishing a Pentateuch for the Young People's Club of Wertheim. The consecration of the new *sepher* was to take place on the Saturday preceding the holiday of Rosh Hashanah.

Reb Auscher not only had to put the finishing touches on the sacred scroll but he also had to construct what is called the *binian*.

The *binian* is a little artificial mountain that is constructed in a private home and on which the *sepher* is placed from the time it is finished until the moment when it is solemnly transported to the synagogue. It's a miniature Sinai from which the law comes down once again to Israel. The true believer's fervor is not satisfied with the representation of any old hill, however. Usually it has to be surrounded with all kinds of picturesque details, with a little forest made out of tree branches, a grotto, a path, and even sometimes a waterfall. If the sofer fancies himself an artist, he will place in the distance a cardboard castle whose style in relation to the Sinai makes for a curious anachronism, but which never seems to shock the eyes or the taste of the spectators. Lit up by Venetian lanterns on which verses of the Bible have been painted, the little display is placed before the public on the eve of the Sabbath on which the solemn delivery of the *sepher* to the temple will take place.

Reb Auscher was very skilled at this meticulous kind of work. Perle, who displayed both taste and creativity, helped him in his labor.

The sofer devoted himself with such ardor to the task because the ceremony would have a double significance for him. His son Samuel, even though he had left Wertheim, remained a member of the Young People's Club, and it had been agreed that he would officiate in the synagogue of Wertheim that Saturday in honor of their celebration. This was of course a great honor for the young cantor and a source of joy for his family. Perle also worked hard on the decoration of the famous *binian* that was taking shape in the house of the parnass, the administrator of the community, who also had a son among the members of the Club. Nor did Gabriel neglect to devote his spare time to helping Perle, as he put it, or perhaps merely to being near her, as his friends would have it.

All anyone in the village could talk about was the *binian*, and all week people streamed into the house of the parnass, curious and impatient to see what progress had been made. Praise, criticism, and commentary buzzed about the ears of Reb Auscher, and he already more than once had had the opportunity to employ his favorite proverb: "Never show madmen a house before it has been constructed."

Despite all this, the *binian* really did promise to be superb. In the background was the mountain, all covered with moss and flowers. In front stood a portico of greenery whose columns formed lines around which big pine branches had been affixed in order to resemble a forest. On each side could be seen a pedestal, one for Moses, the other for his brother, Aaron.

One morning Reb Auscher nestled the two figures, which had been cut out of cardboard and vividly colored, into their respective places. Moses held the tables of the Law in his hand. Aaron, the great priest, held nothing.

This lack of symmetry shocked the parnass, who in his capacity of head of the community had pretentions to erudition. In reality, his great learning was limited to a few morsels of text found in five or six little Hebrew-German books that he had been reading over and over for years.[3] In short, he was an ignorant man.

"Why are the hands of Aaron Hacohen empty?"[4] he asked Reb Auscher. "You should have given him something to hold just as you did Moshe Rabbenu.[5]

"What are you talking about?" responded Reb Auscher impatiently.

The parnass had just at that moment finished his morning prayer, at the end of which one recites the text of the Ten Commandments and the thirteen articles of faith.

That coincidence inspired a bright idea, according to him, which he didn't want to let slip by, nor with it the chance to show that he knew something about the Law.

"I'll tell you what," he said. "Since Moses is holding the table of the Ten Commandments, give Aaron one with the thirteen articles of faith!"

"You are an *am haaretz*," responded Reb Auscher, employing his habitual phrase. Rabbenu Moshe Ben-Maimon wrote the articles of faith more than two thousand years after the death of Aaron. How can he hold them in his hand?"

The parnass offered no reply, but the phrase *am haaretz* had offended him deeply. He went about his business while Reb Auscher attached the Great Lawgiver and the High Priest to their pedestals.

III.

While Reb Auscher, his daughter, and even Gabriel were absorbed with the preparations for the special day that was approaching, and were

---

3. "Hebrew-German," i.e., Yiddish.
4. Aaron the Cohen, or Priest.
5. Moses, our teacher. [Author's note.]

thus hardly thinking of Zadoc the Redhead, the latter was thinking a lot about them, even though he was at that moment in Germany, where he had come to sell hemp.

The wife of Reb Auscher was born in the Grand Duchy of Hesse. Her parents were dead, but she still had a sister about whom she had spoken a few times in the presence of Zadoc. At that time, the railroad hadn't yet enlaced Europe with its ever tightening network. Communications weren't easy and traveling to Germany or just across the Rhine was reserved for the adventurous. Correspondence wasn't frequent so it comes as no surprise that the wife of Reb Auscher hadn't heard from her sister in years. All she knew was that the sister had finally married after having worked for a long time for the Rothschilds in Frankfurt, who always provided for the future of their servants.

That year, Zadoc's business brought him to Frankfurt for the first time. He naturally stopped at the Street of the Jews: since it was a Friday, he attended the evening service in the great synagogue, then went to have dinner in the restaurant of Madame Hecht.

There were a lot of people around the table, and when they learned that the foreigner with the red hair was Alsatian, the questions about the Jews of his region came raining down hard. Zadoc, who had always studied the fluctuations in the price of hemp more carefully than the influence of political turmoil on his coreligionists in France, responded as well as he could to the often quite subtle interrogation of these good Germans. In the course of his answering their questions, he mentioned the name of Wertheim.

"Wertheim, you say," interrupted Madame Hecht, who always took part in the conversation of her many patrons. "Wertheim! My tenant, the old Feilché sometimes speaks to me of Wertheim. She has a sister in the area."

Zadoc pricked up his ears.

"That sister," the innkeeper continued, "married a sofer, I think. Tell me, do you know him?"

"But of course," Zadoc responded in an indifferent tone, although he was already speculating on the implications of this meeting.

"Well," Madame Hecht replied, "I think you would give her great pleasure if you went to see her. The poor woman rarely goes out or else I wouldn't tell you to go visit her."

Zadoc promised the innkeeper he would visit old Feilché, and indeed, the next day, after the morning service, he went to see her.

The old woman was thrilled to see someone who knew her sister. When Zadoc had given her every possible detail about her, her husband, and their two children, it was the old woman's turn to speak.

"See here, my good man," she said. "I'm very happy to have met you. I have a small fortune. Thanks be to God! Oh, it's not a lot, to be sure. God in his goodness did not give me any children and my husband died two years ago. So here I am like an old tree without branches. So who should I be thinking of? My sister and her family, since I'd like to leave them what I have when they shut my eyes. I would have wanted to talk about it a long time ago with my sister, her husband, and her children, especially Perle, as you called her, since the young girl bears the name of our departed mother, may she rest in peace. See here, I know how to pray in my *tephila* and read the *Tsene-rene*.[6] But I never learned to write. Nobody here," she continued, lowering her voice and looking around cautiously, "nobody here, my dear sir, knows that I have six thousand nice écus.[7] If I drew up a will, or if I had my family in France draw one up, the entire community of Frankfurt would know about it."

"Six thousand écus!" repeated the redhead to himself.

"Madame Hecht, who is not a mean-spirited woman," continued Feilché, "would raise my rent, the city would tax me, the synagogue would demand a contribution, the poor fund would demand a contribution, and so on. Oh, you can't imagine how people are around here. I would soon be ruined, do you understand?"

"Yes, I do," Zadoc responded mechanically, while in his head he heard the jangling sound of metal: Six thousand écus! Six thousand écus!

"That is why," the old woman continued, "I am so happy to see you. Since you're a friend of the family, you will carry my message so that I don't have to write it down. You can't trust papers, you never know..."

"As you say," Zadoc repeated, "you never know."

Zadoc returned to his inn, his mind racing. In contemplating a marriage with Perle, he had occasionally entertained the possibility of an

---

6. The traditional Jewish women's bible, written in Yiddish.

7. The écu was a prerevolutionary French coin worth six livres. In the nineteenth century, the term *écu* usually designated a five-franc coin.

inheritance from the young girl's aunt. But he had never imagined it would be such a fortune: Six thousand écus!

"I'm such a fool," he said to himself when he was alone in his room. "I must have heard them talk about that aunt who was the Rothschild's cook twenty times. I should have known she'd be rich. Six thousand écus that could belong to me since I know the sofer would have given his daughter to me twenty times over if I had asked for her hand in marriage. Instead, like a real imbecile, I let this golden opportunity get away from me. I saw that sweet-tongued Gabriel circling the girl, courting her, and I let him do it. I let love enter the equation. What am I saying? I was even happy to see that they were falling in love . . . But could I guess? . . . Gabriel on the other hand . . . he must have known something! Love came over him awfully suddenly . . . Yes, his father plays the Frankfurt lottery in secret, I know. He must have learned something from him, and now his son will pocket the old woman's money . . . Six thousand écus! What business I could do . . . but we shall see. He doesn't have them yet . . . yes, we shall see."

With these words the redhead stood up.

He had made a decision.

He couldn't do anything that day since it was Saturday. But the next day, Sunday, he finished up the little business affairs he had begun and instead of continuing his voyage to the north of Germany, he returned on the road to Strasbourg.

He had only one idea in his head: to separate Gabriel and Perle. How would he do it? He didn't know, but the most important thing was to be on the scene as soon as possible. It was a question of six thousand écus! A nice pile! And this was without counting Perle, with whom the stingy Zadoc once again suddenly found himself more in love than ever.

Never had Zadoc found the road back to Wertheim so long. He thought that once he got there, an idea of how to succeed in his enterprise would come to him. In the meantime, the leisure of travel gave him some time to think.

He had already realized that he shouldn't attempt a frontal attack by trying to stir up trouble between Perle and Gabriel. But their parents were another matter: he could sow discord between the sofer and the cantor. The one was stubborn, the other was short-tempered; the first was quick to take offense, the second was a careless talker. There was surely some way to divide them, but unfortunately there was no professional relation between them.

Zadoc thought about it long and hard but couldn't find the point of contact out of which the conflict of interests, the clash of passions, might grow.

He became obsessed with finding a solution; it absorbed him completely. He was still searching when he arrived in Strasbourg. The same difficulty presented itself as he entered Reb Auscher's house: what point of interest linked the two men?

The sofer and his wife welcomed Zadoc graciously, for the upcoming celebration had lifted everyone's spirits. Even Perle was nice to the newcomer. They were grateful to him for hastening his return so as to be present at the consecration of the *sepher* and brought him up to date on all that had been done and all that was planned for the celebration. They also informed him of the imminent arrival of the son of the house, the young hazan who was going to officiate on Saturday at the synagogue of Wertheim.

This was the first that Zadoc had heard of this detail that was so important to the family of the sofer. He was delighted to hear the news, which of course appeared completely natural for a friend of the family and a former comrade of the young cantor. Neither the sofer, nor his wife, nor even Perle, suspected the real motive for Zadoc's happiness.

Indeed, a ray of light had just penetrated the confusing maze of thoughts that had confounded him for three days: the point of contact that he had searched for had finally been found.

The son of the sofer was coming to officiate in the place of the cantor! What a perfect base from which to launch his operations. All that remained was for him to exploit it skillfully.

IV.

That evening, confident in the plan he had hatched, Zadoc took a stroll through the part of the village where Reb Gerson lived. He paused, as if by chance, near the cantor's door, and casually exchanged a few words with him. He allowed himself to be persuaded to enter the house, even though deep down he was burning with desire to be invited in by this worthy dignitary.

After some small talk, the conversation naturally turned to the upcoming celebration.

"Here, finally, is a Saturday," Zadoc said to the cantor, "when you don't have to work, since Samuel is coming to officiate."

"Yes," said Reb Gerson, "I'm looking forward to it."

"Naturally, at a certain age one likes rest."

"Oh, I'm not there yet."

"Feh! What would be the problem if you retired, since your son is doing well enough in business."

"What the devil kind of idea is that?"

"My God, seeing Samuel come to officiate here on Saturday, I thought that it was a kind of test, that you and the sofer had come to an understanding."

"What kind of understanding?"

Zadoc looked like he had said too much. "Let's not speak of it anymore then," he said.

"On the contrary," responded the cantor, who was made more curious by his calculated reticence. "I see that you know more than you are willing to admit. Speak up, I'm discreet."

"This is not to say that anybody confided anything in me," Zadoc said with studied casualness. "Let's just say that I'm speaking on my own account. Clearly you're a good hazan. But Samuel, of course, is young. He has a certain reputation. Comparisons will be made that won't be favorable to you. And who knows if the community won't decide it wants a young cantor and to make you retire with some kind of pension. You know what that will be like."

"But you can't have invented all this."

"What a funny man you are! What's it to you? I'm certainly the sofer's friend, and I find it completely natural that he would want to see his son take your place . . . But I won't say anything more since I don't want to get caught up in all this."

"But I won't mention your name."

"I'll tell you again, nobody has confided anything in me, do you understand? And I for my part haven't said a word about it. But of course this doesn't concern me at all. I'm but a simple merchant. Only when I want to sell a load of hemp I don't go around talking up the competition. But I repeat, I have nothing to say on the matter."

"Very well then," said the hazan, "it's understood."

With this, Zadoc wished Reb Gerson good evening and returned home, well satisfied by the success of the first stage of his plan.

Indeed, the innuendo and careful reticence of the redhead had hit their mark. The cantor was convinced that the plan that was laid before him was hatched by the family of Reb Auscher. What could have motivated Zadoc to invent such a story? Nothing.

Reb Gerson was indignant at what he considered to be the treason of a friend, and such an old friend at that! But there could be no doubt. He certainly couldn't delay trying to parry the blow, which wouldn't be very hard, he reasoned. It was just a matter of preventing Samuel from officiating at the temple that coming Saturday.

Reb Gerson didn't want to oppose it directly since he wasn't sure of having the parnass and the community on his side. What is more, he didn't want to create a stir. He thus decided to make a detour that would bring him all the more surely to his goal.

The next day, at the end of the morning service, the hazan stopped the parnass on the threshold of the synagogue, as they were the last to leave. "Was it you," he said, "who decided that the son of Reb Auscher would officiate on Saturday at the consecration of the new Sepher?"

"Why are you asking me that?" responded the parnass.

Reb Gerson knew the administrator was jealous of all the rights that were his, and even those that weren't.

"Because if it were you, I would find it quite natural," Reb Gerson said.

"But I decided nothing at all. They didn't even consult me."

"As for me," added Reb Gerson, "I have nothing to say about it. In the end, it's all the same to me. I gain a day of rest by it."

"As for me, it's not all the same," responded the parnass, struck in his weak spot. Moreover, he was still angry that the sofer had called him ignorant. "Are we a community with rules or are we not? My authority derives from the Consistory and I will show them that nothing happens in the synagogue without me."[8]

---

8. The Consistory was the governmental body established by Napoleon that controlled all aspects of Jewish religious practice in France. Each region had a local consistory, elected by Jewish notables, under the umbrella of the Central Consistory in Paris.

"However," replied the hazan to stoke the fires of his interlocutor's jealousy, "if the Young People's Club, who had the *sepher* copied . . ."

"The Young People's Club!" replied the administrator, "Who are they? I'm the parnass."

"After all," the hazan began again, "if Reb Auscher announced that his son will officiate, without first asking you, it must be that he just didn't think of it, that's all."

"Oh! no," the parnass responded angrily. "He didn't forget. I know the sofer. He scorns everyone for being ignorant (the administrator couldn't digest the word). Well then, I'll show him . . . Never will his son stand in front of the Torah. You are our hazan. You will officiate."

"I don't know."

"I do know. That's how it will be."

V.

Everyone knows how little time it takes for a bit of news, and especially a bit of bad news, to make its way through a village and how much it gets embellished during that initial, rapid trip. An hour after that conversation, there was not a Jewish house in Wertheim that was not discussing the sudden decision of the parnass regarding the son of the sofer.

The hazan would have gladly left the full responsibility to his superior, but the affair concerned him too directly. In spite of himself, he spoke of it with too much passion for the ingrained spite of the villagers not to recognize him clearly behind the parnass. Moreover, they had been seen talking together that morning after leaving the synagogue, and if all this together didn't suffice to shed light on the affair, Zadoc was there, and his adroit insinuations would have compensated for more precise information.

The news produced true consternation in the home of the sofer, and it was mainly there that Zadoc, through some well-placed observations, let it be known that the blow must have come from the cantor.

If the two friends had discussed it, the difficulty would have been resolved, or at least would not have divided them so profoundly. But Zadoc knew the sofer's character all too well. When he had reason to complain of somebody, he would withdraw immediately into his shell. Like an honest man wronged, he kept his distance and said nothing.

Thus there came to pass exactly what the redhead had predicted. Reb Auscher immediately kept his distance from the hazan. The latter, in response to the tacit accusation, reproached his former friend all over town, and his loquacity led him to say on multiple occasions much more than he really thought.

As in similar cases, the formerly good relations and the mutual aid given served to increase the animosity of the two men—all silent and sullen in the first case, all noisy and voluble in the second—rather than diminish it.

Before she even learned the details, Perle instinctively sensed how fatal this unhappiness would be to her. If Gabriel had been present, things would have turned out differently. He would have brought the adversaries together in an instant. Unfortunately, the young man was still in the Vosges. When he returned on Friday, the evil was done: the hazan and the sofer had become irreconcilable enemies.

During the first few days after the sudden rupture between the cantor and the sofer, the latter, as was his custom, had hardly spoken a word about it to his family. He had simply decided that since his son Samuel could not officiate at the temple, he would not come to Wertheim to take part in the celebration. Perle studied her father's smallest movements with great anxiety, seeking to guess his thoughts by reading his face. She would have liked to have known how deep his resentment really ran and what should be her conduct in the future, not only with respect to the hazan, but also with respect to those that belonged so closely to him.

This uncertainty was a cruel torment to her, but her father said nothing. Friday came, and Perle had already seen Gabriel wave to her from afar, as he always did when he returned from his weekly voyage, and still her father had not spoken. Finally, that evening, upon returning from synagogue, he said to Perle the following words without any other introduction: "You know, my daughter, I swore that from now on you will no longer speak to Gabriel."

Perle felt her blood run cold and her teeth began to chatter. Those few words passed like a destructive wind over all the joy and happiness in her life. Her father had sworn: she never considered disobeying or resisting. And as for changing her father's opinion, the poor child knew all too well that it would be impossible. The rupture was total.

The ceremony for the consecration of the *sepher* was much saddened by the unfortunate quarrel. The little jealousies and childish grudges that take up so much space in the ordinary lives of these little communities always disappear amid the expansiveness and joy of religious holidays. But the regrettable circumstance weighed heavily on all.

Gabriel suffered no less than Perle from the blow that had been dealt to their fondest hopes. This was the first Friday night in a long while that he hadn't spent by her side. The next day he searched for an opportunity to speak with her, but the poor child didn't leave her house. She now feared seeing Gabriel. Would she have the strength, should she meet him, to obey her father and not speak to him?

On Sunday, however, Gabriel caught sight of the young girl as she crossed the street. He signaled to her from afar and she stopped.

"Are you also angry with me?" he asked her when he had caught up to her.

Perle didn't respond. She had tears in her eyes. Gabriel sweetly took her hands in his.

"Your father has forbidden you to speak to me, hasn't he?"

Perle nodded her head, crying.

"Well then," he said bravely. "That means nothing. I won't abandon you just like that because our fathers are having a stupid quarrel. Will you have courage and patience?"

"I will," Perle murmured, sobbing, as she broke free of the young man's hands, scared to speak to him and especially scared to be seen by her father doing so.

Despite the sadness that had overtaken the community of Wertheim that Saturday, Zadoc could not have been happier. His plan had worked to perfection. In order the better to hide his maneuvers and allay suspicion, he took great pains, for the time being, not to change his manner with the family of the sofer. He rarely went to see the father and showed complete indifference to the daughter. He even pursued this tactic to the point of simulating a false attack, like a general who, in order to demolish a besieged city, attempts to outflank the enemy.

He went to pay his provisional and very ostentatious respects to another young Wertheim girl who was of marrying age. She was an orphan named Gudule, but she had no fortune: an uncle had promised to help her but the amount of her dowry wasn't known, a question that preoccupied above all else the redheaded and greedy hemp merchant.

VI.

The solemn days of autumn, the new year, Kippur, and the festival of Tabernacles came and went, but did not change the situation. Perle now only saw Gabriel from afar, when the young man made friendly signs to her while passing in front of the window of her house. He had even found a way to say a few words to her and to engage her in his plan to foster a reconciliation between their parents. He thought he could bring his father around and Perle would try with hers. The young girl promised to do her best but didn't have much hope. She knew her father all too well and was accustomed to bend before his will. All her feeble attempts failed when confronted with that cold and inert character, which was like a polished surface eluding her grasp.

The poor child shut her sorrow away in her heart. Neither the sofer nor his wife guessed the profound and passionate attachment that Gabriel had inspired in their daughter, and they never suspected the secret sadness of that tender and timid soul, which an exquisite sense of modesty prevented her from revealing.

Perle had lost that sweet gaiety that brightened everything around her. She attended to her duties silently, devouring her tears and sorrow in secret. The sofer's house had become sad and monotonous. Winter had come. The year had been bad with poor harvests everywhere, bringing the return of hard times to the house of Reb Auscher, whose fortunes diminished with the general decline. Zadoc, who always had found work for the sofer, no longer brought much. Always able to profit from circumstances, the redhead schemed to indebt the sofer to him, and if he wasn't perverted enough to refuse orders for Reb Auscher during his travels, he no longer made the effort, as before, to get him any. At the same time, he had generously offered his services to the poor man. The latter, pressed by need, had accepted them. He already owed Zadoc a large sum, especially for a man in his situation.

Little by little, Zadoc had increasingly begun to frequent the sofer's house. At the same time that he ceased his attentions to Gudule, he became more assiduous toward Perle.

The young girl grew terrified at these signs of a renewed passion. In her situation, it was the worst evil that could befall her. At first, she had taken that rebirth of affection for one of the redhead's passing fancies, but soon she could fool herself no longer. Zadoc had clearly expressed his intentions and formally asked for her hand.

The sly merchant had taken care to color his actions with the tint of generosity. As long as Perle, he said, had had some hope of marrying the man whom she seemed to prefer, he had sacrificed his hopes and stood on the sidelines. Now that she could no longer hope for a union with Gabriel, he was the one who could assure her happiness.

The sofer and his wife were not displeased to see Zadoc return to his earlier project. He was an excellent match for Perle and a much more advantageous one than they could have dreamed of for their daughter.

Poor Perle was weighed down by all these blows, but as if her own sadness weren't enough, she also felt sorry for the unhappy Gabriel. His family also was struggling in these difficult times, the revenue of the hazan had diminished, Gabriel had lost the good humor that attracted customers, his affairs were going badly, and the boldly proclaimed plans of Zadoc goaded the demon of jealousy within him. He had found a means to see Perle and during that interview, he begged her on his knees not to bring about their unhappiness by giving in to the wishes of his rival.

Perle had promised to try her best and to tell her parents everything. A hundred times, she was on the verge of revealing to them the state of her heart, but her timidity prevented her from speaking. She was waiting for the right moment and put off the painful confession day after day. Day after day, Zadoc meanwhile became more pressing. Perle didn't see a way out of her position. She saw no help or support anywhere and felt herself slipping into the abyss.

At night, her sleep was feverish and agitated by painful nightmares. She would dream of a poor little fly caught in a spider's web, and then the fly would be her. The spider, a horrible red monster, would close in on her with horrible claws, look at her with big green eyes, encircle her and envelop her little by little with his sticky thread. The repulsive insect was Zadoc, who would throw himself on her in order to devour her. Then she would wake up and return to a reality that was just as terrible as these frightful games of her nighttime imagination.

One night when she was lying agitated on her bed, unable to sleep, she overheard, despite herself, a conversation between her parents who were still awake. They were speaking of her and Zadoc. Both the father and mother considered this marriage a real blessing for their daughter and for themselves. The sofer was beginning to feel old and work was becoming harder for him. A well-off son-in-law like Zadoc, to whom he was already indebted, was becoming a necessary support for both of them in their old age.

The words of Reb Auscher were the *coup de grâce* for Perle. She had finally found the strength for which she begged God every day in order to withstand her sad destiny: the idea of sacrificing herself to provide for her parents in their old age made anything possible. From this moment on, her fate was sealed.

Only one other time did her mind wander to the sweet times gone by. Her thoughts caressed one by one all her beautiful old dreams. Then she bid them a final farewell, locking away in the deepest folds of her heart, like a precious perfume of her youth, her love for Gabriel. She bowed her head with resignation and fell asleep murmuring a distressed prayer to God.

The following days, Perle shed a few more tears thinking that Gabriel would think she had betrayed him, but when her parents spoke to her of the union with Zadoc, the courageous child responded without hesitation: I will do as you wish.

It was thus agreed that Perle would marry Zadoc, although the date had not yet been fixed. Zadoc first needed to make a vital business trip to Germany. The engagement would take place upon his return, promptly followed by the marriage, which was not normally the custom. Zadoc had his reasons for proceeding in this manner. A prudent man never commits himself definitively without making sure of every eventuality, and he wanted to guarantee there would be no problem with the inheritance of Aunt Feilché of Frankfurt. He thus wisely resolved to first have the good woman sign a proper and legal will. As the future nephew, he could guide her in this direction in spite of her ill-founded repugnance for such a formality. After this, he would return to Wertheim and marry the pretty heiress with the six thousand écus waiting for her in the green boxes of a notary of the free city of Frankfurt.

In the meantime, he asked the sofer and his wife not to speak to anyone of these arrangements, and for this too he had his reasons. He knew that Gabriel was constantly trying to reconcile his father with

Reb Auscher. These attempts had not met with success, but the premature announcement of Perle's marriage could bring the young man to the sofer's house and thereby threaten to undermine the whole plan, which despite its clever construction rested on a lie that could easily be exposed.

The wily merchant also feared trouble from Gudule's family, even though the young girl hardly seemed to have noticed that he had cooled toward her. But Gabriel often went to see her; it was even his ordinary means of communicating with Perle, who was her friend. Zadoc worried about this indirect contact, telling himself: "I won't let this business drag on. Once I'm back from Frankfurt, I'll hurry things along so that they won't even have time to blink between the engagement and the marriage."

VII.

It was the Sunday before the festival of Hanukah. Gabriel, as usual, had left for the Vosges, after having, yet again, repeated his entreaties to his father, who accompanied him out of the village. As always happens with fiery and loquacious people, the resentment of the hazan had slowly calmed down, and if he wasn't willing to take the first step, neither would he reject a hand that was outstretched toward him, even if he wouldn't admit it.

Returning home, he had to pass in front of the sofer's house. Indeed, he noticed Reb Auscher standing in the window. The poor man looked anxious and seemed to be lost in serious and painful thoughts, for he didn't even notice that he was being watched.

The pitiful face of his former friend struck the cantor all the more strongly in that he too was not in a happy state. The road marked by adversity that they had traveled together, sometimes even happily because of their mutual support, presented itself before his eyes, and he regretted for the first time that such a long and tested friendship had ended in such a pitiable manner.

The hazan returned home with this on his mind. On the threshold of his house he met the postman, who gave him a large letter. Reb Gerson recognized immediately that it came from Frankfurt. The envelope bore the stamp of Maurice Stiebel and Co., the lottery agency for the free city. It will be remembered that the cantor had a habit of tempting the goddess Fortune, who lived in Frankfurt.

But he had for so long received from the agency long missives containing interminable boilerplate statements of regret concerning his ill luck and even sickly sweet expressions of hope for a happier future, that he opened the letter only by habit, almost with indifference.

However, while unfolding the list of the winning numbers, he immediately noticed a number underlined in red pencil.

He had the winning ticket.

At first, the cantor could scarcely believe his eyes, but he grew even more incredulous when he saw the amount attached to the number selected, which he had chosen. Reb Gerson had won three thousand florins.[9] His legs buckled. He grew pale. His vision darkened. And he barely had the strength to call his wife and to show her the paper.

She was frightened when she heard the strange note in her husband's voice, but soon she understood. "Three thousand florins," he finally said. "That's a fortune."

"The Lord our God knows what He does," replied the wife piously. "We really need the money."

Reb Gerson, however, had gone in search of the ticket. He compared it carefully to the underlined digits. It really was his number. There could be no doubt.

Once the first excitement had passed, the hazan resolved first and foremost not to divulge to anyone that happiness that had befallen him. It couldn't serve any good purpose. and might even cause him a lot of harm. Then the husband and wife began to make plans. That happy activity occupied them the whole evening and even into the night, long after they had gone to bed.

In the middle of his happy dreams of a golden future, the cantor suddenly saw rise before his eyes the face of the sofer, standing somber and worried behind his window.

"Well," the cantor said to himself, "we've never either of us had any luck. But the real *schlemiel*, the man who has always been truly unlucky,

---

9. The gulden, a unit of currency used in southern Germany between 1754 and 1873, was often called a florin.

is him. Now, for the first time, I could be truly useful to him and here we are in a fight. It's really unfortunate: the tithe of my winnings belongs to the poor. Whom would I rather give it to than him? If only I knew he would accept it . . . but no, he will refuse."

It is said that the night brings counsel, and it appears that that particular night did its duty conscientiously. The next day, the cantor left for Strasbourg and after having converted his ticket into money, he went to the see the notary Strohmeyer.

He explained to the administrative officer that having won three thousand florins in the Frankfurt lottery, he wanted to give a tenth of his winnings to one of his friends, Reb Auscher of Wertheim, without the latter being able to know who had given it to him. The notary should therefore send the money to the sofer saying it is an inheritance from some distant relative, no matter from where. To make it more realistic, the notary should send the money in florins.

Mr. Strohmeyer found this all quite unusual.

"I don't see any problem," he said. "If you like, the money can come from one of my colleagues in Frankfurt."

"Perfect," replied Reb Gerson, rubbing his hands together contentedly. Then he wrote a letter to Gabriel telling him to hasten his return so that he could tell him a bit of good news.

The next day, when the letter from the notary of Strasbourg arrived, the sofer, his wife, and Perle all found themselves at home. Zadoc was there as well. He was leaving the next day for Frankfurt and had come to say goodbye. Perle was barely paying attention to what the young man was saying. She had resigned herself to her fate and was indifferent to all the rest.

A thick envelope always caused a stir in the sofer's house. Reb Auscher opened it and while he was reading, his wife, Perle, and Zadoc followed with equal attention the growing expression of surprise that painted itself on his face.

"So what is it?" the wife of Reb Auscher asked.

"Good God, heaven is sending us a small inheritance at a good time. It comes to us from Frankfurt. The letter isn't really clear, but here are some papers that are."

Zadoc grew pale.

Had death anticipated and forestalled his maneuvers?

"An inheritance," said Perle, for whom every accident became a ray of hope.

"Yes," said Reb Auscher, "three hundred florins!"

"Three hundred florins! God be praised," said the mother.

"Three hundred florins!" added Perle, "That's a lot."

"Three hundred florins!" Zadoc said in turn, still in shock, his prudence giving way to disenchantment. "But that's not possible. You've been cheated, robbed . . . you've . . . "

He stopped, for he perceived that he had given away half his secret.

"How? What?" replied the three other interlocutors at the same time! "So you know something about it?"

"I know and I don't know," responded an embarrassed Zadoc. "If it's all the same to you, let me take care of this. I won't stand by as honest people—almost my own family, right?—get cheated. No, no, let me take care of this. I'll leave this very night and I will make sure you get what's owed to you."

The redhead struggled to avoid the questions they asked, which were proving more and more embarrassing. With his customary farsightedness, he realized that there remained only one way to avoid a shipwreck in the port: he had the sofer's word. If he went to Frankfurt and succeeded in returning to him the aunt's money, which could still be ripped out of greedy and indelicate hands, then the sofer would be doubly bound and Perle would become his wife despite this unfortunate mishap.

VIII.

The sudden departure of Zadoc and the knowledge that the redhead had of this unexpected inheritance made the sofer think. He vaguely surmised that there must be some connection between his falling out with the hazan, the remoteness of Gabriel, the advances of Zadoc, and the well-kept secret of the mysterious inheritance from Frankfurt. Wheels were turning in his head without his realizing it, but they kept bringing him back to the moment that he broke with his friend the cantor.

Perle had begun to hope without quite knowing why, but she understood vaguely that something in the situation had changed.

Gabriel had just returned from the mountains after receiving his father's letter. He was greatly intrigued to know the good news they had mentioned. His father was about to satisfy his curiosity when the community administrator entered.

"Reb Gerson," he said to him, "I have come for a very pleasing commission. A person who shall remain nameless sent me thirty florins to give to you today. He said it was the restitution of an old debt. Here they are."

The cantor smiled. So the sofer also had thought of his friend in a moment of happiness. Like Reb Gerson, and despite their recent separation, he had recalled their long and old friendship and gave him a part, the tithe, of the money that God unexpectedly sent him.

"You're discreet," Reb Gerson said to him, "but I shall go myself to thank Reb Auscher."

"Hazan," said the astonished parnass, "you must either be a sorcerer or a kabbalist."

"I'm neither the one nor the other, but I'll explain it all to you later. Come," he said to Gabriel, "we're going to see Reb Auscher."

Gabriel thought he would burst with joy. The good news that awaited him surpassed his wildest expectations.

The father and the son went out accompanied by the parnass who was going in the same direction.

What a surprise when the two men entered the house of the sofer who, as was his custom, had said nothing to anyone about the thirty florins, the tithe of the supposed inheritance, that he had sent secretly to a former friend.

Perle couldn't believe her eyes. She saw Gabriel and instantly almost fainted into his arms.

"Well," said Reb Auscher, "shaking the hand of the hazan, the parnass must have talked, I should have known he would."

"Not in the least," responded the hazan, "I would have surely guessed the truth, even if you had taken the precautions I did to make you accept the three hundred florins."

"What do you mean, the three hundred florins?"

"But of course. Mr. Strohmeyer's letter, the inheritance from Frankfurt, all that came from here," he said, tapping his forehead. "I am the one who sent you the three hundred florins because I won three thousand. I made a tithe, as did you."

The sofer became more and more surprised.

"But then," he said, sliding his velvet skullcap back over his occiput, which was for him the ultimate sign of astonishment. "But then, what was the inheritance from Frankfurt that Zadoc mentioned?"

"An inheritance from Frankfurt. Zadoc! That is indeed curious. You must have dreamt it."

"But no. My wife, and you Perle, you also heard it, didn't you?"

But Perle had other things to do than to concern herself with inheritances and florins. She was talking to Gabriel. Both were speaking at the same time. Perle had to explain and be forgiven for accepting the redhead's marriage proposal. But how could Gabriel blame her? She had yielded because of such a beautiful and touching sentiment! The young girl only became dearer to him because of it. Moreover they felt so happy that the past had already disappeared and they concerned themselves only with the future didn't pay the least attention to what was going on around them.

Thus the sofer was obliged to repeat his question.

"Indeed," responded Perle, "there must be something to it, since the redhead who has been to Frankfurt knows more about it than we do."

"No matter what you think," replied the cantor, "I know that I won my three thousand florins, because I have them."

"You won three thousand florins, father," Gabriel said in turn, who was following the conversation now that the charming Perle was no longer talking to him, "and you didn't tell me?"

"Didn't I tell you? That's true. I didn't want to mention it in front of the parnass. But that second story from Frankfurt that Zadoc was talking about strikes me as odd."

"It will all be explained one of these days," replied the sofer. "Just tell me how you could have gotten it into your head that I wanted my son to replace you."

"By Jove, it's Zadoc who told me that. He heard it here."

"The redhead again!" responded the sofer. "That man wants to meddle in all my affairs. But he's the one who assured me that you had invented it. So he's the one who sowed discord between us! Why?"

Love is blind, or such anyway is its reputation. Nevertheless it was love that saw the situation most clearly. Gabriel was the first to untangle the threads that had been so carefully and secretly woven by the maneuvers of his rival.

The redhead had learned that an inheritance was going to give Perle a nice dowry and in order to possess both he had sowed discord between the two families.

It was all plain as day. If a doubt lingered in any of their minds, Zadoc himself soon came along to dispel it. He had left that same evening for Frankfurt, needled by the disappointment of seeing his carefully laid plans come to naught. To his great astonishment, he found Aunt Feilché in good health.

Our crafty dowry chaser couldn't understand what had happened, and wondered whether all the Jews of Frankfurt had made the sofer their heir. While he was there, he presented himself as the future husband of Perle and put on such a show in front of the aunt that she agreed to draw up a new legal will in favor of her niece. Zadoc had nothing more pressing to do than to inform the sofer of the result of his actions in order to take advantage of his efforts and of his success as one more reason to be welcomed into the family.

I will leave to the reader's imagination the laughter that greeted his missive. Gabriel especially cackled at the thought of a rival taking such good care of his interests, and he couldn't stop himself from telling everyone how the sharpest man in Wertheim had gone all the way to Frankfurt to settle the affairs of his rival, thinking they were his.

When the poor boy returned he was the laughingstock of the entire village. God knows what mockery he suffered and what names he was called: the mortification was doubly cruel for a man with such a great reputation for cunning.

Two months later the rabbi of Fegersheim came to bless the union of Perle and Gabriel. The three thousand florins of the Frankfurt lottery had allowed the young man to greatly expand his commerce. Instead of taking pains to bring his merchandise to the customers, he could from now on wait for them to come to his own store.

His business prospered and he soon convinced his father to resign his duties so that Samuel, the son of Reb Auscher, could replace him.

Since the position was a good one, the sofer did not delay in giving up his as well.

From that day on, the two friends, like good rabbinists, divided their time equally between distraction and study: in the morning they deepened the Talmud with an army of all sorts of commentaries; the evenings were normally devoted to games of piquet.

Aunt Feilché lived many more years but, as Gabriel used to like to say, thanks to the efforts of Zadoc, they could be sure of the inheritance.

The sofer and the hazan soon made up with the latter, and they didn't miss the chance to mock him, for the redhead often came to see the family. Only Gabriel couldn't forgive him for all the unhappiness he caused his dear Perle, but the latter was so happy that she easily forgot about the wrongdoings of her former and too crafty suitor.

Moreover he was sufficiently punished by the continual jokes that tormented him: the story of the inheritance from Frankfurt would not go away.

He got so tired of it that he resolved one fine day to prove to the world that his heart contained enough space to love something else besides money. He went to ask for the hand of Gudule despite the fact that her uncle had given her an excessively small dowry.

But it was then that the people of Wertheim realized that even the smartest people often don't know what is going on around them. Nobody had ever doubted that behind Gudule's friendship for Perle lurked a serious affection for Samuel, her brother. They had promised a long time ago to get married once the young man had found a suitable position.

And when Zadoc went to see the uncle, he met the young cantor with Gudule. They had just set the date for the engagement and three months later they celebrated their marriage.

Zadoc is still single.

Samuel Gordon, "Daughters of Shem: A Study in Sisters" (1898)

Samuel Gordon (1871–1927) was born in Buk, Prussia (now Poland), of a Russian father and Polish mother. The family emigrated to England when Gordon was twelve years old. He was educated in London and at Cambridge University, where he studied Classics. He led a cosmopolitan life, traveling widely in Europe and living briefly in America. In London, he spent much time in the East End in the company of the campaigning journalist and dramatist George R. Sims.

Gordon was also closely connected to the leadership of the Anglo-Jewish community. His father was the cantor of the prestigious Great Synagogue in Duke's Place, Aldgate, in the City of London—the leading London congregation which included members of the established elite of Anglo-Jewry as well as recent immigrants resident in the nearby East End. Samuel held the office of Secretary there between 1894 and 1913. He was among the first generation of Jews to graduate from Cambridge University but, unusually, he combined a secular higher education with active involvement in organized religious life.

Much of Gordon's fiction focused on the lives of contemporary Jews both in Russia and London and was published by mainstream publishing houses. His first collection of stories, *A Handful of Exotics: Scenes and Incidents Chiefly of Russo-Jewish Life* (1897), aimed to restore the humanity to the much-discussed subject of the Russian Jew, but also drew attention to the "unfathomable policy of systematic and gratuitous cruelty" of the imperial regime. The book attracted considerable critical praise, but Gordon never enjoyed great commercial success. He went on to publish several novels, including *Unto Each Man His Own* (1904), on the question of marriage between middle-class London Jews and Christians, and *The Ferry of Fate: A Tale of Russian Jewry* (1906), as well as a further volume of stories, *God's Remnants: Tales of Israel among the Nations* (1916). Gordon described himself as an "optimist" and unlike many of his Jewish and non-Jewish contemporaries regarded the immigrants as a resource of Jewish moral and racial vitality. In his most well-known

In the Hebrew Bible, Shem was the son of Noah and in Jewish tradition regarded as the progenitor of the Semitic peoples.

novel, *Sons of the Covenant: A Tale of Anglo-Jewry* (1900), two East End brothers, one an enterprising capitalist and the other a university man, work together on a scheme to regenerate East End Jewry by establishing a training institute in order to diversify Jewish occupations and residence. They wish to eliminate the ghetto mentality of immigrant Jews but not to erase their collective allegiance.

It was in this context that Gordon produced English-language versions of the "ghetto tale" genre. *Daughters of Shem and Other Stories* was first published in 1898 and reprinted as *Strangers at the Gate: Tales of Russian Jewry* (1902) by the Jewish Publication Society of America. In 1906 Gordon produced a stage version of "Daughters of Shem" in London. Like his other stories it depicted Jewish life in the Russian empire as constrained by both external and internal forces, but also warned against intermarriage. Yet even the *Jewish Chronicle* remarked on the ambivalent note that is struck at the end of the story with the Jewish heroine's tragic renunciation of her gentile lover. In 1901, Gordon said that the "danger ... of religious disintegration, which is threatening Jewry and Judaism with extinction" was a crisis facing "the civilised world in general." In other words, he intended his stories of Jewish protagonists torn between love and tradition to be understood in universal terms, as an expression of the wider shift toward secularization.

I.

The shop stood in the very centre of the town. One could determine this with almost mathematical precision, for the place was styled a town less on its merits than by geographical courtesy; as a matter of fact it consisted of a single street, all frontage, which, starting from the shop, took a few strides to the right, as many, or as few, to the left, and then broke off abruptly. It enjoyed, however, the distinction of being one of the half dozen frontier stations within the railway radius, the main object of which is to render the lives of travellers passing in and out of the land of the shadow of the Czar as much a burden to themselves as possible.[1] Woe to the improvident passenger whose passport shows the slightest flaw or discrepancy. The double-headed eagle of Russia has sharp eyes and sharper claws, and he can strike hard, unless one has the means and the presence of mind to soothe the ruffled feelings of his myrmidons. As a rule, palm oil will be found very effective. If you succeed in running the bureaucratic gauntlet, you are allowed to get off with the freight, and the conviction that the Russian frontier is

---

1. The town is at the border between Prussia, the dominant state in the German empire, and Russia, its enemy empire.

a beautiful thing in retrospect. If you do not, you become an object of tender solicitude to sundry gendarmes, till advices arrive as to whether and whither you are to be expedited by special escort.

To begin again, then. The shop stood in the middle of the town. It was a miscellaneous depot of salt herrings, treacle, Limburg cheese, and everything else that could go to make it a large-sized spice-box. Its atmosphere, in consequence, was a downright extravagance; condensed in jars, it could have been sold as an original kind of condiment. But Zillah was used to it by now. She had been born into it, though she could never make out how, under the circumstances, she had survived her birth.

Just now she was serving in the shop, as usual; that is, she was seated behind the counter absorbed in her book, while Yeiteles, the boy-of-all-work,[2] attended to the customers, and handed her the money, which Zillah never checked. For Zillah did nothing but read—not the homespun lucubrations of the Jargon literature, but real German novels by Franzos, and Marlitt, and Spielhagen.[3] When she was nine, and her sister, Salka, seven, they had been sent to their uncle, a well-to-do shopkeeper in an East Prussian provincial capital, to get a little schooling. Salka did not go back to him after the first holidays, because all the time she had been dying of home-sickness; not even the beautiful name of Rosalie, which her girl-cousins had promised to give her, could prompt her to return. But Zillah went back, term after term, till she was sixteen, because she did not notice the silent protest in her parents' eyes, the unspoken admonition that it was time she should cast anchor at their hearth; and when at last there came tangible cause for her to stay with them, she obeyed, but with a heart gnawed to the core by discontent.

It was her mother's illness that had called Zillah back to the hole-and-corner life in the dreary frontier town,[4] just as her eyes were beginning to open on the manifold glories and the gladness of the outer world, her ears to catch the loudening echoes of its thousand-voiced laughter, her soul to feel its life-joy, which leavened her placid girlhood

---

2. Servant.

3. Karl Emil Franzos, witty chronicler of Eastern European Jewish life (and friend of Leopold Kompert), E. Marlitt (Eugenie John), bestselling romance writer and Friedrich Spielhagen were among the most popular German novelists of the period. "Jargon literature" is popular Yiddish literature.

4. *Hole-and-corner* means "clandestine."

with a subtle presage of possible delights. Aye, just then she had to leave it all; but she brought the memory of it, a precious contraband, back with her into captivity, three months of which had ripened her into a woman. One grows old quickly in prison. And to her woman's fancy, which intensified the girl's dream, these things seemed more desirable, more alluring, because of the iron restraint that hemmed in her young life. Not fifty yards from the house loomed up the cross-barred frontier-gate, where the sentries' bayonets gleamed night and day, and fierce-eyed, impatient bloodhounds yelped disconsolately. And beyond them lay the fairyland from which she had been banished, the gladsome companionship of the wider, larger life she so often dwelt on with hungering memory. Every evening, as she heard the rattle of the massive ring chain being drawn across the gate-posts, she felt the world was locked out amid the hard metallic laughter of her malignant fate.

That was her horizon without. And within, the same narrowness, the same choking of the tether. Three human souls, just three, peopled her universe. The bedridden, unrepining mother; the equally patient sister, who had made it her task to fan the flickering life back to a fuller blaze; and the sturdy, quick-witted father, who was constantly traversing the country's breadth to pile yet higher the contents of the stout oaken safe; and report had it that Anshel Markovitz was a prosperous man. On these three, then, Zillah expended what emotions were not crushed within her by the leaden routine. She gave them all her heart; and yet, when they thought her closest to them, she was roving through an enchanting wonder-world whither they did not accompany her—the world she had fashioned for herself out of the books she was forever reading, reading, reading.

Five years lay between her final return from Germany and this sultry late-summer afternoon. There was little or no business, and Yeiteles had utilized the fact by going to sleep in an empty herring barrel; the salt smell made his throat very dry and he wheezed raucously. Zillah sat in a wicker chair, her hands toying idly in her lap with the book they held. She was dreaming—the same old dreams of the far-away, the unattainable. She got tired of that as well. Wearily she rose and stepped to the door; the shop was stifling. The street appeared empty, but no—just then old Torkov, the hunchback idiot, came hobbling round the corner. Just in front of Zillah he stopped, his gaze caught by a putrefying apple on the pavement—the pigs had over looked it because they preferred to nose in the garbage of the open road. With a squeal of joy Torkov snatched up his treasure-trove, and devoured it as he shambled on. Zillah looked after him with a curious smile on her face.

"God was good to you, Torkov," she murmured at last, "better than to me. If only I had been born like that, inwardly and outwardly."

Then she went back to her wicker chair and the German novel. Yeiteles, awakened by her step, sat up with a snort, and rubbed his eyes. Another footfall was heard from the back of the shop, and Salka came in softly.

"Mother is asleep," she said. "I'll just run down to the post and see if there is a letter from father. If mother calls . . ."

Zillah nodded silently. She always saved words where signs sufficed; perhaps it was that which had stamped the pathos on her lips.

Salka was considerably longer over her errand than was usually the case, so much so that she felt it necessary to give an explanation on her return.

"The Police Commissioner is dead—died suddenly," she said; "I stayed to hear all about it. Everybody is wondering what the new man will be like. There is a lot of excitement."

"Yes, a death is the only thing that makes folks here know they are alive," commented Zillah. "Is there a letter?"

"Oh, I nearly forgot," stammered Salka, confused at having apparently neglected their father on account of a stranger; "yes, a big one—I can feel by the envelope. Shall we wait till mother wakes up?"

"No," said Zillah, "if there is good news she will hear it twice—once from our telling and again from the reading. If, God forbid, something is not as it ought to be, we shall know what to leave out."

And slowly she ripped open the cover, while Salka looked at her with shining eyes. It was a very big letter—twice the ordinary length; it began by saying that the writer was well, and that business was flourishing, and went on to detail with much circumstance the bargains he had driven, as well as the course of his journeys. A puzzled look came over Zillah's face as she read.

"I don't know," she suddenly interrupted herself, "father never writes like that. There's something he has to say and is putting off—ah, here it is!"

She had skimmed the next page hurriedly, and had found what she was searching for. It ran as follows: "And now, my dear ones, I have joyful tidings for you; like a miser his gold, so have I been eking out the pleasure of them to the utmost. I am returning to you this day week,[5] and not alone. I am bringing with me—but I shall not say whom, only that a great honour is being done to our house. You will be pleased with me. So content yourselves meantime with the knowledge that wherever I go, whatever I do, my children's happiness is nearest my heart."

Zillah paused and looked questions at her sister. The latter answered only with a mischievous smile.

"Tell me, what does it mean? You seem to be in the secret," urged Zillah.

"You know, too. If not, I shall give you a hint: you were twenty-one this summer."

"Well?" asked Zillah, keeping down her upstruggling suspicion of the truth.

"And father took your photograph away with him."

Zillah started back, pale to the lips. Then she looked round quickly; the shop was empty. Yeiteles had sneaked out to verify the report of the Commissioner's death.

"It means—my marriage," she whispered.

Salka was about to assent, with a merry laugh at the well-planned surprise; but she stopped short when she saw Zillah's mouth contract as with the pain of a sudden wound.

"Oh, anything but that," came piteously from the puckered lips, "anything but that, Salka. Why should it be? Do I complain? Do I say I am dissatisfied? All I ask is to be left to myself. I don't want to belong to anyone else. I want to be my own—and yours. I am to be given to a man into whose face I have never looked, whose voice I have never heard, to be his inalienably, while I may be gasping for liberty; what shall I do, sister of mine, what shall I do?"

Salka's eyes drooped because they were heavy with the mist of tears. "Trust father," she replied, after a while; "he is not the man to make mistakes. I am certain he has satisfied himself that your husband-to-be is all one can desire. Does he not say he is always thinking of our happiness?"

---

5. This day next week.

"Who says I am not happy?" asked Zillah, eagerly. "Am I to go about laughing and singing with the shadow of mother's illness in the house? I shall promise him he will never see a frown on my face, never a vexed look; but he must not force me to this."

"It will grieve him—and mother," said Salka, quietly.

Zillah clenched her hands.

"I have never thought of myself," she said, almost harshly, "it was always of them; well, they must also be generous for once." Then her eyes lit up. "Suppose the man does not care for me, after all?" she broke off suddenly.

Salka came a step nearer, and silently she turned her sister's face to the light; then as silently she shook her head.

"You think he will approve of me?" said Zillah, despairingly.

"Who would not?" replied Salka.

There was a slight tapping overhead.

"Mother's awake—that's her knock," continued Salka, hurriedly. "Come, we must read her the letter."

Zillah held her back.

"Not a word—don't tell her how I think of it," she whispered; "another time, when she is stronger."

Salka nodded, and led the way up to the spacious, airy bedroom. A pale, wasted woman smiled on them happily, as they entered.

"Good news from father," cried Salka; "listen—"

But the next moment Zillah had taken the letter out of her hand.

"I am the elder," she said simply. Steady and clear, her voice gave out every word, without a quaver, even when she came to the tidings at which her heart had rebelled.

The happy smile deepened in her mother's eyes, and then the thin little voice said:

"Thank God! So he has succeeded. Zillah, kiss me. That was a cold kiss, but perhaps it is my fault; my lips are never warm. In a week's time, then?"

Salka stood at the window.

"Some people have gone into the shop, Zillah," she called.

And Zillah went downstairs, thanking Providence for such a sister.

II.

It was the following afternoon. From the doorway of the shop Zillah was staring into infinity. Over night she had had ample time to grasp the situation more clearly and to gaze deeper into her heart; both of which things did not tend to make her happier. It was not merely the thought of being handed over, bound hand and foot, to an utter stranger, which agonized her; but with such a marriage she knew full well her last chance of redeeming herself from the trammels of her present bondage was gone irretrievably. For the man who had gained the approval of her parents so signally as this projected husband of hers seemed to have done, could not but stand in complete accord with their views and ways and wishes. And their views and ways and wishes were not always hers. Their wishes had always found her obedient; all the rebelling she had done had usually been against herself. But now she was asked to lock the portals of her prison and throw away the key. She was to be burdened with duties that were but a euphemism for menial service. She would be a household drudge, weaving day to day and year to year, without a knot in the texture to mark where an event had broken the faceless uniformity. That was the fate of all the women she knew; only they had harnessed themselves willingly in their traces—nay more, they flaunted them, as a badge of honor, in the eyes of those who had not yet become yoke-fellows. But these women had not been given understanding; the world's cry rang in their ears inarticulate, they did not even know it was capable of interpretation. She, too, would have to forget that to her it was once fraught with a great meaning; she would forget easily once she got into the groove of haggling over the price of vegetables and descanting on the merits of the tinker who doctored her pots and pans. It escaped her that this did not define the scope and function of the average housewife of her race, or any race; but when one is sore with oneself, one is least likely to do justice to others.

Her eyes ached with the cloudless glare of the afternoon sky. She was glad of it—the physical pain seemed somewhat to lessen her heartache, and it was a pain she could relieve more easily than the other. In front of her stretched a strip of greensward carpeting the opposite side of the road. Presently she rested her eyes upon it. A tall man was walking across the grass, his sabre clanking musically against his spurs. As he passed, he turned his face on Zillah's, casually and carelessly; he evidently did not care what there was to be seen. Then his gaze tightened; it became a stare. Zillah stood unconcerned. She was used to this, had been used to it since she was fifteen. Most people looked at her; some went to the trouble of adjusting their *pince-nez* for a proper focus. From that she knew she was beautiful; the glances of young men make a reliable mirror.

The tall man walked on, but at a slower pace. Two or three times he looked round, but the worship of his eyes was wasted on Zillah, for she was busy resting her own on the grass-patch opposite. And when she found they were relieved, she retired to her wicker chair and went on with her book. Business was slack, as usual at this time of the day, and she could look forward to a long stretch of leisure. Her story was getting near to the climax; rapidly, ravenously almost, she was turning the pages, fascinated by the power of its genius—yes, she knew what genius was. Suddenly a cry of vexation broke from her; a shadow had fallen across the leaf, and would not go away. She looked up; the tall young officer of half-an-hour ago stood in the doorway, his attitude one of irresolution. Her upward glance seemed to decide him; he stepped into the shop, touching his cap politely and keeping his sabre from clattering. Zillah remained quietly seated.

"What do you speak here?" he asked. And just then he caught sight of the book Zillah had laid open upon the counter, and continued in excellent German: "Ah, the language of Heine; we shall understand each other."

His voice sounded firm, yet mellow—not an unkindly voice.

"What is your wish?" asked Zillah, self-possessed.

The young man forgot to answer immediately; he was immersed in her eyes. He recovered himself with a little laugh.

"I am bewitched; I suffer from an absurd fancy for smoked flounders. You Jews can prepare them as no other people can; if only you would never do anything worse."

Zillah's face was as that of a statue.

"How many do you require?" she asked, nonchalantly as before.

"Just a couple will do for the present."

"Yeiteles, a pair of flounders for the gentleman; wrap them up neatly," said Zillah.

The next moment she had resumed her book, and was leaning back in her chair, apparently oblivious of everything.

A quiet smile hovered on the officer's lips as he watched Yeiteles clumsily struggling with his task; but from where he stood he could likewise observe Zillah's profile and her long lashes, even to noting how they curled up at the ends. Yeiteles was not so clumsy after all; at any rate he seemed to have taken a marvellously short time over his parcel.

"What have I to pay?" asked the purchaser.

"Twenty copecks, please," answered Zillah, turning over-leaf.

Leisurely the young man pulled out his pocket-book, and from it selected a hundred-rouble note. Zillah took it up, and glanced at it.

"I can't give you change for so much," she said coldly, handing it back to him.

"Then I can't have any flounders, I suppose? I have nothing less," said the other. The smile was there all through.

"No matter; you can send the money round afterward."

He did not take that for his dismissal; he stood tapping the counter with his knuckles.

"Your book must be very interesting," he said at last.

"Yes," returned Zillah, curtly.

"So interesting that you do not observe this is an historic event—a precedent, to say the least."

Zillah raised her head, but not her eyes.

"You ask how?" he continued. "Well, in this way. An officer of his Majesty the Emperor comes to make a purchase in a Jewish shop while the mistress is present, and she allows him to get served by the errand-boy, the state of whose fingers is not above reproach. I consider the fact distinctly original."

This time he forced her to look at him.

"When an officer of the Emperor buys something in a Jewish shop," she echoed, "he buys that which he pays for; he does not buy its owner as well."

"In this case she is certainly beyond price," he interrupted banteringly.

"But I am sorry about Yeiteles," she continued eagerly. "Yeiteles, go and wash your hands, and give the gentleman two other flounders."

"Pray don't trouble the excellent Yeiteles," smiled the young man; "I never intended to eat the fish myself; surely you must have known that all along. I came here—can you tell me why I came here?"

"Yes," she replied quickly, "to cast insult at my people."

"Oh, that rankles," he said with a short laugh; "but I did not intend it for an insult, I assure you. It was just an experiment."

Neither by word nor by gesture did she ask his meaning.

"You are certainly not inquisitive," he proceeded; "but I feel sure you would like to know all the same. I wanted to see if the placid, unruffled exterior you presented to me harboured any emotions. You foiled me at first; I am glad I stayed long enough to get a reward for my diplomacy. A volcano beneath an iceberg is a rare phenomenon. I wish you good-day."

At the door he turned again; his former smile had resumed possession of his face.

"Do you know what I should suggest to you for an occupation? You might make a tour in the Greek orthodox villages and exhibit yourself as the Madonna Rediviva. Your eyes alone would bring you many believers."

Five minutes after he was gone Zillah happened to glance at Yeiteles; he looked troubled.

"What is the matter, Yeiteles?" she asked.

"I don't know," stammered the boy; "but if I were you, I should have been more—more friendly to the gentleman. He is the new Police Commissioner."

"And what if he is?" smiled Zillah.

"He might take away your shop license."

"And then?"

"And then I should be without work, and should have to go back home to starve with the others."

III.

Zillah sat idle; her book lay discarded. She was reading something more interesting—her own thoughts, to wit; that, after all, was her favourite literature, as it is with all who live their lives in solitude. The form of her thoughts was the same as usual, and yet withal there was a different tone and colour to them. She was trying to account to herself for the change, and failed. It seemed to her that the far-away wonder-world to which she had all these years been stretching forth her hands in impotent longing had quite suddenly stepped close and touched her on the arm. She had heard its voice speak loudly at her ear, for a moment only, it was true, but the touch still thrilled her, the utterance had not ceased to reverberate. It was a pleasant sensation, this sudden brightness that had flitted across the midnight of her desolation. Only that the mystery of it frightened her. Surely it owed nothing to the young Commissioner who had talked to her yesterday afternoon? What made her suppose it did? Young men had talked to her before, more conciliatingly than this rude stranger had done. It would be paying him a compliment to connect him, however distantly, with anything that gave her pleasure.

And meanwhile her doubts redoubled. Then it struck her it was the close-packed atmosphere of the shop that clogged her power of analysis. Perhaps if she went out into the heart of the forest, among the leafy, nodding wiseacres, they would whisper suggestions to her, and interpret her to herself. She did not wait for more promptings; the next moment she had reached down the crook-handled sunshade of faded pink from its peg—a few rapid touches to her hair, and she was ready.

"Yeiteles," she called from the doorstep, "I shall be back in an hour; be attentive, and don't eat too much treacle."

Quickly she stepped down the road. Outside the last house but one lounged a group of girls and young married women, laughing, chatting, munching pears, and ill-treating innocent pieces of calico with needles and thread. As Zillah approached, their merriment grew hushed. She nodded pleasantly; one or two responded, but no one asked her where she was going, or if she would join them. Zillah passed on untroubled; she had noted the sudden silence that had greeted her appearance—nay more, she had expected it. Whose was the fault? Not theirs, she admitted that. Her whilom playmates had given her cordial welcome whenever she had appeared in their midst; they had overlooked the chariness of her response as long as they could disguise it. Then gradually they had become aware that Zillah was the daughter of the richest man in the place, that her beauty was beyond compare, that she possessed knowledge of things far out of their ken; and all this entitled her to her strange aloofness. Pride they called it for short; but to Zillah it sometimes seemed a curse that rested upon her. She could not otherwise account for the perverseness that made her an exile in body, because her soul felt like an anchorite. She did not regret it, not even after all these years of loneliness. If a pang stung her heart, it was that she had forced her sister to follow her into this self-banishment. Salka had to choose between her former associates and Zillah; and Salka had chosen as one would expect of her. Loyal little Salka!

The thoughts of it kept Zillah company as far as the forest border. Then she remembered she had come out for a special purpose, and dismissed them. The wood itself had too much tangle and undergrowth to make pleasant walking, but the road-path into which it had been widened was good thoroughfare for foot and vehicle. Zillah kept well within the shadow of the trees. It was quiet as the grave; if she could not now puzzle her heart clear of its doubts, they would only vanish in the greater darkness of eternity.

Behind her rang out the sound of a horse's hoofs. That did not trouble her; she knew no one who rode a horse, at least at that speed, and therefore she did not fear interruption.

The rider came abreast, cast a quick, sidelong glance at her, and pulled up with a jerk. The next thing she knew was that he had dismounted, and was walking beside her, leading the chafing animal by the bridle.

"Good-day," he said pleasantly; "this is lucky—I can pay my debt now."

She looked at him; their eyes were almost on a level. A flush was on her face, but it might have been only the reflected tint of the pink parasol.

"But you had no value for the money; you did not eat the fish," she said.

"That's true, but my Phylax enjoyed them tremendously. You should have heard his bark after, it sounded like a thanksgiving. By the way, do you often take walks—alone?"

"Whenever occasion offers," she answered equivocally. She was thinking what, according to Yeiteles, would happen if she were not "more friendly to the gentleman." He could take away their shop license. Not that it would make much difference to them—they could live on the contents of the oaken safe; but Yeiteles would be thrown out of employment, and would have to starve. She would sacrifice her feelings of resentment for poor little Yeiteles' sake, and show herself sociable to the Commissioner.

The latter did not appear to feel there was cause for apology.

"Yes, in these nutshell places one has no room to be alone," he said, apropos of nothing; "I have been here twenty-four hours, and already I am gasping for breath. So I came out for a canter."

"The road farther on is very good," she could not, despite her resolution, forbear to remark.

"Ah, you don't get rid of me so quickly," he laughed. "The road further on will improve by waiting. I can make its acquaintance later, seeing I may have to stay here some time."

"Unless in the meantime you die from want of breath," she jested.

"It's not so serious as all that," he replied; "I referred only to the moral atmosphere, of course. Otherwise small towns have their advantages. For instance, one cannot waste any money in them—except on flounders."

She ignored his jest. "Not one's money, but one's time," she said gravely. What she really wanted to say was: "One's youth."

"Time, time," he exclaimed with a flippant wave of his hand; "what is time when one is in the twenties? You feel like throwing it away in handfuls. One can start to economize it when one gets old, and the store scanty."

She made no answer. Should she tell him she was jealous of every day, every hour that sped on and left her where she was?

"Why do you look sad? You are not very old," he began again, half playfully, half in earnest.

"Not very, and even if I were, it would make no difference to me," she prevaricated.

"Still you *do* look sad," he persisted, profiting by the opportunity to obtain a good critical look at her; "I noticed it yesterday. Do you know, when I left you, I felt sure you were no stranger to me; I seemed to have known you for years."

"I don't understand," she said.

"I did not understand myself at the time; the explanation came afterwards. It was because I had met so many of your sisters—your national sisters, I mean. I have met them in the capitals of the world—in St. Petersburg, in Berlin, in Paris. They were all beautiful, and they were all sad, despite their diamonds and coronets. You reminded me of them. And why not? Do they not inherit their beauty and sadness from the same stock as you—from the women who sat wailing by the waters of Babylon?"

"I am like them, you say?" she reiterated.

"Yes, except that you surpass them in both things. I wonder how you would look in diamonds."

"It's very kind of you to express curiosity about anything that concerns me," she said lightly; "it's more than I should do myself." Somehow she felt she had let him come within an inch of trespassing on forbidden ground.

They walked on in silence. Zillah's heart throbbed. Again the strange feeling of before had come over her—the vague exultation at having approached near the nameless goal of her desire. It must have arisen from the mention of the beautiful women in coronets. And that was due to the man at her side; he had seen them as close as he saw her now. So it was he, after all, who had brought the wonder-world into her horizon. But its wonders were no longer shadows; they had become real. They gathered themselves into pomps and pageants that trailed by her in splendour and magnificence; she could almost feel them catching and whirling her off her feet. So she had not come in vain to the forest-oracles; they had given her the knowledge for which she craved. And somehow she did not resent that knowledge being such as it was.

With a little gasp she stopped. "I have walked too far—I must turn back," she said.

"So must I," he echoed quickly.

"No, please"; she lifted her eyes as she spoke—she knew where her eloquence lay. "Take your canter; I should hate to think I deprived you of it."

"As you wish," he said disappointedly. "By the way, though, I haven't settled my account after all."

For a moment she was silent; an answer was struggling to her lips, but to give it utterance would be playing with fire. And yet it was pleasant to play with fire when one felt cold in soul or body. And, therefore, she became reckless.

"I never transact business outside the shop," was what she said.

She was halfway out of sight before he caught the full drift of her words; then a smile spread over his face, and he stood nodding his head till she had disappeared.

Yes, she was right—the road further on was very good riding.

IV.

Salka was watching her sister in the twilight. Her patient was sleeping soundly upstairs, and that was Salka's only opportunity for escaping from the sick-room. When she was not watching her mother, she was watching her sister, and from long observation she had learnt to construe rightly the external indications of her every mood. But the expression Zillah had been wearing all day could not be catalogued under any particular heading. So Salka could only conjecture.

"You seem to be expecting someone," she blurted out at last; "you have been looking like that ever since you came back from your walk yesterday."

"Whom should I expect?" asked Zillah, gazing straight at her. She knew she could do so with safety in the twilight.

"And you have eaten nothing all day," continued Salka severely. "Do you want to turn the house into a hospital?"

"No, and that's why I don't eat when my appetite plays truant."

"So you admit that?" said Salka, quickly; "then I believe my suspicion is correct."

"What suspicion?" asked Zillah, sitting up suddenly.

"You are, after all, eager to see this intended husband of yours; I can imagine that interfering with your appetite."

Zillah did not reply; she was recovering breath. But Salka mistook her silence.

"Did I not know it?" she went on hastily. "It merely needed a little time to get yourself reconciled to the idea. Yesterday the look in your eyes was that of apprehension, today it is impatience."

"And to-morrow it will be neither, little spy; and you will have no chance of prying and drawing wrong conclusions. Shall I tell you the truth? This intended husband of mine has not cost me a single thought. I have made up my mind on him."

"Without thinking?"

"Without thinking. I intend to wait till the article arrives and put the label on it then."

"Zillah, don't talk like that; remember you might have to spend your life in the company of the article—label and all."

"I might—I might not."

Zillah clasped her hands behind her head, and sat back.

"What are you thinking of, Zillah dear?" asked Salka uneasily.

"If you promise not to be frightened, I shall tell you."

"Is it so terrible?"

"That depends on the way you look at it. I should like to be right out of it, Salka—right out of it."

"Out of what?" queried Salka, pretending to be calm.

"Out of this crawling, tedious monotony, this fathomless solitude, this death-in-life."

"Zillah!"

"Oh, I know what you mean by that; I know it's black sacrilege to talk in this way of home, of paradise as it should be. But one can feel discontented even in paradise; Adam and Eve did, and I was not born quite so near Heaven as they were."

"Was that what your look meant?"

"That among other things. I won't tell you what other things. I can hear your teeth chattering loudly enough as it is. I ought not to have answered you at all. But I could not keep it back—this time."

A little sob came from Salka; then she quavered:

"If I know so much, let me know all. Tell me, little sister, what do you want to do?"

"Go out into the world and wear coronets."

"But you can do that here; mother has a beautiful little crown, the one, you know, with the seven stones that glitter red and green and blue. And then there is her golden chain—thick as my little finger, that winds twice round the neck and still reaches down to the waist. She would let you wear them if you asked her."

Gently Zillah stroked the little figure that had come crouching towards her chair.

"You fluttering little stupid," she murmured; "what good would that do? What use is the badge without the office. Diadems mean rule, and power, and homage; but what is there here to rule except one's own rebellious heart that cries out with the pain whenever it has to be bound with fetters? And then there is the danger of its dying with the restraint, and that would be a bad day for you all. Salka, can you imagine what it is to be near a live thing with a dead heart?"

"I cannot imagine why you should be afflicted with thoughts that are so little in keeping with your life," said Salka wearily. "What has brought it on you? Some trespass you have committed? Then it must have been a grievous one, since your punishment is the hardest that can fall to the lot of a human creature—to battle against its destiny."

"Ah, Salka, but I am not fighting against my destiny: I am fighting for it. If you are not given something you desire, you must try to take it. Is not the mere desire evidence that it was meant to belong to you?"

Salka shook her head.

"I don't know how to argue against you," she said sadly. "I only know you are attempting what is impossible. If there were some hope, I, loving you as I do, would be the readiest to urge you on. And now you can gauge the depth of my love by my protest. Tell me—how is it to be done?"

"Yes, how is it to be done?" repeated Zillah, mechanically.

"You see, I am right," went on Salka more zealously. "Listen to me, sister. You are a daughter of the race that taught the world what resignation means—the secret of being strong through weakness and proud through humility. Zillah, that secret is part of our heritage—why should you lack it? Look for it in yourself, and you will find it."

"And when I have found it?"

"You will marry the man father has chosen for you; it is him you will make your vassal. He will put a queen's crown on your head and worship you."

"And will he expect me to do nothing in return?"

"Nothing—except to make him happy."

"Yes, I suppose he would expect that," said Zillah reflectively; "he would almost be able to claim it as a right. But the exchange is not fair; his task would be easier than mine."

"How can you tell?" asked Salka eagerly. "Time will drive your strange fancies out of your head; you will begin to take pride in your household, in your husband's affairs, and when the little ones arrive—"

"I hear voices, but the rest is darkness," said someone from the door.

Salka started up with a little scream, but Zillah kept her seat. Nay, her tone was quiet and commonplace, as she said: "Make a light, Salka. That rascal of a Yeiteles is late, as usual, on his errands. I suppose he has looked in at his mother's."

While she spoke, Salka had lit the two gas-jets of which the shop boasted. There on the doorstep, smiling and blinking with the sudden glare, stood the Commissioner.

"I am something of an apparition, evidently, but that is the fault of the surroundings," he said genially, showing his white teeth. "I want to settle that debt of mine badly—it has been giving me pangs of conscience. Permit me."

He held the coin out to Zillah, who took it silently.

"I should have called before, but I couldn't," he went on. "A political infidel, for whose society the police felt very anxious, wriggled himself across the frontier, and I had to take a trip into Prussia to escort him back."

Salka stood rigid at the counter, staring large-eyed at the intruder. Zillah saw the stare.

"I forgot to tell you, Salka," she explained hurriedly. "This gentleman gave us the honour of his patronage the other day, and had no change at the time."

The young man had followed her glance.

"Your sister, I suppose?" he said.

Zillah nodded and flushed with embarrassment; was he going to let slip anything about their chance meeting in the forest the day before? She would prefer very much that Salka should hear of it—if she heard at all—from her own lips, and without witnesses. But the Commissioner had not in vain learnt logic at college; from Zillah's reticence about his first appearance, he deduced she had not mentioned the second. In short she had made a secret of it, and the fact pleased him mightily. And so his next words reassured her.

"What a dreary little place this is," he said, addressing himself to Zillah. "I can find absolutely nobody to talk to, so out of sheer desperation I took a spin on my nag yesterday, thinking my good luck lay outside it. I was right. I got some fine views; I also met one or two interesting people. It was very enjoyable."

"How could it be otherwise—out in the sunshine?" said Zillah. It was quite safe to say that.

"It did not depend on the sunshine," he replied, his eyes fastened on hers. "It was the mood. Just then I felt I could have passed a night in a Carpathian snowdrift and thought I was sleeping on eiderdown. Pity these moods come so rarely, and then only by accident."

Zillah did not avoid his gaze; it did her good—it made her heart glow. And the covert meaning of his words! She suddenly realised, as he already had done, that there was a secret between her and this man, and the thought did not make her quail; but it kept her silent.

"Does—does the gentleman want to buy anything to-night?" faltered Salka. Her bewilderment was making havoc of her comprehension. This man, this stranger—this Gentile, was conversing with her sister familiarly like an old acquaintance. And her sister betrayed no astonishment, no resentment at the fact.

"That is a pretty broad hint," he said, turning to her good-humouredly, "and it comes just in time. The passenger train from Riga arrives in ten minutes, and I must be at the station to examine the passports. By the way"—he faced Zillah—"you implied you were fond of the sunshine. If you will take the advice of an experienced man, you will find that there is no better way of enjoying it than by taking a walk in some shady place—a forest-road by preference—between the hours of two and three in the afternoon. Good evening, ladies."

He walked out and left silence behind him.

Salka spoke first. "What does he mean, Zillah?" she asked, her face and voice full of puzzled anxiety.

"How should I know?" replied Zillah pettishly. "Any one would think from your question that I had a most intimate acquaintance with his way and manner of speaking."

"But you are so much cleverer than I—that's why I asked."

"Well, then, I take it he was simply laughing at us; he was telling us something every child knows, and then intended us to be impressed by his abstruse wisdom."

"You are right, Zillah; you are always right," said Salka, with a deep breath, as though her mind were disburdened of some great uneasiness. "He was merely laughing at us; he did it before, when he was talking about his moods. Let him—you don't care, Zillah, do you?"

"Not in the least," and Zillah shrugged her shoulders for emphasis; "let him scoff. He thinks we are lawful spoil for ridicule. Has the world not tried to scoff us out of existence these many centuries? Another jeer or two will do us no harm."

Then Salka went upstairs to attend to her patient, and Zillah turned the gas low and pulled her chair to the door, where she sat looking into and listening to the star-lit night. But really she was thinking of the Commissioner and his theory on the sunshine, and wondered since when she had learnt to lie to her sister so lightheartedly.

Yeiteles was late that evening. He had not been to see his mother—he had been playing soldiers with the other boys. His guilty conscience made him expect much scolding and little supper. But Zillah only said:

"Close up the shop, and then there is a piece of cold fowl for you. You will find it in the forest road—I mean in the pantry."

V.

The Commissioner was strolling up and down the alley of trees which formed the vestibule of the forest. This was the third afternoon he did so. The sun was hot overhead, but he did not seem to mind that. Occasionally he walked right to the top of the approach, whence he could peer down the row of houses, and stood watching for five minutes at a stretch. Then he shook his head, and resumed his ambulatory activity. People passed him, made a low reverence, and went on hastily; it was not politic to show curiosity in a Commissioner's movements, especially when he was looking serious and preoccupied. But the birds up in the branches were not afraid of him; they kept on hopping and twittering quite unconcernedly, just to show the human race what a good thing it was to be a bird—sometimes. But it was just as well for them that the Commissioner did not hear enough of them to disturb him, otherwise they might have made acquaintance with the revolver which he kept in his pocket, and which he knew how to handle. He was listening to a voice much more musical than theirs; it was less than a week since he had first heard that voice, and already it seemed to him that by comparison with it all other melodies were jangled discords.

And therefore he had done sentry duty here for three days in succession, in order that he might listen to it again. She had not come—his patient waiting had been in vain. But not all in vain. The long solitary ambushes had done their work effectually—they had been to him a trap and a snare from which he could no longer struggle loose. How they had gripped him and entangled him, these meshes of memory and longing! Several times he had attempted to rend them, and give himself liberty, till he saw the hopelessness of the effort: was he not his own captor as well as prisoner?

And that being so, he started again wondering why she did not come, until his heart was one agonising query. He might have gone to the shop to ask her, but that would be humiliating; he would not risk his pride so far—no, were she a hundred times more beautiful. Had she not understood his hint, she who had shown herself adept in letting her meaning peep skilfully from under the mask of words? And then a sudden thought made him bite his lip: had it all been only a trick of practised coquetry? If it was, what would he do to her—what could he do to her? Harass her and her people with petty indignities and annoyances, such as it was in his power to inflict? He laughed at the notion; if he had been made ridiculous in her eyes, he might at least preserve his self-respect in his own. Better not think of it at all—better think of the great luminous Madonna-eyes, from which truth had looked at him if ever it had faced him out of human countenance. And was he not right? His heart leapt exultantly, for round the bend of the road a pink parasol came floating towards him, shading a tall willowy figure—one would think it not so much a shade as an aureole. Quickly he strode towards her; her hand lay in his—she knew not how.

"We are fated to meet," she said, smiling tremulously.

"Why will you dissemble?" he asked, almost roughly. "You know this is a fate of our—of my making. Why did you not come yesterday, and before?"

"You forget my time is not my own; there was a great deal of business—who was to attend to it?"

Her lashes were on her cheek; so she could best tell her falsehood. Could she disclose to him why she had not come before? Could she avow the soul-distracting struggle she had lived through in those days? In the sunshine and in the darkness, in her waking hours and in her slumber, she had wrestled with herself as with a deadly enemy. And now it was ended. Should she count it victory or disaster? It seemed almost ungrateful to ask, because whichever it was, it was fraught with delight ineffable. What mattered whether it was the gladness of triumph or the sweetness of surrender? And so she had ceased questioning, and had gone forth with the spirit of prophecy upon her, for she knew she would find him here.

He seemed to read as much in her face, for he said:

"You had faith in me; I feel honoured—I thank you. But it was just as well you did not strain your belief to its utmost. I should have come again to-morrow, and the following day, and perhaps yet once again; but after—"

"After, you would have mounted your horse and have taken a spin cross-country. That is all."

"It might be all; I put myself the question a little before you came, and dared not answer it. And now," his eyes flashed, "and now it requires no answering—not, at least, for the present. It's a fool that haggles with the golden present about the future."

"A fool," she echoed; but it was not so much in corroboration as in misgiving. She could not afford to ignore the future—not for very long; it might turn out to have been bought very dear with the gold of the present.

"Come out of this glare," he said, buoyantly; "I can feel the freckle microbes whisking about thick as hail; they make short work of peach-bloom—come."

She followed him unresistingly, with a half smile at his compliment; and as the trees closed round them, closer and yet closer, a sullen anger came into her heart at her own folly for having thrust off from her this happiness for three long days—a prodigal, useless sacrifice. Once or twice she stumbled amid the tangle of the creepers, but she refused the arm he proffered her. No, do not touch him—that would be unwise. It would remind her too clearly whence she derived her joy, and that it was iniquitous. Afterwards, perhaps—when she had entirely forgotten to think, and could only feel.

"You have told me nothing of yourself, of your people," he said, as soon as they had come to a little clearing.

"Because there is nothing to tell. My mother has been bedridden for years; my father is a good deal from home; my sister you know."

"A remarkable family history," he laughed; "but no doubt the historian will make up for its brevity by discussing herself in more detail."

"I never talk of myself."

"I see," he bantered, "from an overwhelming sense of modesty; you could say nothing about yourself that would not redound to your credit. Then nothing remains for me but to discover these excellencies for myself. I shall be very searching, I warn you."

"The search will take you a long time."

"The longer the better." He remembered something, and his face clouded. "And yet," he went on slowly, "I may have to break it off suddenly. My stay here is precarious. Any moment—what a fool I am; I speak of having to leave you, and here I go wasting precious time in idle apprehension. Quick, what shall we talk about?"

"Tell me about the beautiful women you have seen," she answered quickly.

"Did I say I had seen beautiful women? It must have been an optical illusion, or at least a grave error of judgment. I apologise to you."

"Don't jest—I am serious."

"Then I hasten to be serious as well," he said, with a lingering glance at her; she felt it though she did not see it. "I shall tell you about one of them in particular; I forget where I saw her—in some big city. She had come there goodness knows from what God-forgotten solitude. A week after her arrival she was famous. She passed from palace to palace with a retinue of slaves. They had left their studies, their easels, their barracks, their counting-houses to follow her wherever she went, for to look at she was like the morning star. But more than all, her husband loved her as his very life, and earth to her was heaven."

"And what became of her?" whispered Zillah.

"You think there ought to be a climax to all this? But there is not. She just came into my mind because you asked me."

"Was she, too, of the sad-faced ones?"

"Yes, she looked sad, but only with excess of her happiness; she had so much, and others so little. Or, perhaps, springing from a race that believes in the evil eye, she was afraid lest her joy should have a downfall if she paraded it, and therefore she feigned the sadness she did not feel."

"Are you sure it was feigned?" asked Zillah, staring before her. "Perhaps she had brought to the palaces only half a heart; the other half she might have left behind in the solitude whence she came."

"At first it might have been real," he replied, after a little thought; "but when one has once survived this cleavage of the heart, it grows again rapidly until there is not even a scar to show where it has been sundered."

Zillah roused herself—she was getting afraid, sorely afraid; his words seemed to come home to her so very closely, as though they were the answer to her inmost questionings. She must not listen to such answers, not when they came from anyone save herself.

"Why do we talk so solemnly?" she said, with a little laugh. "Doesn't it feel like desecrating all this gladness and glory around us?"

"You distract me," he exclaimed, in mock despair. "Just before you complained of my jesting, and now you are displeased at my seriousness. I shall be silent altogether."

But Zillah felt that the silence would be more perilous than talk of any kind. And so she got him into swing again on indifferent topics. But even with such the time can slip away very quickly, and when they had made their way back to the avenue of trees Zillah realised with a start that the vanguard shadows of the dusk were upon them.

"When are you coming again?" he asked, holding her back almost by force.

"To-morrow, or the day after—I can't tell," she murmured, struggling to get her hand loose.

"Listen. My orderly will come to the shop every morning to make a purchase; you can give him the message. But it must be soon—do you hear?—soon!"

He released her and kissed his fingers, still warm with contact of hers. She did not see the gesture, because she was speeding on in front. She was running away from the fleet-footed fear that had tracked her home the last time she left him.

Five minutes after, she stood again in the shop.

"Miss Zillah has come," shouted Yeiteles, up the staircase.

And before Zillah could ask him to explain the reason of his vociferousness, Salka had hurried down full speed.

"Where have you been?" she queried, excitedly; "we have been looking for you everywhere."

"I—" began Zillah.

But Salka did not give her time for another syllable. "Here is a letter from father; he has finished his business more quickly than he expected and is coming home to-night. You must help me prepare for them."

"Them?" asked Zillah.

"Yes; have you forgotten?"

The truth was, Zillah had forgotten.

VI.

The sick-room upstairs had undergone so complete a transformation that it was probably troubled with doubts as to its identity. It had taken to itself a cheerful and festive look. The cumbrous invalid couch had been pushed into a corner and concealed from view by thick and many-hued hangings. In the centre stood a stout mahogany table, clothed in gleaming napery; upon it, beginning with a pedestal of porcelain, upreared the lamp of massive bronze, with a silver candlestick planted on each side for adjutant.

Salka was in the kitchen seeing to the last batch of her fritters in an agony of trepidation. Zillah's assistance had proved worse than useless, and after upsetting a basket of eggs, and almost producing an irremediable catastrophe in the cheese-cakes by handing the salt when Salka had asked her for sugar, she had been ignominiously informed that her further services could be dispensed with. She had submitted to the disgrace with cordial indifference. She had felt more or less an automaton from the moment she had received the news of what was in store for her that evening. And now she sat in the transfigured sick-room, alone with her mother—the latter solicitously bestowed in the wool-stuffed armchair. Zillah kept close to the chimney nook, because that was the spot into which all the shadows had crowded. She was more comfortable among the shadows.

"They are late, are they not?" said the invalid.

It was the third time she had asked the question, and each time Zillah had replied patiently as she did now:

"No, mother—the train does not arrive till a quarter to nine; it isn't that yet, and besides, we shall hear the engine whistle as it steams into the station."

"To be sure, to be sure," murmured the sufferer. "I cannot see your face, child, but I know you are pleased."

"Of course I am pleased, little mother; do we not always consider it a sort of festival when father comes home?"

"And this time more than all others. Why don't you say what is itching on the tip of your tongue? But it was the same with me when Anshel came the first time. How I remember it! I was sitting in a corner, just as you are now, only that I was pretending to be busy mending socks. And the youngsters—there were more of them than you are here—the youngsters were huddling at the other end of the room, giggling and whispering mischievously; and Yekel, the eldest and wildest of them—he has been quiet enough these many years under the sward away in the Caucasus—aye, Yekel I remember it was who struck up suddenly: "Every maid a sweetheart has, I alone have none," as the old song goes. And then the others burst out laughing, while I sat trembling with fear and vexation, till, to make things worse, I pricked my thumb with the darning-needle and ran from the room, sobbing angrily. You see, my daughter, these things are no secret to me; you need not hide your feelings so jealously."

Zillah writhed as though the chair on which she sat had become a rack. But she held herself in check and turned lovingly to her mother—this poor unsuspecting mother whom happiness made so garrulous.

"Do you think I would grudge you anything?" she smiled. "If I felt what you think, would I be chary of letting you see it?"

"Ah, then you do not feel it?" came the query, full of sadness and disappointment.

"How can I? Mother, you will not blame me for letting my heart go at its own speed, before I know that I can safely give it the rein. Would you have me whip it?"

"You are different, Zillah—different to what I was. I loved my husband before I saw him, because in loving him I was obeying the commandment which bids us honour our parents. Well, what is to be shall be. What do they say? 'Joy delayed is joy redoubled.'"

Zillah looked at her with the same smile; she could not divest herself of it, for it had become frozen on her face. And this was only the beginning; from this torment there could be no escape till that further agony, to which the present would be as a garden of roses to a bed of brambles. And over it all was to be the mask of her smile, like a "Welcome" written over the entrance to a charnel-house; and before it her dear ones would stand, singing songs of gladness, and not knowing that they were recalling the dead remnants of her feelings to life only in order to make them writhe afresh.

Desperately her lips struggled to frame an answer, but she was saved the trouble. The invalid suddenly sat up—her ears, tight-strung by the peg of suffering, had caught the screech of the approaching train.

"In ten minutes they will be here," she said rapidly; "now you shall see, Zillah. Quick, set the chairs straight—the lamp-shade is a little to one side. If only my limbs were strong enough to carry me as far as the door to give him greeting the moment he enters," she sighed; "but, please God, I shall dance at your wedding, Zillah, as lightly as I did at my own—the Cossack dance, your father and I—and you and Salka will stand by clapping your hands. How I remember—"

And then she rambled back into the distant past, going over the old well-worn details which always were a fresh delight to her listening children. But now they came on Zillah's dazed senses as the murmuring of far-off waters. If only she could keep like that—hear nothing, feel nothing, know nothing. No; presently she would have to become alive. What, so soon? Could they not give her a little more respite, only a very little? Down below in the street were heard the footfalls of men walking rapidly—aye, two men; now they were halting at the door, and the next moment Salka's joyous cry of "Father!" rang out as in triumph.

Zillah rose, her nerves firm, her gaze steady. Was she a child? Would she let this stranger frighten her from her duty of going to meet her father open-armed? If she showed herself craven even before she was fronting the foe, what would be the issue of the conflict? But her resolution had come too late; before she reached the door it had already opened, and her father stepped in, flushed and eager.

"Now this is what I call honouring a guest," he cried, the glow on his face deepening with pleasure as he noted the inviting appearance of the chamber; "I accept the compliment, even though I have a suspicion it isn't all meant for me. Esther, you are looking twenty years younger, and are getting strong as a lion, Salka tells me."

Then he turned to Zillah.

"You have been taking care of mother?" he whispered, kissing her; "that is right, and for reward I have brought some one to take care of you."

And then Zillah noted with a fugitive glance the figure still and motionless in the doorway.

Anshel looked round.

"Where are you, Enoch?" he exclaimed; "we are coming to a fine state of things when men like you are afraid to show their faces."

And the next thing Zillah knew was that her father had led the stranger to her side, holding him by the hand, and was saying:

"Zillah, this is Enoch Gontaller. When you were yet in your cradle his father's name had already travelled to the four corners of the world. It is a name to be proud of, and the son is worthy of the father; need I say more? Come, Enoch, this is my wife—and now you know us all. You have had a silent welcome, but that is only because it comes so deep from the heart."

Zillah turned pale to the lips. So this was the high honour at which her father had hinted—the alliance with the house of the great Rabbi-Talmudist. Ah, that made everything more difficult. She wanted to go on thinking how much more difficult, but her father's last words, which had sounded almost like a reproach, recalled her.

"You have had a wearisome journey," she said to the guest, her eyes downcast; "pray be seated, and give us your indulgence for a few minutes. We shall soon have our best ready for you."

He did not seem to hear her; he remained standing, his melancholy eyes, luminous in their blackness, riveted upon her. Anshel shot a quick side-glance at him; it was a good sign, this silence of his—it spoke many things. And so it was with a smile of pleasure that he took up the conversation.

"You did not expect us quite so early, I suppose? You almost did right there. For if we are here now, it is something of a miracle. No, there was no danger," he interrupted himself in answer to his wife's anxious look of inquiry, "but—well, here is the whole thing as it happened. I was coming from Berditcheff, where I had stayed several days, and where Enoch joined me. To save delay, we travelled by the next train that was available, and I had no time to get my passport countersigned by the police. But that did not trouble me, because old Tomalov, the police Commissioner here, and I—well, it would not be the first time we had settled such a matter by accommodation. And it was not till the train stopped at Bogilno, three stations from here, that I heard he was dead, and that his successor was already appointed. You can imagine I did not bless the tidings. I did what I could. First I counted out a hundred roubles for an emergency; and secondly, I took out the Book of Psalms, and made good use of it till we arrived here. Outside the gendarmerie stood the new Commissioner. I don't know whether you have seen him, Zillah—he is tall, with an iron look on his face. My heart sank; already I saw myself in the train back on my way to Berditcheff to get my passport signed. I handed it to him, such as it was; he glanced at it, and his brow wrinkled. Suddenly it became smooth again. 'Is your name Markovitz?' he asked. I told him it was. 'Do you keep a cheese and herring store?' he went on. 'I do, your honour,' I replied in astonishment—how did he know? 'Your passport is quite in order, you may go,' he said pleasantly. Is it not miraculous?" And Anshel expanded his broad chest to recoup himself for the breath he had consumed in the narrative.

"It is indeed strange," replied Zillah, to whom the last query had been addressed; "and yet—considering you were repeating psalms all the time . . . "

Anshel tapped his forehead and looked at Enoch.

"And so a woman has shamed us men in understanding," he said almost solemnly.

Enoch cleared his throat of some imaginary obstacle before he answered; his voice was as dreamy as his eyes. "Perhaps you take that for a still greater miracle," he said; "to me it is only as it should be. When God has made a thing that is perfect in its outward semblance, why should He stop half-way and not complete it inwardly? And because it is not always His will to achieve His work, is that any reason to wonder when He does?"

A short silence followed his words, and then Anshel turned smilingly to his daughter.

"What do you say to that?" he asked.

"That the words are ill-applied," she said with a flush, perhaps of modesty, but possibly of anger. "Our guest puts too high an estimate on me. I am only a poor thing at best, full of defects and blemishes; if he says I am one of those on whom God has laid the seal of perfection, he utters blasphemy."

Enoch's pale face became still paler, but his eyes took a new splendour to themselves as he saw the flush creep over her. Anshel sat as in a dream. The greatest mystery in his life was how it came that such a creature should call him father; and now he thought it time to give up hope of ever solving it.

"You see, Enoch, one never knows when one is going to receive a stone for one's bread," he laughed.

"And yet there are cases where one must offer the bread, although one knows one is going to get a hailstorm of stones in return," said Enoch quietly.

"And talking of bread, Zillah, will you see that Salka brings up what there is to eat?" broke in the invalid. The mother's eye had suddenly seen a look of unutterable pain flit over her child's face. Yes, embarrassment was sometimes a physical agony.

Zillah obeyed, and a minute or two after, Salka and Yeiteles, the helpful, brought up the steaming dishes, and the homely clatter of plates frightened the spirit of restraint out of the room. Anshel's homespun joviality and Salka's merry prattle acted as a barricade against its return. If Enoch was a little monosyllabic, and Zillah entirely silent, it was only natural under the circumstances. It was also natural that she should withdraw before the others did, pleading a headache. But had anyone seen her throw herself on her bed in a tempest of tears and with disconsolate wringing of hands, he might have found more reasonable cause for comment.

VII.

"You ask why a lender who has taken security from the borrower in a piece of tillage, varying in quality, may only claim in repayment of his loan that portion of the land which is the less productive?" Enoch was saying to Anshel on the second evening of his visit, a good while after supper had been disposed of. "The reason is this. Suppose a man of affluent means should desire for its fertility a piece of the field belonging to a neighbour who happens to be in monetary straits. Well, this man might say to himself: 'I shall inveigle my neighbour into taking a loan to be repaid on a certain day, and take his estate for a pledge. And then, by some chicanery or underhand act, I shall make him fail in the payment, so that his lands might become forfeited and I might take my choice of them.' But then comes this law of our Rabbins, which says he may recoup himself only with the inferior portion of it. And in this way there is a curb laid on the avarice of the ungodly."

Anshel listened to him ecstatically: this scholar, this sage, this oracle, who seemed able to expound all the secrets of heaven and earth, was to be his son-in-law. Salka was also sitting at the table. She was not so much listening to Enoch's words as looking at his face, with its eloquent change of expression and the wonderful glow of his eyes. She marvelled why she was watching it so hard. Zillah was seated near the window, which seemed of late to have a peculiar fascination for her. She was reading the new instalment of Spielhagen which had arrived that morning. She neither listened nor looked. Had she paid any attention at all, she could not have failed to notice that very often the sound of Enoch's voice travelled to her in a straight line, although he was sitting sideways. Even if she had, she would never have associated the fact with a possible intention of Enoch that all this store of learning was to be laid as a tribute at her feet. But perhaps most women would connect love-making more closely with the rattle of spurs and the clank of sabres than with an exhibition of the most brilliant antics of casuistry.

"And now, Enoch," said Anshel, "only one question more; the evening is late—see, mother has fallen asleep already. But I would just have you explain the strange saying of Rabbi Chaninah in the Treatise Baba Kama;[6] that those who keep our holy precepts when they are enjoined to do so can hope for greater reward than those who keep them when there is no such obligation upon them. It seems to me there is more merit in the latter case."

For a moment or two Enoch wrinkled his forehead in thought, and then smiled as the solution of the problem flashed upon him.

"Is not the first instinct of man's nature that of freedom?" he answered. "Does not every reasoning and unreasoning thing rebel against alien control? And so, when we are under a command that enjoins a certain behest on us, there is, as it were, a yoke and a shackle laid upon the very mainspring of our life, for our will and inclination may perhaps be carrying us to the very opposite. Thus the obeying of the injunction entails a certain amount of self-mastery, which makes it more laudable than when it is the result of a spontaneous desire."

Zillah's ear caught the concluding sentence without knowing from what premises it was the deduction. There seemed to be in it something that bore a special significance; and with that an involuntary resentment came over her. Yes, it might be a grand and laudable thing to make a

---

6. A tractate of the Talmud, the compilation of ancient rabbinical writings and commentaries that forms the basis of Jewish religious law. In this period Talmudic study and debate was mainly the preserve of men.

martyr of oneself, but she had lost the taste for it. She had done enough of self-mastering in her brief life to give herself for once the luxury of abandonment.

The two men and Salka had risen to their feet.

"No doubt you think me an exacting host," jested Anshel; "I make you pay for my hospitality with gems of wisdom. Fortunately you are so well provided with the capital that there is no fear of your having to turn bankrupt."

"You are welcome to it," said Enoch; "it is a pleasure to be prodigal in wealth of this sort if one can only find a receiver for it. I know it isn't current coin everywhere."

Salka had a tolerable notion of the particular bearing of his complaint. She said nothing, but she made a resolution that it should reach its address.

"Zillah, our guest is about to retire," remarked Anshel.

The remark was necessary, for Enoch had stepped close to her, and she had not lifted her head.

"Good night," she murmured in confusion. Perhaps it had just struck her that whatever else she lacked there was no reason why she should lack in ordinary courtesy.

"Good night," he said simply: and yet it was as though he had wanted to say something more. But the two words had done that without his knowing it.

"It's a queer thing with these women," said Anshel, lighting Enoch to his attic; "how skilfully they will ignore a thing of which every one knows they are aware. And yet this reserve—does it not give zest and flavour to them?"

"It does, indeed," replied Enoch, but only in a half-hearted sort of way.

Salka was helping to bed her mother, who had awakened from her doze.

"Are you comfortable, little mother?" she asked.

"Quite, thank you."

"And you will not want anything else just now?"

"Nothing—except to sleep. You are very good, child."

"Then Zillah may come down with me to the kitchen and help me put things in order there. Will you, Zillah?"

"Of course—did I ever refuse?"

Silently the two sisters made their way downstairs. Zillah gave a little cry of surprise.

"Why, everything is spick and span! What else is there to do?"

Salka smiled at the success of her ruse, but immediately became grave again.

"We can't talk upstairs, we shall disturb mother."

"Is there anything you have to tell me?"

"So many things that I shall end by saying nothing, for I don't know where to begin. However, what happened to you yesterday?"

A great fear struck into Ziliah's heart. Had they been seen—overheard?

"When?" she quavered.

"In the evening."

"I told you I had a headache; I don't think that requires much discussion," said Zillah, with a breath of relief.

"Listen, Zillah," said Salka. "Last night, as I came to our room, I stooped over you to kiss you in your sleep; but on your mouth there was such a strange, cruel look that I refrained. I was afraid you might bite me."

"In my sleep?" laughed Zillah, but mirthlessly.

"How did that look come there? It was so different to the one you brought home in the afternoon. It seemed to me it spoke of some terrible hatred—against us, perhaps, Zillah: it made me cry."

"Then it served you right for being a little goose. Are you sure you have never seen me look like that when I am awake?"

"No, I have always seen you beautiful."

"If I appeared cruel, Salka, have I not cause for it?" broke out Zillah passionately. "Am I not cruelly dealt with? And though I bear my mask of meekness by day, can I help it that my thoughts are written on my face at night? But you need not be afraid of me, waking or sleeping. When I wake, my heart is full of love for you all; and my dreams will not do harm to any one, save myself. Only you must not begrudge me them."

"You are talking wildly," moaned Salka. "Who is dealing cruelly with you? Up till yesterday you had perhaps some reason for thinking yourself aggrieved, but now—"

"Why only till yesterday?"

"Because till then I was sharing your dread of the stranger with whom you were to couple your life. He might have turned out to be a hunchback, or repulsive in face and manner—his father's fame and greatness were no guarantee against that. But when he is beautiful as an archangel, and—"

"Is he beautiful?" queried Zillah, coldly.

"You may well ask; you have not vouchsafed him a glance since his arrival. And therefore you have not noticed how hungrily his gaze is bent on you and the untold pain of his eyes, although his voice rings so steady and his words show such calm self-possession. All the time you sit poring over that stupid book of yours—as though you wanted to read yourself dead."

"It does not work; I have tried it."

"But it serves another purpose," went on Salka hotly; "it keeps you from noticing your mother's silent reproach and your father's wonder and embarrassment. And when I look at him—at Enoch, with his patient smile—the tears well into my eyes."

Zillah was silent for a moment, then she said suddenly:

"I suppose our parents wish him for a son-in-law?"

"Suppose?" echoed Salka, looking at her sister as if she doubted her reason.

"Well then," continued Zillah calmly, "have they not another daughter?"

Salka changed colour three times in as many seconds. "You might have spared me that, Zillah," came from her quietly. "It sounds almost like a taunt. You know that no man who has seen you and me would hesitate about his choice. And he has made his, I assure you."

Zillah caught her in her arms and gently forced her face up.

"Do you think I should say such a thing unless I meant it?" she whispered. "Salka, if ever I wished I were horrible as a toad to look upon, I wish it now."

The words had broken from her in the rush of her passion, but the next moment they had rolled back upon her as though they knew they were the false echo of her thoughts. Did she really wish it? Was it not yesterday, as she was treading the forest shadows, that, in her heart, she had given thanks to God for her beauty? Had there been any reason that she should prize it then, and, if so, why had she now spoken of it almost as a curse?

"You see, Salka," she hurried on, "it could be arranged. Suppose father promised for your dowry one or two thousand roubles more—"

With a strangled cry Salka tore herself loose from her embrace; then she laughed bitterly. "Do you really think two thousand roubles will make me equal to you?"

"You are a thousand, thousand times better than I am; I am not worthy to kiss your feet," came like a torrent from Zillah; "you love your parents, and I feel as though I were their murderess. And, therefore, in your thousand-fold goodness, I want you to do me this service. Use all the wiles of our womanhood; I will think them out night and day, and teach you them. Do everything to make him love you. You will succeed I am certain. Oh, promise me, Salka, promise me."

Salka shook her head. "It is beyond us both," she said brokenly. "Father says from the moment he saw your picture he went about like a sleepwalker. And then father will never, never consent that his younger daughter should marry before the elder. He would rather have us both remain under his roof till we were grey-headed. It is you, Zillah, who must make the effort."

Zillah stood looking dazed and vacant till Salka got frightened.

"What will you do?" she whispered, stealing an arm round the other's neck.

"What can I do? I must find out," said Zillah, voicelessly. "If you cannot do me this service I ask you, Salka, you will at least do me another."

"Quick, tell me."

"It is a mere trifle by comparison. Just a little falsehood that will hurt nobody in the world. To-morrow afternoon father will be going to Nirshava, and—and our guest will be thrown on our company. I shall want to leave the house for a little time—an hour or so—and I want you to bear me out in saying that I have urgent necessity for it."

"Why, where are you going?" asked Salka, apprehensively.

"Nowhere in particular," said Zillah, glancing away from her; "I only want to be alone; quite alone to take counsel with myself. The solitude will do me good—as it did yesterday. I must come to a decision about this; did you not say so yourself?"

"Is that all? I wish you would give me a harder task to test my love."

"I gave you one."

"That was not a task—it was a forlorn hope."

"Well then, wait; I shall perhaps take you at your word a little later. In the meantime there is tomorrow. Don't forget."

Salka did not fall asleep for a long time; she lay staring wide-eyed into the darkness. Pictured upon it, as on a sable canvas, stood Enoch's pale face with its lustrous eyes. Why should it come to her here in the gloom? It was a punishment she had laid up for herself: she should not have looked at it so much in the light, and then it would not trouble her now, and keep her from her slumber. And more strangely still, like a refrain to a song of her own singing, rang in her ears Zillah's words: "Make him love you!" Her tongue had flouted the suggestion—but her thoughts? Aye, it was child's play to speak with the lips, but the heart could not be tutored so easily into speaking the words it should; and just now the language of her own sounded contrary and wayward. It was urging her to the task her sister had set her, although she herself had dubbed it impossible. Somehow it did not now seem so impossible. Oh, no; it was not because she wished it otherwise. She did not—at least, she told herself so. And then she thought of Zillah's request and what it meant to herself: an hour of undisturbed companionship with him—not in vision as now, but in living deed, with sight and sound to convince her it was not a phantasy. The thought took hold of her; she tried to drive it away—it would not go. And then she gathered it to her bosom, and strained it close till she felt it tingle into life, and throb with alternate pulses of fear and gladness.

VIII.

"You are punctual," said the Commissioner to Zillah, looking at his watch; "you told my man at three; it's three to the minute."

"I was eager to thank you for your kindness to my father," said Zillah, taking no trouble to conceal the breathlessness which evidenced the swiftness of her walk.

"Why not look on that as a matter of course?" he asked a little disappointedly; "I should have preferred had you come with—with a less definite motive."

"How do you know that without it I should have come at all?"

"Oh, there was no guarantee whatever," he said. So long as she was there, what matter if she fenced and quibbled about it?

"But it *was* kind of you," she iterated; "you saved him considerable inconvenience, simply because—"

"Because?"

"Because you are too broad-minded to see a criminal in every man who has not conformed to the absurd ordinances of official tyranny."

"This is treason—rank treason," he exclaimed, with a make-believe frown; "is that the way to speak of the institutions of our all-wise Government?"

"Then you are not broad-minded?"

"I have had a duty given me which I must fulfil without questioning," he said seriously.

"Then why did you neglect it in the case of my father?"

He looked at her full; then he said smilingly: "Because he happened to be the father of his daughter."

"If so, why do you refuse the daughter's gratitude?"

"I will accept it if she makes it an incident of her coming, not its main motive."

"I offer it to you; make it what you like," she said.

"That's much better," he said approvingly. "By the way, before we dismiss the subject, who was your father's fellow-traveller? Hardly your brother—there was no resemblance. His passport was invulnerable, which unfortunate fact robbed me of a chance of earning some additional gratitude and credit for tolerance."

Zillah's lips closed very tightly; she was afraid lest the impulse to echo his "before we dismiss the subject" would be too strong for her. Why, this particular department of the subject required a world of words all to itself. She tore a little shoot from the nearest fir-bush and commenced stripping it of its needles.

"I have no brothers." she replied at last; "I thought you understood that. It's a friend of my father."

"He comes from Berditcheff," remarked the Commissioner, puzzled despite the clear drift of her reply; "what is he here for—on business?"

"Yes, on business," she repeated mechanically, while her tense lips drew themselves asunder into the caricature of a smile. He was quick to notice it.

"Please put on your sad mien," he begged earnestly; "that smile looks like a murdered thought."

"Why should I look sad?" she asked jauntily, recklessly. "It's most amusing, I assure you. That man—"

She broke off abruptly. The full bearing of what she was about to do came rushing in upon her and frightened her into silence. She was going to tell this stranger, this mushroom acquaintance, of the things that concerned her life most closely; she was going to vent her ridicule upon them, or, worse perhaps, exact his sympathy. But thank God, it was still not too late; she could yet retrieve herself.

The Commissioner watched her lynx-like.

"That man," he prompted impatiently.

She took a step backward and gazed round her desperately, like a hunted fawn.

"It is nothing of consequence, I assure you," she gasped; "and now please excuse me; I must really go, this very minute."

But the Commissioner knew better. "Will you be good enough to give me the particulars you intended giving me concerning this man?" he said, his voice harsh and strained. Zillah remembered her father had called him stern; he was not stern—he was cruel. And yet how his cruelty became him.

"I repeat to you," she said more collectedly, "that it is nothing—nothing worth speaking about."

"Well, then, I must bring more pressure to bear on you. What is it with this man? I ask in my official capacity."

"Indeed, in that it does not concern you in the least," she said eagerly. "Will you not take my word for it?"

"Then it concerns me only personally," he observed, softening his tone. "That man, you were going to say, is intended for your husband; the project does not please you—you were about to speak of it with bitterness and ill-will. Am I right?"

She stared at him dumb and petrified.

"Believe me," he went on gently, "I have not been tracking the cunning and craftiness of crime all these years without being able to unmask the subterfuges of innocence when I come across them."

"You have no right to tax me with subterfuges."

He shrugged his shoulders.

"I don't insist on it as an assertion—I am merely venturing a suggestion. I leave you the right of rebutting, of denial."

For a moment her pride upreared itself rebelliously. Why should he think she owed him confidences? Why should she stand before him like a culprit confessing to a transgression? But then again she felt this power he was wielding over her was as balm to her soul; this dominion of his was a mould into which her heart fitted and seemed safe against life's jutting edges. She lifted her eyes to his fearlessly, and said:

"I do not deny it—I cannot."

Quickly he came close to her. "I felt sure I had spoken for you," he said softly; "and do you know what remains for me now? To think for you—think for you what you have not the courage to think for yourself; to ask the questions which you would go on asking without ever answering them. Shall I?"

Her nod gave him leave.

"Why have our paths crossed, Madonna? Why have we touched each other's hands—why have we looked into each other's faces? Why have I counted the hours, the minutes, till I should touch and look—why have you sent me a message defining the term and limit of my counting? Look, we are standing here wrapping ourselves in the solitude of each other's company, and yet feeling as though the world were filled with our fulness. What does it mean? We that are distinct and separate by all the differences which should thrust two human beings asunder, we have found each other with but little searching. Tell me, what does it mean?"

She stood listening with clasped hands and parted lips. As he stopped, she turned to him and breathed: "Go on thinking for me—go on questioning."

He bent close to her, till their foreheads almost touched.

"No, I have questioned enough; it is time to make answer. It means that we are to clasp each other's hands for all our life, and read each other's faces till we are blind in death. You and I and the future, Madonna—have I not answered right?"

"Yes, you have thought for me, questioned for me, answered for me," said Zillah, trembling; "you have done it well—only too well. And, therefore, the end must be—"

"Must be what?"

"As though there never had been a beginning."

He almost staggered; then he set his teeth hard.

"I see," he grated out, "this has all been a deep-laid plan, a device of cunning and trickery. You said to yourself: 'I shall weave this Gentile's heart into my toils, and then I shall let him writhe; so shall I avenge the wrongs his brothers have done to my sisters.' Girl, from where did you get the courage for that?"

She looked at him steadily.

"Courage?" she said, slowly. "I have none. I am not as Jael—she of the milk-bowl and the iron spike. If I could help my suffering race by any service of mine, I should do it gladly; but never with weapons of treachery. Where would such vengeance lead to?"

"I have wronged you—forgive me," he replied humbly; "my disappointment made me unjust; not my disappointment, my misunderstanding rather. You meant something else than your words said. Speak—I shall be very patient."

He waited a minute—two—but there was no sound from her. He took her hand and stroked it tenderly.

"Madonna, Madonna," he whispered, "do you not love me?"

Again there was no answer, but instead she darted at him a look, half ineffable agony, half passionate entreaty. He had been expecting that look; it served his purpose.

"Now we can speak," he said, his voice quivering with suppressed exultation. "Do you remember the woman of whom I told you—the one who was sad because she was overburdened with happiness? Do you know who that woman was? Yourself—yourself as I pictured you in the years to come. You shall walk in the gilded palaces of which I, your husband—do you hear me?—your husband, shall open for you the portals. Goddess mine, do you grasp all that this means? Ah, you do not know the splendour, the grandeur of it—the intoxicating gladness, the exquisite heart-throbs of secure affluence, the surpassing triumph of bended knee and absolute homage. But you shall taste it all, I promise you. And when you are tired of it, I shall make my love your undying delight. Come with me."

"Whither?" she asked dreamily.

"Whither? Away from here. Is this the place where I could ever redeem my promise?"

"Then I must leave my parents," she said, awaking from her trance.

"Do you expect to gain everything and make no sacrifice whatever?"

"I would make any sacrifice, but not this," broke from her like a wail. "Oh, why did you not let me go before—why have you made me listen to all this? Be merciful—do not tempt me too hard. I cannot leave my parents, and yet—and yet, oh, I want to go with you."

The Commissioner clasped both her hands tightly.

"Yes, you shall come with me. And soon. Hear me. You know I am here only on intermediate service. Within the next few days I expect orders to go far inland to take over control of a large revenue department which I have been promised. By then you must be ready to follow me. You must be prepared any moment. In the morning I shall send you a message by my man, and that same evening we must be gone. That is settled."

"Not quite—not quite," she whispered fearfully; "please do not yet take everything for granted. I know if I were now to say yes, I should be bound to it, not only by my heart, but by my conscience also—"

"Then say yes," he interrupted eagerly.

"But I must give myself breathing-space, more for your sake than for mine," she said, ignoring his words; "I must fortify myself to it by clear thought and reasoning that shall sweep away all hindrances now, and all reproach, should there be any, hereafter. For I shall then be able to say to myself that it was not your importunity, but my own free will, which made my life such as it shall be. Believe me, it will be better for both of us. And one other thing: till then avoid me. Let me come to my decision unprompted, spontaneously. The sight of you would probably be to me more bewilderment than argument. Will you grant me this?"

He cast at her a quick look of suspicion; and then, as her clear eyes met his, he felt ashamed of it. He nodded.

"I will, but in return I shall ask you for something too. You have not yet told me what your heart says to mine."

"Has my silence not told it more clearly than any words of mine could?" she queried.

"I want your words as well. Say after me: 'Otto, I love you.'"

She obeyed—even when he said he wanted to hear it twice.

"Do you know what my purpose was?" he went on. "I wished you to say it because I know the utterance will ring in your ears and admonish you when your surroundings will call to you too loudly. You will remember it, and you will not falter. Or perhaps you count that undue influence?" he added, with the faintest touch of jesting.

She smiled wearily. "No, because you have put me on my guard against it."

"Yes, that is right," he exclaimed quickly, his face suffused with joy; "guard yourself against it. This will probably be the last time you will partake of the experience."

She looked puzzled.

"Because," he explained, "after that it will be my office to safeguard you, to watch over you, to be your armour and shield. And therefore I ask you now, for this once more, to be your own protection. Drink the sensation to the dregs; you will then be better able to appreciate the contrast."

"My armour and shield," she echoed softly, measuring him from head to foot; "that must feel good—I shall think of it. Good-bye." She held out her hand.

"Is that all?" he asked, taking it in his.

"All till—"

"Till we meet again with no parting before us," he said fervently; "I ought to be satisfied with that."

He had to be, for the next moment she had left him and was making her way swiftly and sure-footedly through the tangled undergrowth; but he had caught the look with which she had turned from him—it was better than a caress.

Outside in the clearing Zillah moderated her pace. At this rate she would get home too soon, before her blood could settle down into more temperate motion, before she had gained control of her voice and tongue, and could force them to the requisite restraint of everyday speech. Otherwise her feelings would become as a flood on which her secret would be borne to the understanding of anyone who chose to listen.

Not yet; her secret would see light soon enough.

The autumn day was crimsoning out into sunset. The flaming orb overhead had gathered back into itself the myriad shafts it had been brandishing all day, and seemed melting away with the fury of its fire. The clouds flared up like a furnace, as though to infuse the shrinking sky with a little warmth against the numbing touch of the night.

Zillah looked up. Glory and splendour—but before long, the darkness. These things were riddles, even as her own life.

IX.

Softly Zillah entered the shop. Yeiteles was weighing out bags of sugar near the window. It was a task that could well be entrusted to him. Rhadamanthus, Chief Justice of the heathen Sheol, was surely not more critical in his verdicts than Yeiteles in his judgment of the scales. He never gave over-weight; he kept that for his perquisite.

From the kitchen came voices. Ah, of course, it was Salka and the wooer. He had slipped Zillah's memory. Well, one could not remember everything, and she had so much to think of. A few steps brought her into their presence. At her entrance Salka started up and fixed her with an eager, anxious glance. The dry fir-logs on the kitchen-hearth flared up like torches and made Zillah's features stand out as in daylight. Yes, thought Salka, she had come to her decision; her face showed serene with certainty; the furrows of self-questioning had disappeared, and round her lips played a smile, like a halo of victory.

A quiver of rebellious pain trembled through Salka's heart. Why had she thrown away her chance when it had been thrust upon her unsought? The intimation which had crept into her brain the night before, and which that afternoon had ripened into conviction—why had it come so late—too late? Had she known then what she knew now she would have set herself to win him, whatever might betide thereafter. She had trifled with her good fortune, and this was how it worked its revenge. But she must not show anything; she must be brave, brave and maidenly—the one thing meant the other.

"I am glad she is better," she said calmly, in reply to Zillah's remark anent the condition of an imaginary friend suffering from a fictitious illness; "very glad indeed. Guess what we shall have for supper."

Zillah shrugged her shoulders.

"Sour cabbage stew and blue potatoes."

Zillah opened her eyes.

"It's Enoch's favourite dish—he just told me so," explained Salka.

"Is it?" queried Zillah in neutral tone.

But Salka accentuated the question her own way; to her it sounded instinct with solicitous interest. "Ah, she has a right to know his favourite dishes," she thought bitterly.

"My dead mother preferred it to all others," said Enoch, quietly. "She was a good woman, and I think one can honour the memory of a good woman, even by the eating of cabbage stew."

Zillah glanced at him strangely; his words rang so full and true. Then her bosom heaved with a sudden, nameless anger; why had chance hurled this taunt in her teeth? It was a grand thing to boast of the love one bore to one's mother. Not everybody could do that; she least of all.

"She must have been good," said Salka, unable to resist her impulse; "she has left testimony of it in—" she stopped short, flushing.

"In her son?" supplemented Enoch, with a deprecatory smile; "Oh, I am no paragon—I am full of faults and blemishes;"—Zillah recognised the words—"for instance, I impose myself on people to whom my presence is irksome. That is only one of the great precepts of humanity as laid down by our Rabbins that I am violating. Again—"

Salka started up suddenly. "Mother is tapping for me," she said, hurrying out. It was strange that neither of the others had caught the signal.

There was silence between the two; Enoch had forgotten the second point of self-accusation and stared mutely into the fire. Zillah took the initiative; her lips were trembling, but her voice was firm.

"I have deserved your reproach," she began, "I have deserved it—can I say more? And now that you have heard me owning to my wrong, will you do justice to me?"

He signed her to continue.

"Then listen. Why are you here? I have not sent for you. You cannot claim that I have broken faith with you; there has been no promise of mine I have omitted to make good. Is there any blame you can attach to me?"

"No, none," he said wearily, after a little pause. "You cannot help being what you are; I cannot help feeling what I feel. But why trouble over it? There is a remedy: I shall go."

An idea flashed on Zillah. No, he must not go away; he must stay on to be the prop whereon her parents might lean their shattered, battered lives when the blow came—how it pleased her to torture herself with the thought. He was so good and kind—he had studied the "great precepts of humanity"; he would comfort them and become their son for charity's sake.

"Go?" she echoed. "Who tells you to do that? Why not rather say you have not yet given yourself a fair trial? Why, once you are gone—"

He started up and looked at her with straining eyes.

"Yes?" he prompted.

"Your hopes go with you, I suppose."

"Hope? Then there is really hope?"

"You must not press me for an answer; who knows?"

The equivocation came easily from her lips. What did it matter—one lie more or less? And this was perhaps the only one that might be registered to her credit in heaven. The fir-logs crackled and sputtered as the tongues of flame licked each new vein of resin; both pretended to be listening to them. Thus they could more plausibly give ear to the rush and whirr of their own thoughts.

"So busy, children, that you don't even hear my gossamer footsteps?" Old Anshel's voice broke in on them cheerily from the door; "I suppose now that I have sounded the alarm I may come in?"

He answered his own invitation by striding into the kitchen; his quick eye observed in both something that looked very much like embarrassment. The observation pleased him greatly; this meant making headway.

"I was half-way on to Tuschk when I met the very man I wanted; he was coming to me on the same errand. So we finished our business in the open road, and here I am again in good time and in still better appetite. Where's Salka?"

"With mother," said Zillah; "but don't be afraid—the supper's cooking. Enoch and I are cooking it, aren't we, Enoch?"

"The bill of fare was certainly my suggestion," answered the latter, with a flush of pleasure at her appeal; "but that is all I can take credit for."

"Thank God," muttered Anshel, "that saucepan has done the business. It preached to her the pleasures of housewifery. A marriage cooked in a saucepan; I should laugh if only I were sure she has learned the sermon well by heart."

It was the pleasantest evening spent since Enoch's arrival. He caught the inspiration of it, and his parables, sophisms, and dialectic fireworks came out thick as hail. Many a time he drove Anshel into a nasty corner, but Anshel only chuckled with delight, like a three-year-old toddler who has found a grownup man to play with him. Salka alone went about subdued and out of sorts, with a touch of red about her eyes which might possibly be attributed to an overhasty drying of tears.

Zillah had been sitting the whole evening on the edge of her mother's armchair, stroking the wan cheeks and fondling the nerveless hands. She kept her place there even after the two men had retired upstairs and Salka had retreated to the kitchen.

"Just five minutes all to ourselves, little mother," she said; "it is such a long time since we spoke to one another without a listener."

"Yes, quite two days; I am forgetting the sound of your voice—I mean the voice you keep all for myself."

"Should you not begin to accustom yourself to its absence?" asked Zillah pensively.

"Then you have settled with Enoch, and all is well—is it true?"

"Tell me, mother," said Zillah, ignoring the question and avoiding the joy-lit look that accompanied it; "tell me: was it for the honour of our house that this match was arranged?"

"What a strange thing to ask, child," was the answer. "For our honour? Of course not—for your happiness."

"Then so long as I had that, so long as you knew all my heart's desires were being gratified, would that satisfy you?"

"Quite; what more are we to expect? Zillah, what do you mean? Why do you frighten me with riddles?"

"Forgive me—I was clumsy," stammered Zillah; "I only meant to assure you that when I shall be away you shall hear of my happiness; I shall write you very, very often—"

"Yes, but what need is there of the assurance? Do not these things go without saying? I make no conditions with you, Zillah; I do not ask you to promise anything. I only want you to be a true daughter of mine. The rest I leave to you. Come, I am very tired; put me to bed."

Silently Zillah did as she was bidden; she could not have uttered a word although it had been to beg her life. A sense of foiled, abortive effort gnawed in her mind. She had attempted to feel her way. She had achieved nothing. Ah, yes, something. She had instilled into her mother the vague apprehension which would afterwards dull the shock by its saving foreknowledge. Zillah wondered that she could calculate these things with such precision, could put upon them their proper value; and from that she learnt that her heart was all out of gear—and perhaps not only her heart but her reason as well. If not, the two would not have made common cause to blunt the sting of her offence.

Slowly she made her way downstairs into the kitchen. Salka, too, was probably fatigued with the long day's toil.

"I might as well lend her a hand while I can," thought Zillah; "next week, perhaps, she will not mind the labour. It will help her to forget she had a sister."

Salka hardly looked up at her entrance.

"So you have made up your mind," she began, after a moment's silence.

"Yes, I have," replied Zillah, reckless and defiant; "I am going away from here."

"I know Enoch's father wants you to live near him," said Salka.

"Enoch's father? I am not going with Enoch—I am going with the Commissioner," she continued calmly, noting Salka's look of stupefaction, "the man you saw in the shop the other day. He asked me to marry him this afternoon. I told him I would consider, but he knows very well what my answer will be. And now you can go and kill mother with the news if you like."

The heavy silver ladle in Salka's hand clattered to the ground and lay there disregarded. Then a short inarticulate cry wrung itself from her lips. Zillah did not heed it; she sat down and carefully, dispassionately smoothed back a tress of hair which had struggled loose.

Salka listened: the words she had just heard were vibrating with a strange after-note. At first it was but an indistinct suggestion, then it shaped itself into recognisable sounds, until it rang out clear and resonant:

"Enoch is free—Enoch is free!"

So he was not lost to her after all? Fate had been kind to her—had not taken offence at her former rebuff. To waste this second chance would be deliberately pushing aside the extended hand of God.

"Zillah, do as your heart bids you," she said slowly.

With a bound Zillah was at her side, peering deeply into her eyes.

"Salka, are you really telling me to do that?" she panted. "Are you really in earnest? No, I can see you are not speaking to me in mockery.

Ah, the true little sister you are. Do you know, Salka," she went on, almost sobbing, "I had expected you would overwhelm me with your reproaches; I thought you would burst out crying, and make me falter with your appeals and passionate entreaties. And perhaps you would not have needed to go so far; just one little word of remonstrance might have turned me from my purpose—and I love him so. But you say I am doing right; that is the heaven-sign for which I have been waiting. Oh, Salka, Salka!"

Salka wrenched herself loose from her embraces; she did not deserve them.

"What is the use of your staying here eating your heart out?" she said quickly. "Would it be more pleasant for me to see you do that than to know that elsewhere you are tasting love and life to the full? I should scold myself for a selfish, whining weakling if, because of the pain of parting with you, I should dissuade you from following your truest impulse."

She paused for a moment; then her eyes brightened and her voice rose.

"But that is not the only reason why I ask you to go, Zillah. A great mission awaits you. You will accomplish much for which you would never find the scope here. Out there, in the midst of our enemies, to whom we are but a name and an execration—among them in secret and in ambush, as it were, you will be able to champion our struggling race. It is not our professed advocates, who make a great noise and shout themselves hoarse in the world's market-places, that shall work our redemption. No; it is the quiet example, the living lesson, the subtle, voiceless persuasion by act and deed, however small, which shall teach our adversaries how they misjudge us. We want many, many such teachers scattered abroad. Think of it, Zillah, you will be one of them, and not the idlest. I know. Did my fate call me, ill-equipped though I am, I should go likewise."

A great sigh rose from Salka's inmost heart as she finished. That sigh was a prayer of gratitude. God was merciful, and had given her something wherewith to salve her conscience. It was no longer an ignominious falsehood, a despicable device, which made her send her sister adrift; but a great and glorious purpose which had ennobled selfishness into self-sacrifice.

Zillah seemed to think so too. The colour in her face ebbed and flowed, her fingers twined and untwined as she listened.

"Can I ever thank you, Salka?" she said, finally. "Whence did you take that inspiration? I might have gone on thinking and thinking—it would never have come to me. Salka, as you love me, let me not hear another word from you to-night. I want to soak my brain in what you have said—to teach our enemies to love us! What a task you have set me. One thing you can be sure of—I shall be loyal to it. I shall sing the songs of the Lord in a strange land as no one has sung them yet. Believe me, my life shall not be lived in vain. Do I not know it? I must wipe many a tear from the face of our nation's misery, I must apply many a bandage to its sufferings, before I can hope to earn atonement for the wounds I am inflicting on those that gave me life."

She stopped and listened; down the street a horseman was passing at a furious gallop.

"That is he," she muttered, her finger to her lip; "hark, how his restlessness is scourging him. Come, Salka, if mother should wake she will wonder what we are doing. Are you not lucky, Salka? Only a few days more and you will have no need to share your mother with anyone else."

When Yeiteles entered the kitchen next morning he had quite a shock. On the floor, rubbing shoulders with the plebeian fire-tongs, lay the silver ladle, disconsolate and neglected.

X.

It was the fourth morning following. Anshel had started out quite early the previous day to collect accounts in the neighbouring villages, and was not expected back till late that evening. Zillah was in the sick-room; she had hardly stirred from it during the last three days. Her mother wondered at it, but she took it as she took every other blessing, without enquiry. She knew it was dangerous to question one's good fortune.

Enoch had been hovering about the house aimlessly. He thought he had something to wait for—had not Zillah told him so? He had repeated her words to himself time and again; at first they sounded sweet, comforting, inspiring. And then—was it from the endless iteration?—they began to lose the edge of their import. And now, as he recalled them, sitting in his attic with the tremendous tome of Talmudic lore in front of him, they seemed hollow and lifeless, for they roused in him no responsive thrill. From that he knew he had lost faith in them. Anchorite though he was, he had learnt enough of the world's ways that if a woman wanted to show favour to a man, her features, however tense with pain, would soften at his approach, her vacant eyes would become suffused with light and life. Zillah's did nothing of the kind. Ah, it was a difficult question—much more difficult than any of those propounded in Treatise Baba Kama. But he would have it answered this day.

Salka was in the shop. Somehow she was glad of this new partition of labour between her and her sister; it kept her for the most part out of her mother's presence, and what had formerly appeared to her a deprivation now came to her as a relief. She felt guilty; she had not yet taken account of the extent and origin of the feeling, because so far it was sufficiently strong as to override all attempts at self-analysis. It resulted in a state of helpless bewilderment, which as often as not overshadowed her perception of outward things.

That was apparently the case with her at present, or else she would long ago have noticed the lanky gendarme who was promenading up and down the street, and casting a vexed look into the shop each time he passed it. And so she started up half-frightened as suddenly he clanked in.

"I want two copecks' worth of pipe-clay," he said, looking round inquisitively.

"Pipe-clay? We don't sell any here."

"Yes, you do—I bought some the other day; the tall young lady with the big, shining eyes served me."

A light dawned on Salka. Swiftly she walked to the backdoor.

"Zillah, I want you," she called up.

Her voice trembled, but she did not know it.

A minute passed and then Zillah appeared; her first glance caught the gendarme.

"A message?" she asked.

The man nodded and looked towards Salka, who had stepped to the other counter.

"She does not matter," Zillah impatiently replied to the look.

"I was ordered to give it to nobody but you," he explained, handing her the note, "so as to make sure it reached you."

Zillah read it through, read it again and again, as the man divined from the time she took perusing it; it was not such a very long letter.

"I shall send the answer later, through someone else," she informed him at last.

The man hesitated. Zillah repeated her words. Then he went, his head high in the air. He was rather proud of the pipe-clay idea.

"Here," said Zillah, holding the letter out to Salka. The latter took it, although her trembling fingers almost refused her service.

"My despatches have arrived," she read; "I am to be given the post on condition that I report myself at Samarkand by noon on the fifth day from this. We must go by the seven o'clock train tonight: or, at the latest, we can leave at nine in the locomotive car, which will be in time to meet the South Line train at the junction. If you have not sent your answer by seven, I know you will bring it yourself at nine."

"To-night, then," said Salka, her gaze riveted on the missive. Zillah did not answer, so that Salka fancied she had only thought, not spoken the words.

"To-night, then," she repeated, more loudly.

"God! do I not know it without your dinning it into my ears?" cried Zillah.

"I thought you would be glad," ventured Salka, timidly.

"Of course I am glad—so glad that I am jealous of showing it. Only I thought it would not be so soon."

"When did you expect it?"

"In a month, in a year—and there would be a chance of my being dead before then. It is true, though, he gave me warning that he would want me speedily, now that I come to think of it," she went on, almost rambling, "but I did not believe he meant it; I did not believe this meant anything save a blind, undiscerning happiness that looked neither behind nor in front. And now that I must use my sight it hurts. Yes, Salka, it hurts."

Entreatingly she turned her blanched face to her sister; in the garish sunshine it looked piteously wan and drawn.

Salka crushed the Commissioner's letter with feverish fingers.

"You are not going," she said, coming closer to Zillah; "you don't want to go. Your courage is failing you."

A glad smile relaxed Zillah's features. She clutched Salka's hand.

"Ah, you are my angel, as ever," she broke out; "you need but open your lips and help comes. Indeed, it is merely my courage has deserted me—not my desire. Only I did not know it till you told me. Should I not be frightened to give myself into a stranger's keeping, one of whom I know nothing save that I love him? And perhaps love may not be a safe touchstone—perhaps there is some alloy where my heart would fain only discover refined gold. All these things are a hazard, a life and death hazard, and is it to be wondered at that a weak woman like me shrinks from staking her all upon it? But now there remains only one course: to cast misgivings to the wind, to be brave and fearless, to trust that what God makes us do is surely for the best. Salka, I shall go."

Pensively the younger sister gazed out at the apple-tree that stood sentry outside the shop, and now seemed shaking its yellowing leaves as though in disapproval.

"Is it worth it?" she asked, at last.

"You mean is it worth father and mother and you? I don't know; did I not say it was a hazard? I only know that if I lose, I shall not be sorry—because I should not dare to be."

A long silence followed. Salka spoke first.

"Father will not be home before eight."

"Yes, I have been thinking of that," said Zillah.

"You will want to see him; and so you will not be able to go before nine. In the meantime the Com——, he will be waiting for an answer. Let me take it to him."

Salka's dispassionate voice contrasted curiously with Zillah's eager accents as she replied:

"Oh, Salka, I had intended asking you, but I was afraid. I want to be with mother all I can; every hour I see her between now and tonight might have to serve me with its memory for a year."

"Why should you be afraid to ask me? Don't you remember, I still owe you a service?" answered Salka, in a most business-like tone. One would think she had not noticed the pain that quivered through her sister's last words.

"I shall go over to the railway station shortly before seven," she continued; "I shall be sure to find him on the platform. Would that not be best? You see he does not expect a message much before then."

And smoothing the crumpled paper she held it before Zillah. The latter nodded; she had no need to look—she knew it well by heart.

"You are doing your best to make it hard for me, little sister," was all she said. And Salka knew what she meant.

Without another word Zillah went back to her mother. She must not waste the precious time; she must take a deep impress of the dear, dear features—deep enough to last her all her lifetime. Oh yes, that was what it would come to; they would never forgive her—she would be dead to them. Her father would sit in the mourner's chair, mourning her for the prescribed seven days, and ever after observe the date of her flight as the anniversary of her passing. With a sob she pressed one hand to her eyes, but the terrible picture would not vanish.

So she groped her way up the stairs. At the top she came face to face with Enoch. He looked at her with the curious hungry gaze with which she was well acquainted, but before he had time to utter a word, she had opened the door and disappeared.

With a sinking heart he crept down into the shop. But Salka had heard him coming, and was stooping over an account-book, adding up long rows of figures. Calmly she went on with them as he entered. Enoch watched her a little, waiting vainly to see her turn her face upon him, and then with a sigh he went back to his attic. So his fate was sealed. Even Salka, kind, sweet-voiced, warm-hearted Salka whom he had made the receptacle of his doubts and anxieties, and who had ever requited his confidence with her sympathy, even Salka flouted him. Yes, he was only torturing himself in vain.

But it was not the ledger Salka was so busy with; it was a reckoning of her own, and she was well aware that the sight of Enoch might in some way interfere with her result. And at that result she must arrive quickly; time was pressing.

The day sped on, both for Zillah and Salka, with relentless rapidity. Zillah was calm—the stillness of a dammed-up torrent. But Salka held her feelings less under lock and key. As the afternoon wore on a fever of impatience painted her pale face with crimson eagerness. Her brain had become a machine of blood and tissue, and its wheels were revolving restlessly, straining their sweep and compass without mercy, to achieve their task betimes. And at last, towards evening, the colour began to fade, for her thoughts no longer hustled and jostled each other; they were shaping themselves out of chaos into a compact resolve. So she sat back in her chair, closing her eyes like one who has done his work well and can afford to wait patiently for the issue.

About a quarter to seven, Zillah, or something that looked very much like her, came down and said:—

"Had you not better go now?"

"Yes," and Salka rose readily; "what shall I tell him?"

"Tell him that I shall come at nine."

Salka had to strain her ears so as to catch the words. With a swift movement she drew down Zillah's head and touched her lips with her own. At the same time she looked deep into her eyes.

What she saw in them made her heart give a bound of delight. Clearly she read there as from a manuscript on which Zillah's soul had penned: "Save me from myself!"

The next moment Salka was out in the street, traversing the distance to the station with flying feet. Quickly she recapitulated to herself the reflections which had helped her to her resolution. She would save her sister—that had been her starting-point all along. It was not fulfilling a duty, it was only a chance, given her by God's mercy, of redeeming herself from a deadly sin. At the eleventh hour, as it were, the film of blindness had been withdrawn from her vision. She had seen, and had stood shuddering as before an abyss. She had been content for the sake of an iniquitous love, of which the gratification was at best uncertain and precarious, to pay the price of a sister's undoing and disownment, to pay for it with her parents' broken hearts. She was the parricide—not Zillah. Had Zillah not said, that but for her prompting, her encouragement, she might never have had the fortitude to cast herself afloat on those strange seas beyond?

And the sinful desire which had not yet entirely taken its sting from out of her bosom? It did not matter; it would count as nothing beside the gladness of her self-retrieving. It was a weed, and it would die of its own loathsomeness.

Thank God there was yet time.

She had come to the station turnstile that admitted on to the platform. The locomotive was getting up steam; porters and passengers were hurrying in the wild pell-mell that precedes immediate departure. But in the midst of the confusion the tall figure of the Commissioner was striding up and down leisurely, his hands in his pockets. He knew the train would not leave without him unless he willed it so. Outwardly he was calm—so calm that no one would have suspected for a moment that he was envying the locomotive for being able to give vent to its feelings without running the risk of comment.

As he turned back he caught sight of Salka in the dim lantern-light, and came quickly towards her.

"I was sure she would send a messenger," he said, eagerly; "so I must wait till nine?"

Salka's breath came fast. God help her now.

"You need not wait; my sister is not coming," she answered, without a quaver.

Then she stepped back; in a moment the storm would break. Presently he would begin to fume and rave and threaten: already she seemed to feel his blows tingling on her face.

But no—he remained silent; and yet this silence was more terrible than would have been an avalanche of rage.

After a while his lips moved.

"Why not?" She almost had to guess the question.

"Because she belongs to a race which imparted to the world the commandment: 'Thou shalt honour thy father and mother'" replied Salka, mechanically. She had conned her lesson well.

"Where is she?" he asked suddenly.

"At home."

"Then I shall fetch her," he said, turning on his heel.

Salka's heart beat like a sledgehammer.

"It is useless, your Honour," she said, following him and laying her hand on his arm; "it is useless, I assure you. You will find her at her mother's bedside. Her mother has not left her couch for three years, but she will be strong as a tigress when it comes to struggling for her child, and I think you can guess on whose side will be the victory."

He had stopped and was looking at her dazed; then he said: "Yes I can guess. She asked you to tell me all this—she, your sister?"

"She asks you to forgive her, and to forget her. She says she will pray every day to our God for your welfare; she will beg Him to make you the equal of the greatest in the land, to be good to you for the sake of the goodness you had promised her."

He seemed to be waking from his trance.

"Goodness?" he uttered, with a bitter laugh. "What goodness? I had promised her my love, my name,—but there was no kindness in that; it was only selfishness. I wanted her heart though she brought it to me bleeding from a thousand wounds. And therefore your God has punished me for it, and has taken from me what I coveted so greedily, in the very hour I had hoped for its attainment Ah! this old God of yours is very powerful; yes, let her pray to Him for me, to send me comfort, even as He has sent punishment. Oh, must I believe it? She will not come—is she sure she will not? There is still time, you know—"

Salka shook her head; her heart was too full for speech. He was strong indeed, the God of Israel, and more than that, He protected His children.

The iron horse on the rails stood champing and quivering; presently it snorted. The Commissioner came close to Salka on the spur of a sudden thought.

"When did you kiss her last?" he asked.

The girl looked at him in terror—had he gone mad?

"When?" he repeated.

"Just before I came here," she replied, trembling.

The next instant he had caught her tight, his beard was grazing her face, his lips burnt on hers. Then he let her go.

"I have not been cheated out of that at least," he said; "it was to have been mine when we were to meet with no parting before us. Tell her she has given it to me by proxy. My Madonna of the frontier! She will know how much I loved her, if I can leave her."

He turned quickly and made his way into the compartment.

The guard signalled—the steam horse gathered itself up and moved. The Commissioner stood at the window and waved his hand to Salka.

* * * *

Salka remained on the platform long after the rear-lights of the train had become swallowed up in the darkness. With a sigh that was more a sob, she started on her way home. She was safe—her sister was safe.

All that now remained was to tell her so. When she reached the house, she found Zillah in the kitchen counting the contents of a little iron casket.

"This is all I am going to take with me," she said, without looking up; "about a hundred roubles I have saved; I may need them."

"You will not need them—at least not tonight," replied Salka.

Zillah raised her head.

"Then he has put off his departure?" she asked, her eyes radiant with a flash of hope. "Have his despatches been revoked?"

"No, they have not been revoked. He has gone."

"Gone?"

"I saw the train carrying him away—I swear to you I saw it. I told him that you had changed your mind, that you could not bear to desert your parents on earth and your Father in heaven—that you would die of it; and he went away to prove how he loved you. You can kill me for it, but I could not do otherwise."

Zillah listened and her face became transfigured.

"You say that this was your doing?" came slowly from her. "You flatter yourself. It was not yours—it was my good angel's; he has entered into you, he has taken your shape and voice. I have missed him these last days; he had abandoned me and had taken my conscience with him. Or else would I not have heeded my mother when she asked me to be a true daughter to her? I knew I was rushing into the arms of my evil destiny, but I did not struggle, for dimly, darkly I felt that help would come in the extremest hour of the peril. Salka, what can I do to repay you?"

"You can marry Enoch," replied Salka, quickly; "you owe it, not to me, but to your parents; it will be your reparation for the wrong you all but did them. Hush!"

She held up her finger warningly. Enoch was heard descending the staircase.

"Can you oblige me with a piece of cord?" he asked, stopping at the door.

"For what purpose, pray?" asked Salka.

"I am packing—my train leaves at five tomorrow morning. I cannot afford to neglect my affairs any longer."

"Wait here a moment," said Salka, hurrying out. "I shall look for some upstairs."

He took a step forward and stood gazing vacantly into a corner. Suddenly he felt a light touch on his hand. Zillah was quite close to him.

"And suppose I am one of your affairs?" she asked, with downcast eyes.

"Zillah!" he shouted.

She raised her glance and looked at him solemnly. She saw the tears in his eyes and silently tightened her clasp on his hand.

Five minutes afterwards Anshel's vehicle pulled up outside the door. Salka stood on the step.

"News, good news," she whispered to him.

But Anshel needed no telling. He had guessed.

Section 2 *Historical Fiction and
the Sephardic Experience*

Grace Aguilar, "The Escape: A Tale of 1755" (1844)

Grace Aguilar (1816–47), the first widely read Jewish writer in Britain, was born in the village of Hackney close to London. Her parents were Sephardic Jews of Spanish and Portuguese ancestry whose grandparents had been merchants and plantation owners in Jamaica. Typically for a girl of her class and generation, she was educated at home. Her religious influences were eclectic: in London her father was a prominent member of the Spanish and Portuguese Jewish congregation and Grace may have been taught Hebrew. However, during her teens the family spent several years in a Devon coastal resort, for her father's health, and here Grace attended Protestant churches. Much of her fiction was written during her late teens and remained unknown until her father's health declined further and Grace became the family breadwinner, running a boys' school with her mother and publishing poetry and her earlier prose works. After Grace's death at the age of thirty-one her mother, Sarah, continued editing and publishing her daughter's manuscripts.

Aguilar's first major published works were on Jewish subjects. Reflecting the contemporary Jewish preoccupation with the threat of Christian conversionists, she produced three works of apologia on behalf of Judaism: a translation of Baltasar Orobio de Castro's *Israel Defended* (1838); *The Spirit of Judaism* (1842), an explanation of Jewish beliefs and practices which was published in America; and *The Jewish Faith: Its Spiritual Consolation, Moral Guidance, and Immortal Hope* (1846), which took the form of letters addressed to a Jewish girl encouraging her to remain loyal to her faith. She also aimed at a female readership in *The Women of Israel* (1845), a book of essays on Old Testament heroines. Her "History of the Jews in England," published anonymously in 1847, declared support for Jewish political and civil equality. Her books aimed to foster pride in Judaism but also to argue for religious tolerance and to demonstrate the affinities between Judaism and English Protestantism. Her emphasis on the importance of reading the Bible, the authority of the individual to interpret Scripture, and her opposition to rabbinical authority—all indications of the influence of contemporary Evangelicalism—incurred some criticism from the Anglo-Jewish press and her American editor Rabbi Isaac Leeser but contributed to her popularity among Protestant readers.

Aguilar was also the author of a number of bestselling domestic and historical novels for a general female readership, which celebrated the role of the middle-class mother in teaching the virtues of charity, obedience, and piety, including *Home Influence: A Tale for Mothers and Daughters* (1847), which went through nearly thirty editions, and *The Days of Bruce: A Story from Scottish History* (1852). Her popular novel *The Vale of Cedars; or, The Martyr* (1850) combined the domestic novel with gothic melodrama in a Jewish historical setting. This tragic tale of the persecution and heroism of a Jewish woman during the Spanish Inquisition appealed to the strong anti-Catholic feeling of the period and became one of her most successful books. It was also translated into German and influenced German-Jewish writing.

The story included here, "The Escape: A Tale of 1755," first published in a short volume, *Records of Israel* (1844), also highlights the suffering of crypto-Jews in Iberia. Aguilar frequently refers to the memory of the Inquisition as alive and formative for contemporary Jews, and often takes the opportunity to pay homage to the tolerance of England, where Judaism could be practiced openly. Her use of the dramatic historical event of the 1755 Lisbon earthquake and tidal wave as a denouement for her story is particularly interesting. Whereas Evangelicals read the earthquake as a sure sign of the imminent End of Days, Aguilar casts it in quasi-biblical terms as a miraculous act of retribution upon Portugal for its persecution of the Jews and a reward for the loyal faith of the protagonists and their resignation to divine will. Like *The Vale of Cedars*, "The Escape" was also translated into German in the 1850s and appeared in Ludwig Philippson's *Jüdisches Volksblatt*, the same journal that published the story that follows "The Escape" in the current volume, Philippson's "The Three Brothers."

*

> Dark lowers our fate,
> And terrible the storm that gathers o'er us;
> But nothing, till that latest agony
> Which severs thee from nature, shall unloose
> This fixed and sacred hold. In thy dark prison-house;
> In the terrific face of armed law;
> Yea! on the scaffold, if it needs must be,
> I never will forsake thee.
>
> Joanna Baillie[1]

---

1. Joanna Baillie (1762–1851), popular Scottish poet and dramatist, close friend of Walter Scott. The epigraph is taken from her tragedy *De Montfort* (1798), and spoken by a loving sister to her murderous brother, but Aguilar quotes the lines out of context to suggest instead the unwavering faith of Jews.

About the middle of the eighteenth century, the little town of Montes, situated some forty or fifty miles from Lisbon, was thrown into most unusual excitement by the magnificence attending the nuptials of Alvar Rodriguez and Almah Diaz; an excitement which the extraordinary beauty of the bride, who, though the betrothed of Alvar from her childhood, had never been seen in Montes before, of course not a little increased. The little church of Montes looked gay and glittering, for the large sums lavished by Alvar on the officiating priests, and in presents to their patron saints, had occasioned every picture, shrine, and image to blaze in uncovered gold and jewels, and the altar to be fed with the richest incense, and lighted with tapers of the finest wax, to do him honour.

The church was full; for, although the bridal party did not exceed twenty, the village appeared to have emptied itself there; Alvar's munificence to all classes, on all occasions, having rendered him the universal idol, and caused the fame of that day's rejoicing to extend many miles around.

There was nothing remarkable in the behaviour of either bride or bridegroom, except that both were decidedly more calm than such occasions usually warrant. Nay, in the fine, manly countenance of Alvar ever and anon an expression seemed to flit, that in any but so true a son of the church would have been accounted scorn. In such a one, of course, it was neither seen nor regarded, except by his bride; for at such times her eyes met his with an earnest and entreating glance, that the peculiar look was changed into a quiet, tender seriousness which reassured her.

From the church they adjourned to the lordly mansion of Rodriguez, which, in the midst of the flowering orange and citron trees, stood about two miles from the town.

The remainder of the day passed in festivity. The banquet and dance and song, both within and around the house, diversified the scene and increased hilarity in all. By sunset, all but the immediate friends and relatives of the newly wedded had departed. Some splendid and novel fireworks from the heights having attracted universal attention, Alvar, with his usual indulgence, gave his servants and retainers permission to join the festive crowds; liberty, to all who wished it, was given for the next two hours.

In a very brief interval the house was cleared, with the exception of a young Moor, the secretary or book-keeper of Alvar, and four or five middle-aged domestics of both sexes.

Gradually, and it appeared undesignedly, the bride and her female companions were left alone, and for the first time the beautiful face of Almah was shadowed by emotion.

"Shall I, oh, shall I indeed be his?" she said, half-aloud. "There are moments when our dread secrets are so terrible; it seems to forebode discovery at the very moment it would be most agonizing to bear."

"Hush, silly one!" was the reply of an older friend; "discovery is not so easily or readily accomplished. The persecuted and the nameless have purchased wisdom and caution at the price of blood—learned to deceive, that they may triumph—to conceal, that they may flourish still. Almah, we are NOT to fall!"

"I know it, Inez. A superhuman agency upholds us; we had been cast off, rooted out, plucked from the very face of the earth long since else. But there are times when human nature will shrink and tremble—when the path of deception and concealment allotted for us to tread seems fraught with danger at every turn. I know it is all folly, yet there is a dim foreboding, shadowing our fair horizon of joy as a hovering thundercloud. There has been suspicion, torture, death. Oh, if my Alvar—"

"Nay, Almah; this is childish. It is only because you are too happy, and happiness in its extent is ever pain. In good time comes your venerable guardian, to chide and silence all such foolish fancies. How many weddings have there been, and will there still be, like this? Come, smile, love, while I rearrange your veil."

Almah obeyed, though the smile was faint, as if the soul yet trembled in its joy. On the entrance of Gonzalos, her guardian (she was an orphan and an heiress), her veil was thrown around her, so as completely to envelop face and form. Taking his arm, and followed by all her female companions, she was hastily and silently led to a sort of anteroom or cabinet, opening, by a massive door concealed with tapestry, from the suite of rooms appropriated to the private use of the merchant and his family. There Alvar and his friends awaited her. A canopy, supported by four of the youngest males present, was held over the bride and bridegroom as they stood facing the east. A silver salver lay at their feet, and opposite stood an aged man, with a small, richly-bound volume in his hand. It was open, and displayed letters and words of unusual form and sound. Another of Alvar's friends stood near, holding a goblet of sacred wine; and to a third was given a slight and thin Venetian glass. After a brief and solemn pause, the old man read or rather chanted from the book he held, joined in parts by those around; and then he tasted the sacred wine, and passed it to the bride and bridegroom. Almah's veil was upraised, for her to touch the goblet with her lips, now quivering with emotion, and not permitted to fall again. And Alvar, where now was the expression of scorn and contempt that had been stamped on his bold brow and curling lip before? Gone—lost before the powerful emotion which scarcely permitted his lifting the goblet a second time to his lips. Then, taking the Venetian glass, he broke it on the salver at his feet, and the strange rites were completed.[2]

Yet no words of congratulation came. Drawn together in a closer knot, while Alvar folded the now almost fainting Almah to his bosom, and said, in the deep, low tones of intense feeling, "Mine, mine forever now—mine in the sight of our God, the God of the exile and the faithful; our fate whatever it be, henceforth is one"; the old man lifted up his clasped hands, and prayed.

"God of the nameless and homeless," he said, and it was in the same strange yet solemn-sounding language as before, "have mercy on these Thy servants, joined together in Thy Holy name, to share the lot on earth Thy will assigns them, with one heart and mind. Strengthen Thou them to keep the secret of their faith and race—to teach it to their offspring as they received it from their fathers. Pardon Thou them and us the deceit we do to keep holy Thy law and Thine inheritance. In the land of the persecutor, the exterminator, be Thou their shield, and save them for Thy Holy name. But if discovery and its horrible consequences—imprisonment, torture, death—await them, strengthen Thou them for their endurance—to die as they would live for Thee. Father, hear us! homeless and nameless upon earth, we are Thine own!"

"Aye, strengthen me for him, my husband; turn my woman weakness into Thy strength for him, Almighty Father," was the voiceless

---

2. Jewish readers may have recognized these practices as comprising the Jewish marriage ceremony; for non-Jewish readers the revelation of their meaning is delayed a further few pages.

prayer with which Almah lifted up her pale face from her husband's bosom, where it had rested during the whole of that strange and terrible prayer; and in the calmness stealing on her throbbing heart, she read her answer.

It was some few minutes ere the excited spirits of the devoted few then present, male or female, master or servant, could subside into their wonted control. But such scenes, such feelings were not of rare occurrence; and ere the domestics of Rodriguez returned, there was nothing either in the mansion or its inmates to denote that anything uncommon had taken place during their absence.

The Portuguese are not fond of society at any time, so that Alvar and his young bride should after one week of festivity, live in comparative retirement, elicited no surprise. The former attended his house of business at Montes as usual; and whoever chanced to visit him at his beautiful estate, returned delighted with his entertainment and his hosts; so that, far and near, the merchant Alvar became noted alike for his munificence and the strict orthodox Catholicism in which he conducted his establishment.

And was Alvar Rodriguez indeed what he seemed? If so, what were those strange mysterious rites with which in secret he celebrated his marriage? For what were those many contrivances in his mansion, secret receptacles even from his own sitting-rooms, into which all kinds of forbidden food were conveyed from his very table, that his soul might not be polluted by disobedience? How did it so happen that one day in every year Alvar gave a general holiday—leave of absence for four and twenty hours, under some well-arranged pretence, to all save those who entreated permission to remain with him? And that on that day, Alvar, his wife, his Moorish secretary, and all those domestics who had witnessed his marriage, spent in holy fast and prayer—permitting no particle of food or drink to pass their lips from eve unto eve; or if, by any chance, the holiday could not be given, their several meals to be laid and served, yet so contriving that, while the food looked as if it had been partaken of, not a portion had they touched? That the Saturday should be passed in seeming preparation for the Sunday, in cessation from work of any kind, and in frequent prayer, was perhaps of trivial importance; but for the previous mysteries—mysteries known to Alvar, his wife, and five or six of his establishment, yet never by word or sign betrayed; how may we account for them? There may be some to whom the memory of such things, as common to their ancestors, may be yet familiar; but to by far the greater number of English readers, they are, in all probability, as incomprehensible as uncommon.

Alvar Rodriguez was a Jew. One of the many who, in Portugal and Spain, fulfilled the awful prophecy of their great lawgiver Moses, and bowed before the imaged saints and martyrs of the Catholic, to shrine the religion of their fathers yet closer in their hearts and homes. From father to son the secret of their faith and race descended, so early and mysteriously taught, that little children imbibed it—not alone the faith, but the concealing of it, so effectually as to avert and mystify all inquisitorial questioning, long before they knew the meaning or necessity of what they learned.

How this was accomplished, how the religion of God was thus preserved in the very midst of persecution and intolerance, must ever remain a mystery, as, happily for Israel, such fearful training is no longer needed. But that it did exist, that Jewish children, in the very midst of monastic and convent tuition, yet adhered to the religion of their fathers, never by word or sign betrayed the secret with which they were intrusted; and, in their turn, became husbands and fathers, conveying their solemn and dangerous inheritance to their posterity—that such things were, there are those still among the Hebrews of England to affirm and recall, claiming among their own ancestry, but one generation removed, those who have thus concealed and thus adhered. It was the power of God, not the power of man. Human strength had been utterly inefficient. Torture and death would long before have annihilated every remnant of Israel's devoted race. But it might not be; for God had spoken. And, as a living miracle, a lasting record of His truth, His justice, aye, and mercy, Israel was preserved in the midst of danger, in the very face of death, and will be preserved forever.

It was no mere rejoicing ceremony, that of marriage, among the disguised and hidden Israelites of Portugal and Spain. They were binding themselves to preserve and propagate a persecuted faith. They were no longer its sole repositors. Did the strength of one waver, all was at an end. They were united in the sweet links of love—framing for themselves new ties, new hopes, new blessings in a rising family—all of which, at one blow, might be destroyed. They existed in an atmosphere of death, yet they lived and flourished. But so situated, it was not strange that human emotion, both in Alvar and his bride, should, on their wedding-day, have gained ascendency; and the solemn hour which made them one in the sight of the God they worshipped, should have been fraught with a terror and a shuddering, of which Jewish lovers in free and happy England can have no knowledge.

Alvar Rodriguez was one of those high and noble spirits, on whom the chain of deceit and concealment weighed heavily; and there were times when it had been difficult to suppress and conceal his scorn of those outward observances which his apparent Catholicism compelled. When united to Almah, however, he had a stronger incentive than his own safety; and as time passed on, and he became a father, caution and circumspection, if possible, increased with the deep passionate feelings of tenderness toward the mother and child. As the boy grew and flourished, the first feelings of dread, which the very love he excited called forth at his birth, subsided into a kind of tranquil calm, which even Almah's foreboding spirit trusted would last, as the happiness of others of her race.

Though Alvar's business was carried on both at Montes and at Lisbon, the bulk of both his own and his wife's property was, by a strange chance, invested at Badajoz, a frontier town of Spain, and whence he had often intended to remove it, but had always been prevented. It happened that early in the month of June, some affairs calling him to Lisbon, he resolved to delay removing it no longer, smiling at his young wife's half solicitation to let it remain where it was, and playfully accusing her of superstition, a charge she cared not to deny. The night before his intended departure his young Moorish secretary, in other words, an Israelite of Barbary extraction, entered his private closet, with a countenance of entreaty and alarm, earnestly conjuring his master to give up his Lisbon expedition, and retire with his wife and son to Badajoz or Oporto, or some distant city, at least for a while. Anxiously Rodriguez inquired wherefore.

"You remember the Senor Leyva, your worship's guest a week or two ago?"

"Perfectly. What of him?"

"Master, I like him not. If danger befall us it will come through him. I watched him closely, and every hour of his stay shrunk from him the more. He was a stranger?"

"Yes; benighted, and had lost his way. It was impossible to refuse him hospitality. That he stayed longer than he had need, I grant; but there is no cause of alarm in that—he liked his quarters."

"Master," replied the Moor, earnestly, "I do not believe his tale. He was no casual traveller. I cannot trust him."

"You are not called upon to do so, man," said Alvar, laughing. "What do you believe him to be, that you would inoculate me with your own baseless alarm?"

Hassan Ben Ahmed's answer, whatever it might be, for it was whispered fearfully in his master's ear, had the effect of sending every drop of blood from Alvar's face to his very heart. But he shook off the stagnating dread. He combated the prejudices of his follower as unreasonable and unfounded. Hassan's alarm, however, could only be soothed by the fact, that so suddenly to change his plans would but excite suspicion. If Leyva were what he feared, his visit must already have been followed by the usual terrific effects.

Alvar promised, however, to settle his affairs at Lisbon as speedily as he could, and return for Almah and his son, and convey them to some place of greater security until the imagined danger was passed.

In spite of his assumed indifference, however, Rodriguez could not bid his wife and child farewell without a pang of dread, which it was difficult to conceal. The step between life and death—security and destruction—was so small, it might be passed unconsciously, and then the strongest nerve might shudder at the dark abyss before him. Again and again he turned to go, and yet again returned; and it was with a feeling literally of desperation he at length tore himself away.

A fearful trembling was on Almah's heart as she gazed after him, but she would not listen to its voice.

"It is folly," she said, self-upbraidingly. "My Alvar is ever chiding this too doubting heart. I will not disobey him, by fear and foreboding in his absence. The God of the nameless is with him and me," and she raised her eyes to the blue arch above her, with an expression that needed not voice to mark it prayer.

About a week after Alvar's departure, Almah was sitting by the cradle of her boy, watching his soft and rosy slumbers, with a calm sweet thankfulness that such a treasure was her own. The season had been unusually hot and dry, but the apartment in which the young mother sat opened on a pleasant spot, thickly shaded with orange, lemon, and almond trees, and decked with a hundred other richly-hued and richly-scented plants; in the centre of which a fountain sent up its heavy showers, which fell back on the marble bed, with a splash and coolness peculiarly refreshing, and sparkled in the sun as glittering gems.

A fleet yet heavy step resounded from the garden, which seemed suddenly and forcibly restrained into a less agitated movement. A shadow fell between her and the sunshine, and, starting, Almah looked hastily up. Hassan Ben Ahmed stood before her, a paleness on his swarthy cheek, and a compression of his nether lip betraying strong emotion painfully restrained.

"My husband! Hassan. What news bring you of him? Why are you alone?"

He laid his hand on her arm, and answered in a voice which so quivered that only ears eager as her own could have distinguished his meaning.

"Lady, dear, dear lady, you have a firm and faithful heart. Oh! for the love of Him who calls on you to suffer, awake its strength and firmness. My dear, my honoured lady, sink not, fail not! O God of mercy, support her now!" he added, flinging himself on his knees before her, as Almah one moment sprang up with a smothered shriek, and the next sank back on her seat rigid as marble.

Not another word she needed. Hassan thought to have prepared, gradually to have told, his dread intelligence; but he had said enough. Called upon to suffer, and for Him her God—her doom was revealed in those brief words. One minute of such agonized struggle, that her soul and body seemed about to part beneath it; and the wife and mother roused herself to do. Lip, cheek, and brow vied in their ashen whiteness with her robe; the blue veins rose distended as cords; and the voice—had not Hassan gazed upon her, he had not known it as her own.

She commanded him to tell her briefly all, and even while he spoke, seemed revolving in her own mind the decision which not four and twenty hours after Hassan's intelligence she put into execution.

It was as Ben Ahmed had feared. The known popularity and rumoured riches of Alvar Rodriguez had excited the jealousy of that secret and awful tribunal, the Inquisition, one of whose innumerable spies, under the feigned name of Leyva, had obtained entrance within Alvar's hospitable walls. One unguarded word or movement, the faintest semblance of secrecy or caution, were all sufficient; nay, without these, more than a common share of wealth or felicity was enough for the unconscious victims to be marked, tracked, and seized, without preparation or suspicion of their fate. Alvar had chanced to mention his intended visit to Lisbon; and the better to conceal the agent of his arrest, as also to make it more secure, they waited till his arrival there, watched their opportunity, and seized and conveyed him to those cells whence few returned in life, propagating the charge of relapsed Judaism as the cause of his arrest. It was a charge too common for remark, and the power which interfered too mighty for resistance. The confusion of the arrest soon subsided; but it lasted long enough for the faithful Hassan to escape, and, by dint of very rapid travelling, he reached Montes not four hours after his master's seizure. The day was in consequence before them, and he ceased not to conjure his lady to fly at once; the officers of the Inquisition could scarcely be there before nightfall.

"You must take advantage of it, Hassan, and all of you who love me. For my child, my boy," she had clasped him to her bosom, and a convulsion contracted her beautiful features as she spoke, "you must take care of him; convey him to Holland or England. Take jewels and gold sufficient; and—and make him love his parents—he may never see either of them more. Hassan, Hassan, swear to protect my child!" she added, with a burst of such sudden and passionate agony, it seemed as if life or reason must bend beneath it. Bewildered by her words, as terrified by her emotion, Ben Ahmed gently removed the trembling child from the fond arms that for the first time failed to support him, gave him hastily to the care of his nurse, who was also a Jewess, said a few words in Hebrew, detailing what had passed, beseeching her to prepare for flight, and then returned to his mistress. The effects of that prostrating agony remained, but she had so far conquered, as to seem outwardly calm; and in answer to his respectful and anxious looks, besought him not to fear for her, nor to dissuade her from her purpose, but to aid her in its accomplishment. She summoned her household around her, detailed what had befallen, and bade them seek their own safety in flight; and when in tears and grief they left her, and but those of her own faith remained, she solemnly committed her child to their care, and informed them of her own determination to proceed directly to Lisbon. In vain Hassan Ben Ahmed conjured her to give up the idea; it was little short of madness. How could she aid his master? why not secure her own safety, that if indeed he should escape, the blessing of her love would be yet preserved him?

"Do not fear for your master, Hassan," was the calm reply; "ask not of my plans, for at this moment they seem but chaos, but of this be assured, we shall live or die together."

More she revealed not; but when the officers of the Inquisition arrived, near nightfall, they found nothing but deserted walls. The magnificent furniture and splendid paintings which alone remained, of course were seized by the Holy Office, by whom Alvar's property was also confiscated. Had his arrest been deferred three months longer, all would have gone—swept off by the same rapacious power, to whom great wealth was ever proof of great guilt—but as it was, the greater part, secured in Spain, remained untouched; a circumstance peculiarly fortunate, as Almah's plans needed the aid of gold.

We have no space to linger on the mother's feelings, as she parted from her boy; gazing on him, perhaps, for the last time. Yet she neither wept nor sighed. There was but one other feeling strong in that gentle bosom—a wife's devotion—and to that alone she might listen now.

Great was old Gonzalos' terror and astonishment when Almah, attended only by Hassan Ben Ahmed, and both attired in the Moorish costume, entered his dwelling and implored his concealment and aid. The arrest of Alvar Rodriguez had, of course, thrown every secret Hebrew into the greatest alarm, though none dared be evinced. Gonzalos' only hope and consolation was that Almah and her child had escaped; and to see her in the very centre of danger, even to listen to her calmly-proposed plans, seemed so like madness, that he used every effort to alarm her into their relinquishment. But this could not be; and with the darkest forebodings, the old man at length yielded to the stronger, more devoted spirit with whom he had to deal.

His mistress once safely under Gonzalos' roof, Ben Ahmed departed, under cover of night, in compliance with her earnest entreaties, to rejoin her child, and to convey him and his nurse to England, that blessed land, where the veil of secrecy could be removed.

About a week after the incarceration of Alvar, a young Moor sought and obtained admission to the presence of Juan Pacheco, the secretary of the Inquisition, as informer against Alvar Rodriguez. He stated that he had taken service with him as clerk or secretary, on condition that he would give him baptism and instruction in the holy Catholic faith; that Alvar had not yet done so; that many things in his establishment proclaimed a looseness of orthodox principles, which the Holy Office would do well to notice. Meanwhile he humbly offered a purse containing seventy pieces of gold, to obtain masses for his salvation.

This last argument carried more weight than all the rest. The young Moor, who boldly gave his name as Hassan Ben Ahmed (which was confirmation strong of his previous statement, as in Leyva's information of Alvar and his household the Moorish secretary was particularly specified), was listened to with attention, and finally received in Pacheco's own household, as junior clerk and servant to the Holy Office.

Despite his extreme youthfulness and delicacy of figure, face, and voice, Hassan's activity and zeal to oblige every member of the Holy Office, superiors and inferiors, gradually gained him the favour and goodwill of all. There was no end to his resources for serving others; and thus he had more opportunities of seeing the prisoners in a few weeks, than others of the same rank as himself had had in years. But the prisoner he most longed to see was still unfound, and it was not till summoned before his judges, in the grand hall of inquisition and of torture, Hassan Ben Ahmed gazed once more upon his former master. He had attended Pacheco in his situation of junior clerk, but had seated himself so deeply in the shade that, though every movement in both the face and form of Alvar was distinguishable to him, Hassan himself was invisible.

The trial, if trial such iniquitous proceedings may be called, proceeded; but in naught did Alvar Rodriguez fail in his bearing or defence. Marvellous and superhuman must that power have been which, in such a scene and hour, prevented all betrayal of the true faith the victims bore. Once Judaism confessed, the doom was death; and again and again have the sons of Israel remained in the terrible dungeons of the Inquisition—endured every species of torture during a space of seven, ten, or twelve years, and then been released, because no proof could be brought of their being indeed that accursed thing—a Jew. And then it was that they fled from scenes of such fearful trial to lands of toleration and freedom, and there embraced openly and rejoicingly that blessed faith, for which in secret they had borne so much.

Alvar Rodriguez was one of these—prepared to suffer, but not reveal. They applied the torture, but neither word nor groan was extracted from him. Engrossed with the prisoner, for it was his task to write down whatever disjointed words might escape his lips, Pacheco neither noticed nor even remembered the presence of the young Moor. No unusual paleness could be visible on his embrowned cheek, but his whole frame felt to himself to have become rigid as stone; a deadly sickness had crept over him, and the terrible conviction of all which rested with him to do alone prevented his sinking senseless on the earth.

The terrible struggle was at length at an end. Alvar was released for the time being, and remanded to his dungeon. Availing himself of the liberty he enjoyed in the little notice now taken of his movements, Hassan reached the prison before either Alvar or his guards. A rapid glance told him its situation, overlooking a retired part of the court, cultivated as a garden. The height of the wall seemed about forty feet, and there were no windows of observation on either side. This was fortunate, the more so as Hassan had before made friends with the old gardener, and pretending excessive love of gardening, had worked just under the window, little dreaming its vicinity to him he sought.

A well-known Hebrew air, with its plaintive Hebrew words sung tremblingly and softly under his window, first roused Alvar to the sense that a friend was near. He started, almost in superstitious terror, for the voice seemed an echo to that which was ever sounding in his heart. That loved one it could not be, nay, he dared not even wish it; but still the words were Hebrew, and, for the first time, memory flashed back a figure in Moorish garb who had flitted by him on his return to his prison, after his examination.

Hassan, the faithful Hassan! Alvar felt certain it could be none but he; though, in the moment of sudden excitement, the voice had seemed another's. He looked from the window; the Moor was bending over the flowers, but Alvar felt confirmed in his suspicions, and his heart throbbed with the sudden hope of liberty. He whistled, and a movement in the figure below convinced him he was heard.

One point was gained; the next was more fraught with danger, yet it was accomplished. In a bunch of flowers, drawn up by a thin string which Alvar chanced to possess, Ben Ahmed had concealed a file; and as he watched it ascend, and beheld the flowers scattered to the winds, in token that they had done their work, for Alvar dared not retain them in his prison, Hassan felt again the prostration of bodily power which had before assailed him for such a different cause, and it was an almost convulsive effort to retain his faculties; but a merciful Providence watched over him and Alvar, making the feeblest and the weakest, instruments of His all-sustaining love.

We are not permitted space to linger on the various ingenious methods adopted by Hassan Ben Ahmed to forward and mature his plans. Suffice it that all seemed to smile upon him. The termination of the garden wall led, by a concealed door, to a subterranean passage running to the banks of the Tagus. This fact, as also the secret spring of the trap, the old gardener in a moment of unwise conviviality imparted to Ben Ahmed, little imagining the special blessing which such unexpected information secured.

An alcayde and about twenty guards did sometimes patrol the garden within sight of Alvar's window;[3] but this did not occur often, such caution seeming unnecessary.

It had been an evening of unwonted festivity among the soldiers and servants of the Holy Office, which had at length subsided into the heavy slumbers of general intoxication. Hassan had supped with the gardener, and plying him well with wine, soon produced the desired effect. Four months had the Moor spent within the dreaded walls, and the moment had now come when delay need be no more. At midnight all was hushed into profound silence, not a leaf stirred, and the night was so unusually still that the faintest sound would have been distinguished. Hassan stealthily crept round the outposts. Many of the guards were slumbering in various attitudes upon their posts, and others, dependent on his promised watchfulness, were literally deserted. He stood beneath the window. One moment he clasped his hands and bowed his head in one mighty, piercing, though silent prayer, and then dug hastily in the flower-bed at his feet, removing from thence a ladder of ropes, which had lain there some days concealed, and flung a pebble with correct aim against the bars of Alvar's window. The sound, though scarcely loud enough to disturb a bird, reverberated on the trembling heart which heard, as if a thousand cannons had been discharged.

---

3. An *alcayde* (Spanish/Arabic) was a prison governor.

A moment of agonised suspense, and Alvar Rodriguez stood at the window, the bar he had removed, in his hand. He let down the string, to which Hassan's now trembling hands secured the ladder and drew it to the wall. His descent could not have occupied two minutes, at the extent; but to that solitary watcher what eternity of suffering did they seem! Alvar was at his side, had clasped his hands, had called him "Hassan! brother!" in tones of intense feeling, but no word replied. He sought to fly, to point to the desired haven, but his feet seemed suddenly rooted to the earth. Alvar threw his arm around him, and drew him forward. A sudden and unnatural strength returned. Noiselessly and fleetly as their feet could go, they sped beneath the shadow of the wall. A hundred yards alone divided them from the secret door. A sudden sound broke the oppressive stillness. It was the tramp of heavy feet and the clash of arms; the light of many torches flashed upon the darkness. They darted forward in the fearful excitement of despair; but the effort was void and vain. A wild shout of challenge—of alarm—and they were surrounded, captured, so suddenly, so rapidly, Alvar's very senses seemed to reel; but frightfully they were recalled. A shriek, so piercing, it seemed to rend the very heavens, burst through the still air. The figure of the Moor rushed from the detaining grasp of the soldiery, regardless of bared steel and pointed guns, and flung himself at the feet of Alvar.

"O God, my husband—I have murdered him!" were the strange appalling words which burst upon his ear, and the lights flashing upon his face, as he sank prostrate and lifeless on the earth, revealed to Alvar's tortured senses the features of his WIFE.

How long that dead faint continued Almah knew not, but when sense returned she found herself in a dark and dismal cell, her upper garment and turban removed, while the plentiful supply of water, which had partially restored life, had removed in a great degree the dye which had given her countenance its Moorish hue. Had she wished to continue concealment, one glance around her would have proved the effort vain. Her sex was already known, and the stern dark countenances near her breathed but ruthlessness and rage. Some brief questions were asked relative to her name, intent, and faith, which she answered calmly.

"In revealing my name," she said, "my intention must also be disclosed. The wife of Alvar Rodriguez had not sought these realms of torture and death, had not undergone all the miseries of disguise and servitude, but for one hope, one intent—the liberty of her husband."

"Thus proving his guilt," was the rejoinder. "Had you known him innocent, you would have waited the justice of the Holy Office to give him freedom."

"Justice!" she repeated, bitterly. "Had the innocent never suffered, I might have trusted. But I knew accusation was synonymous with death, and therefore came I here. For my faith, mine is my husband's."

"And know you the doom of all who attempt or abet escape? Death—death by burning! and this you have hurled upon him and yourself. It is not the Holy Office, but his wife who has condemned him," and with gibing laugh they left her, securing with heavy bolt and bar the iron door. She darted forward, beseeching them, as they hoped for mercy, to take her to her husband, to confine them underground a thousand fathoms deep, so that they might but be together; but only the hollow echo of her own voice replied, and the wretched girl sunk back upon the ground, relieved from present suffering by long hours of utter insensibility.

It was not till, brought from their respective prisons to hear pronounced on them the sentence of death, that Alvar Rodriguez and his heroic wife once more gazed upon each other.

They had provided Almah, at her own entreaty, with female habiliments; for, in the bewildering agony of her spirit, she attributed the failure of her scheme for the rescue of her husband to her having disobeyed the positive command of God, and adopted a male disguise, which in His eyes was abomination,[4] but which in her wild desire to save Alvar she had completely overlooked, and she now in consequence shrunk from the fatal garb with agony and loathing. Yet despite the haggard look of intense mental and bodily suffering, the loss of her lovely hair, which she had cut close to her head, lest by the merest chance its length and luxuriance should discover her, so exquisite, so touching, was her delicate loveliness, that her very judges, stern, unbending as was their nature, looked on her with an admiration almost softening them to mercy.

---

4. Deuteronomy 22.5 prohibits cross-dressing. Despite the familiarity of disguised clothing as a literary plot device in romance (e.g., Shakespeare), Almah's anxiety would have resonated with Aguilar's first readers in early Victorian England, when the ideology of separate spheres was gaining prominence.

And now, for the first time, Alvar's manly composure seemed about to desert him. He, too, had suffered almost as herself, save that her devotedness, her love, appeared to give him strength, to endow him with courage, even to look upon her fate, blended as it now was with his own, with calm trust in that merciful God who called him thus early to Himself. Almah could not realize such thoughts. But one image was ever present, seeming to mock her very misery to madness. Her effort had failed; had she not so wildly sought her husband's escape—had she but waited—they might have released him; and now, what was she but his murderess?

Little passed between the prisoners and their judges. Their guilt was sufficiently proved by their endeavours to escape, which in itself was a crime always visited by death; and for these manifold sins and misdemeanours they were sentenced to be burned alive, on All Saints' day, in the grand square of the Inquisition, at nine o'clock in the morning, and proclamation commanded to be made throughout Lisbon, that all who sought to witness and assist at the ceremony should receive remission of sins, and be accounted worthy servants of Jesus Christ. The lesser severity of strangling the victims before burning was denied them, as they neither repented nor had trusted to the justice and clemency of the Holy Office, but had attempted to avert a deserved fate by flight.

Not a muscle of Alvar's fine countenance moved during this awful sentence. He stood proudly and loftily erect, regarding those that spake with an eye, bright, stern, unflinching as their own; but a change passed over it as, breaking from the guard around, Almah flung herself on her knees at his feet.

"Alvar! Alvar! I have murdered—my husband, oh, my husband, say you forgive—forgive—"

"Hush, hush, beloved! mine own heroic Almah, fail not now!" he answered, with a calm and tender seriousness, which seeming to still that crushing agony, strengthened her to bear; and raising her, he pressed her to his breast.

"We have but to die as we have lived, my own! true to that God whose chosen and whose firstborn we are, have been, and shall be unto death, aye, and *beyond* it. He will protect our poor orphan, for He has promised the fatherless shall be His care. Look up, my beloved, and say you can face death with Alvar, calmly, faithfully, as you sought to live for him. God has chosen for us a better heritage than one of earth."

She raised her head from his bosom; the terror and the agony had passed from that sweet face—it was tranquil as his own.

"It was not my own death I feared," she said, unfalteringly, "it was but the weakness of human love; but it is over now. Love is mightier than death; there is only love in heaven."

"Aye!" answered Alvar, and proudly and sternly he waved back the soldiers who had hurried forward to divide them. "Men of a mistaken and bloody creed, behold how the scorned and persecuted Israelites can love and die. While there was a hope that we could serve our God, the Holy and the only One, better in life than in death, it was our duty to preserve that life, and endure torture for His sake, rather than reveal the precious secret of our sainted faith and heavenly heritage. But now that hope is at an end, now that no human means can save us from the doom pronounced, know ye have judged rightly of our creed. We ARE those chosen children of God, by you deemed blasphemous and heretic. Do what ye will, men of blood and guile, ye cannot rob us of our faith."

The impassioned tones of natural eloquence awed even the rude crowd around; but more was not permitted. Rudely severed, and committed to their own guards, the prisoners were borne to their respective dungeons. To Almah those earnest words had been as the voice of an angel, hushing every former pang to rest; and in the solitude and darkness of the intervening hours, even the thought of her child could not rob her soul of its calm, or prayer of its strength.

The 1st of November, 1755, dawned cloudless and lovely, as it had been the last forty days. Never had there been a season more gorgeous in its sunny splendour, more brilliant in the intense azure of its arching heaven than the present. Scarcely any rain had fallen for many months, and the heat had at first been intolerable, but within the last six weeks a freshness and coolness had infused the atmosphere and revived the earth.

As it was not a regular *auto da fè* (Alvar and his wife being the only victims),[5] the awful ceremony of burning was to take place in the square, of which the buildings of the Inquisition formed one side. Mass had been performed before daybreak, in the chapel of the Inquisition, at which the victims were compelled to be present, and about half-past

---

5. Correctly spelled *auto da fé*: act of faith (Portuguese). The execution of a sentence imposed by the Inquisition, usually the burning of a heretic.

seven the dread procession left the Inquisition gates. The soldiers and minor servitors marched first, forming a hollow square, in the centre of which were the stakes and huge faggots piled around. Then came the sacred cross, covered with a black veil, and its body-guard of priests. The victims, each surrounded by monks, appeared next, closely followed by the higher officers and inquisitors, and a band of fifty men, in rich dresses of black satin and silver, closed the procession.

We have no space to linger on the ceremonies always attendant on the burning of Inquisitorial prisoners. Although, from the more private nature of the rites, these ceremonies were greatly curtailed, it was rather more than half an hour after nine when the victims were bound to their respective stakes, and the executioners approached with their blazing brands.

There was no change in the countenance of either prisoner. Pale they were, yet calm and firm; all of human feeling had been merged in the martyr's courage and the martyr's faith.

One look had been exchanged between them—of love spiritualized to look beyond the grave—of encouragement to endure for their God, even to the end. The sky was still cloudless, the sun still looked down on that scene of horror; and then was a hush—a pause—for so it felt in nature, that stilled the very breathing of those around.

"Hear, O Israel, the Lord our God, the Lord is ONE—the Sole and Holy ONE; there is no unity like His unity!"[6] were the words which broke that awful pause, in a voice distinct, unfaltering, and musical as its wont; and it was echoed by the sweet tones from woman's lips, so thrilling in their melody, the rudest nature started. It was the signal of their fate. The executioners hastened forward, the brands were applied to the turf of the piles, the flames blazed up beneath their hand—when at that moment there came a shock as if the very earth were cloven asunder, the heavens rent in twain. A crash so loud, so fearful, so appalling, as if the whole of Lisbon had been shivered to its foundations, and a shriek, or rather thousands and thousands of human voices, blended in one wild piercing cry of agony and terror, seeming to burst from every quarter at the self-same instant, and fraught with universal woe. The

---

6. The first words of the Shema, avowing the unity of God, traditionally recited by those about to die.

buildings around shook, as impelled by a mighty whirlwind, though no sound of such was heard. The earth heaved, yawned, closed, and rocked again, as the billows of the ocean were lashed to fury. It was a moment of untold horror. The crowd assembled to witness the martyrs' death fled, wildly shrieking, on every side. Scattered to the heaving ground, the blazing piles lay powerless to injure; their bonds were shivered, their guards were fled. One bound brought Alvar to his wife, and he clasped her in his arms. "God, God of mercy, save us yet again! Be with us to the end!" he exclaimed, and faith winged the prayer. On, on he sped; up, up, in direction of the heights, where he knew comparative safety lay; but ere he reached them, the innumerable sights and sounds of horror that yawned upon his way! Every street, and square, and avenue was choked with shattered ruins, rent from top to bottom; houses, convents, and churches presented the most fearful aspect of ruin; while every second minute a new impetus seemed to be given to the convulsed earth, causing those that remained still perfect to rock and rend. Huge stones, falling from every crack, were crushing the miserable fugitives as they rushed on, seeking safety they knew not where. The rafters of every roof, wrenched from their fastenings, stood upright a brief while, and then fell in hundreds together, with a crash perfectly appalling. The very ties of nature were severed in the wild search for safety. Individual life alone appeared worth preserving. None dared seek the fate of friends — none dared ask, "Who lives?" in that one scene of universal death.

On, on sped Alvar and his precious burden, on, over the piles of ruins; on, unhurt amid the showers of stones, which, hurled in the air as easily as a ball cast from an infant's hand, fell back again laden with a hundred deaths; on, amid the rocking and yawning earth, beholding thousands swallowed up, crushed and maimed, worse than death itself, for they were left to a lingering torture — to die a thousand deaths in anticipating one; on, over the disfigured heaps of dead, and the unrecognized masses of what had once been magnificent and gorgeous buildings. His eye was well-nigh blinded with the shaking and tottering movement of all things animate and inanimate before him; and his path obscured by the sudden and awful darkness, which had changed that bright glowing hue of the sunny sky into a pall of dense and terrible blackness, becoming thicker and denser with every succeeding minute, till a darkness which might be felt enveloped that devoted city as with the grim shadow of death. His ear was deafened by the appalling sounds of human agony and Nature's wrath; for now, sounds as of a hundred water-spouts, the dull continued roar of subterranean thunder, becoming at times loud as the discharge of a thousand cannons; at others, resembling the sharp grating sound of hundreds and hundreds of chariots driven full speed over the stones; and this, mingled with the piercing shrieks of women, the hoarser cries and shouts of men, the deep terrible groans of mental agony, and the shriller screams of instantaneous death, had usurped the place of the previous awful stillness, till every sense of those who yet survived seemed distorted and maddened. And Nature herself, convulsed and freed from restraining bonds, appeared about to return to that chaos whence she had leaped at the word of God.

Still, still Alvar rushed forward, preserved amidst it all, as if the arm of a merciful Providence was indeed around him and his Almah, marking them for life in the very midst of death. Making his rapid way across the ruins of St. Paul's, which magnificent church had fallen in the first shock, crushing the vast congregation assembled within its walls, Alvar paused one moment, undecided whether to seek the banks of the river or still to make for the western heights. There was a moment's hush and pause in the convulsion of Nature, but Alvar dared not hope for its continuance. Ever and anon the earth still heaved, and houses opened from base to roof and closed without further damage. With a brief fervid cry for continued guidance and protection, scarcely conscious which way in reality he took, and still holding Almah to his bosom—so supernaturally strengthened that the weakness of humanity seemed far from him—Rodriguez hurried on, taking the most open path to the Estrella Hill. An open space was gained, half-way to the summit, commanding a view of the banks of the river and the ruins around. Panting, almost breathless, yet still struggling with his own exhaustion to encourage Almah, Alvar an instant rested, ere he plunged anew into the narrower streets. A shock, violent, destructive, convulsive as the first, flung them prostrate; while the renewed and increased sounds of wailing, the tremendous and repeated crashes on every side, the disappearance of the towers, steeples, and turrets which yet remained, revealed the further destructiveness which had befallen. A new and terrible cry added to the universal horror.

"The sea! the sea!" Alvar sprung to his feet and, clasped in each other's arms, he and Almah gazed beneath. Not a breath of wind stirred, yet the river (which being at that point four miles wide appeared like the element they had termed it) tossed and heaved as impelled by a mighty storm—and on it came, roaring, foaming, tumbling, as if every bound were loosed; on, over the land to the very heart of the devoted city, sweeping off hundreds in its course, and retiring with such velocity, and so far beyond its natural banks, that vessels were left dry which had five minutes before ridden in water seven fathoms deep. Again and again this phenomenon took place; the vessels in the river, at the same instant, whirled round and round with frightful rapidity, and smaller boats dashed upward, falling back to disappear beneath the booming waters. As if chained to the spot where they stood, fascinated by this very horror, Alvar and his wife yet gazed; their glance fixed on the new marble quay, where thousands and thousands of the fugitives had congregated, fixed, as if unconsciously foreboding what was to befall. Again the tide rushed in—on, on, over the massive ruins, heaving, raging, swelling, as a living thing; and at the same instant the quay and its vast burden of humanity sunk within an abyss of boiling waters, into which the innumerable boats around were alike impelled, leaving not a trace, even when the angry waters returned to their channel, suddenly as they had left it, to mark what had been.

"'Twas the voice of God impelled me hither, rather than pausing beside those fated banks. Almah, my best beloved, bear up yet a brief while more—He will spare and save us as He hath done now. Merciful Providence! Behold another wrathful element threatens to swallow up all of life and property which yet remains. Great God, this is terrible!"

And terrible it was: from three several parts of the ruined city huge fires suddenly blazed up, hissing, crackling, ascending as clear columns of liquid flame; up against the pitchy darkness, infusing it with tenfold horror—spreading on every side—consuming all of wood and wall which the earth and water had left unscathed; wreathing its serpent-like folds in and out the ruins, forming strange and terribly beautiful shapes of glowing colouring; fascinating the eye with admiration, yet bidding the blood chill and the flesh creep. Fresh cries and shouts had marked its rise and progress; but, aghast and stupefied, those who yet survived made no effort to check its way, and on every side it spread, forming lanes and squares of glowing red, flinging its lurid glare so vividly around, that even those on the distant heights could see to read by it; and fearful was the scene that awful light revealed. Now, for the first time, could Alvar trace the full extent of destruction which had befallen. That glorious city, which a few brief hours previous lay reposing in its gorgeous sunlight—mighty in its palaces and towers—in its churches, convents, theatres, magazines, and dwellings—rich in its numberless artisans and stores—lay perished and prostrate as the grim spectre of long ages past, save that the fearful groups yet passing to and fro, or huddled in kneeling or standing masses, some bathed in the red glare of the increasing fires, others black and shapeless—save when a sudden flame flashed on them, disclosing what they were—revealed a strange and horrible PRESENT, yet lingering amid what seemed the shadows of a fearful PAST. Nor was the convulsion of nature yet at an end—the earth still rocked and heaved at intervals, often impelling the hissing flames more strongly and devouringly forward, and by tossing the masses of burning ruin to and fro, gave them the semblance of a sea of flame. The ocean itself, too, yet rose and sunk, and rose again; vessels were torn from their cables, anchors wrenched from their soundings and hurled in the air—while the warring waters, the muttering thunders, the crackling flames, formed a combination of sounds which, even without their dread adjuncts of human agony and terror, were all-sufficient to freeze the very life-blood, and banish every sense and feeling, save that of stupifying dread.

But human love, and superhuman faith, saved from the stagnating horror. The conviction that the God of his fathers was present with him, and would save him and Almah to the end, never left him for an instant, but urged him to exertions which, had he not had this all-supporting faith, he would himself have deemed impossible. And his faith spake truth. The God of infinite mercy, who had stretched out His own right hand to save, and marked the impotence of the wrath and cruelty of man, was with him still, and, despite of the horrors yet lingering round them, despite of the varied trials, fatigues, and privations attendant on their rapid flight, led them to life and joy, and bade them stand forth the witnesses and proclaimers of His unfailing love, His everlasting providence!

With the great earthquake of Lisbon, the commencement of which our preceding pages have faintly endeavoured to portray, and its terrible effects on four millions of square miles, our tale has no further connection. The third day brought our poor fugitives to Badajoz, where Alvar's property had been secured. They tarried there only long enough to learn the blessed tidings of Hassan Ben Ahmed's safe arrival in England with their child; that his faithfulness, in conjunction with that of their agent in Spain, had already safely transmitted the bulk of their property to the English funds; and to obtain Ben Ahmed's address, forward tidings of their providential escape to him, and proceed on their journey.

An anxious but not a prolonged interval enabled them to accomplish it safely, and once more did the doubly-rescued press their precious boy to their yearning hearts, and feel that conjugal and parental love burned, if it could be, the dearer, brighter, more unspeakably precious, from the dangers they had passed; and not human love alone. The veil of secrecy was removed, they were in a land whose merciful and liberal government granted to the exile and the wanderer a home of peace and rest, where they might worship the God of Israel according to the law he gave; and in hearts like those of Alvar and his Almah, prosperity could have no power to extinguish or deaden the religion of love and faith which adversity had engendered.

The appearance of old Gonzalos and his family in England, a short time after Alvar's arrival there, removed their last remaining anxiety, and gave them increased cause for thankfulness. Not a member of the merchant's family, and more wonderful still, not a portion of his property, had been lost amid the universal ruin; and to this very day, his descendants recall his providential preservation by giving, on every returning anniversary of that awful day, certain articles of clothing to a limited number of male and female poor.[7]

---

7. A fact. [Author's note.]

Ludwig Philippson, "The Three Brothers" (1854)
Translated from the German by Jonathan M. Hess

Ludwig Philippson (1811–89) was born and raised in Dessau, the capital of the small German principality of Anhalt-Dessau. The son of a prominent Hebrew printer who died when Philippson was three, he was among the first generation of Jews to become university-trained rabbis in the German lands. Philippson studied first in Halle and then in Berlin, where he attended lectures by Hegel and other luminaries while pursuing his Jewish education privately, outside the university. After earning a doctorate in classical philology in 1833, Philippson accepted a position as a rabbi in Magdeburg, the capital of the Prussian province of Saxony. During his close to thirty-year tenure in Magdeburg he was known as a moderate reformer. Philippson supported himself during his student years by writing for a variety of newspapers and journals, and in Magdeburg he emerged as one of the premier Jewish publicists in Europe. In 1837, he founded the *Allgemeine Zeitung des Judentums* (Universal Jewish Newspaper), which quickly established itself as one of the leading Jewish periodicals in the world. Philippson's paper, which he edited until his death in 1889, was published continuously until 1922, when it was absorbed by the newspaper of German Jewry's largest organization, the Central Association of German Citizens of the Jewish Faith.

As editor of the *Allgemeine Zeitung des Judentums*, Philippson actively promoted the development of Jewish literature, publishing regular installments of his older brother Phöbus's short novel *Die Marannen* (The Marranos) in the first volume. Philippson wrote two major novels and numerous short stories and novellas, many of which were first published in the *Allgemeine Zeitung des Judentums* or in the *Jüdisches Volksblatt* (Popular Jewish Paper), a weekly supplement launched in 1853 that was eventually incorporated into the paper as its separate arts and culture section. As the cofounder of the Institut zur Förderung der israelitischen Literatur (Institute for the Promotion of Israelite Literature, 1855–73), a pioneering Jewish book club, he helped place two hundred thousand copies of the club's fifty-five titles—including his own novels *Sepphoris und Rom* (Sepphoris and Rome, 1866) and *Jakob Tirado* (1867)—in Jewish homes and libraries on both sides of the Atlantic. He also produced a popular German translation of the Hebrew Bible, wrote widely on theological matters, and coedited with his brother Phöbus the literary anthology *Saron*, which went through numerous editions in the nineteenth century. Much of Philippson's work was translated into Hebrew, Yiddish, and Ladino as well as into many non-Jewish languages in the nineteenth century.

"Die drei Brüder" (The Three Brothers), originally published in serial form in the *Jüdisches Volksblatt* in 1854, was reprinted frequently in *Saron* and other nineteenth- and early twentieth-century German anthologies of Jewish prose. Historical fiction foregrounding the heroism of the Jewish past was Philippson's favored genre of German-Jewish literature, and much of his fiction focused on the history of Spanish Jewry. In "The Three Brothers," he builds on the popularity of Grace Aguilar's novel *The Vale of Cedars* (1850), the German translation of which was among the offerings of the Institute for the Promotion of Israelite Literature. Like Aguilar, he tells a tale of a family hiding from the Inquisition in a mountain refuge. But through the stories of the three brothers that he grafts onto Aguilar's melancholy look at the last days of Spanish Jewry, Philippson moves beyond the idealization of Sephardic Jewry typical of nineteenth-century Jewish culture. He gives his readers a whirlwind tour of the world around 1500, drawing on both the exoticism of literary genres like the Oriental tale and the adventure novel and the rage for reading travel literature that dominated the nineteenth-century book market. In the tale of the third and youngest brother, Sanzo, Philippson offers a corrective to the Austrian writer Adalbert Stifter's celebrated 1842 novella "Abdias," creating a model of a Jew in the Sahara that is the antithesis of Stifter's highly ambivalent title character. Unlike Aguilar, who celebrates feminine piety, Philippson's model of heroism in this text is an unequivocally male one. Each of the stories of his three brothers outlines the ways Jewish men managed to overcome the trauma of the expulsion from Spain to stake out new public roles for themselves in the Iberian diaspora.

I.

This story takes place at the beginning of the sixteenth century, in a deep gorge in the Sierra Nevada, whose picturesque mountains traverse the Spanish province of Granada.

The steep cliffs all around were gazing boldly upward, and wherever one looked, one saw either exposed rock or brushwood and the densest primeval forest imaginable. It was as if no human being had ever set foot here. Nevertheless, on various sides of the gorge, almost entirely hidden from view, there were small trails leading down from the tops of the cliffs through the cracks and crevices of massive boulders. These hardly deserved to be called trails. They were actually just steep tracks down the cliffs that only an experienced mountaineer would notice. After traveling just a few minutes down the dangerous section of the trail, however, the descent became less precipitous, rewarding the bold hiker with a dense canopy of trees. Down in this seemingly inaccessible gorge, strangely, there was no rushing brook; it was as if the scraggly peaks that formed this canyon barred the outflow of water all around. But there was a small, ice-cold spring trickling forth at the bottom of the gorge. The imposing limestone cliffs on the northern side of the ravine rose out of the ground like a massive wall, and from the bottom, it became clear that the gorge was in fact much wider than one would have supposed from above. In the middle of the canyon, where the spring was, the dense shrubbery of the forest receded a bit, as if it had been cleared by human hands, and in the center of this small round area stood a modest, square structure. This building was humble in scope and had simple walls without windows. It was difficult to imagine why someone would have worked so hard to remove these materials from the cliffs and the forest to construct such a crude structure here.

It was the month of August 1504, and the sun was already beginning to set in the west when a tall and dignified figure stepped forth from behind the building. The man's powerful gait, his unyielding demeanor, the masculine features of his face, and the sparkle in his eyes all indicated that he was far from old age, even though his undulating beard had more than a few hints of gray and the hair on his head was practically silver. He came out of a small gate at the backside of the structure and then strolled back toward it, sitting down on a stone bench on its evening side. Lost in thought, he spoke to himself: "Today is the ninth day of the month of Av,[1] and it was on this day ten years ago that our father died. If my brothers have not arrived here by the time the sun sets in the evening, I shall mourn all of them and consider myself all alone on God's earth. Oh, to lose both of my brothers, that would be a severe test!" His chin fell onto his chest as he recalled earlier times. Ten years is a long time for a human being to live through, as easy as it may be to reflect back on such a period of time once it has passed.

---

1. The ninth day of Av (*Tisha B'Av* in Hebrew) is a solemn fast day commemorating the destruction of the first and the second temple in Jerusalem. It is also used to commemorate other major tragedies, including the expulsion from Spain.

Whom was he thinking of? Ten years ago three brothers said farewell to each other at their father's grave, each going his separate way out into the world. They had spent two years living a hidden life in this gorge with their father before he died in their arms. They buried him here, doing their best to create this simple structure over his grave, and then they left their mountain refuge, making each other the solemn vow that wherever they might be on the tenth anniversary of their father's death, they would return here to see and embrace each other again. If one of them should not be able to be present, the others would have to mourn his death. And why were they banished from the world in this way? Not voluntarily. Jews had experienced centuries of happiness and peace in Spain. There had been long periods of magnificent scholarship and science, upstanding contributions to the arts, trades, and agriculture, and numerous services performed for king and fatherland. But then Ferdinand and Isabella, the bigoted founders of the Spanish Inquisition, issued an order of expulsion for all Jews in Spain, without respect to position, fortune, age, and way of life. Only those who prayed to the cross in the Roman Catholic manner were allowed to breathe on Spanish soil. It made no difference here whether these Jews were rightful property owners or not—or that many of their ancestors had settled in this country long before Christianity appeared on earth. All of them, without exception, were ordered to leave behind their beloved homes, the cradles of their children, and the graves of their fathers.

At the time of the order of expulsion, Don Luigi was an old man of eighty, and his three unmarried sons were all still living in his home in Carthagena.[2] The serious, learned Don Abraham was approaching forty; the clever Don José was thirty; and the athletic Sanzo, who was well versed in the arts of chivalry, was twenty-five. Don Luigi could not resolve to leave Spain. Before the day came that the royal decree had set for the Jews' departure, a gang came into the city to ransack Jewish homes. Sanzo set his father on a mule, and bearing a sword, he accompanied him and his two brothers out of the city and into the Sierra Nevada. They traveled on rudimentary, little-used trails until they reached this gorge, which he had somehow discovered on his ramblings with his young noble friends. They settled in as best they could in the

---

2. A port city in southeastern Spain.

splendid climate of the gorge. Sanzo, using a diverse set of disguises, would leave the gorge to go out and supply them with the food they needed, and the forests also did their part here by furnishing them with natural traps and snares to catch game. They lived in this way until the messenger of the lord sent for their elderly father. At that point the sons knew that they could not continue to spend their life in this place. After the one who kept them together passed away, they had to rejoin the rest of the world. They thus went their separate ways with profound sorrow, making the vow that we mentioned above.

The eldest, Don Abraham, had arrived a week earlier in the gorge. He had spent the last seven days hidden from the hustle and bustle of the world, praying at his father's grave and anticipating his brothers' arrival. His hope was now beginning to yield to doubt. He gazed at the setting sun full of melancholy, as if the life of his brothers depended on its final rays for the day.

But behold, he had hardly spent half an hour lost in reflection sitting on that stone bench when it sounded as if someone were working hard to break his way through the brushwood. Branches crackled and limbs shook. Don Abraham quickly jumped up, and there before him stood his brother José. He recognized him immediately, even though his slender frame was bent over somewhat, his brow had become furrowed, and his dark black hair had thinned considerably. Abraham's loving eye quickly took in the great changes in his brother; clearly this now forty-year-old man had experienced unspeakable hardships and had had more than his share of difficulties and worries. But when he caught sight of Abraham, José ran to his brother faster than one might have imagined. He embraced him and exclaimed in a clear and sonorous voice: "You're here already, brother Abraham? You look like yourself! Have you been waiting long? For several days I was captivated by the marketplace in Almeria, where I landed. I had to see whether the old traffic in the known commodities was still flourishing, whether one could still buy 'apes and ivory and peacocks and silver,' as scripture says.[3] Oh, Abraham, how beautiful Spain is. But alas, it is no place for us. You know, I saw places we knew. No, let's not talk about that. Isn't Sanzo here yet? How have you been, dear brother? You've changed. But I myself have

---

3. 1 Kings 10:22. [Note in the original.]

stayed the same, don't you think? Well, we all age, and life is difficult, particularly for refugees like us."

Such were the comments that spewed forth from the agile man's lips. He carefully placed the bags he had with him onto the stone bench and without ever once letting go of his brother's hand he sat down. He and Abraham were lost in each other's eyes. It was as if his tongue were chatting away while his spirit, high above, were pondering profound thoughts that his tongue could not even fathom. Then he jumped up and embraced his beloved brother once again, and tears poured down his cheek. "Abraham," he whispered, "have you come to our father's grave all alone?"

"My life's journey has been a solitary one," Abraham responded. "I have never known the pleasures of domestic life."

"And I, Abraham, I buried them after tasting them intensely for a very short time." He desperately clung onto his brother's hand, and his head fell onto his brother's shoulder.

The brothers sat down. Abraham went to get some food that he had prepared, and their thoughts drifted on to their third brother, the chivalrous Sanzo. They did not dare utter his name, for the sun was about to set. When the sun finally set, nightfall set in quickly, filling the forest with dense darkness, and Sanzo had still not appeared. José had quickly prepared a fire in the middle of the clearing so that Sanzo, if he were still to come, would have a light to lead him to their refuge. Soon a sliver of moon rose up over the cliffs in the east, and they heard a quiet and gentle sound in the distance. It sounded like a horn, but it was a faint noise moving through the branches and leaves of the trees that was hard to make out.

"What is that?" José exclaimed.

Abraham listened. The sound repeated itself. "It may be a message from our brother."

"But how? Could he possibly . . . ?"

"No, not from beyond the grave, José! Listen, the sound is getting stronger, he must be approaching!" Quickly, he grabbed a torch and entered the forest, where the sound was coming from. José did the same, both of them raising their voices crying "Sanzo! Sanzo!"

"Hark!" a powerful voice responded, "over here, Abraham, over here, brother José." Sharp, youthful sounds resounded through the man's call.

A few minutes later a tall, strong man in his prime became visible in the firelight. He was armed, with a sword at his side. He was holding, in his left hand, the hand of a splendid eight-year-old boy. On his right side he was carrying a tender, six-year-old boy whose fearful head of blond locks was buried in his father's shoulders. This was the way Sanzo appeared to the old Abraham and the declining José in the hidden gorge in the Alpujarras.

The reader should not expect that we will be describing the first hours the brothers spent together. Indeed, having a sense of the stream of feelings that was raging so powerfully through the hearts of the three men would make it superfluous to tell their stories. And how the brothers told each other about the fates they had met up with is precisely what we want to relate here.

II.

"It was a very difficult road that brought me here," Abraham began. "Unlike you, I could not choose to land in Almeria or Malaga. I had to take the land route, traveling from the land of the Franks over the Pyrenees through all of Spain. It was a journey full of difficulties, dangers, and pain. I could not risk showing my face in large cities and populated areas, where you find the thugs of the Inquisition monitoring and persecuting everyone who looks like a foreigner. I had to go to small villages to seek out the meager food that the law allows us to eat, and I had to conceal my name and position, my nationality and religion, as carefully as possible. I traveled only by night and sought out solitary areas during the day. And many times I was almost discovered and captured, which would have meant the most frightful death imaginable! But my journey was not just marked by fear. Everywhere in Spain today human folly is destroying the traces of the people of Israel, who had flourished here until recently, and this pained my heart. Israel's magnificent schools have been turned into monasteries. Synagogues have been transformed into chapels or storehouses for grain. Jewish graveyards have been made into pleasure gardens and vineyards. It pains me so to see our much beloved Spain in this state! Robbed of its hardworking and chivalrous Moors and its industrious and learned Jews, it lies largely desolate, with whole portions of its population cleared away. And now it's sending its most vigorous men to the new, recently discovered India![4] Where will all this end? This was the route I took to the meeting place we had agreed on, and it is similar to the path my life has taken in the ten years we have been separated. It has been a constant stream of difficulties, dangers, and pain. All alone, I have had to find my own sustenance and support, and I have had to wander in the dark so as to avoid the gaze of those who hate us. Yet I have not perished. After all, I have returned here to find you both, dear brothers. In the same way, I managed to live and prosper.

"I don't want to burden you with further details of my journey through Spain, just as I don't need to tell you about every moment of my life story for the last ten years. You know how divine providence often brings one's fortunes together, as if into a knot, only to loosen this knot so that our fortunes can spin forth on their own in peace? Let me tell you about the knot in which the web of my fate was bound.

"You know, of course, about my life before. I dedicated myself to the study of our sacred teachings and our divine law. I studied and taught, and that was the main occupation of my life until that terrible expulsion and our escape. Let me tell you that there still are those who feel my absence today, and I'm not speaking just of those from our community. Many non-Jews came to study secular subjects with me. I found the world beyond Spain entirely different. I went to France and found that our coreligionists there had descended into an appalling state of primitive ignorance. There was no trace of culture and education, but only squalor, both in the way that they lived and in the way that they kept the legacy of our great tradition alive. Philosophy and mathematics, grammar and history are subjects that are entirely unknown in their schools. All they do there is to answer questions about the casuistry of the law, and when such questions don't exist, they invent them. Through such tests they strive to sharpen their acumen, and herein lies their claim to fame. In much the same way, I found them estranged from the rest of the world. A deep gulf cuts them off from the rest of humanity. They live in both spiritual and social ghettoes! Oh, how different was it in our Spain! I found many of our refugees in southern France, but they were still wandering around, and few had settled down. I tried to give lec-

---

4. America, which was first seen as the east coast of India. [Note in the original.]

tures in several places, but either the local rabbis wouldn't permit me to speak or the people didn't understand me, and I had to take my walking staff and move on. Their religious services had also fallen into such an extraordinary state of chaos. I shudder when I think of the way they pronounced the sacred language, or the way they put the most befuddled and incomprehensible prayers one can imagine into the service where they didn't belong. And then there's their restlessness and chatter during prayer! Spaniards used to a different style of prayer were naturally so repelled by all this that they could not stand for it. It's no surprise that whenever a sufficient number of Spanish and Portuguese refugees gathered in a certain place, they created their own congregation with their own services and institutions. Inevitably, this would deeply offend the existing community. I saw a rift arising between the children of one tribe that could not have been bigger had it been between members of two different religions. This was bitterly painful for me to observe. In the best case these two groups avoided each other entirely. Certainly, no one would have thought of mixing, intermarriage, or anything of that sort. Our people, to be sure, are to be faulted here for pride, arrogance, and condescension. And the French Jews made the mistake of crudely turning away the unhappy wanderers from their doors!

"Recognizing these problems made me very unhappy. I could envision these divisions persisting for centuries. We would become even more deeply humiliated, and they would rush to catch up with us, and then to surpass our cultural achievements and level of education. I tried to speak to our people about this issue, but to no avail, and this estranged many of them from me.

"One day I was walking on my way to the gates of the city of Nîmes. It was an oppressive, humid day, and the main road was deserted. I myself was creeping through the large forest extending on for miles between me and my destination. I had hoped I would be able to cool off in the woods, but instead of refreshing shade, the pine trees were filling the air with the stifling stench of pitch. Nevertheless, I gathered my energy and did my best to keep moving along. I was expected in Nîmes, for it was the day before the "Sabbath of Repentance,"[5] and I had been

---

5. The Sabbath of Repentance (Shabbat Shuvah) is the Sabbath between the beginning of the Jewish New Year (Rosh Hashanah) and the Day of Atonement (Yom Kippur).

asked to give the usual sermon in the small congregation that had been founded there a year earlier. A Spanish Jew whom I had arranged to meet in a small city along the way had held me up with a very difficult question concerning marital law. I thus had to hurry to reach Nîmes in time, and I was already concerned that I was so tired that I might not make it at all.

"All of a sudden I heard a desperate call for help. The road ahead of me led over and around several hills, and it was thus impossible for me to see who was calling out. But I was sure that I was hearing women ahead of me who were about to be attacked, and their cries of desperation were growing fainter. I knew that there were bandits who made this region unsafe and I assumed they were behind this commotion. I had no weapon apart from my gnarled walking staff, which was filled with lead, but I bravely rushed ahead, being clever enough to yell out as loudly as I could, 'Help, help! We're coming, we're coming! Benno, Henri, Jacques, come help, hurry, women are screaming!' While calling out, I hit my stick against stones and trees so as to make as much noise as possible. When I made it around the bend, I saw a scene that filled me with fright and horror. A servant lay on the ground swimming in blood; his skull had been shattered. Two dreadful-looking fellows were about to tie up two women by their hands and feet. They had already taken them out of a small, open coach and stuffed pieces of cloth in their mouths. I did not hesitate for a moment. Continuing to call out to my alleged comrades, I went for the two evil doers, swinging my staff. I do not know whether it was the fear of God that came over them or my sudden appearance coupled with the fear that others were close behind. But the bandits left their victims and jumped over the ditch into the forest. I followed them, and with superhuman power I hit one of them so hard that he fell down. The other escaped. I hurried back, freed the women from their bonds, and calmed them down as much as I could. I then helped them get back in the coach, for I was scared that the one who had escaped would go seek assistance. He might decide to return when he saw from the thicket that I was alone. I whipped the horses to get them moving, and the animals seemed to recognize the dire situation we were in. They rode away from the scene of the crime in a mad gallop, leaving behind the dead servant and the bandit I took for dead.

"We drove on for over an hour in silence. We passed through numerous villages and saw other travelers and coaches. Finally, we considered ourselves safe, and at that point I turned around and gave the women a friendly greeting. They had just embraced each other. They were an older and younger woman, and I saw quickly that they were mother and daughter, and likely fellow Jews. The daughter lay on her mother's breast, pale as a ghost, with tears running down her cheeks. Her mother had regained her composure and was caressing the girl's face. I had hardly slowed down the horses and turned to greet them when the mother expressed her most sincere gratitude to me with a look of deep appreciation; the daughter quickly grabbed my hand and kissed it. I asked them to compose themselves and to join me in thanking God, who always puts danger in our path and sends us help at the right time. They continued to express their gratitude and praise the devotion I had shown them. I could not get them to stop, and when they found out that I was a Jew, they opened up the treasure chests of their hearts to me even more. I learned that they were the wife and daughter of the rabbi of the local congregation in Nîmes, and that they had been traveling to visit the woman's sister who was near death. Today, because of the upcoming holiday, they had to return home, and they did so without being able to bring any hope with them. We reached Nîmes, and following the women's instructions, I drove the coach directly to the rabbi's house. It was getting late, so I resisted their pleas to go in and went on to my host. The small group that came to hear my sermon was pleased, and they hired me to spend the winter in Nîmes and run a Beth Midrash there.[6]

"Several days went by, and I was kept too busy to have the chance to go see how the women whom I had saved were faring. After the Day of Atonement had passed, the rabbi sent for me and invited me to his home. When I arrived, I found a shrunken little gray-haired man who did not tire of expressing his gratitude to me. This was a strange feeling. There I stood, with the respectable height and breadth that the Lord gave me, in my stately Spanish dress. Here was this little man—the representative of French Jewry—jumping back and forth in front of

---

6. A Beth Midrash is a house of study, a place where Jewish men traditionally gather to study the Torah, Talmud, and other sacred writings.

me, and he spoke in rather the same fashion. He mixed in a word from scripture and then a saying from the Talmud, applying everything to the current situation often in a very forced manner, as if he were composing an epigram. He would then make a 'hee, hee' noise and laugh, raising his eyebrows and opening up his toothless mouth while his little white goatee danced up and down. But then the door opened, and in walked his daughter. Slim and sublime, she was dressed in simple but becoming clothes. Her magnificent face was glowing, and her brown eyes were shining brightly. Her mother, the stately matron, followed her in. I bowed deep down in reverence, but the women stepped toward me and they both expressed the depths of their gratitude. Since they insisted, I agreed to dine with them for the Festival of Booths.[7] Oh, I can still see the little hut decorated with mediocre pictures and copper hanging baskets. Those were very blissful hours that I spent there. Despite the shallow chatter, the rabbi's 'hee, hee' and his forced application of proverbs, the girl's gaze and her mother's words encouraged me to open up to them. I told them about Spain, about our past, and about you both. Oh, why don't I get to the point, dear brothers? I, the forty-two-year-old refugee who had known nothing but scholarship and the word of God up until that point, experienced love in that hut. I felt and I awakened love. I professed my love, and it was reciprocated, and her parents were pleased."

Memories overcame Abraham as he told this story. He stopped talking, and his eyes became teary. But soon he pulled himself together and continued. "We all know," Abraham went on, "that passion that sets in late in life is particularly forceful. Oh, I had dedicated my entire youth to studying, committing myself exclusively to scholarly pursuits. Now, in my prime, I finally experienced the power of what people call love. It overcame me and overpowered me, and I gave into it without resistance. Did I do the right thing? I often wondered about this in those few days, but since everyone around me seemed to be in agreement, and since my bride looked at me with such satisfaction and happiness, I quickly dispelled all my concerns. I did not even consider whether

---

7. The Festival of Booths (Sukkot in Hebrew) is a holiday following Yom Kippur that celebrates the fall harvest and commemorates the forty years the Israelites spent wandering in the desert. In memory of the period of wandering, observant Jews spend Sukkot living and dining in temporary dwellings.

I, still a refugee, should even consider binding another being to myself. As you know, we were not entirely without means when went our separate ways, and I still had most of the jewels that were mine. I thus thought it would be easy to settle down. In addition, my sermons in the small Spanish congregation were meeting with much approval, and, as I mentioned before, they were entreating me to spend the winter in Nîmes to teach a series of classes in a small Beth Midrash. I thus settled in Nîmes, and it was decided that I would marry the rabbi's daughter in the spring, before Passover.

"My engagement to Dina quickly made me the talk of the town in the rather large Jewish community, and the enthusiasm that the Spanish Jews showed for me also did its part in making me an object of curiosity. When I began my lectures in the Beth Midrash, the room could barely hold the audience. After giving one or two, I soon had to look for a larger room to accommodate all those who came to hear me. The topic I had chosen for the series of lectures was one that lay close to my heart. I found my fellow Jews faithfully and firmly observing the law, and their teachers were also committed to studying it. This in and of itself was a cause for joy and inspiration. But nowhere did the *spirit* of religion seem to be flourishing. No one felt the need to grapple with doctrinal questions or with issues of morality. They thought that observing the law was sufficient in and of itself. Everywhere I looked I saw a spiritual drought, a horrific emptiness that threatened to issue in intellectual poverty and degeneration the likes of which Judah had not yet seen. The great thinkers of Spanish descent were almost entirely unknown, and I thus began speaking about the writings of Albo, Bechai, and Abarbanel. I went on to Yehuda Halevi and closed with the *More*.[8] That is, it was my plan to proceed in this way.

"All these ideas were new for my audience, and they had never heard anything like it. It may have been the novelty of the material I was presenting, or perhaps it was the accessible and rousing style I used in my lectures, but they were all carried away, and the enthusiasm they shared with each other was so tremendous that I was soon surrounded by love and adoration. This encouraged me more and more, and I felt a type

---

8. The reference here is to Maimonides' *Moreh Nevochim* (Guide for the Perplexed), a twelfth-century masterpiece of medieval rationalist philosophy.

of satisfaction that I had never felt before. Soon I thought it was my calling to herald in a spiritual revival in this region. Oh, what blessed hopes came over me as I imagined the growing influence I could have! Ultimately, however, I was not to be exalted in my efforts. Instead, I was humiliated.

"All the Jews in Nîmes who had some degree of education enjoyed my lectures and spoke of nothing else. My future father-in-law, the local rabbi, was annoyed by this. When everyone but a few ignorant people started to leave his Beth Midrash for mine, he was rankled even further. He himself was supremely narrow-minded and poorly educated, and he knew he had no way of competing with me to retrieve his lost flock. This drove him mad. Unfortunately, I did not see the storm that was brewing. I believed that my small triumphs in my lectures were sowing love for me, unaware that hatred and anger were scheming to take it all away from me. At first when I visited my bride, I did not notice that my future father-in-law was never there, and for a long time I failed to notice that Dina herself always looked so oppressed and unhappy. Whenever I held her in my arms, she became tempestuous and passionate. She would cry, and I couldn't figure out why. I was too naïve, and inexperienced as I was, I thought this was just the way girls were. This is how it was for quite some time.

"In the winter, many of the Spaniards were out of town and there weren't enough around to form a *minyan*.[9] I thus tended to go to the French synagogue at this time. For three weeks I had been only seeing my future father-in-law during services, after which he always ran off in a hurry. One Sabbath, the week after I had announced that I'd soon be dealing with the great *Moreh Nevochim* in my lectures,[10] the rabbi stepped in front of the lectern and rambled on for a long time, going from one topic to the next. With his usual nitpicking manner, he explained passages from scripture and Talmud that did not even appear to be related to each other. He then took a short break from talking. When he started up again, he surprised me with his remarkable agility. He forced together all the passages that he had cited to form a

---

9. The Hebrew word *minyan* refers to the minimum number, ten adults, required for a Jewish prayer service.

10. The great philosophical work by Maimonides (Rambam). [Note in the original.]

diatribe against pseudo teachers who, like locusts, are chased out of one region only to descend on another where these undesired pests devour the land and its people. I was excited, for he was giving a new and lively speech, and I had no idea where this all was going. It seemed as if the small man were getting bigger and towering in the air. Then he began to scream: 'And you people, is it right that you are leaving the fields that have supplied you with the bread of proper doctrine for so long? You are reaching for the poison that is being given to you because it is coated with honey, because it seems new, and because you do not know it yet. What is going on? You want to learn about a book that the greatest and most pious rabbis in France see as the grounds for excommunication (חרם). This book is worthy of being burned in the fires of hell, even though it carries the name Rambam. Is this how we are being mocked? Is this gratitude for the hospitality which we have shown these strangers? They're trying to defile and eradicate our sacred religion in our pious fatherland, after God punished them for destroying it in their own land. Curse them, curse them! Let us not keep company with the villains. Whoever takes them in is a sinner; whoever seeks them out is an evil-doer; whoever spends time with them is a malefactor. *Let us give the sinners no peace!*'

"I was not the only one mortified as I listened. So was everyone else. My innermost soul was raging in anger, but I didn't know quite what to do. Suddenly, I found myself stepping forward, almost involuntarily, and my mouth opened up to answer the screeching, cursing little man who was pounding on the lectern and jumping up in the air while sending lightning bolts and basilisks at me with his small, wide-open, green eyes. As I moved toward the lectern, everyone stepped back, and soon I stood directly across from the rabbi. I had hardly opened my mouth to say, 'How can you? In a holy place?' when I noticed a group of fellows dressed in rags. They had either been paid off or incited by fanaticism, and they screamed out furiously: 'Let's get rid of the Spaniard! Let's get rid of the heretic!' A deluge of curse words was then heard in the sacred hall, and I noticed these fellows coming after me with their fists. I looked around and saw pale, cold faces putting on distant looks as they withdrew cowardly. No one stood by me. No one joined forces with me. Just an hour earlier these people had shown me nothing but affection and courteousness. When I looked around now, they seemed pathetic to me, and I turned and left the building. Their silence and proud composure was enough to silence dogs. When I was outside, though, I heard them yapping and rumbling. I paid no attention.

"Back at home, I pulled myself together and reflected on what had happened. Given how the people had behaved when they heard the wrongheaded and hateful rabbi's curse of excommunication, I realized that I could only continue my lectures if something were done explicitly to redress what had happened. But was this really to be expected? There weren't enough Spaniards for me to lecture just to them. And who was the one who dealt me this blow? The father of my future wife! Could this have happened without the firm intent to destroy the bond that connected me to him? The more I thought about what the angry rabbi had said, the more I became sure of it. Both my honor and my love were about to become the casualties of a shipwreck caused by the folly of a wounded spirit who could not bear being challenged. I couldn't make sense of all this. But when a courier came and handed me a letter that had been composed the day before, on Friday, things began to make more sense. The letter contained the final words of the rabbi's sermon and his signature, nothing else. This little man had carefully thought through his maneuvers. Everything he did had been prepared in advance!

"I was outraged. I felt I had only one choice, to publish an open letter to the man who had hurled the curse of excommunication at me. I would publicly accuse him of the crudest ignorance and claim that he was not capable of occupying a rabbi's post with honor. I had plenty of proof for this. I would also challenge him to a public disputation and invite him to have a tribunal of other rabbis judge our case. I had resolved to take this route. But how did Dina feel about all this? Hadn't she also already destroyed the bonds that connected her to me? I spent an entire day in unspeakable anguish. No one came by. But then I pulled myself together. I paid a visit to my bride's aunt, who had always been good to me. She took me in, and what is more, she accepted me with tears and deep pain. She was a woman full of proper feeling. She recognized what had motivated her brother-in-law's actions, and she did not just assume that he was mistaken. She knew he was going after me intentionally. But this was bitter consolation for me. She acquainted me with the pitiful situation in which Dina and her good mother found themselves. Dina was caught between her love for her fiancé and her father's threat of excommunication. What could she do? She was suffering so under this cruelty. I asked the aunt whether I might have an audience with Dina in her home, and she agreed.

"We met at dusk in the honorable woman's home. I had forged and hatched so many plans by then. It was a painful reunion. For a long time, Dina lay at my breast without being able to compose herself. She apologized for her father, who had behaved so poorly toward the homeless stranger in their midst and who had chosen such an awful way to show his gratitude to the man who saved his wife and child. She assured me of her deep and eternal love for me. The girl's desperation brought me to my senses. I spoke clearly and simply to her. Either she could honor the sacred vow she had made and go with me, or she could respect her father's orders and we would have to go our separate ways. There was no third choice, I explained, and it was time to make a decision. I could not remain any longer in this town, where I had had such sweet but also such bitter experiences. She understood what I was saying, but what could she do? She threw herself again into my arms, saying she could not leave me and did not want for us to be apart. We were still deep in conversation thinking things through and reassuring each other when we heard a screeching voice coming after us with execrations and threats. Somehow the old rabbi had learned of our meeting. He grabbed his daughter with arms of iron and took her away. He would not listen to my objections and my words of wrath. And Dina! The presence of her father broke her courage. I left.

"The next day I received some words of farewell from Dina. She swore she'd always be faithful to me, and she asked me to leave Nîmes. Perhaps her father's anger would abate, she said, but for his sake she asked me to refrain from taking any steps against him. Because the man was supposed to have become my father-in-law, I respected her plea. I left Nîmes with a broken heart, and it took some time for the wounds to heal. It was my first love, a belated love, and my last love. It's been eight years now, and men age quickly. I've long since recovered from this ordeal.

"But my stay in Nîmes did not ultimately prove to be completely unproductive. A respected man from Amsterdam heard me lecture there, and he soon invited me to visit him. I moved there, and after a year had passed I had become the associate rabbi in this, the greatest congregation of the western world. I'm next in line to succeed the honorable old man who is the pride and joy of Spanish Jewry."[11]

"What! That's you?" both brothers exclaimed at once.

"Yes, my dear ones, and I cannot thank the God of Israel enough for the grace he has shown me."

"And Dina, dear Abraham?" José whispered.

"After some time, she got married to her father's successor, and her father ended up dying of a stroke a few weeks after I left."

III.

"I landed at the port of Almeria, dear brothers," José, the second brother began, "and this tells you that I came in from the east. Indeed, I came here on a Turkish ship that I own myself. I've made my fortune in Turkey, and I thus pray to God that he'll keep my noble lord Sultan Selim II in his good graces. When I speak of fortune, I mean riches and grandeur, and I've had more than my share of this type of good fortune. But there's another, realer, and more enduring type of riches: true happiness. I'd gladly sacrifice all my treasures and honors for that. I've had true happiness, but only to have it taken away from me. But quiet, you don't want complaining or bragging. You want to know how I've fared, and that's what I want to tell you.[12]

"After I left our mountain refuge, I went to the port city of Almeria and boarded a ship bound for the Netherlands, which I learned was where so many of our refugees were headed. I arrived safely in Antwerp. Once there I began using our former family name, which for some mysterious reason our father of blessed memory, Don Luigi, gave up to call himself Micquès. My name thus became Don Joseph

---

11. Amsterdam had no organized Jewish community until a century later, and this fact was amply reflected in contemporary historical literature with which Philippson was familiar. Philippson is self-consciously creating historical fiction here, taking liberties with the historical record that enable him to underscore how, after some initial trials and tribulations, the spirit of Spanish Jewry proves easy to transplant to northern Europe, where it functions as an agent of enlightenment and modernization.

12. Most of what follows is historical and taken from a biographical article by Carmoly in the *Archives Israélites de France* 15, no. 1. [Note in the original.]

Nasi.[13] In Antwerp I exchanged my jewels for money and engaged in commerce. I had great success, and everything I touched prospered. I was one of those who only had to open his fists, and the lead that I was holding would turn into gold. But I did not enjoy such peace for long. I don't know exactly how it started, but the large numbers of Spanish and Portuguese Jews settling in the Netherlands were causing unrest, and suddenly, there was a decree banning all those among us who had not spent ten years in the land already. I left and went to Lyon. Once there, though, I soon had troubles. I brought together a group of Italian and Spanish bankers to invest in Lyon's fledgling silk industry. Right after we began, however, the silkworms had a bad year, and the price of red silk rose steeply. The Lombards also wanted to take the silk out of circulation and bought up all the raw materials. In short, we soon lost all our capital, and mine was gone as well. I was able to pay off all my debts, and this allowed me to cover up the true state of my assets. I was close to despair, for I could not go on much further, and I was at a loss as to what I should do next.

"One day I was taking a walk along the banks of the Rhône when I saw a man walking toward me. I soon recognized him as a Jew. He did not speak to me, but he was humbly dressed and his face was furrowed by troubles and deprivation; he was clearly suffering. I went up to him and gave him some money that I had with me, saying 'Milla be'sela mashtoka bi'trein' (If a word is worth a coin, then silence is worth two).[14] He responded to me 'Melaḥ mamon ḥasser' (The salt of money is charity).[15] Then he started to speak, saying, 'I don't know who you are or what your name is, but I know that the book that I'm handing to

---

13. In what follows, Philippson grafts the historical person of Joseph Nasi (1524–79) onto a fictional character born thirty years before 1492. In this way, once again, he creates historical fiction that stresses how quickly the legacy of Spanish Jewry translates into a powerful model for the diaspora. Contemporary historical sources (such as Carmoly, above) noted that the historical Joseph Nasi was raised in a crypto-Spanish family in Portugal. He went on to become a banker in Antwerp before becoming the Duke of Naxos and the Lord of Tiberias, a Turkish-Jewish statesman and financier who was a celebrated intercessor on behalf of Ottoman Jewry. He served during the reign of Sultan Selim II, referred to above, who was also not born until 1524, that is, two decades after Philippson's story is set.

14. Megillah 18. [This note, a reference to the Talmudic saying invoked here, is in the original.]

15. Ketubot, 66.2. [This note, similarly a reference to a Rabbinic source, is also in the original.]

you now is addressed to you and no one else . . . ' With these words he handed me a book. I looked at the volume, and while I was doing so the man disappeared. It was a treatise in Spanish about dreams, *Tratado de los sueños*, and the conclusion of this treatise prophesied that the person to whom the treatise was being handed would one day be in the service of his highness of the Turkish empire. The author called himself Moses Almosnino.[16] I looked for him in vain. It was not until several years later that I finally met up with him again, and at that point I was fortunately in a position to enable him to live out his remaining years without cares.

"Reading this prophecy, I have to confess, encouraged me to pay particular attention to a shipment of Damascus blades from the Levant that the French authorities were offering for sale. Boldly, I worked hard to secure credit so that I could take on this venture. It turned out well, and I undertook other such business ventures, myself traveling to Constantinople, where the French ambassador gave me an introduction to the sublime ruler Suleiman the Magnificent. I knew that the Sultan loved pearls and diamonds, and I used all my connections to make certain I would be able to give him gifts of the most precious pieces of jewelry of this type; every time I visited the Sultan in his palace, in fact, I presented him with such treasures. I thus rose in his graces from day to day and managed to secure his permission to allow a large number of Jewish families from Iberia to immigrate to Turkey, where they found not just security but stable work. I had made business connections with the Netherlands, France, Spain, and Portugal, and the Sultan was happy to see how easily and how abundantly western wares poured into his capital city. All that had to be done was to pay for these goods with products from his extensive empire.

"Then I hatched a plan to go even further. Inspired by my eagerness to serve the Sultan and my desire to secure a decent existence for the huge numbers of Jewish refugees, I suggested that the Sultan follow the model of Christian states and set up textile plants to produce fabric and linen for his subjects. I proposed the holy land of our forefathers as the ideal site

---

16. Moses Almosnino (1515–80), a rabbi, philosopher and Jewish communal leader in the Ottoman empire, was a close associate of Joseph Nasi. His treatise on dreams, published in Spanish in Hebrew letters, was composed at Nasi's request and contained a lengthy description of Nasi's palace. Philippson here, again, self-consciously builds on and takes considerable liberties with the historical record.

for these plants. He approved this plan and settled on the city of Tiberias, granting me the most extensive mandates and privileges. I received an imperial mandate signed by both Sultan Selim and his son Murad. I myself moved to Tiberias, and the Sultan issued the pasha of Damascus and Safed an order that they were to grant me whatever I wished.

"When I arrived in Tiberias, alas, I found that this once blessed city had become a desert full of ruins! But I've never been one to complain. I immediately got to work. The ruins were full of useful stone, and the Sea of Galilee had plenty of sand we could use. But then another obstacle presented itself. There is an old Turkish legend that as soon as Tiberias awakens from its slumbers, the Muslim religion will turn to dust. Suddenly, this legend was on everyone's lips, and the workers put down their tools and refused to work. I informed the pasha of Damscus about these developments, and he arranged for the ringleaders here to be arrested. One of them was hung, and soon enough everyone was back at work and working hard.

"I remained in Tiberias for several years. Alas, I was very happy there, and not merely in my business ventures. I'll tell you about that later. Now, my brothers, I want to tell you quickly about the trajectory of my career. I planted mulberry trees that prospered magnificently and provided nourishment for innumerable silkworms, and we processed the silk that was produced there on site. I ordered wool from Spain and used it to create Venetian cloth. I employed as many Jews as I could in all these efforts, and numerous communities arose in Tiberias and the surrounding region. Because of these fortunate business ventures, my wealth and my reputation grew tremendously. Everyone praised me. Once the textile plants and buildings were well underway and business was blossoming, the Sultan called me back to his palace to put my knowledge of the west and my insightful advice in the service of his governing council. I hurried back to Istanbul, leaving a faithful steward, Joseph ben Adruth, in charge of my business operations in Tiberias. I left my magnificent estates there, alas, without ever seeing them again.

"Beloved brothers, should I give you an extensive description of everything I did in my new position and how influential I became? This great empire had so benevolently taken me in, along with hundreds of thousands of fellow Jews, and I cared deeply about its well-being. I thought of nothing other than the power and dignity of my monarch and was incorruptible, unable to be enticed by favors or scared off by hatred. It often happened that I had princes at my feet who had been mistreating Jews in the most hostile way. They would court my favors, and I would grant them what they wanted only if they agreed to return home and treat my coreligionists well. Turkey is so powerful now that this had major consequences for our oppressed brethren. It was because of my efforts that Turkey humiliated Venice and took away its power over the Mediterranean. When this proud republic had been defeated, I turned my attention to Spain. I advised Sultan Selim, who succeeded Suleiman the Magnificent, to declare war on the king of Spain in order to gain ever greater influence in Europe. I first negotiated an alliance between Turkey and the Netherlands and then encouraged us to take on Spain and its tyrannical yoke. My monarch soon gave Spain so much trouble that he couldn't even think about Holland. In Antwerp people were so receptive to these ideas that a large collection was organized to support Turkey, and this turned out extraordinarily well.

"Thus the years went by. Let me mention just two incidents that will give you a sense of the position I had in Istanbul. A while back the ambassadors of Emperor Maximilian II appeared in Constantinople to negotiate an advantageous peace treaty.[17] They did not just pay respects to me. They gave me, along with all the other senior ministers of the palace, a gift of two thousand ducats in the name of their lord. I accepted this gift, but only to donate it to the poor, splitting it equally between Turks and Jews. A little while later there was a horrible fire in Constantinople, the likes of which hadn't been seen in living memory. Thirty-six thousand houses burned down. The fire started in the Jewish quarter, which suffered an unusually high number of casualties. I did not just do everything in my power to alleviate the adversity. I had the honor of being appointed by the Sultan to oversee the state's efforts to alleviate the suffering and repair the damage. I spared nothing to make Istanbul rise up from the ashes more resplendent than ever, and soon everyone was thanking me in their prayers.

"Finally, my brothers, a few months ago I reached the height of what mortals can achieve on earth. The Duke of Naxos had done some dubi-

---

17. Maximillian II was the emperor of the Holy Roman empire from 1564 until his death in 1576.

ous things in the battle against Venice. Through a clever ploy the palace managed to get hold of his papers, and what had appeared dubious was in fact perfidious treason. The Sultan summoned him to Istanbul and divested him of all his titles. One morning a state messenger unexpectedly ordered me to come to the palace. I threw on my vestments and hurried to follow the order. When I arrived at the palace I was taken into the large ministers' chambers and presented to the Sultan and the council of state assembled there. I was summoned right up in front of the throne. I still had no idea was this all meant, and I was bowing down deeply when the Sultan addressed me. He praised all that I had done for his empire and announced that he was naming me Duke of Naxos, Paros, Andros, and the other Cyclades, giving me complete sovereignty under the suzerainty of the Sultan.[18]

"You can easily imagine what I was feeling in this moment, dear brothers. I was proud that I, a poor Jewish refugee, had risen to such heights, and I was grateful for the divine providence that alone 'bringeth low and lifteth up.'[19] At the same time, I was conscious of the distressing solitude of my life. There was no one close to my heart with whom I could share my joys and my successes. I dutifully expressed my gratitude to my sovereign but also requested several months leave before setting forth for my new homeland—so that I could rush off to see the two of you. I have come at the right time.

"This, my dear brothers, is the crude outline of what I've experienced over the course of the last ten years. I look back with satisfaction on the brilliant role that fell to me. How rare this is in our days for a son of Judah! But you're asking, I'm sure, 'Was this your *entire* life? What about affairs of the heart? Isn't there a story to tell us apart from the changing external circumstances of your life?' Oh no, brothers, I had a wife, and I had a child. This, alas, is all part of the past now!

"Not far from Tiberias, on the south side of the lake, lie the ruins of Sennabris, which once was a rather large city. I came across these ruins when I began staking out Tiberias's surroundings to look for the best soil and the most appropriate place for my business ventures. My people had set up their tents at a distance. I went out alone so that I would not

---

18. This too is historical. [Note in the original.]
19. A reference to 1 Samuel 2:7–8.

be disturbed while casing out the site. Climbing among the ruins, I suddenly heard people talking. The volume of the conversation fluctuated considerably, and then finally I heard an unpleasant male voice screaming: 'You can't go any further, and your father can't go further. You have to decide now. Either your father will languish, and you'll languish, or you'll be mine. Swear here on the spot that you're willing to become my wife. I have a jar full of water, a pouch full of wine and a bag full of dates. Look, your father has already lost consciousness, and you're about to pass out yourself. Make your choice, you only have a moment!'

"I couldn't hear a response even though I was straining hard to listen. But suddenly I heard a fearful woman's voice crying for help. I jumped forward, climbing over a pile of ruins with my sword all ready to go. I found a girl lying on the ground with a man holding a whip over her. I ran up to them and struck the scoundrel on his arm with my saber. He promptly fell down. The girl had just passed out, and next to her was an elderly man who was completely unconscious. I placed my horn to my mouth to call for my people, and before several minutes had passed, they heeded the signal and hurried to where I was. My men, following my instructions, lifted both of them up and carefully carried them to our tents. In the meantime the villain who had beaten the girl had disappeared. My efforts were crowned with success, and soon both father and daughter regained consciousness. They recovered visibly, and I took them with me to Tiberias, where I gave them pleasant accommodations and took care of all their needs. The man wanted a job. But since he didn't have a lot of qualifications and had even less strength, I gave him a sort of supervisory position so that he'd have the sense that he was making a living for himself and his child. The girl saw through this, and she was thankful.

"Would you like to know who these people were? Let me tell you about something that transpired two months later, and you'll know all you need to know. I was sitting in the simple but very nice house that I had had built for myself in Tiberias. My favorite spot in the house was a room with a huge bay window and a breathtaking view. From there one could see the entire city, half of which was still buried in ruins, half of which had been rebuilt and was full of life. There was a view of the reflection of the lake, and on clear days you could see the lowlands on the east bank of the lake as well. I was sitting on a sofa at this window, lost in thought. I had given orders that no one should disturb me, and I soon escaped to the realm of dreams. Past and present, memories and hopes, were all flowing into each other, when I suddenly saw a man standing in front of me, an ugly, callous, red-haired fellow. I recognized him immediately and quickly got up, my hand grabbing for my sword. It was the man who had held the whip over the girl.

"'Stop, sir,' he started quietly, 'I come in peace. I just want to speak to you, and you owe me this much.'

"'Who are you? How did you get in here?'

"'Listen to me, sir,' he responded, 'and you'll understand everything.' I gestured at him to continue. 'You have thwarted my plans, and I am coming to ask what gives you the right to do so. The people whom you have taken in here and are taking care of, they are mine and I want to have them back. Listen, we're all Jews from Hebron, and the man is my uncle, my father's younger brother. He has always lived beyond his means, and he never could seem to hold on to anything that he owned. He's inept and gullible, and on top of that, he's malformed and sick. To make a long story short, he became a beggar, and his wife died in misery. That's when I took them in. His daughter Miriam grew up, and she became splendidly beautiful, and I loved her. For years I supported both of them. They ate my bread, drank my wine, and dressed themselves in my clothes. Then I courted her, but Miriam rejected me, and she and her father left my house that very same night. As a result, they soon suffered extreme hardship. I offered them my help, but they rejected me, forbidding me to cross the threshold of their home. This was the thanks I got! Finally they resolved to come here to look for work, as they had heard of your business ventures and that you are happy to employ Jews. I followed them. Soon they were wandering about without food, without shelter, exposed to game animals, hunger, and thirst. I protected them, but they wouldn't take anything from me. At one point their suffering became dire, and both of them were near death. They couldn't escape me. You appeared then, and the goal that I had pursued for years suddenly slipped away from me. I know that you're unmarried, Sir. You'll court Miriam, and she won't reject you. But that's why I'm coming, to appeal to you directly. My rights are prior to yours. You are such a wealthy man, and I'm so poor. Please don't steal away the only thing that I own.'

"For a long time I looked at the man in silence. Then I got up and, without saying a word to him directly, sent for Miriam and her father. When they arrived, the girl was horrified to see her cousin in my home. I asked her to come closer and said, 'Miriam, here is a man who wants you to be his wife. Are you open to considering this courtship?' Pale with fright, she stepped back and responded, 'Nevermore!' 'Why don't you present your case yourself?' I appealed to her cousin. Then he began to beg and plead with her. He repeated what he had told me. He reminded her of all that he had done for her, how he had always stood ready to help. He overpowered her with the onslaught of his words. Miriam suddenly trembled and then she exclaimed, 'Stop, you liar! Do you think I don't know now that you were the one who deceived my weak father and stole everything he had? You and your villain friends laid traps for him until he sank into misery and my mother passed away. When we left your home full of loathing for you, you slandered us and chased after us. Do you think I don't know all this? Whenever we looked for work, you scared off the people with deception and threats. No, no! You chased us out of our native region. You prevented people from giving us lodging and food during our journey, and we had to sleep on stones in the fields. No, no! Sir, do not cast us off,' she appealed to me, 'do not surrender us to this horrible man.'

"As soon as he was exposed, however, the man had run off.

"Abraham, Sanzo! Miriam became my wife, and I was very happy.[20] Admittedly, in my happiness I often sensed that the devil was somehow close by. I found threatening notes along my path, and small accidents happened that I could not attribute to any other cause. All of this made me even more vigilant. I enfolded my wife with the most diligent care, and her smiles enabled me to forget the storm rumbling from afar. She gave me a boy, who was given the name of our father of blessed memory. What a delight!

"One year later I received an order from the Sultan to come to Istanbul immediately. My wife was about to give birth again, and she

---

20. Here as well, Philippson is taking poetic license with the historical record. As contemporary sources indicated, the historical Joseph Nasi married his first cousin Reyna, daughter of Gracia Mendes Nasi (1510–69), a prominent international businesswoman of her era who was a prominent figure in Ottoman politics and one of the major forces behind efforts to promote Jewish settlement in Tiberias.

was having a difficult pregnancy. I could not subject her to such a quick journey, and yet I could not think of staying back myself. The Sultan's order was clear-cut, and not to obey would have meant losing my position and perhaps even endangering my life. Oh, brothers, what a farewell this was! Miriam did not want to be separated from her husband and her son at the same time, so I had to leave behind my son, my greatest treasure. I arranged for the most loyal guards possible and left them with appropriate orders. And I promised to send for my family as soon as possible. Nevertheless, brothers," José covered his face in pain, "I never saw them again. When I arrived in Beirut I was given a letter. I opened it to read the words, 'Miriam and Luigi are alive no longer! I have been avenged.' I was livid with pain. I immediately had the fastest camel saddled and, throwing all caution to the wind, returned to Tiberias. When I arrived, I found out that, the day before, a cobra viper had broken into the bedroom and killed my sleeping wife and the boy in her arms. Surely, a human hand had thrown the viper into the room through an opening in the roof. I had lost everything.

"Brothers! I have borne this misery, but my hair turned silver-gray over night."

IV.

It was now time for the third brother to begin his story. Sanzo had been resting his head pensively in his right hand for a long time. He lifted it up suddenly, and he had an unusual sparkle in his eyes. His two boys were standing in front of him, waiting for him to start talking.

"Dear brothers, unlike you, the honorable rabbi, and you, the experienced merchant and statesman, I am not a man of many words. All you can expect from me, therefore, is a simple report of the manifold things that have happened to me.

"Ten years ago, the ship that I boarded had hardly left the port of Malaga when it got caught in a storm. Its mast was split into pieces, its sails were torn apart, and its rudder broke apart. For some time, the waves carried the ship on in its helpless condition. Suddenly a Moorish pirate climbed on board the wreckage and took us all captive. No one resisted, for what on this destroyed ship was there to defend? I thus became a slave, and at the marketplace in Tunis I was sold to a

Bey who wielded unlimited power over a small dominion in the interior of the country. I eagerly sought to perform all the tasks I was assigned, and I persevered, never complaining. Because of this, and because of some small duties I performed especially for him, the kindly Bey took notice of me and soon grew fond of me. He observed that I did not worship the Prophet, and finally one day he asked me what religion I belonged to. I answered, 'I am a son of Yehuda, a son of Judah.' 'What?' he said, 'are you one of those children of the desert who live in the south, where they have conquered the great plains and take orders from no one but themselves?' I shook my head, indicating that I knew nothing about these people. I told him about Spain, my fatherland, and about the battle between the Moors and the Christians. I told him about the Moors' defeat, and how the same rulers that toppled Abo-Abdeli from the throne also attacked us Jews and insisted on driving us out of places that our forefathers had inhabited long before Christians and Moors did. The Bey then told me about the wild tribes of the Beni Yehud. The Bey's dominion was bordered in the south by a chain of high mountains,[21] right beyond which lay a great desert that that no human being had been known ever to cross.[22] That is where these tribes lived. They happily maintain peaceful relations with other tribes, but they never fraternize with others, and they never recognize anyone else's authority but their own. They drive their plows with their swords in their right hands, and they graze their herds carrying their bows in their left arms.

"I found myself strangely captivated by this information. I was of the same religion and stock as these people, and they lived a free and independent life, wielding a sharp sword in their fist, subject to no one other than the leader they chose themselves. These people were on my mind all day long, and they were in my dreams at night. I did my best to learn more about the region where they resided, but no one with whom I came into contact had any relevant knowledge. I tried to be clever and get more information out of the Bey, but he saw through me and would say nothing more than that he had met with them once under some very special circumstances. In this way, I spent six months in slav-

---

21. Atlas. [Note in the original.]
22. Sahara. [Note in the original.]

ery. What else could I have done? I had to leave everything in God's hands. I did not want to run away from my master, for he was good to me and had purchased me through legal means. And where would I go? There was nowhere where I would have been treated better.

"One day the Bey went on a hunt in the mountains, accompanied by a large entourage. I was there as well. I was unarmed, except for a small knife that I carried on my left side; my job, like that of the other slaves, was to carry food for the Bey and his friends. We took our breakfast in a beautiful clearing under palm trees that were high as heaven, and from there we set out to go directly into the mountains. We were hunting antelope, ostrich, and buffalo. The hunting party inadvertently split into two groups, and I and five other slaves happened to be the only ones who were left with the Bey. We had just entered into a canyon, when suddenly a terrifying lion jumped out of the bushes in front of us and ran right up to the Bey. The Bey's horse took fright and threw him off, and he landed with one leg right under his steed's belly. The other slaves screamed in horror as they ran off. I, however, took one look at my master in his helpless state and became filled with courage. I fearlessly placed myself between my master and the lion, hoping to stare the lion down by looking directly into his eyes. He responded by putting his right paw on my arm, but I remained standing like a man, looking him sharply in the eye. I refused to move. The lion closed his eyes for an instant, keeping his head with its open jaws pointed right at me. My left arm was immobilized under the weight of his paw, but my right arm was free, and I took advantage of this moment. I grabbed the small knife I had with me, and before the lion could open his eyes, I sank it right into his heart with a powerful thrust. The lion jumped up for a second, lifting his right paw off me in order to hit me. But God was with me, for in that very moment I rotated the knife in the wound, and he fell down dead. My left arm was torn up a bit, but apart from that, I suffered no injury. I turned around to see how the Bey was faring; he didn't understand that the danger had been averted. I helped him up, and his gratitude and appreciation were boundless. He embraced me and offered me all his possessions and all his treasures. He said that I should become his vizier and he would give me a palace, gardens, and slaves and fulfill all my wishes. I rejected everything, hanging on only to his final words. I explained to him that all I wanted was to have my freedom so that I might join the Beni Yehud. The only other thing I really needed was for him to give me directions. The Bey was startled to hear this disclosure, and as we were heading back home, he did everything in his power to disabuse me of this wish. He even offered me his own daughter in marriage if I were to stay with him. I refused.

"Several weeks later the Bey supplied me with a horse and weapons and accompanied me himself to the borders of his dominion, at which point two able guides took over and led me over the mountains. I don't want to describe for you in detail the dangers I had to endure, the troubles I had to deal with, and the challenges I had to overcome. The main thing is that I conquered them all. Admittedly, I lost one of my guides, who disappeared down into a crevice in a glacier when we entered the region of eternal snow. We had to climb over a mountain that was as high as the heavens, where there were no trails, and even my guide didn't know the precise route. Lions were lurking down in the valley, and up on the mountain we faced the dangers of bears and vultures. With God's help, however, we overcame all these obstacles, and we descended the southern face of the mountain to find a fertile landscape. The Bey had given me a letter of recommendation that enabled me to be well received. We soon found ourselves at the edge of an immense desert, and that is where my path led. When I woke up at our last camp before entering the desert, I found that my second guide had disappeared. He had slipped away, and I couldn't blame him. Unlike me, he did not have a people and a homeland to find.

"My steed entered into the silent desert. I was alone and could not find a trail to follow. I had been told that the Beni Yehud now resided in several oases in the desert far away from the caravan paths in the east. I thus made my pilgrimage toward the morn, trusting in God, who reigns over the desert as well and doesn't allow it to consume prey that is not its own. As a result of a recent series of battles, the Beni Yehud had become even more mistrustful of foreigners. They were living now in even greater isolation, and for years no one had heard anything certain about them. It was thus going to be very difficult to gain entry to them. You all will say that it was foolish on my part to chase after a phantasm without any guarantee of success. Yet this phantasm was my reality; it was the only way I could envision a future for myself. I was not a scholar able to influence others through his teaching, nor was I a merchant able to make a life for myself through commerce. I had had enough of being badgered in the lands of Christendom and the crescent without a place of my own and without honor. I took one more look at the beautiful landscape behind me and then looked up at the heavens 'from whence cometh my help.' I then rode on into the seemingly endless desert.

"I don't want to tire you out telling you of the horrors of this route. During the day it was the sun, and during the night it was the moon that served as my guide leading me to the east. Tornadoes came and covered me and my faithful steed almost entirely with the sand of the desert, practically suffocating me and my horse with the desert blaze. With the sun beating directly down on us all day long, we easily became exhausted, lacking the respite of shade, rain, or cool breezes. The haze was deceptive, creating mirages that would lead me away from my path. During the night, horrible predators wandered about, and I owe it to God's good graces alone that they hurried past me and my steed. Soon my water supply was finished. My two pouches were empty to the last drop. My horse and I were close to fainting. I had long since dismounted and my horse was creeping behind me as I carried myself slowly forward. I couldn't go any further and sank down onto a small sand dune. My horse stood next to me, about to languish, and I lost consciousness.

"I don't know how long I had been lying there when suddenly, in the middle of my foggy state, I felt a prickling sensation on my tongue. This pain awakened me, and I opened my eyes to see a long, bearded, dark brown face bending down over me. A man in customary Bedouin dress was feeding me drops of water out of a short leather flask. The water was lukewarm, but it revived me, and I was saved. When I looked around, I saw several men on horseback. One of the horsemen grabbed me and hoisted me up with his left arm, and we rode off in a raging gallop. I lost consciousness several more times. Finally, I felt a cool breeze being fanned onto my burning face. I opened up my eyes to see a heavenly garden with a brook running through it. I saw grass, palm trees, cornfields, and tents. I soon found myself fed and settled in a bed, where I slept for several days straight.

"I quickly got my strength back and began to feel better. When I was finally ready to get out of bed, a venerable old man came into the tent to talk to me. He wore snow-white Bedouin dress, had a long snow-white beard, and on his head he wore a snow-white turban that revealed locks of silver hair. From the four corners of the upper half of his robes hung down fringes, into which a blue cord was braided. The old man shook my hand and addressed me in Arabic. He bid me peace and told me that the men of his tribe were riding through the desert when they found me lying unconscious on top of my dead horse. They had brought me here. But now I had to tell them who I was, for the strict law of their tribe does not allow them to keep a stranger in their midst any longer than is absolutely necessary to save his life.

"'Venerable old man,' I answered him, 'I'd like to tell you openly who I am, where I come from, and where I want to go. I am a Ben Yehud from the land across the desert, the mountains, and the sea, and I am looking for the Beni Yehud who live behind the sea, the mountains, and the desert.'

"'You are a Ben Yehud?' exclaimed the old man and jumped up in the air. 'How can you prove that?'

"'Old man, do you know the Beni Yehud and their law so well that I could prove it to you?' I responded.

"'Well, you should know that you are now among the highest tribe of the Beni Yehud. The chieftain of this tribe is standing before you now.'

"Now it was my turn to jump up, and I grabbed the old man's hand and covered it with kisses. 'So God in his good grace has served as my guide, and I have reached my destination!' I tore open my shirt and showed the old man the knotted fringes on my prayer shawl. They didn't have a blue cord, so he didn't find them quite right. I spoke to him in Hebrew, which he didn't seem to understand apart from a few words from the Torah and the Psalms. I then told him about our patriarchs Abraham, Isaac, and Jacob, about the holy land and Jerusalem, of David and Solomon. The knowledge he had about these figures and places was different from mine, but we were using the same names for our ancestors, and he finally accepted me as a member of his people and his religion. I was happy; I was among the free sons of the desert. But would I be permitted to stay with them? Would they grant me asylum? These questions were on my mind when the old man quickly stepped out to share the news with his brothers.

"The old man soon came back, accompanied by several older people. They all sat down around me and beseeched me to tell them my story, where I came from, who I was, and how I managed to reach them. How surprised these good people were when I told them of the numerous Beni Yehud that live dispersed among the peoples of the earth, where they are oppressed and persecuted. 'Why don't they come here?' they asked. 'The desert has room enough for all of them!' They could not comprehend how anyone would not prefer the austere and dangerous freedom of the desert to a comfortable life spent in dependence and shame. They had no difficulties understanding why I left behind the luxury of the Bey to make the dangerous journey to them.

"'Well then,' they said after I had finished, 'you are welcome here as a son and brother. From now on, regard yourself as one of us, as our flesh and blood. We will defend you, and you will defend us as well. What is ours is yours!' They also told me of the legends of their tribe. Many, many centuries ago, their fathers—the tribe called itself the Beni Qurayza—were attacked by Muhammad, the prophet of the Ishmaelites, in the land of Arabia. The men were slaughtered, and the women and children were all sold off as slaves.[23] Only a small number who had happened to be away from their main place of residence at the time had been able to save themselves, and they went from land to land, from desert to desert, fleeing from the power of the Ishmaelites. They finally came here, where they have held their own for a very long time. To be sure, this has not been easy. They've moved eastward and southward when necessary, and they've also had more than their share of difficult battles. After a while I became more familiar with their way of life. I found them to be brave, honest, God-fearing, and full of domestic virtue and innocence—and yet also crude, ignorant, and full of superstition. They had inherited a few holy scrolls from their forefathers, among which I found the Torah, the Psalms, and the powerful book of Isaiah. Yet they could not

---

23. Philippson here builds on a historical event that took place in Arabia in 627 C.E., creating a story about fictional descendants of the Beni Quarayza. Philippson was hardly alone in fueling fascination with such groups of Saharan Jews. Indeed, with French inroads into North Africa in the early nineteenth century, tales about such Jewish Bedouins started to be widely circulated in Europe. But Philippson's tale is not just building on contemporary travel narratives. In many ways, as noted in the preface, Sanzo's story reads as if it were created to be the antithesis of the highly ambivalent Jewish figure created by the Austrian writer Adalbert Stifter in his celebrated 1842 novella "Abdias."

understand the contents of these writings. They observed laws which were basically traditional customs that they performed following their fathers from generation to generation. And they had some set phrases which they taught their children to pronounce, even though these were often deeply garbled.

"I'm sure that you want to know what I did among and for these fine people. If I had been a scholar, I might have taken them to the gates of scholarship. If I had been a businessman, I might have convinced them to move and live among civilized peoples. But as you know, I only acquired superficial knowledge in my youth and spent all my time practicing the arts of chivalry. I firmly believed, however, that what the Beni Qurayza required to find salvation was neither knowledge nor riches. They needed to have the type of security and peace that would allow them to develop on their own. And soon events happened that put all other thoughts aside. The Beni Qurayza village that had taken me in consisted of approximately three hundred tents, with roughly one family per tent. These families lived simple and reclusive lives. The women in particular were hardly seen outside their tents, and each family generally kept busy with its work, paying visits to other families every once in a while. The tents were set up fairly close to each other, and the children spent their time playing in the lanes between the tents. As a safety measure, horsemen were sent out every day to roam through and patrol the surrounding area. If they gave the alarm sign, all the men would gather and arm themselves. Half of them would go after the enemy, and the other half would remain back to defend the village. If the enemy seemed large in number, the tents would be quickly dismantled, and they would move in an organized fashion, taking as many of their possessions as possible to another site that had already been chosen in advance. You see, they proceeded with great simplicity but with even greater caution, and after centuries of such experiences, this had become second nature to them. They had left me in the foreigner's tent since they had not yet been able to determine what they thought about the extraordinary case of a Ben Yehud that didn't belong to one of their tribes.

"I quickly began to regain my powers. Three days later, at noon, the patrol expedition raced back to report that a very large number of armed men of an enemy Bedouin tribe was approaching. The alarm sign was sounded, and in a quarter hour the crew was armed and ready. But this time things were different. The men riding guard could not agree on a strategy. Some of them thought the enemy was so great in number that resistance would be futile. Others thought that if we used all our men, without dividing up into two groups, we would be strong enough to fight back. No one really knew what to do. But I soon managed to get an overview of the situation. I raised my voice and expressed my opinion briefly and with determination. This tribe of honest men agreed with me, and I'm not quite sure how this happened—this went against all their customs—but we were in a pressing situation, and soon I took on the commando. I had them dismantle their tents and use them as protective covering on top of their property. I then had the group form a quadrangle on the ridge of a nearby hill. I put the women, children, horses, and donkeys all in the middle. I placed the spear throwers and bowmen in the second and third rows. I myself and about fifty of the bravest men were on horseback forming a vanguard and mobile platoon. It took us an hour to get all set up, and we then waited quietly for the enemy. Soon a band of almost a thousand enemy horsemen came at us with a ferocious battle cry. When they were close upon us, the vanguard split up and flanked the rest of us. By having our bowmen alternate between shooting and preparing their bows to shoot, we were able to send a constant cloud of arrows out of our quadrangle. And our spear throwers were also mounting an unrelenting attack on the enemy horsemen. Once these offensives got started, we, the vanguard, attacked the enemy from the sides, using irresistible force. The enemy receded and then came back at us. They receded yet again and mounted a third attack. The enemy was suffering more and more losses. Then I gave a sign, and the majority of our men mounted the horses that stood ready for us. We went after the confused and battered enemy in such a way that they never managed to recover. Our victory was complete. More than five hundred of their dead and wounded covered the battlefield, and we had lost relatively few men. The tribe was elated. That very same evening the tents were set up again, and the entire tribe came to the foreigner's tent to express their gratitude. They accepted me into the tribe in a celebratory manner with plenty of ceremonies and led me into the tent of the old man, the tribal chief, who adopted me as his son.

"Now, dear brothers, the old man had neither wife nor children, but he shared his tent with the daughter of his younger brother, who had fallen in battle. I could not spend a long time under the same roof as Aisha without her enchanting beauty, her virtue, her industriousness, and her friendly demeanor winning over my heart. She became my wife and for the past nine years she has never ceased to make me happy. She gave me these two boys and two little girls that remained at home with her.

"But I am not finished with my tale. The battle that I just described, along with repeated attacks that happened soon thereafter, gave me great reason for concern over the circumstances of the tribe. I realized that if two of our enemy tribes would unite against us, they would be able to crush us to death, despite all our bravery. Soon the men of the tribe chose me to be their leader and general. I pursued a threefold plan. First, I made a journey to the Bey, taking a small number of men and all the precious metal that we had in the tribe with me, so that we could buy rifles and cannons, weapons which were unknown in the desert. Led by these men who knew the desert well, we traveled safely until we came to the cultivated land. We then crossed the mountains and reached the Bey. He was happy to sell us the weaponry and all the ingredients the tribe needed to make gun powder, and after two months I was already on the way back home. God was with us. We were gone for half a year but came home to find everything in the best condition. You should have seen how surprised these men were when I showed them the way the rifles worked and how to use these deathly weapons. Our enemies were even more amazed. I took the very first attack as an opportunity to seek out our enemies in their most deeply hidden nests and annihilate them. The weaponry soon earned our tribe a reputation. I then moved on to the second stage in my plan. I wanted to unite all the tribes of the Beni Qurayza so that we could resist still greater opponents even if the use of cannonry should penetrate into these remote regions. I succeeded here, and soon I stood at the head of two thousand tents and ten thousand warriors. This made it necessary for us to look for a larger oasis, which we did. In our new oasis—this was the final element of my plan—I sought out an appropriate site for a fort. We found the perfect location, and we constructed a well-built fort. We were so successful in all these efforts, in fact, that for the last six years, no enemy has dared to tread any place where a son of the Beni Qurayza has stood. In the meantime I also sought to educate our tribe in other ways. I taught a number of our youth our sacred language so that they could understand the scrolls of the Torah, the Psalms, and the book of Isaiah. I also taught them some useful knowledge and let them then take my place, teaching what they had learned from me to children and anyone eager for knowledge.

"Amid such activities, which God has blessed, the tenth year soon approached, and ten moons ago I sallied forth with my boys and a capable entourage to fulfill my vow to you both. We passed through the great and horrible desert without languishing. We climbed over the powerful mountains reaching up to heaven without perishing. We crossed through the wide and hostile plains without a calamity. I left my entourage on the other side of the sea and landed safely in Malaga."

Sanzo had hardly completed his story when Don José, the Duke of Naxos, called out to him, "So are you Adon-Midbar, the celebrated 'Lord of the Desert,' whose reputation reaches all the way to Istanbul?"

"That's what they call me, brother."

The three brothers embraced each other, and then they each got down on their knees and said a heartfelt prayer of thanks to God almighty. For a long time they spoke with each other about how God had led them in such different directions, enabling all three of them to achieve great things they would never had suspected. The oldest had become a teacher in Judah with a world-renowned reputation. The second had become a great man in the service of the Ottoman monarch. The third had become a benefactor and leader of a free tribe whose name was known throughout the silent desert.

For fourteen days they remained with each other at their father's grave. Then it was time for them to go their separate ways. Each of the brothers had rooted himself so firmly in his new home that he could no longer part from it. They embraced each other again, weeping one final time in each other's arms, and they shook hands one last time. There was no vow this time to meet each other again, for their advancing age would not permit this. Then the rabbi went to the north, the statesman to the east, and the warrior to the south. An hour later the silent gorge was filled with the sound of a horn coming from the peak on the southern face of the gorge. The bright sound echoed softly and then died away bit by bit. On the mountain on the north side of the gorge, a gray-haired man listened and said a blessing. On the mountain in the east a hunched-over man listened as well. He lowered his head as tears streamed forth from his eyes. Then each brother turned toward his homeland. They never saw each other again.

David Schornstein,
"The Marannos: A Spanish Chronicle" (1861)
Translated from the French by Maurice Samuels

Schornstein's "Les marannos: Chronique espagnole" (The Marannos: A Spanish Chronicle) is very different from his other work collected here, "The Tithe."[1] Whereas "The Tithe" looks back nostalgically at the vanishing world of traditional Ashkenazic life in a small town in France's eastern provinces, "The Marannos" depicts the adventures of a family of crypto-Jews as they attempt to flee the Spanish Inquisition. Whereas "The Tithe" offers a gently ironic and almost anthropological look at a culture on the verge of disappearance, "The Marannos" is a fast-paced adventure tale, told in the cloak-and-dagger style of Alexandre Dumas *père*. With its graphic representations of torture and persecution, "The Marannos" is anything but nostalgic for the past. On the contrary, it uses the traumatic history of the Inquisition and expulsion from Spain to promote Jewish solidarity in the present. A narrative of Jews suffering in order to remain Jews, it provides a historical basis for affiliation at a time when Jewish identity was threatened not by the Inquisition but by the temptations of assimilation.

"The Marannos" was published serially in a short-lived French Jewish journal, *La Vérité Israélite* (The Israelite Truth). Founded in 1860 by Joseph Cohen, the journal mostly offered scholarly articles on Jewish history and the Jewish religion and counted both Alexandre "Ben Baruch" Créhange and Alexandre Weill among its contributors. The six historical novellas Schornstein wrote for the journal, all of which depict the horrible persecution faced by Jews in Spain and Germany during the early modern period, stand out from the sober articles surrounding them and were no doubt meant to draw a wider readership to the journal. And yet, like the other articles in the journal, Schornstein's fictions formed part of the modern attempt, begun by the scholars of the Wissenschaft des Judentums movement in Germany, to call attention to more recent periods in Jewish history, which had long been neglected by rabbinic scholars.

Marannos means "heretics." This term was used in Spain for converted Jews and Muslims, as well as for their descendants who were suspected of secretly practicing the religion of their fathers. [Author's note. This story has been abridged for this translation.]

1. See the introduction to "The Tithe," in Section 1, for biographical information on Schornstein.

Typical of the fascination with the Sephardic experience that marked a certain strain of acculturated Ashkenazic Jewry in the nineteenth century, "The Marannos" depicts Jews who blend in so well to their surroundings that nobody suspects them of being Jews. But the characters in "The Marannos" are models not because of their social integration but because of their desire to remain Jews in spite of it— even at great peril. Ultimately, this story points not to Spain but to France as the true Jewish promised land, despite the fact that Jews had been officially banned from the kingdom of France since the end of the fourteenth century and the several thousand "new Christians" who sought refuge from the Inquisition could not practice Judaism openly there until the eighteenth century. This story inscribes the Sephardic experience in a larger narrative of progress with emancipation and modern French citizenship as its goal.

*

The last rays of the setting sun that gilded the steeples of the ramparts of Saragossa were about to give way before the shadows of the night. The sounds of the day died out little by little and the rare passersby crossed already silent streets. At this moment, a young man who had just left the city stopped in front of the Red Tavern, which was situated just outside the walls, on the road that leads to France.

The doors and windows of the building were open so that one could easily see inside the tavern's main room and examine the curious faces of its inhabitants. They were a mix of gypsies, smugglers, associates of the Inquisition, outlaws, and brigands belonging to the Gardugnas, a powerful and well organized band that had long plundered Spain. They were sitting around various tables, busy drinking, gambling, and talking. A few smoky oil lamps lit the scene and their reddish, dim light fell on bronzed faces with strong features and ferocious expressions, endowing the meeting with an extraordinary, almost infernal appearance.

After looking into the low room of the Red Tavern for a few moments, the young man gestured impatiently. Evidently he didn't see the man he was looking for. He took a step toward the building, as if to enter. He must have changed his mind, though, for he then began to pace slowly in front of the tavern, occasionally peering in with an inquisitive look. Suddenly, some of the drinkers let out a cry. They had noticed the young man observing them from outside the building. Most of them had already had run-ins with the authorities and they all had various peccadilloes on their conscience, so the mysterious man observing them made them ill at ease.

"By Saint Jacques," exclaimed one of them, a *guapo* or high-ranking bandit in the Gardugna, who was athletically built and had just returned from the galleys a short time before. "I want to know what this is about." And he left the room, followed by a few of the others. Looking around him in all directions as if he suspected some kind of treason, he approached the young man.

"What brings you here, signor?" he asked in a tone that reflected both his fear and his insolence, for the brigand did yet know to whom he was speaking.

"I'm looking for Mateo," responded the young man calmly.

"Mateo," the *guapo* responded, still in the same tone. "But why are you pacing in front of this tavern? You're making these honest men nervous. You would do better to enter and wait for your man inside."

"Yes, come inside," several voices repeated.

"Thanks for the offer, but I prefer to wait here."

Grumbling and threats surrounded the young man.

"Make him come in!"

"We have to see who he is."

"He comes with us or else."

"Silence!" said all of a sudden a new voice, full of authority.

"He's a spy," responded some of the men.

"He's watching us," added the others.

"Signor Mateo," said the young man, who recognized the newcomer.

"Silence!" repeated the latter to the men who were surrounding him. "You can see that you're wrong. It's signor Fernando, the friend of Diego d'Almora. May God preserve his life . . . and his money," he added laughing. "Hello, signor Fernando, how may I be of service?" [. . .]²

"Signor Mateo, you know that in a few days there will be a big celebration in the city of Saragossa. Our gracious sovereign, His Very Catholic Majesty Philip II, has demanded that his victories in Portugal be celebrated in all the capitals of the kingdom."

"I know," responded Mateo in a satisfied tone as he thought of all the profits that the Gardugna was going to derive from the occasion.

---

2. Indicates an abridged passage in this translation.

"The whole province wants to attend the brilliant festivities that will take place here. Some friends of signor Diego d'Almora will also be coming and . . ."

"They wouldn't mind arriving in Saragossa safely. I understand, signor Fernando."

"Naturally," the latter responded.

"How many of your friends are coming?"

"I don't know for sure, five or six. But I will pay you for more just in case."

"I accept," said Mateo, taking the money that Fernando offered him. "The old password will work for your friends. If there are more than you say . . ."

"We will pay you for them."

"I'm sure you will. But I was going to say that they will arrive safely. I haven't forgotten what Diego d'Almora did . . ."

"Let's not speak of it, signor Mateo."

Having said these final words, the young man, after saluting the *capatoze*, returned to the town while Mateo entered the Red Tavern.

The leader of the Gardugna was greeted with cries of joy by the *guapos* in the tavern. They knew there was always a lot of money to be made whenever Diego d'Amora asked for something. [. . .]

"Signor Diego d'Almora, there's a pearl of a man," said one of the *guapos*.

"It's true," responded Mateo. "He's generous, charitable, and a good Christian."

"Just last week he gave a gilt crown to Notre-Dame del Pilar."

"If all Catholics were like him, we wouldn't need the Inquisition."

"Chito!" said three or four voices at once. "Chito!"[3]

A silence ensued.

Such was the terror that the implacable tribunal inspired that its name alone sufficed to scare men who didn't shrink before any crime, but who didn't dare neglect the slightest religious duty for fear of being denounced as a heretic and falling into the hands of the Holy Office. They all grew pale and eyed each other suspiciously. The man who had spoken stayed as silent as the others. Was he a fool or a spy?

---

3. Silence. [Author's note.]

"Is it true," asked a gypsy woman, "that Diego d'Almora is going to have his daughter Juanita marry Fernando?"

That question succeeded in dispelling the unpleasant atmosphere produced by the previous speaker. Everyone heaved a sigh of relief and the conversation once again flowed naturally.

"It seems that it's a done deal," responded another woman.

"I don't believe it," said a *guapo*. "D'Almora is rich and Fernando has nothing."

"They've been talking about this marriage for a long time and nothing has happened yet."

"Which hasn't prevented Juanita from refusing a number of offers."

"They say she even refused the son of the powerful Count Francisco de Ramira, from this city."

"Enough of your yapping," shouted Mateo suddenly. "God only knows what you people would say if I let you. Mind your own business and leave honest people alone." [. . .]

The habitués of the Red Tavern were not the only ones in Saragossa speaking of the more or less imminent nuptials of Fernando and Juanita. It was an interesting subject of conversation, and more important, offered little danger. In that period, such subjects were hard to come by. The terror that the Inquisition inspired was indeed universal. Nobody, however highly placed he might be, was safe from its reach. An imprudent reflection, a thoughtless word, an enemy's denunciation, all sufficed to condemn an innocent man for heresy and to lead him to the stake. Nobody was safe any longer. Things had become so bad that the most highly regarded men and the proudest nobles curried favor with secret agents or associates of the feared tribunal. This was the only way to escape from the perpetual danger suspended over everyone's heads. For the Holy Office required its associates to take a terrible oath by which they swore to renounce all family bonds and to report any words contrary to the faith that they heard spoken. They had to denounce their closest relatives, their father, their mother, their wife, even their children. Thus had all mutual trust ceased even within families. No more sweet nothings, no more intimate whispers. Friends feared friends, brothers suspected brothers, and fathers avoided their own children. Like all Spanish cities, Saragossa had become sad and silent. Life was no longer gay or lively. Everyone spied on everyone else and approached each other with the greatest circumspection. Every word was weighed and people only spoke of indifferent matters.

So people in Saragossa spoke often of the upcoming marriage of Juanita and Fernando despite their unequal fortunes. For people generally agreed that Diego d'Almora must be very rich and that Fernando was poor. He had arrived in the city one day from nobody knew where. He lived for a while in shabby conditions until the day when fate, it was said, put him into contact with Diego d'Almora. The latter took an interest in the young man and offered him aid and protection, which surprised nobody since Diego was the most charitable man in Saragossa. Never had an unfortunate or poor man addressed him in vain. Fernando was able to enter into the good graces of his protector. The latter had initiated him into all his affairs. He had confided in him and, everyone believed, he was about to give him his daughter's hand in marriage.

It's true that these were only rumors and nobody knew for certain that the marriage would take place. Diego d'Almora was an honest and kind-hearted man. He always welcomed with perfect equanimity all those who came to see him in his modest dwelling. But, at the same time, he was extremely discreet and never spoke of private family matters. Fernando, for his part, always responded evasively to questions that the other young men put to him when they joked about his good fortune in the tavern. The one thing that was certain was that Juanita, the daughter of Diego, had already refused several excellent offers and the habitués of the Red Tavern were well informed when they cited among these the son of the Count de Ramira, a deputy from Aragon, and the descendant of one of the first and oldest families in the province.

Magnificent and proud, the count led an opulent life, more in keeping with the status of his name than with the state of his fortune. His business affairs were not going well and he was scared of what the future would bring. It was in these circumstances that the count had thought of an alliance between his oldest son and the daughter of Diego d'Almora, an alliance that could help rebuild the fortunes of his house. But, to the count's great surprise, Diego d'Almora, instead of hurrying to accept such a flattering offer, had responded to his overtures with embarrassment, in vague terms that resembled a refusal. Humiliated, the vindictive count, who had thought he was doing a great honor to a simple *hidalgo* in offering him such an alliance, developed a violent hatred for Diego d'Almora and swore to enact vengeance for the affront.

In the first moments of his fury, he had thought of denouncing him as a heretic to the Inquisition. Nothing could have been easier. All you needed were two witnesses, whose names were never revealed during the proceedings, to have a man locked up in the dungeons of the Holy Office, and once there, people rarely came out again. The infernal tortures that the accused were subjected to made them confess to anything, and if they had the force to resist the awful torments, they were still lost: they were condemned as impenitents and obstinate heretics. Moreover, the fortune of Diego d'Almora itself was sufficient to arouse the interest of the Inquisition. Many unfortunate men who died in the dungeons or on the stake had no other crime to reproach themselves with than being rich. For the Holy Office confiscated the property of its victims, whose dishonored descendants were declared incapable of holding any office or position and were reduced a life of misery and despair. But this is precisely what the count didn't want. Vengeance was no doubt sweet, but he hadn't given up all hope for the marriage and for the new fortune that it would bring his house. Diego's refusal had not been formal. Nothing confirmed the rumors of the marriage between Fernando and Juanita. The count had therefore resolved to wait for a favorable occasion to renew his request. He could always enact vengeance later. [. . .]

One morning, a few days after the scene we have described, Diego entered the garden with Juanita, as was his custom. While walking with her under the old trees that spread a delightful coolness around them, he contemplated from time to time with pride and happiness the pure and charming features of the young girl, lit up by black eyes and shiny, luxuriant hair. The father's eyes betrayed such a profound expression of tenderness and solicitude that it was easy to see that he loved his child with a double bond of attachment. Indeed, Juanita's childhood had lacked a mother's affection and Diego had raised her alone, with all the devotion, all the love that a father's heart is capable of when it is focused on a single being. As for Juanita, she felt happy in the arms of her father, whom she venerated and adored. For her, Diego seemed like the embodiment of every virtue and perfection. She was proud to belong to him and her respect for him was without limits, as was the touching effusion with which she returned his love.

However, on that day, there was something even more penetrating than usual in the way Diego looked at his daughter, something more vibrant in his voice when he spoke to her. Something inexplicable agitated his entire being. He either walked in silence, absorbed in his thoughts as if he didn't notice Juanita's presence, or he overwhelmed her with caresses. Occasionally, he would interrupt his steps and turn to face his daughter. He seemed to want to say something to her but he remained silent, as if new reflections stopped the words on his lips. Juanita had noticed her father's agitation. She herself seemed singularly moved. Twenty times she seemed on the point of asking him what was wrong but she stopped herself, held back by an invincible force. The walk seemed to have worn Diego out, for after a short time, he stopped.

"Let's go back in, my child," he said to Juanita. "I'm tired. Moreover, I need to speak to you, and with what I have to say, we will be better off in my office than in the garden." The tone in which he said these words made the young girl shudder.

"Let's go back in, father," she said, her voice quivering with emotion.

If Diego wanted to speak in private to his daughter, the circumstances were propitious. Or rather, he had prepared the circumstances himself. Fernando had gone out for a few hours with his friends who were visiting Saragossa. Diego had ordered his only servant to accompany them. As for his housekeeper, she was busy with domestic chores and with the added duties caused by the visitors. The house was thus silent and deserted as Diego and his daughter entered. He climbed the steps leading toward his office, situated in a distant wing of the abode. When Juanita entered the office, he closed the door and carefully shut the windows and pulled the drapes, after having made certain that nobody was in the courtyard. Juanita followed her father's mysterious movements with growing bewilderment. A vague uncertainty had taken hold of her. It certainly must be an important matter her father wanted to discuss to have necessitated such precautions.

While the young girl was preoccupied with these matters, Diego approached her. He took her two hands in his and pulled her gently toward him, looking at her for some moments in silence. Then he spoke in a penetrating voice:

"Juanita, my child, do you love me?"

"Do I love you, father?" responded the young girl, surprised at such a question. "Do I love you? But isn't my only happiness loving you, father?"

"And him—Fernando?" asked Diego in a half-serious, half-joking tone.

"Naughty father," responded Juanita with a charming pout, wagging her finger in a gesture of reproach. "Aren't you the one who taught me to esteem him? Aren't you the one who told me he had the most noble and generous heart?"

"Yes my child," interrupted Diego. "The most generous, the most worthy of my Juanita. And if I am asking you today if you love me, my child, it's not because I doubt it but because I need a great proof of your affection."

"Of my affection? Speak, father," said the young girl who was growing more and more worried.

"Silence, child. Silence, in heaven's name! What I have to say to you requires the most profound silence. One word of what I have to tell you, of what I must confide in you, and before me would appear the most terrible, implacable enemy, who knows neither pardon nor pity."

"An enemy! You, my father?" responded Juanita, in whom worry had given way to terror. "Who can hate you and why would they accuse you? What can you have done, you who are so good and just?"

"Rest easy, child. You needn't be ashamed of your father. What I have done I can confess before God if not before men. My crime is performing the holiest of duties and obeying a voice from on high. And yet, there are men who would pursue me, who would kill me if they knew my secret, or if they only suspected because of an imprudent remark you let escape."

"Never, father," responded Juanita, trembling and barely daring to raise her voice. "Never will I reveal what you tell me, whatever happens . . . But what do you have to fear? Everyone loves and esteems you. You are a loyal subject of the king and a devoted follower of our holy church."

"Child," said Diego, lowering his voice once again. "You are young and you don't know what torments are concealed by those brows that seem the most calm and tranquil. No doubt," he added, and his gaze landed with an indefinable expression of irony on the numerous holy objects with which the walls of his office were covered. "No doubt, the most Catholic house in Saragossa does not have a more beautiful Christ nor as many pictures of martyrs as you see here. And yet, my child!" continued Diego with a growing emotion, whispering the words that seemed to emerge painfully from his heaving chest. "Do you know what I pray for, when I am kneeling in church in front of the crucified God, in front of the images of mortals like me? While my lips repeat mechanically the words of faith and adoration, do you know what thoughts rise from my heart toward heaven?"

"Father," said Juanita, pale with terror.

"I ask forgiveness of God for profaning his holy and venerable name. I ask forgiveness for prostrating myself in front of sculpted figures and human images when God himself came one day to say to my ancestors: 'You will make no image, and you will worship nothing next to me!' I ask this God forgiveness for not observing the true law and the holy commandments that He gave himself to Moses, in the midst of the flames of Mount Sinai! Do you understand my crime now? Do you know who my enemies are now? Oh, my Juanita! I am a Maranno. I am a Jew! And the Inquisition is watching us!"

At the mention of the Inquisition, Juanita drew back instinctively, dropping Diego's hands, then stood frozen in terror. Pale, breathless, she looked from her father to the objects that surrounded him, as if to ask if all that she had just heard could possibly be true or if she wasn't under the influence of some horrible dream.

Frightened by his daughter's movement, Diego observed her with profound anxiety. He would have liked to have been able to read her heart to see if that terrible revelation had erected a barrier between them, or if she felt the bond of love that united them grow even tighter.

"And now, my child, I know that they have taught you . . . What am I saying? I myself have taught you that the most sacred of duties is to denounce those who, like me, are false children of the Church to the Holy Office . . . "

"Who? Me? Denounce you, father? Deliver you to the Inquisition!" murmured Juanita, who drew closer to her father. One of her arms encircled Diego while she raised the other one before him, as if to protect him from the enemy. "I want to share your dangers and your faith. You are my father and my master. What you believe must be the truth. The God whom you adore I will adore also."

Diego embraced his daughter in ecstasy.

"I expected nothing less of you, my Juanita! Oh! You are truly my blood and soul, valiant child!" And he hugged her again even more tenderly in his arms.

"But you are very pale, my daughter," he said a second later. "Don't be too afraid. You see you have always lived without any trouble. Prudence and mystery, that's all that's necessary."

Indeed, the poor child was profoundly shaken by what she had just learned. A moment ago life seemed to open its arms to her, happy, free, and beautiful, and now suddenly she saw herself surrounded by dangers, assaulted by terrors, held back by an eternal constraint and threatened by unknown enemies without number and without pity! Diego saw all that was going on in Juanita's heart.

"Pardon me, child," he said to her after an instant of silence. "Pardon me for having initiated you into the anguish and sorrow of this mysterious struggle. I would have wanted to spare your youth the fears and battles that are our lot. I would have wanted to leave you in ignorance of the terrible secret that now cast such a pall on your dreams of happiness. I hesitated a long time before telling you, but before God, could I keep silent? Didn't I owe you the truths that I possess? For it is at once our duty and our greatness to transmit to our descendents, amid perils without number, in the face of the cruelest torments, of death and infamy, the gift of that faith that makes for the hope and the support of our people across the centuries. And yet, in the midst of our trials, we have some rare but sweet compensations. Later, when you know more, you will understand what poignant satisfaction, what bitter pride we feel in the accomplishment of our holy but painful mission. You will understand how we are made greater by our unshakable attachment to the faith of our fathers and by our hidden but invincible resistance to the cruelest and most fearsome powers, despite dungeons, tortures, and the stake! And how these eternal dangers, these incessant threats, only serve to tighten the sweet bonds that unite us! Believe me, my daughter, I have always loved you, all the more so since I had to raise you amid implacable enemies and to save you from their ambushes. Well, you are a hundred times dearer to me since you have decided so courageously to share those perils of which you are now aware! Oh! I have already suffered greatly for my faith! I have overcome cruel vicissitudes, but I am amply repaid in this moment by your affection and your filial devotion!"

The voice of Diego trembled as he spoke these words, for he was profoundly moved. Seeing her father's emotion, Juanita forgot her own violent fears and only thought of him. She threw herself, palpitating, into Diego's arms.

"Oh, my father," she said in a hushed tone. "I will always love you." She could not continue. Sobs choked her voice. Father and daughter remained silent for a few moments, hugging each other tightly. Juanita was the first to break the silence.

"Father, don't say any more right now. You see how moved you are, how you are trembling! Another time . . . "

"Oh no, my Juanita, let me speak. It does me so much good. I have wanted to share this terrible secret with you for so long. I have always refrained, but it seems to me that only now are you my daughter, now that I can without hesitation tell you of my hopes, my beliefs, and all that I have already suffered!"

"Poor father!" Juanita said, clinging to Diego's neck. [. . .]

"Oh, I have asked myself many times if our fathers shouldn't have died as martyrs rather than accept conversion and force us to practice this eternal dissimulation. But could they? They faced the most bloody persecution. Death or baptism! That was the cry of their implacable enemies who had already wrenched their children away to bring them to the altars of Christ! What could such unfortunate people do? To die for the faith would have been great and worthy of the perseverance of Israel, worthy of themselves. But their baptized descendants, mixed with Christians, would have been strangers forever to the law of Sinai. They would have been lost for Israel. So it was necessary to lower their heads to receive baptismal waters, but their hearts stayed devoted to God's true law that they transmitted in secret to their sons and their daughters, at the cost of a thousand dangers, a thousand sacrifices. Thus my father revealed his faith to me one day. Thus he taught me to know the law of our master Moses, as I reveal it to you today, as I will teach you in turn. Like you, I was shocked for an instant, but the thought of my duty sustained me. That is why, child, you must be courageous and prudent. Act like you did before, fulfill just as regularly all those vain ceremonies in order to deflect suspicion. But in your deepest heart, raise your thoughts to the one and invisible God. He will forgive you and He will accept your prayer, for you are pure and innocent and He is just . . . Don't confide in anybody. Don't respond to any sign, for spies are prowling everywhere . . . Watch out for the servants, Iago and Joséfa . . . I have been very generous with them, but they would think it their duty to denounce me . . . Forget everywhere that you are a Jewess, except when you are alone before God or with me."

"And him? Fernando?" asked the young girl trembling.

"Child," Diego responded, as a smile returned to his lips and his eyes took on a profound expression of tenderness. "Child, do you believe that I cared so little for your happiness that I would choose a husband who is a stranger to your faith? He also, dear Juanita, belongs to the persecuted and indomitable race! Generous heart! He also knows what it is to suffer and keep silent. But you are upset, my child. Let's end this discussion. I think I heard a noise. People are entering the courtyard. Let's go, my daughter, and remember to be prudent and calm!" [. . .]

It was not the public celebrations, nor the parties thrown by the city, that had attracted Diego's friends to Saragossa. They were all Marannos like him. He had merely taken advantage of the occasion to bring them together without arousing suspicion. They had arrived last so as to be sure to find no room at the inns and be forced to stay under Diego's roof. Nor was Fernando, that abandoned child who came from nobody knew where, who had led so precarious a life until a happy chance had placed him in Diego's path, unknown to the latter. He had expressly brought him to Saragossa with the intention of providing for his future and giving him his daughter in marriage. Fernando was the son of an unfortunate Jewess whom Diego had seen die in an *auto-da-fé* and whom the king of Spain, despite his compassion for the youth of the victim, had not dared tear away from the butchers of the Inquisition. Happily for the child, he was not living with his mother, but had been given to a wet-nurse who didn't know who his parents were. They pretended Fernando was an orphan, for as the son of a heretic who had died on the stake he would have been barred from entering a profession or holding office, nor allowed to bear arms, nor to deal in gold, silver, pearls, silk, or fine wool. It would have been very dangerous for the young man to violate any of these prohibitions if the Inquisition had discovered the secret of his birth. In any case, it was prudent that Diego pretend not to know any of this so as not to be compromised along with Fernando if anything unfortunate should happen to him.

Diego saw the young Fernando for the first time at one of those nighttime assemblies where the Marannos celebrate in secret the ceremonies of the Jewish religion and where they initiate their children into the true faith. They were among the most critical and terrible moments in the lives of these families. For young girls, they could choose the time of these revelations, according to circumstances, sometimes waiting, as Diego had done, until they were old enough to marry. Before going to the church, the bride and groom, in the silence of the night, always received the nuptial blessing according to the law of Moses. As for boys, however, at the age of fourteen, they were suddenly introduced into the religious assembly of their nation. They were told of their birth and of the laws that condemned them. They were asked to choose between the God of their fathers and that of their persecutors. A sword was placed in their hands and if they wanted to stay Catholic, they were told to cut their parents' throats rather than denounce them to the Inquisition, as their religious faith demanded them to do. After such a revelation, faced with such a cruel alternative, these children sometimes were struck dumb, but nobody hesitated for long between their parents and the Holy Office.

When the young Fernando was presented with a sword at one of those ceremonies and told to kill his benefactors, instead of turning them into the Inquisitors, after they told him how his parents had died, the courageous boy energetically seized the weapon. His head held high and his eyes aflame, he stood before the assembly:

"Yes, I want to strike with this sword," he said. "But I want to strike our enemies. Let me keep this weapon, so that I may avenge all of you."

This courage, this generous impulse of indignation at such a young age, charmed Diego. He resolved to adopt the poor orphan and to make him the husband of his only daughter. We have seen what precautions he had to employ to accomplish this good work. What is more, the planned marriage between Fernando and Juanita fit in well with Diego's plan to emigrate. For this was the goal of all the Marannos: to escape from that country that had been ravaged by the fury of the Inquisition. But how much prudence was needed to manage it! There were many Marannos whose Jewish extraction was unknown. Normally, three or four generations had intervened since the abjuration that had been forced by persecution. But the Inquisition had its traditions and didn't lose sight of the descendants of the new Christians, as they were called, surrounding them with spies and informers. Their attempt to escape was fraught with danger and often cast the unfortunate people into the very abyss from which they were trying to escape.

For a long time, the city of Saragossa had been home to very few Marannos, even though formerly its most notable inhabitants were descended from converted Jews. But most of them had been killed or dispersed. [. . .] A few had managed to escape to France. Others, still more rare, had been able to dissimulate well enough to fool the Inquisition itself. Later, one by one, they left the province and even managed to leave Spain, employing endless precautions and leaving at well spaced intervals. In the period that we are speaking about, there remained in Saragossa only a few monks locked away in their convents, Brother Enriquez, the secretary of the Inquisitor Molina de Medrano, and finally Diego and his family.

The latter had been preparing his departure for a long time. While waiting, he affected the most profound piety. He was liberal to the church and to the priests and covered the statues of the Madonna and saints with ornaments. From time to time, he also took care to buy some property to allay suspicions of a flight. But alongside his open affairs, he also managed, with the help of his coreligionists in other cities, to engage in an active business that was unknown in Saragossa. It was for these men that he so often had recourse to the good offices of the Gardugna. He paid handsomely for their services and never bargained. He thus gained the good graces and the protection of the famous society, which was no small matter. He and his associates possessed the password that was known by all the Gardugnas in the provinces, and the name of Diego sufficed to stop the hands of the most fearsome brigands, wherever they were met. While Diego appeared to immobilize his fortune in landed wealth, in reality he moved the greater part of his revenues abroad, in order to prepare his resources for an eventual flight when the time was right.

But this departure demanded the greatest circumspection and the deepest care. Diego's plan was skillfully and perfectly calculated. Here is what he had imagined to allay all suspicion. On the day in question,

Fernando would go on a business trip to one of the ocean ports, where English or Dutch ships were always docked. Once there, he would send word to Saragossa that he had suddenly fallen seriously ill. Diego would go to join him there with his daughter and they would leave Spain together. The execution of this plan necessitated first of all the marriage of Fernando and Juanita, so that she could join him as his wife. Otherwise it would not have seemed natural for a young girl to undertake such a voyage, and such a strange determination would have inevitably aroused the attention of the Holy Office and its innumerable spies.

But, before celebrating the marriage in church, Diego wanted to unite the two young people according to the law of Moses. He had long awaited a favorable circumstance that would allow him to reunite at his home some of his coreligionists in order to accomplish this secret ceremony. The recent public celebration in Saragossa had furnished the occasion that he had desired. Diego's friends had come to his home, not only to settle their business affairs but also to serve as witnesses to the marriage of Juanita and Fernando. Such were the explanations that Diego gave that day to his daughter and this was why he had finally revealed to her the secret of his true religion.

That same night, Diego, his family, and his friends, who had been brought together under his roof for a double purpose, were all united in his office, at the far end of the apartment. The monk was also there. He had entered under the cover of night while the servants weren't looking. The thick drapes covering the windows were carefully closed, the doors all locked. A thick carpet stifled the noise of footsteps. Christ and the pictures of the saints had all disappeared. A sole lamp lit the room and threw a feeble light on the characters of this nocturnal, silent scene.

Fernando and Juanita stood together in the middle of the office, next to Diego and one of his friends. The monk approached the group. He had set down the crucifix he always wore and had covered his tall head with a white wool shawl, the kind Jews wear during religious ceremonies. A similar shawl was spread over the heads of the bride and groom. The monk pronounced, in a low voice, slow but distinct, the seven nuptial benedictions. And the spectators responded, each time: "Blessed is the name of the Lord, amen." Then the monk took a cup, filled it with wine, blessed it, and presented it to the groom. Fernando pressed it to his lips and offered it to Juanita, who did the same. Then Fernando took a ring and placed it on the finger of the young girl, pronouncing, still in a low voice, the sacramental formula: "Henceforth, you belong to me according to the law of Moses and of Israel."

It was at once sad and striking, this mysterious ceremony, this union celebrated in the middle of the night, by the flickering light of a lamp, this initiation, perilous in itself, of two young people in love into an existence full of danger and struggle. These grave and solemn moments reminded the spectators of all that was terrible about their situation. These men who were accustomed to living amid enemies and ambushes, who were familiar with every sacrifice, were profoundly moved. They passed the hands of Fernando and Juanita among them in silence as a sign of congratulations. Only Diego embraced his daughter and held her for a long time against his heart. A quarter of an hour later everything was once again quiet in Diego's house. As for Brother Enriquez, he had left by a side door, which was on the other side of the house from that used by the servants. As a monk belonging to the Inquisition, moreover, he could go wherever he wanted and at whatever time without causing surprise.

But while Diego was taking the most minute precautions against the enterprises of his redoubtable enemies, another danger was brewing for him and his loved ones: the vengeance of the Count de Ramira. Always having assumed he would be able to achieve the union between his son Alonzo and Juanita that would reestablish his family's much diminished fortune, he was all the more confident in that until then Diego had not formally confirmed the rumors that he was giving his daughter to Fernando. But the motives that Diego had for keeping quiet no longer pertained once he was sure of being able to marry his daughter secretly according to the prescriptions of his true religion. Thus, once his friends had arrived in Saragossa, Diego had announced the coming union of Fernando and Juanita, which would be celebrated after the public festivities.

Upon hearing that piece of news, the anger and vexation of the Count de Ramira knew no bounds. He felt his pride had been wounded and he resolved to avenge this insult against his name—of which, as a true Spaniard, he was extremely proud. But if the pride of the count was great, his greed was greater, and the financial troubles that threatened him made him look for a way to satisfy both his vengeance and his desire for wealth. To denounce Diego to the Inquisition was not the way to arrive at this double goal. The Holy Office always confiscated the property belonging to heretics. The count therefore did not even consider this means of vengeance, but the Gardugna was there, ready to sell its services to the highest bidder. The count had at first thought of having Fernando killed by brigands. But if this crime would prevent his marriage, the father could still persist in his refusal. It was therefore his resistance that must be broken. Diego had to die. Once he was out of the way, the count had enough influence to be able to manipulate events so as to achieve his goal.

Once the celebrations in Saragossa were over, and the many inhabitants of the provinces they had attracted began to disperse, all the roads and mountain trails around the city were filled with travelers going home. Many went along in bands to protect themselves against brigands and thieves. Diego's friends had left with the others one evening and Fernando had accompanied them to the edge of town. But an attentive observer would have noticed them, in groups of two or three, leaving the main roads for the small paths that covered the sides of the mountains. Some of them seemed to go left, others right. But when night came, black and silent, all these men were once more near the city and slipped carefully and silently between the trees and brush, arriving one after the other at a secret rendezvous, long known only to them.

It was a mysterious and deserted spot that was called the Ruins. Indeed, it contained the remains of an ancient temple consecrated, no doubt, to some Roman divinity. But the centuries had covered it with a venerable debris of thick vegetation. Popular lore depicted it as a rendezvous for ghosts, a theater of diabolic scenes, where witches celebrated their sabbath, dancing around Satan. The new Christians who met there to celebrate, at night, the ceremonies of the Jewish religion, fostered these superstitious rumors because they helped keep away curious and spying eyes. Whenever people passed the Ruins during the day, they made the sign of the cross, and even the bravest men would never have ventured there during the night.

It was in the middle of the Ruins, under fallen arcades, in a pit dug by nature herself, that the Marannos held their mysterious meetings. That cavern was impenetrable for those who weren't intimately familiar with the labyrinthine detours that hid the entrance. In former times, the cavern was barely big enough for all the Marannos who came for the secret services, but the emigrations and tortures had considerably diminished the number of those who attended these celebrations, which were becoming more and more dangerous and therefore more and more rare.

In the middle of the cavern there was a little outcropping of rock that formed a kind of table for the reading of the holy book. They had placed there a single torch that lit the scene, throwing a reddish light, along with thick clouds of black smoke, on the low ceiling of the overhanging rock. It was around this stone table that the Marannos stood, as they arrived one by one. Two of them stood by the entrance to the cavern. Every time a newcomer arrived, these guards held a sword to his throat. Without displaying any fear, the newcomer would calmly repeat in a low voice the password *lo ammi*,[4] or else he was a traitor and paid with his life. A relatively large number of Marannos had gathered this time in the cavern—not only Fernando and the friends of Diego, but other coreligionists, who lived spread out in different cities in Aragon, had taken advantage of the circumstances to reunite in Saragossa for this meeting in the underground Ruins.

There were nobles, bourgeois, men of the people, workers, monks, two or three agents of the Inquisition. The men spoke to each other in low voices. It had been a long time since they had all met. Many of those who attended the last meeting were not present at this one. Some had been able to leave Spain. These were the lucky ones. Others hadn't dared to come. Many were dead. Some had fallen into the clutches of the Inquisition and had died as martyrs to their faith. Still others were hidden away in dungeons waiting to be tortured and die on the stake.

Suddenly all eyes were drawn to the entrance of the cavern. Brother Enriquez had just entered. He slowly approached the group around the stone table, greeting them and shaking their hands one by one. Enriquez had taken off his crucifix. He moved a stone from under the table and took out a prayer book as well as a white wool shawl. The other Marannos likewise took out prayer books hidden in different spots while two of them slid a rock to reveal a hiding place where they

---

4. In the Bible *lo ammi*, which means "not my people," is the name given to the people Israel before their reconciliation with God.

had stored the sacred parchment scroll containing the five books of Moses. Enriquez wrapped himself in the white wool shawl. Addressing those gathered, he said in a grave and moving tone: "My brothers, let us pray." And he began to recite the evening prayer, in a low but fervent tone.

It was a strange spectacle, both solemn and poignant, to see all these men praying quietly, with their pale and grave faces, onto which the torch threw a flickering red light. All around them were mysteries and shadows, danger and enemies! The threatening rock suspended above them was like an image of the perils that hovered ceaselessly over their heads. But just as their prayers rose to heaven through the rocks and the earth, so too, they believed, did the purity of their faith arrive before the Lord, even in the form and in the ceremonies of a religion that they considered idolatrous. At this moment, they bowed under the hand of God that weighed heavily upon them. But they drew their strength from the very enormity of the sacrifices that they made. They felt their greatness in the terrible dangers that they faced in order to hold once again a ceremony of the true faith. And they were proud in their suffering, these men who were spied upon, hunted, chased, because they worshipped God as he commanded, in spite of the ambushes of their omnipotent, fanatical enemies, who were implacable in their pursuit and pitiless in their punishment.

When the ceremony was over, the monk, after having taken off the wool shawl, turned around and signaled to the congregants that he wanted to speak to them. They all drew closer and huddled around him in silence. Then Enriquez spoke the following words, still in a low tone:

"Brothers, I had you come here in order to have the ineffable and only too dangerous happiness of praying to God together according to our holy law. But I also wanted to acquaint you with the current situation. Know this: never have the dangers been greater than they are about to become! Only a few days ago, the lead Inquisitor Molina said to me: 'The pernicious doctrines of the monk from Wittenberg are causing us much worry and we need all of our authority to combat the heresies that have emerged from hell and that gain souls for Satan. Thus we have neglected the new Christians for a time, but we still suspect them of judaizing in secret. Depend upon it. Even if the Inquisition can't do everything at once, it still defends the faith! And as soon as the numerous trials of the adherents of Luther are over, we will once again turn our attention to those other enemies of the Holy Church.'

So you see, brothers, we have to redouble our prudence and hide even deeper in our hearts our thoughts and hopes. The God of Abraham, of Isaac, and of Jacob, who has never completely abandoned his people, will watch over you. As for me, I can no longer help any of you! Don't count on me any longer! Who knows, perhaps I also am being watched! Abstain, even in secret, from the least act that could betray your faith. God will forgive you, for he reads your hearts! But transmit to your children the sacred and mysterious legacy of the true religion so that on the day of deliverance, which will come sooner or later, Israel will one day find its children again and will not have to mourn for the loss of its children among the nations.

And now, we have a final task to fulfill: these prayer books, this sacred scroll on which is written the word of God, which we will no longer read, cannot remain in this place if we will no longer return to it. Moreover, it could be discovered and would then be exposed to all sorts of profanations. Let us do like our brothers in Palestine: when they could no longer use their books and sacred scrolls, they confided them to the earth, like we confide the remains of those who are dear to us."

After having said these words, the monk took out a dagger from under his garments, knelt down and used that arm to dig the earth. Some of the other Marannos imitated him, using their daggers or the swords that some of them were allowed to carry as gentlemen. The others stood around and watched the strange scene as mute spectators. After a little while, a deep enough hole had been dug. The monk first placed the prayer books into the ground, then he laid down the parchment Pentateuch. He placed over it the white wool shawl, then covered it with earth so that no trace remained. In Palestine, these sorts of burials, which used to be rather frequent, were not sorrowful occasions. The soil to which they confided the used scrolls is sacred. They would recall the long years that the holy book had served and they would rejoice, so to speak, that it had come to a happy end, not as a result of accident or violence. But here, the ceremony had a bitter feeling. For the Marannos, who had defended their faith for so long against the all-powerful Inquisition, the supreme act that they had just accomplished meant the disappearance of their last hope and the admission of their defeat on Spanish soil. They were not abandoning their faith, but this beautiful country that they had always wanted to consider a homeland. Thus were the men profoundly moved. Most of them shed tears and Enriquez himself, despite the strength of his character, could find no words to console his brothers. He contented himself with shaking their hands as they dispersed, recommending once again prudence and secrecy!

While these moving scenes were happening in the depths of the Ruins, away from profane eyes, another nocturnal interview was taking place right outside the forest. The two men who chose this spot for their meeting were Mateo the *capatoze*, the chief of the Gardugna in the province, and Alonzo, the son of the Count de Ramira. What they had to say needed to be kept secret and where they were they didn't need to fear eavesdropping, especially at night.

"What do you want from me, signor?" asked the *capatoze*, after having assured himself that it was really the young knight that he was meeting near the ruins.

"There is in Saragossa a man whose existence troubles me . . . "

"So?"

"And whose death is necessary to my plans."

"So be it," responded the *capatoze*, taking some money from the hands of the young de Ramira. "Who is it?"

"Diego d'Almora"

"Diego, never! Take back your money!"

"You refuse?"

"Yes."

"Why?'

"While I was away from Saragossa, my wife and my young son Esteban found help and protection in the home of Diego. Never!"

If the *capatoze* had wanted to tell the full story he would have said: during the ten years that I spent in the galleys. It was there, in fact, that he had earned his title of *capatoze*. But he didn't find it necessary for the young man to know about his past.

"My father said that I would encounter resistance. But we will overcome it."

"How? I'm the leader."

"Yes, but there is someone whom even you obey. It's the *hermana mayor*, the supreme leader of the Gardugna."

Mateo didn't respond. The young Alonzo's words struck him and he needed to think.

"Do you want me to tell you his name?" asked Alonzo.

"It's not necessary. Since you know him, you know that his name must never be spoken. I accept."

"You will kill Diego?"

"When must he disappear?"

"We will tell you."

"When?"

"Soon."

"Where?"

"At the Red Tavern. One night a man will say to you: It is time. And you will do it the next day."

"That will work."

"I'm counting on you."

"The Gardugna always keeps its word."

After having uttered these final words in a strange tone, Mateo went on his way. Alonzo, who didn't want to travel with the *capatoze*, followed him with his eyes as long as the night permitted and then set off himself.

At that moment, Fernando emerged from the thick bushes that surrounded the ruins, on his way back from the secret meeting of the Marannos. He moved with the precaution that was typical of the Marannos, moving the branches aside, advancing in silence, lending an ear to the slightest noise, and examining his surroundings through the foliage. Suddenly, poking his head out from the branches that hid him, he saw a human figure standing still a few feet in front of him. Who was that man? What was he doing here at this hour? It was Alonzo de Ramira.

This discovery terrified Fernando. What motive could bring the young knight to this spot in the middle of the night? Suddenly, Alonzo made a movement:

"Now," he said aloud to himself, "they won't escape!" And he set off, heading for the city.

An unspeakable terror took hold of Fernando when he heard these words. Apparently Ramira had spied on him and his fellow Marannos and was now going to turn them in to the Inquisition. What else could he be doing here and what else could his words have signified? Fernando was in a horrible situation. [. . .] He couldn't hesitate. Luckily the Count de Ramira was away from Saragossa for a few days. His son thus had nobody he could tell his secret to before turning them into the Inquisition. Fernando couldn't waste any time. He resolved upon what he had to do.

Alonzo, in order to make his way to the Inquisition (which Fernando felt sure was his plan), had to pass in front of the Buen Ventura tavern. He would surely enter. The violent nature of the young count, his aggressive attitude toward Fernando, would surely bring about a quarrel and a quarrel would surely bring about a duel. This is exactly what Fernando was hoping for. He was betting that Ramira would provoke him. And Ramira was not a fearsome adversary for Fernando, who was skilled at arms, always calm, and able to maintain his sang-froid in the midst of dangers. And a duel with Ramira was the only means he possessed of preventing the denunciation, his only chance of salvation. [. . .]

Fernando and Alonzo soon found themselves with swords in hand in the middle of a crowd of onlookers, while the horrified tavern keeper ran to alert the archers of Sainte-Hermandad. The fight did not take long. After a few furious thrusts by Ramira that Fernando deflected with his usual sang-froid, wanting to strike a decisive blow Fernando left himself completely open and drove his sword into his opponent's chest. Alonzo fell. At the same instant, the Sainte-Hernandad arrived. While Ramira's friends, who were saddened by the outcome of the fight, carried him off to his father's house, Fernando was brought to jail. [. . .]

It didn't take long for Diego to learn what happened. [. . .] A few days passed. Finally, after having hovered between life and death, the youth and vigorous constitution of Alonzo triumphed: the young man was saved. Diego, upon hearing the news, felt relieved of a great weight. A smile reappeared on the pale and sad face of poor Juanita, whereas Fernando's terror only grew stronger.

When he learned in prison that Alonzo had recovered, he felt that all was lost for him and his fellow Marannos. Every morning he expected to be transferred from the prison of the Manifestacion to that of the Inquisition. However, the days went by, the preparations for his trial began. Alonzo was living and still Fernando's fears had not come to pass. He was extremely perplexed. What was Alonzo doing near the Ruins that night and what had his words signified?

Once his son was out of danger, the count once again thought of bringing his plan to fruition. The imprisonment of Fernando was a stroke of luck since after Diego's assassination, Juanita would be without a protector and would fall easily into his hands. One night, a short time later, the *capatoze* was, as usual, sitting in the Red Tavern, outside the gate leading to France, when a man sat down in front of him. Mateo looked at the newcomer whom he did not recognize.

"It's time," the latter said in a dry, indifferent tone. This was the signal established between Alonzo and the *capatoze* for the execution of the crime. The *capatoze* shivered. For a second, he thought he had misunderstood. He stayed motionless in his seat without answering.

"It's time," repeated the unknown man in the same tone, staring fixedly at the chief of the Gardugna.

"Very well," responded the latter, who no longer had any doubt about the unknown man's intentions. "Very well." [. . .]

Some time later, Diego had gone out walking, absorbed in his reflections and his doubts, when at the turn of the road he suddenly found himself surrounded by men wearing large cloaks and hats covering their faces. Diego shivered. He knew only too well the mysterious allures of the Inquisition and the way they liked to surprise their victims at night. He did not remain in doubt for very long, for as soon as the terrible thought had presented itself to him, one of the men approached and whispered in his ear:

"In the name of the most holy Inquisition, follow us."

Although the Marannos were always prepared for this horrible blow, Diego froze in stupor and terror. The Inquisition! All the unheard-of miseries, the supreme punishments that this fearsome word contained passed in an instant before his eyes at the same time as he thought of Juanita, his dear child! However, he attempted to gather his wandering thoughts so as not to appear terrified. Perhaps he was only being called as a witness or for a particular piece of business. So many mysterious things happened within the walls of the Inquisition! To appear terrified was to confess a crime and the Holy Office knew no forgiveness.

"I am always ready to obey the orders of the Holy Office," he said. [. . .]

"Walk," said the man who appeared to be the commander. "If your life means anything to you," the chief whispered into his ear, "then don't say a word and walk." And he added in an even lower voice the regular password that Diego used with the Gardugna for his protection and that of his friends on the dangerous roads of Aragon.

"Mateo!" thought Diego, who grew more and more surprised. It was Mateo who was having him kidnapped in such an extraordinary manner, using the fearsome name of the Inquisition. What a mystery. [. . .] Diego tried to question the chief but he could obtain no response. He therefore continued to walk while reflecting on his situation and the intentions of the *capatoze*, all the while giving in to a mute despair as he thought of poor Juanita, alone now, without protectors and abandoned. The unhappy father finally fell into a sort of stupor that almost made him forget his own situation. He didn't know what he was doing nor what he was thinking and only recovered consciousness when one of his companions, after having led him through some tortuous mountain passes, stopped finally at a cavern, a sort of secret hideaway, one of many used by the Gardugna to hide their booty and cover the traces of their crimes.

After Diego had gone out, Juanita was overcome with sinister presentiments that she couldn't put aside in spite of her courage. Since the day of the revelation, when her father had told her of her true religion, the young girl had completely transformed. Young and happy up to that moment, Juanita had always filled the house with laughter and activity. But lately she had become pensive and serious. Her secret discussions with her father, and all she had learned of the sad and heroic destiny of her nation, had made a profound impression on her. Upon hearing the tales of dangers and suffering, the young girl had at first been filled with fear and horror, but little by little she had felt grow within her the indomitable energy of the girls of her race. Like all the Marannos, she was proud of that mysterious struggle waged for so long by her people, proud of the mission they had undertaken. That mission was hers as well and she considered it a sacred duty to accomplish it with courage and perseverance.

Nevertheless, as soon as she was alone, surrounded by dangers, without a protector or friend, without a single human being to whom she could confess her doubts and suffering, the poor young girl couldn't help but shake, and soon she was crying bitterly. She stayed like that all night, waiting in vain for her father's return, listening for the slightest noise, sometimes hoping, sometimes fearing the most awful horrors. The dawn found her still awake, her eyes reddened by crying and insomnia. The day was spent in the same terror and anguish, interrupted a few times by a vague glimmer of hope, but Diego did not return.

Already accustomed to prudence and circumspection, Juanita didn't dare ask directly at the Manifestacion prison to know whether her father had really been summoned the night before. She merely sent her servant Iago to get news of Fernando. Iago reported that he was doing well, and told her and Diego to rest easy. He had seen one of his judges and the trial was sure to lead to his acquittal. So Diego had not been to the prison. The poor child now saw the implacable Inquisition arrayed before her with its cortege of horrors, extending its bloody hand over her and her family!

Poor Juanita remained plunged in a kind of stupor when, the following day, a sinister piece of news reached Saragossa: some woodcutters in the forest had found, in a pit in the middle of the woods, not far from the city, a horribly mutilated cadaver that was totally unrecognizable. By the clothes alone could they determine that the unlucky man who had succumbed to an assassin's blows was Diego. The motive for the crime was surely theft for they had taken all his money. The cadaver discovered by the woodcutters was in reality that of a poor traveler killed by the Guapos the same day that the *capatoze* had kidnapped Diego. They had hidden the body in one of their caves, near Saragossa. Mateo had taken Diego's clothes and put them on the cadaver, after disfiguring it by shooting his pistol at close range into its face. Then they had thrown the body where it would easily be discovered.

The horrible news found its way into Diego's house. Some words exchanged between Iago and Joséfa had attracted Juanita's attention. She questioned the two servants, who attempted to hide the truth from her, when a loud noise was heard in the street. It was the confused rumbling of a crowd that was advancing slowly. Juanita ran into the courtyard and opened the door, but the unhappy girl drew back in terror upon seeing the spectacle before her. Four men, carrying a cadaver, advanced to the opened door. Despite the blood and the dirt that covered the clothes, Juanita recognized them immediately: these were her father's clothes. She stumbled and had to lean against the door so as not to collapse.

Meanwhile, while Saragossa was occupied with the tragic end of Diego, the Count de Ramira was actively pursuing his plans, which promised success. Indeed, Juanita was alone now. Her father was dead, or so they thought. Fernando was in prison. [. . .] The count saw to it that signor Tueno, a deputy, was appointed her tutor. His first action was to have the young girl placed in the Ursuline convent, where the mother superior was the count's sister. During the first few days she was suffering, Juanita barely knew what was happening. Crushed by so many terrible blows, she let herself be directed and led, as if she no longer had a will. Plunged into a mute resignation, she was grateful for the consolations and attentions that the superior of the Ursuline convent gave her. But little by little, when her sadness had calmed a bit, the young girl began to think about her situation. What terrified her the most was her isolation.

In the midst of her despair, and of all the calamities that had befallen her, not a single friend had appeared. At one moment, she saw the cold and impassive face of the monk Enriquez. The Dominican had given her an almost imperceptible signal: he had furtively placed his finger on his mouth, then he had disappeared. But what could he do for her? He didn't know any more than she did what was awaiting her and what was threatening her, nor what would become of her! Moreover, it wasn't the Inquisition she was afraid of now. In that case, he might have been of some use to her.

Enriquez had paid close attention to the peripeties of the bloody and dark drama that began with the duel between Alonzo and Fernando and that seemed to end with the assassination of Diego. He tried to shine a light on this chaos despite a few points that remained obscure to him. The monk nevertheless felt that a great and even a double danger was threatening the daughter of his unfortunate friend.

A few days after her entry into the Ursuline convent, Juanita learned that Fernando had finally appeared before his judges and that the tribunal had absolved him of the charge of homicide that was hanging over him. That bit of news, which the superior communicated herself to Juanita, brought a ray of hope into the solitude that seemed to surround the girl. Fernando was free and soon she would see him again. But the unhappy young girl had to deploy a great deal of skill to resist numerous attacks from all directions. While signor Tueno had told her that she must no longer dream of a marriage with Fernando, the mother superior, at the behest of her brother, the Count de Ramira, had taken it upon herself to plant in the young girl's mind the idea of marrying Alonzo. If Juanita hadn't already understood the miserable machinations of which she was the victim, these words, so often repeated, should have sufficed to enlighten her as to the cause of her suffering. The continual praise of Alonzo, which the superior managed to slip incessantly into her conversation with the girl, could leave no doubt as to the plans of her enemies.

Absolved by the Aragon tribunal, Fernando left prison, where he had heard of the successive blows that had befallen his loved ones. He only half understood what was going on due to the contradictory statements and amplifications of his narrators. Upon leaving the Manifestacion, he headed straight for Diego's house, where he was met by strange faces. Iago and Joséfa, who had long served the family, had been sent away. Signor Tueno announced to the young man that he had no claim to Diego's succession and that his rights were limited to reclaiming the objects that had belonged to him. Nevertheless, he added, in light of his long presence in the home of the departed, he judged it wise to bestow upon him a certain sum for services rendered and which he could claim from the notary in charge of the estate.

This line of conduct was dictated to the tutor by the Count de Ramira, who wanted to make a show of his fairness and generosity. The count feared that in reducing Fernando to complete poverty, he would drive the young man to despair. Despite his courage and his quick temper, Fernando felt powerless in the face of signor Tueno's cold and inflexible words. Fernando went to the Ursuline convent and demanded to speak to Juanita, but his attempt did not meet with success. Fernando returned to the city. He walked, sunk in sad reflections, asking himself what he should do. Turning a corner, he felt a man brush up against him as he passed alongside. Fernando raised his head. The man who had just touched him wore a Dominican's robe. When he turned around Fernando recognized Enriquez. The two men stared at each other an instant then continued on their way.

Soon Juanita felt her strength diminish. For a moment she thought of dying but then the thought of seeing Fernando again gave her the will to live. However, her situation had become intolerable, and despite her courage, she understood that she couldn't resist forever. Abandoned without defenses to those who coveted her fortune, cut off from the whole world, she couldn't hope for any help in her prison. It was necessary to get out, no matter how. Perhaps she would find a generous heart in whom she could confide her troubles, a protector who would take her side against the family and friends of the count. However, there was only one means of making this happen: to appear to give way to her tutor's desires.

She announced her new resolution to the superior. She informed signor Tueno, who appeared immediately before Juanita. He praised the young girl for finally having made a reasonable decision. She was told to go directly to the home of her future husband, where they would celebrate her engagement to Alonzo. Juanita couldn't argue with this plan, but despite the impatience of her tutor, she needed a few days to recover her strength. She appeared completely resigned to her fate and even seemed almost to hurry to the count's house so as to hide the real thoughts behind her actions.

The young girl was received by the countess in a most cordial manner. The count showed her a great deal of deference. As for Alonzo, he lavished on her all kinds of delicate attentions that betrayed a profound respect. In short, everyone in the house seemed to be concerned only with pleasing her and fulfilling her every desire. But Juanita saw clearly that all these incessant signs of interest were only offered to her in order to win her confidence and to surround her with surveillance, in order to make it impossible for her to communicate with anyone outside their entourage.

A great crowd had assembled at the count's house the night of the engagement. All the principal nobles of Saragossa were there, many of whom were secretly engaged in conspiracies against the king and the Holy Office. The count, however, took care to invite the inquisitors and some of their partisans. Surrounded by noble ladies belonging to families devoted to the count, Juanita anxiously contemplated the brilliant assembly. Her eyes were looking for a protector, a sign of encouragement, but not a single face appeared. Her situation was terrible. United with Fernando by sacred and indissoluble bonds, in a moment she was supposed to pledge her faith to another husband. And she couldn't reveal her secret! The poor child remained motionless, trembling and weak.

The count advanced toward her with a firm and determined air, but his face was somber and full of anger. Juanita stood there pale and about to faint. She found herself, without knowing quite how, next to Alonzo.

"Have pity," she whispered to the young man. "Pity!" And her words emerged only with difficulty from her palpitating chest.

"Silence," murmured Alonzo, who feared she might refuse him.

"For the love of heaven," cried Juanita, joining her hands together. Alonzo did not respond. All the spectators approached, anxious, silent. Juanita took a few steps back, her chest heaving, ready to collapse. At this moment the count turned around to take the young girl's hand.

"I can't," she said.

"Go on," said signor Tueno in a dry, cold, imperative tone that he thought she wouldn't be able to resist. That voice reminded Juanita of the past. She shivered with indignation and this indignation restored her strength. Her pale cheeks took on a lively red color.

"Never," she said in a low but resolved voice.

"Go on," repeated the tutor.

"I can't," responded Juanita.

The unhappy girl had become pale once again. A cold sweat appeared on her brow. The shadows of the dead hovered in front of her eyes . . . She looked mechanically around her and in the middle of all those lords and ladies she suddenly noticed a monk, a Dominican, among the inquisitors. A sudden thought went through her head: Enriquez! Enriquez could save her from the hands of the Holy Office. He had said so . . . It was like a ray of hope amid the horrors that besieged her. But such was the fear that the Inquisition inspired that the young girl drew back instinctively as if someone were trying to grab her.

"Say why you can't," said signor Tueno, pale with fury. "You have to say why!"

Juanita turned bright red. Her teeth chattered with terror . . . her tongue was like ice.

"Why?" she said, making unheard of efforts just to speak. Then, summoning all her strength, and gathering her courage and resolution, she cried out in a hoarse and strangled voice:

"Because I'm a Maranna. Because I'm a Jewess!"

At these terrible words, the whole assembly was struck dumb. A large circle formed around Juanita. Signor Tueno, the countess, and Alonzo all drew away. Seeing the fruits of his crime and of his long maneuvers about to escape him, the count took a step forward and cried:

"Don't believe her. It's a lie!" But he stopped when he saw before him the inquisitor Molina de Medrano.

"That judaizing heretic will be brought before the very holy tribunal of the Inquisition," Medrano said in a slow, clear voice. "As for you, count," he added with a menacing look. "The Holy Office will have to examine your conduct in this affair to see if you knowingly sheltered a Jewess by giving her asylum in your house."

The next evening Fernando and Enriquez once again met in the ruins. Fernando had learned the sad news in the tavern. He had been quick to disappear. Juanita's confession was just as dangerous for him as for her, for the Holy Office never had enough victims. He made his way by cover of night to the ruins, where Enriquez was already waiting for him.

"Stay here for a few days," he told him. "It's impossible to flee right now. All the roads are blocked. Here is some bread, wine, and other provisions. Wait, I will return and I will tell you when the time is right to leave Spain."

"And Juanita?"

"She is in the prison of Aljafería. I haven't yet seen her. For her own good, I must not appear to take an interest in her. But I am watching out for her and I won't abandon her."

"But they will martyr her. They will kill her," said Fernando, wringing his hands in despair.

"I won't let them. I will risk everything. I will flee with her and if fate is against us . . . well then I will call death to help me, a quick and sudden death. We will succumb but we will escape the horrors of torture." And the monk took a vial of poison out from underneath his robe and showed it to Fernando.

The sudden confession of Juanita precipitated a catastrophe that the monk was expecting and it did not take him totally by surprise. It's true that the rapidity of the blow had wreaked havoc on his plans. Enriquez thought he had more time, but he had determined not to back down before any obstacle and to brave the greatest dangers to rescue the girl.

But there was another man in Saragossa that the recent events put in a terrible position: that man was Mateo, the chief Gardugna for the province. What was he going to do with Diego? Juanita's father was still in the cave where they had brought him. But Mateo couldn't continue to keep him. He was hiding a heretic, a Maranno, from the Inquisition. For if Juanita was a Jewess, then Diego must be also. And hiding a Jew from the Holy Office was just as great a crime as heresy. At the same time, Mateo couldn't turn Diego over to the Inquisition because this would mean confessing to the count and Alonzo that he had accepted money for an assassination that he hadn't carried out. The only solution he could imagine was to take Diego secretly to France. It was a dangerous solution but it was the only one.

One evening Diego approached the opening of the cave, where instead of seeing his normal captors he saw Mateo.

"Don't ask me any questions. Follow me." Taking him by the hand, he led the unhappy father out of the gorges and through the mountains, where the two soon disappeared into the shadows of the night, along secret paths unknown and inaccessible to any human foot.

Meanwhile, the Inquisitors had conducted Juanita to Aljafería, where the guards placed her in one of the many dungeons of the somber edifice. It was a horrible place, about three feet long by just as wide and so low you could barely stand up. The floor was muddy and cold. Humidity dripped from the walls, which had a single narrow opening with bars. A nauseating odor filled the space, into which the sun never shined.

In the half light of the dungeon, she suddenly saw one of her inquisitors appear, and next to him stood another man whose face she couldn't see. Behind them were two short, stocky men with hard and stupid expressions. These were the two tormentors of the Holy Office. Juanita shivered.

"What is your name?"

"My name is Juanita," she said.

"Who is your father?"

"Diego d'Almora."

"Death prevented him from receiving the punishment that his crimes merited."

"His crimes?" Juanita cried with indignation.

"Silence!" said the inquisitor. "You have enough to do to defend yourself. You declared that you were a Maranna. You have judaized."

"My father told me I was a Maranna. But I never judaized," responded Juanita. The poor child thought that her answer might save her.

"Don't conceal the truth from the Holy Office. We have ways of making you talk. Don't you have other relatives in Saragossa or in another Spanish city?

"No."

"However you don't live alone with your father. A young man was in your house. What was his name?"

"Fernando."

"Was he a Maranno?"

"I never saw anything that indicated it."

"Don't attempt to fool the Inquisition. It knows all."

"I can only say what I know."

"But you were supposed to marry the young man. He therefore must be a Jew like you."

"I was obeying my father and didn't ask for an explanation."

"Where is he?"

"I don't know."

"Don't lie."

"I told you I don't know. He promised he would leave Spain."

"The Inquisition can't believe a heretic. Confess . . . Don't be obstinate."

"I can't tell you what I don't know myself."

"Go ahead," said the inquisitor to the two men behind him. One of them grabbed the girl brutally by the arm and the other took off the shawl that was covering her shoulders. Juanita let out a gasp of fright and pain.

"Confess."

"Oh! I don't know."

"Do your job," said the inquisitor to the executioner.

One of the tormentors then took a large iron ring with spikes on the inside that tightened like a vice. He placed this horrible instrument of torture around Juanita's arm. Then he looked at the inquisitor.

"Go ahead," he said.

The tormentor tightened the vice of the bracelet that squeezed the white and delicate arm of the girl. She let out a low and prolonged moan.

"Confess," the inquisitor began again.

"I don't know," murmured Juanita in a voice broken by pain. "But even if I did know I wouldn't tell you," she added with a sublime gesture of indignation. The inquisitor made a sign. The tormentor tightened the vice a second time. Juanita let out a piercing shriek. The unhappy child was suffering a double torture: the points of the metal entered into her flesh at the same time as it grew atrociously tight around her. Her whole body twitched.

"Confess," repeated the inquisitor in the same impassive, cold tone.

Juanita didn't respond. The tormentor tightened the screws again. The veins in her arm bulged horribly. Streams of blood ran down her arm around the ring. Juanita was seized with a convulsive trembling. Her pale lips contracted, her teeth chattered and a cold sweat wet her hair. She turned her gaze toward her mangled arm and then her head fell back. Two tears rolled down her cheeks.

"Continue," said the inquisitor.

"It's as tight as it will go."

"Try the other arm."

The first executioner opened the screws while the second took hold of Juanita's other arm. But the young girl collapsed. She had fainted.

"We will continue the interrogation another day," said the inquisitor. "Revive her." And he exited the dungeon, leaving Juanita in the hands of her two tormentors. [. . .]

Enriquez knew only too well what had happened to Juanita in prison. He felt terrible that he couldn't prevent her from being tortured and he paid close attention to events in order to choose the right moment to execute his plan, which he hoped was not far off. While he waited, he went to see Fernando in order to bring him provisions and reassure him about Juanita. In truth, the young man needed these consolations even more than material aid. He had forgotten the dangers that faced him by thinking only of Juanita and he knew all that the Inquisition could do to her. Images of the young girl torn to pieces by the horrible tortures of that odious tribunal obsessed him. He was impatient to see Enriquez and every moment he didn't come only added to his fears and his suffering! He wasn't able to rest or sleep in that hideout, far away from all prying eyes. Finally Enriquez appeared.

"Well, my father?" he cried upon seeing him.

"Be patient a little longer," said the monk in a sad tone. "A little more patience."

"And Juanita? They tortured her, didn't they? You aren't answering. So it's true! Oh, the monsters!"

"It's true," responded Enriquez. "However her trial hasn't yet begun so we still have time."

"Time! But they will kill her! She might already be dead!"

"No, thank God. Be patient my son."

The monk exited after saying these words. Fernando watched him leave. When he was gone, the young man shook his head sadly. All the promises, all the assurances the monk had given couldn't convince Fernando. For him, there was no possibility of escape. Enriquez was surely hoping in vain. For what could he expect from those torturers who would martyr the poor child? Juanita torn to bits by the horrible instruments of torture! And on his account! That horrible thought reduced Fernando to despair. He could stand it no longer.

"No," he exclaimed suddenly. "No, I won't permit it. How can I hide here while they kill her! Oh no! I would rather turn myself in to the Holy Office. And what do I have to lose? Who knows if I will escape their clutches? And what good is my life in any case? My benefactor is dead. There's no hope for Juanita. What am I waiting for?"

That same night a man presented himself at the prison of Aljafería. It was Fernando. He was brought to the same underground dungeon where Juanita was being held. The prisons were full and when the young man turned himself in during the night, the guards brought him to the place where they knew there was room. Then they forgot about him. The two unfortunate young people thus found themselves in the same cell. But the darkness in their cell didn't allow them to recognize each other. Finally, an involuntary moan that Juanita let escape attracted Fernando's attention.

"Who are you?" Juanita recognized his voice.

"Fernando, are you here?" He tried to go to her but his chains didn't allow it. Juanita wasn't chained. She went to Fernando. She was profoundly moved by his sacrifice. Alas! Why would so much devotion be met only by a cruel death?

At this moment, Enriquez came down to the dungeons of the Aljafería. He was accompanied by one of the jailers, who let him into

Juanita's cell. The monk entered with a lantern. Fernando and Juanita both trembled when they saw a newcomer they didn't recognize at first. What did he want from them? Enriquez himself was surprised for an instant when he saw a second person in the cell. However the eyes of the two prisoners finally grew accustomed to the light and they recognized at last the features of the monk. A double cry emerged from both their lips.

"Enriquez!" The monk was no less surprised. He lowered the lamp to examine the unfortunate man locked up with Juanita.

"It is I, Fernando," said the young man.

"Fernando!" exclaimed the monk, struck with terror. "Fernando here! Wait." And he went out. The jailer had stayed outside the door. This witness could be dangerous to their plan.

"I have to question the prisoner before bringing her before the inquisitor," he said to the jailer. "You can go take care of your other business until I call you. The second prisoner is chained so he poses no risk." The jailer left and Enriquez entered the cell again, making sure that nobody else was observing his movements.

"Good God, How did you get here?" he asked when he was once again before the two prisoners.

"I knew they were torturing her because of me. Could I let her suffer?"

"Miserable wretch! What have you done? I have come to save her, to take her out of this horrible place. And now I find you here as well! What a stupid thing. What deplorable generosity. What to do now?"

The monk stayed motionless and silent. This unexpected blow cast all his plans into doubt. At the moment when he could finally save Juanita, he found Fernando in the abyss. The two young people were just as silent.

"I can't save both of you," the monk began again after a few moments. "We would all be lost if I did."

"Oh!" responded Fernando. "Go, Enriquez, go with her. As long as my Juanita escapes they can do with me what they wish."

"No, no," said Juanita. "I want to die with him."

"To die," the monk said. "Oh, my child. The Inquisition doesn't kill so easily, for the dead do not suffer. They torture. They martyr. Don't you know it by now?"

Juanita did not respond, but she drew up the sleeve of her dress and showed her mangled arm, still covered with the bloody traces that the iron bracelet had left. Fernando moaned softly when he saw the barely formed scars. The monk shook his head sadly.

"You are mistaken, my child, if you take that for the Inquisition's torture. That's but a game next to what goes on here. They hoist people up by a rope and let them fall to within a few feet from the ground so that the limbs are torn out of their sockets by the body's own weight. They break people on the rack. They squeeze peoples' feet between two pieces of wood and hold them to the fire and submerge them in hot oil!"

Juanita shivered.

"You have to go," Fernando said to her, horrified at the thought of such tortures.

"Leave?" asked Juanita. "And him? My God! My God!"

"All hope is not lost for him. You are rich, my child, they will never pardon you. However, he is poor so they won't get to him so quickly. The inquisitors have other cases to attend to. At least that's my hope," the monk said, turning to Fernando. "Here is some money. You will give it to your jailer, but only once they know about our escape. He is greedy, I know. Tell him that it is I who gives him that money and that I will have three times as much sent to him if you succeed in escaping. I don't ask that he help you, only that he doesn't betray you. He knows me and won't doubt my words. Be ready, my son," Enriquez added. "You are young and strong. If the occasion presents itself, you will take advantage of it. In the meantime, trust in God."

With these words, the monk made a sign to Fernando and without Juanita seeing it, he slipped into the young man's hands a small bottle. It contained a strong poison. Fernando understood. It was a last resort to escape from their tortures.

"And now, my child," the monk said to Juanita. "Time is flying. The road is long and perilous. But who knows? Perhaps we will all be happy again one day."

Juanita couldn't break away from Fernando. She stayed still, weeping. The young man was obliged to push her away gently. The monk took Juanita by the hand and opened the door. When the young girl turned back to bid Fernando a last goodbye, her voice failed her, but her whole soul passed into the look that she gave the young man. Enriquez hurriedly dragged Juanita outside, closing the door on Fernando, abandoning him in the cell. However, now was not the time to pity the fate of the prisoner, they had to act and couldn't waste a second. They crossed through sinister underground corridors and climbed many staircases, past the dwelling of the first inquisitor, and into the monk's own office. Then he removed a cordelier's costume from an armoire, placing the hood over Juanita's head. He armed himself with another vial of poison as a replacement for the one he gave Fernando. Then, taking some provisions and a bottle of wine, he went back down the stairs and out of the Aljafería with Juanita, not encountering the slightest difficulty. Indeed, nobody would have imagined that the cordelier who was accompanying Enriquez was a prisoner of the Holy Office being freed by the secretary of the grand inquisitor himself.

The night was already well advanced. Nevertheless, Enriquez didn't dare cross Saragossa. Instead they bypassed the city and headed for the mountains. Once they were on the bridge, beyond the gate leading to France, he took off his white Dominican's robe, under which he had hidden a cordelier's robe. Then he took a heavy stone, wrapped the robe he had just taken off around it and threw it into the Ebre. The package floated for an instant on the current, then disappeared rapidly thanks to the weight of the stone. Enriquez listened until all became silent. Then he took Juanita by the arm and they continued on their way.

The monk knew all the roads, all the mountain passes, and all the secret spots where they could hide from the enemy. He had been able to study all these wild spots while accompanying the henchmen of the Holy Office when they hunted fleeing heretics. He had even commanded such expeditions. In this, he was a typical Maranno, directing all his energy to a false goal. Thus while the Holy Office congratulated itself on the zeal deployed on these occasions by Enriquez the monk, the latter was obeying quite different motivations.

They traveled like this for two days, heading toward Pamplona and pretending to be peasants from Aragon who were going to sell their sheep that they had sent by the main road while they themselves took a shortcut. This lie was necessary: it led people to believe that the two voyagers had very little money on them and protected them from attacks by thieves or brigands who haunted the inns. Juanita was able to travel without fatigue since she spent the night in good beds. She felt stronger, more confident, and more resolved to brave the dangers that awaited her.

They needed to take such precautions because the monk was convinced the agents of the Inquisition were on their tails. Indeed, nothing can describe the fury of Molina when he learned of the disappearance of Juanita and Enriquez. He fumed with anger. He had been betrayed by his own secretary, a Dominican friar, in whom he had placed the greatest trust! He therefore sent all the men he could spare into the countryside, in all directions. The henchmen headed out toward the mountains that lead to France, motivated by a large reward. The two fugitives couldn't arrive at the frontier fast enough. Soon the monk and the young girl were surrounded by the enemy.

The monk deployed all the resources of his quick wits to elude them. Calm in times of crisis, he was able to make Juanita share his sang-froid. Sometimes leading and sometimes carrying the young girl across barely beaten mountain passes, along almost inaccessible rock faces, and practically under the gaze of their pursuers, he was able to render all the efforts of their pursuers useless, while making their way bit by bit to France. [. . .]

Juanita was exhausted. For two days the fugitives hadn't taken any other nourishment than some fruits and wild berries. Accustomed to an austere life, the monk was endowed with a powerful life force and an exceptionally vigorous constitution. But Juanita, weakened by her struggles, her suffering and torture, her time in the dungeon, and especially the perilous journey, was almost spent. The promise of France and of liberty revived her for an instant, but the feverish energy that had kept her going in the middle of such terrible struggles abandoned her as soon as they were out of danger. Enriquez saw her grow pale and falter. The courageous monk held her almost lifeless in his arms. He was afraid. After having escaped from so many enemies, so many dangers, was the unhappy child going to succumb at the moment of salvation?

However, Juanita came back to life. She opened her eyes, looked at the monk, and tried to point to an object that seemed to have terrified her. Indeed, the monk was so occupied with caring for the girl that he didn't see a man, at a certain distance, who was standing still as the two of them made their way toward him.

That man was none other than the unfortunate Diego. He had stayed behind in a village where Mateo, the *capatoze*, had left him. They hadn't been pursued by the Inquisition and they hadn't been required to hide during their voyage, like the monk and the young girl. However, they had entered France at the same place. It was at the end of this road that the poor father had stayed for hours on end, looking off toward Spain and commending his dear daughter to heaven.

Soon Juanita was at her father's house, sleeping in a good bed. A few hours later, a doctor was at her side. All the conflicting emotions had affected her health. But her youth, the force of her constitution, and especially the happiness at being united again, after so much unhappiness, with the father she believed to have been dead, triumphed in the end, and soon she was completely out of danger. Only one thing made the poor young girl sad: the thought that Fernando was still in the Inquisition's dungeons and would probably die while everyone else had miraculously been saved. However, Juanita hadn't lost all hope and the monk also shared her faith.

When Juanita had fully regained her health, Diego wanted to move to Bayonne to be near his coreligionists. But just as he had waited for his daughter, so too did she want to wait for Fernando, whom she could not bring herself to give up for lost. Days and weeks passed. The monk went several times to Saint-Jean-Pied-de-Port to ask about what was happening in Aragon. He didn't learn anything of interest and Juanita began little by little to lose her hope of seeing Fernando again.

Then, one day, two Spanish refugees, who had escaped from the Inquisition's jails, arrived in Larran. Their escape had been so sudden that they didn't know what was happening in Saragossa. The two fugitives didn't know Fernando, but a young man had escaped at the same time as they did. They had traveled together for a while. A short distance from Saragossa, the young man had proposed taking a different path which seemed to them so dangerous that they didn't dare follow him. They continued on their way, risking arrest by the henchmen of the Holy Office, while their companion disappeared in the mountains.

Upon hearing this story, Enriquez, Juanita, and Diego didn't doubt for an instant that it was Fernando. He was saved. All three hurried to the end of the road, where they hoped they would see the young man soon. They waited there for a few hours but Fernando didn't come.

The route that he took was much more dangerous than the main road but it was also shorter and the young man should have arrived at the same time as the two fugitives. Juanita began to worry and from time to time she looked at Enriquez, as if to ask him something, but the words stopped on her lips. The monk understood what the young girl didn't dare say: What if something had happened to Fernando? What if he needed help?

"I will go," he said to Juanita.

The young girl thanked Enriquez with a look while the latter gathered some provisions and set off back across the frontier. He once again took the route that they had followed just a short time before while escaping from their enemies, hoping to find Fernando along the way and bring him whatever help he needed. Barely had an hour elapsed when indeed, scanning the mountain peaks, he saw, not too far off, a man crouching in the brush. The man seemed exhausted, but when he saw Enriquez, he suddenly rose as if struck by terror.

"*Lo ammi*," Enriquez shouted to him.

This, as we have said, was the secret password of the Marannos. These words reassured the fugitive.

"*Lo ammi*," he responded, holding out his hand. At that moment, he recognized the features of Enriquez.

"Where is Juanita?"

"She is safe. She's alive and she's waiting for you."

"God be praised! And bless you, our savior."

When Fernando had regained some strength, he rose and together with the monk, they made their way toward the French border. Fernando could hardly wait to see Juanita again. But his impatience grew even stronger when the monk told him about another happiness awaiting him. His benefactor, his father, was still alive and was waiting with Juanita. They arrived at the border. Fernando could already see Juanita and Diego. Enriquez could barely contain the young man, who forgot all about the dangers waiting for them along the road and the prudence that was necessary in walking along it. Finally, they touched French soil, and at the same time Fernando found himself in the arms of his loved ones.

There were cries of joy, tears of happiness. They were so overcome with emotion that none of them could say a word. Fernando was the first to speak.

"So heaven has saved us all. We are all saved."

"Yes," the monk said. "Saved because we are in France and here our enemies can't reach us."

Juanita considered for a moment the land that offered her and her family asylum and protection against pitiless enemies and where hope and happiness once again smiled upon her. Her heart filled with gratitude. She joined her hands together, bowed her head, and said an ardent prayer.

"Blessed are you, o land of deliverance. You also witnessed the persecution of our brothers, but the odious Inquisition at least was never able to establish itself among your generous people. May heaven watch over you always so that you become one day the first among nations, the land of justice and the hope of all oppressed peoples." At this moment, the sun set behind the mountains, its last purple rays fell on the group and illuminated the face of Juanita with a prophetic ray. Diego, Enriquez, and Fernando had listened in silence to the girl's prayer and they all three looked at her with profound tenderness.

Two months after these events, a new auto-da-fé broke out in Saragossa. Along with a large number of Aragonese who were condemned to horrible deaths, sixty-nine unfortunate beings were burned, some alive, some after having been strangled out of pity. Among the tortured were the Count de Ramira and his son Alonzo, along with statues of Enriquez, Fernando, Juanita, and the bones of the unfortunate traveler, buried under Diego's name. While the Inquisition burned them in effigy, Enriquez, Fernando, Juanita, and Diego settled in Bayonne. Diego had long ago sent a part of his fortune to France, as we said. After so many trials, he and his family were finally able to enjoy peaceful times, surrounded by perfect happiness and mutual affection, fortified by the memory of their many past sacrifices.

Section 3 *Experiments in Jewish Realism*

Eugénie Foa, "Rachel; or, The Inheritance" (1833)
Translated from the French by Maurice Samuels

Eugénie Foa (née Rodrigues Henriques, 1796–1853) was most likely the first Jew to write fiction in French and was one of the first Jewish women to publish fiction in any language. She was born in Bordeaux into two extremely prominent Sephardic families. Her maternal ancestors, the Gradis family, dominated France's overseas shipping in the eighteenth century and owned large estates in the French colony of Saint-Domingue (now Haiti). Her father came from a wealthy Bordeaux banking family and sat on the Jewish Assembly of Notables convened by Napoleon, which established the limits of Jewish religious law in France.

Despite her connections to the most elite segment of France's Jewish community—her sister would marry Fromental Halévy, the composer of the opera *La Juive* (1835)—Eugénie led a difficult life. Abandoned by her husband, she moved to Paris and turned to writing in order to support herself and her two children. Between 1830 and 1835, she published no less than seven novels and collections of short stories, including *Rachel* (1833), from which this story is drawn. In addition, she contributed dozens of articles to the burgeoning periodical press, while militating for feminist causes and on behalf of the poor. In the 1840s, she found success as an author of saints' lives and books for children.

Foa's relationship to Judaism was fraught. Although her first novel, *Le Kidouschim* (The Kiddushin [Betrothal], 1830), reflects the orthodox values of her upbringing, her later works display increasing hostility to a Jewish tradition that Foa associated with repressive paternalism. In her historical novel *La Juive* (1835), set in the eighteenth century, a young Jewish woman rebels against her father to join her Christian lover and dies a horrible death. The novel ends with the promise that her child will be able to marry whomever she wants, Jew or Christian. In a later historical novella, "Billette; or, The Daughter of the Jew Jonathas" (1845), set in the Middle Ages, the heroine converts to marry a Catholic and finds solace in the convent after he abandons her. Foa herself converted in 1846, possibly in an attempt to promote herself as a Catholic author.

The story "Rachel; ou, L'héritage (Rachel; or, The Inheritance) bears an obvious autobiographical stamp. While the narrator is named Eugénie, it is the character Rachel who shares the author's Jewishness, bad marriage, and literary vocation. At a time when as many as 50 percent of the professional writers in France were female, the story bears eloquent witness to the difficulties such literary women still faced. Although Foa would eventually leave Judaism behind, her fiction reflects a lifetime of struggle with the burden of Jewish tradition.

April 1833

We had spent the summer at Enghien, in the pleasant Montmorency valley, where every year spring brings, along with its fragrant greenery, the choicest Parisian society. Situated on the shore of a small lake, a spa offering sulphurous baths draws as many foreigners as Parisians to this beautiful area, thanks to the healing powers of its waters. As in all such thermal bathing establishments, people live in what could be called a communal manner, almost like a family. And whosoever would refuse such familiarity arouses curiosity, or perhaps a stronger sentiment, in the other inhabitants of the spa.

This did not fail to happen to a young woman who tried to live apart in the establishment. Alone among this boisterous and animated crowd, who continually seek pleasure and often find it without looking, she carefully avoided the gardens, the shores of the lake, and the other public spaces. We used to see her, always alone, searching out the most solitary spots, the most out-of-the-way sites. Whenever one of us, of whichever sex, approached her, she would quickly move away. If you greeted her, however, she would politely return the greeting, blushing, and pass you by so quickly that she discouraged you from attempting to continue the conversation.

Was this arrogance or pride? The sweetness of her physiognomy gave the lie to such a thought. Was she punishing herself for some secret sin? The nobility and modesty of her bearing quickly dispelled this idea and proved, beyond a shadow of a doubt, that she would not have been out of place in the very highest society. Was it therefore a secret sorrow or a deep disgust with life? Alas! Everything about her came to confirm this sad conjecture.

This woman seemed quite young. Without being exactly pretty, her features, which were hollowed out by suffering, bore an expression of indefinable sadness. Long curls of black hair framed her pale, slightly oval face, which made you suspect she might be of Jewish origin. Her big black eyes, with their soft and melancholy expression, seemed to fear the light of day and to shade themselves on purpose beneath a row of long brown lashes, through which pierced from time to time the rays of her shining pupil. Her frail figure had a remarkable elegance and suppleness. This woman inspired interest in all who saw her. It was more than a banal curiosity, however, that attracted people to her. It was a deep and intimate feeling, but one that was hard to pin down, which took you by the soul and seemed to cry out: "This is an unhappy person! A sufferer! Who knows but that one of your tears would perhaps make hers less bitter? A welcoming smile, a word of friendship, would surely lessen the pain of this poor young woman." And if you didn't cede to this heartfelt instinct that attracted you to her, that made you want to mingle your tears with hers, to take her hand, to call her by her name, it was because you did not dare. It was because you understood that often an unwanted consolation bruises or tears the soul instead of calming its pain.

After a few days, the remarks and conjectures became increasingly consistent and plausible. The young woman's modest clothing, although always clean and in good taste, implied a total lack of fortune, as did her simple and frugal manner of living. Thus the pretense of always wanting to be alone, the fear, the terror even, that overtook her at the approach of a happy and brilliant young person, explained itself: the suffering of a tender soul is more sensitive to pity than insult. It is defenseless against the first of these sentiments and too far superior to the second for it to affect her.

She inhabited a little house that was isolated at the far end of the garden of the establishment. An old woman served her. A young and pretty girl, Madeleine, who worked at the dairy, brought her milk every morning and evening. The presence of that young girl, her naïve and happy chatter, were the only distractions of the *pale lady*, as she came to be called by everyone.

She received no visitors with the sole exception of an old man in oriental dress whose grave and venerable face was adorned by a long white beard. But his great age didn't allow him to make the trip from Paris to Enghien very often. We only saw him arrive on Friday morning and he would always return before sundown.

Did this young woman have a family? Sisters? Brothers? People said so but we didn't know for sure. The horrible thing about misfortune is that it often breaks the bonds of nature and cools the very hearts that should be the most devoted to us. It is necessary to have experienced such cruelty to understand how much bitterness and truth this observation contains.

Autumn was approaching and little by little the woman's thinness became more frightening. A dry cough that at first we barely noticed acquired daily a sharper and more penetrating intensity. Her misfortunes were stifling her bit by bit. Each morning another trace of life would disappear from her face. Each evening found her more worn down and more resigned to her suffering.

One afternoon, after I had received some awful news, I fled my usual company to go and weep on my own. Before I knew it, night had fallen. Thinking myself alone, I gave way to my sadness and allowed the sighs that were tearing my breast apart to escape.

"Are you crying?" said a voice in my ear. "Are you suffering? Oh! Madame, excuse my question! From anyone else it would be indiscreet, but not from me!"

I turned around. The mysterious woman from the garden was at my side. Her look, the sweet expression of her face in the moonlight, said so clearly: *I myself am suffering too much not to sympathize with your pain*, that, giving way to a desire I could not control, I threw myself into her arms. "I lost my best friend!" I cried. And I wept at her breast. This was how our relationship began.

Thus I came to know that her name was Rachel, and that she was married very young to an unworthy man who abandoned her to the most dire poverty.[1] That man's family, who were rich and powerful, had abandoned her as well. One of her uncles took her in. But that uncle was not rich. Formerly the chief rabbi of Jerusalem, now a cantor in Paris, he lived on his wages alone. This was the old man with the white beard who would come to see her on Fridays. I thus learned that she was Jewish.

While Rachel told me that story that was at once so sad and at the same time so typical of the lives of certain of us weak women whom relatives often sacrifice for money or propriety, I looked at that poor

---

1. Divorce was made illegal in France in 1816. Women who had been abandoned by their husbands could therefore not remarry. Given the scarcity of occupations open to women, an abandoned wife like Rachel had few financial options.

victim of marriage: she had been fresh and beautiful, but although she was still young, tears had already left their mark on her. Her frail and thin figure, which had once had healthy curves but was now dried out by sorrow, seemed hardly able to withstand the least little shock. And yet she never complained! She never said how much she suffered. But what words could express more eloquently than her physical decay the moral suffering of that unfortunate woman! Tears had scarred her chest. She was dying of consumption. Still so young, she who was not yet twenty would not see the beginning of winter nor the end of the fine days of autumn. Her fate was sealed, and it was approaching so fast!

"Do you see the leaves that protect us from the sun?" she said to me one day. "Today, they offer me shade. Tomorrow, perhaps, they will wither on my tomb!"

"Rachel! You could still have hope!"

"Oh! It's all over for me!" she said, with a melancholy shake of her head. "All over! And yet, if my heart had not been broken, I would have been able to live a few more years! I used to feel such a strong and vigorous sap in my breast! But now death! . . . Don't pity me, Eugénie! Death is but a respite for a suffering soul. And I have suffered so much!"

Thus it was that a new circumstance, seemingly ordinary but worrisome to us because of the influence that it seemed to have on the patient, sparked my curiosity. Every morning and evening, the hooves of a horse could be heard on the path leading up to the little house. A young man with a handsome, expressive face on which one could read a gloomy and profound sadness, would pass slowly by on his beautiful Andalusian horse, his eyes glued to the blinds of Rachel's room. He would stop in front of the dairy and ask for a cup of milk, but would scarcely bring the edge to his lips before paying generously. Then, affecting an air of indifference, and only to chat with Madeleine, or so he said, he would ask about the health of the woman in the little house, without naming her. He would listen with such attention that it seemed like his life depended on the answer. Then he would spur his horse and ride off at a gallop.

I noticed that the patient grew extremely agitated at the time when the horse was due to pass by. At the first sound of hooves, a light blush would color her prominent cheek bones. When they would stop, the patient's breathing stopped also. And when they went away, it was rare that a tear did not wet Rachel's eyelids.

One day, when she was doing particularly poorly, the doctor took me apart and said, "This young woman has some deep sorrow or is trying to produce a creative work that is killing her before her time. I used to hope that she still had a few months. Now I fear each morning that we won't find her still alive."

Madeleine told us that when Rachel was alone, she would write until exhaustion made the pen fall from her hands . . . A word that she later let slip revealed to me a circumstance that increased my admiration for that fascinating creature. Unable to stand the idea of being a burden to her old uncle, who she knew was depriving himself of the kinds of small luxuries that are so necessary as we grow old, that tender and proud soul tried to earn her keep by embarking on a literary career.

She instinctively understood all the vicissitudes that she would have to undergo, all the disappointments she would have to brush away. But, endowed as she was with an indomitable spirit and a great force of character, nothing discouraged her. Nothing! Neither the tepid advice of a family that disapproved of her plan, nor the biting jibes of so-called friends, nor the bitter sarcasm of a society of empty-headed ladies who think they have fulfilled all the obligations that nature imposes on them by dressing up like dolls, spending their evenings at balls and the theater, and their days sitting in a circle in the garden of the Tuileries, watching other ladies of their acquaintance pass by, who likewise spend their time watching them. Nothing made her abandon her courageous resolution, not even those two disdainful words that greeted her like a slap in the face: *Woman author!* to which she responded, "And why not?" her gaze sparkling with genius. Scornfully throwing off all those frivolous prejudices of an even more frivolous society, Rachel had come to understand life differently from all those people. If only she could have been a wife and mother . . . But destiny had not willed it and she had the strength to submit to her fate.

Thus the young Jewess abandoned herself to the inspiration of her original and melancholy soul and to her warm imagination, which was imprinted with the oriental character of its origin. The poor, dependent woman sought neither glory nor renown, but only a living, however precarious it might be, that would allow for her independence and that she would owe only to herself, to her work and her talent. Alas! Her delicate constitution could not support the strain: her burning mind dried out her body, which gave way beneath the double weight of work and tears.

Soon we realized that the fatal moment was drawing near and with an inexpressible pain and sadness, I understood that the touching Rachel harbored none of the illusions that make life sweeter and death less bitter. One morning, when the horse hooves sounded earlier than usual, I heard her sigh almost audibly: "Poor Gérard!" I took her hand and held it in mine silently.

"He asked for my hand in marriage," she added. "And they refused it to him! Yet his love, Eugénie, was so true, so sincere!"

"And why did they refuse him?"

"His religion differed from mine. My good uncle declared that such unions are never happy . . . Alas!"

"And did you not see him again after your marriage?"

"Oh no! I would not have dared!" she responded with an expression of ineffable love. Then, suddenly, she interrupted herself:

"The trees have lost all their leaves, have they not?"

"Why . . . yes . . . " I responded hesitatingly, for I understood her thought.

"Tomorrow . . . I shall doubtless be no more!" she added in a low and halting voice. "He will come, as usual, to inquire after my health . . . Eugénie . . . don't let them tell him the truth, for pity's sake! . . . It would kill him also! But do me one favor . . . the last . . . God will reward you and poor Rachel will go to heaven blessing you. Here . . . cut off this lock of hair . . . this one that has fallen across my brow and through which I so often looked at him! Then give it to him. Do it. He will understand what it means. You will help, won't you? Won't you do it, won't you be so good as to fulfill the last request of a dying woman? There is no harm in what I am doing, right? I am going to die and he loved me so! Oh, no! There can be no harm in that! Tell me, Eugénie, for the love of God! Is there harm in that? . . . "

Two days later, I had delivered the lock of hair to its destination. Upon seeing this last gauge of a hopeless love, the unfortunate Gérard let out a soul-shattering cry. Then he seized the lock of hair, and without looking at me or saying goodbye or thank you, he took off at a gallop. The cloud of dust that sprang up after him shrouded him from my view.

A few days after that, while we were all still sorrowing over the premature death, an unexpected event offered us a bit of diversion. Madeleine, the pretty milkmaid who had taken care of Rachel with me, was supposed to marry Justin, the son of the bathing attendant. The contract had been drawn and the date of the wedding fixed, when all of a sudden, on the day following Rachel's death, the young girl resolutely told Justin that she could no longer marry him. She told him she had had a great change of fortune, that she had become rich, very rich, that she wished him well in spite of it all, but that he should no longer dream of being her husband. Justin prayed, begged, cried, and threatened, but to no avail. The young girl held firm.

Pitying the son of our bath attendant, we summoned Madeleine to appear before us. The oldest in our group gave her a sermon about fickleness that produced no effect whatsoever. The youngest asked her if she had found some other object of affection. And the young men among us pressed her in order to know if it was the sight of one of them that had performed this miracle.

"Perhaps, dear sirs," she finally said with an air of naïve coquetry, "if you knew how rich I am, you would all be courting me instead of mocking me!"

"We would all be tempted, charming Madeleine!" responded an old general who had come to take the waters in order to cure a stubborn rheumatism that had left him a cripple. "If only we weren't scared off by the idea that if your fortune grew any more you would leave us as well, just as you have done to Justin."

Finally, after being pressed and harassed by our questions, Madeleine admitted to us that an hour before her death Madame Rachel had made her approach her bed.

"I am poor, Madeleine, very poor!" she had told her. "And I don't know how to reward you for your devoted service, my child . . . If heaven had granted me enough life to finish the work that I have started, oh . . . I for one believe that I had in me the source of great wealth! But no matter, even unfinished my treasure is still worth something . . . I give it to you . . . here, Madeleine, take it . . . make good and worthy use of it . . . If you can get something for it . . . it will secure your fortune."

"Then," Madeleine added, wiping away a tear with the corner of her apron, "Madame Rachel gave me the little desk she used to write on that

contained all her papers. I will go get it for you, ladies and gentlemen."
A second later, Madeleine placed before us a pretty little writing desk
made of exotic wood. She opened it and proudly showed us all the loose
leaves: "Here is my fortune!" she cried. "A pretty fortune, the poor lady
said. She was much too nice of a lady to fool me. And you don't tell
tales on your deathbed. No—Justin is a fine boy, I don't deny it. I'll do
something nice for him, I promise. But a lady, for I am going to become
a lady, cannot marry the son of a bath attendant! Don't you agree?"

"It's true, Madeleine!" we all said, laughing. "It's true! Only are you
really so sure of your huge fortune?"

"By Jove! I'm as sure as if I were holding it right here. Tomorrow,
I'm going to go to Paris. I had to take care of my sick grandmother,
which kept me from going until now. But tomorrow, come what may,
I'm heading straight for a notary's office and we'll see about turning
these papers into a fortune."

A young man of our group, who had read a few of the pages while
we were talking, challenged the young milkmaid. "In my opinion,
Madeleine," he said, "you need an editor not a notary. These papers are
stories, my child."

"Stories!" Madeleine cried angrily. "Stories! That's not nice what
you're saying! Madame Rachel was too respectable to tell stories."

"Don't get angry, Madeleine. Listen to me," replied the young man.
"I advise you to patch things up as soon as you can with Justin. That
huge fortune, which has gone to your head, might give you enough, at
the very most, to make you the owner of the dairy where you're working now. In fact, I'll make you that deal, if you give me these papers."

"Fat chance, sir! I'm not as stupid as I look. No offense, but I'll show
you when I come back from Paris! And you better believe it that no
matter how rich I am I won't be proud, no siree! When I have a fancy
carriage with fine horses and fine servants all dressed up, I'll even let you
ride with me, ladies and gentleman. It will be my pleasure." And with
that Madeleine picked up the little writing desk, bid us farewell, and
marched off.

We hadn't set eyes on her for a few days. We had even begun to
speculate that she had been right to refuse the offers of her improvised
editor, when one fine morning we saw her bring us our milk as she had
before. Her sad, ashamed expression revealed her disappointment.

"So, Madeleine!" said the young man who had so generously offered to be her editor. "You still don't want to trade your inheritance for the dairy?"

"Would you include the two cows, sir?" she asked in a plaintive tone.

"But of course, my child!"

"You aren't pulling my leg, are you sir?"

"I don't pull anyone's leg when I talk business, Madeline . . . Okay, then! Do we have a deal?"

"Truly, I don't dare say yes! The dairy and the two cows are so fine that I'm afraid . . . "

"The other day you thought it was too little. Today you think it's too much! Your trip to Paris must have really changed your mind, Madeleine."

"Alas, dear sir, in Paris they didn't want to look at my papers. A fat man the notary sent me to said scornfully, "These are stories. I'm telling you, child, that we have enough stories! Everyone and their brother is writing stories. My wife and children . . . even my porter the other day tried to sell me some stories he had written about all the tenants in the building. Luckily I refrained! If he went floor by floor I was probably on the first page! Take back your stories, child. This merchandise is worth almost nothing. Stories! Who isn't writing stories?' So you see, sir, if what you just promised me isn't . . . "

"I may print them, but thank God, I don't tell them! Come collect your inheritance, little one, come on! And if the public likes it, if your stories have some success, I'll throw in some gold earrings and a pretty crucifix."

"Would you also put in a good word for me with Justin, sir? He's been ignoring me."

"We'll take care of all that! Rest assured."

Now, I will tell you in confidence that I can't wait for the spa season to come again so I can return to Enghien. I'm truly curious to find out if Madeleine got her earrings and her gold cross. Whoever can tell me would be doing me a great service, I dare say.

E——E.

Ben-Lévi, "The March 17th Decree" (1841)
Translated from the French by Maurice Samuels

Godchaux Baruch Weil (1806–78), who wrote under the pseudonym Ben-Lévi, was born in Paris into one of the capital's most prominent Jewish families. His father had come from Alsace and established himself as a porcelain manufacturer as well as a leader of the capital's nascent Jewish community in the early years of the nineteenth century. His great-nephew was the writer Marcel Proust. Educated by a private tutor, Godchaux was something of a prodigy, publishing his first text at the age of fifteen—a scholarly refutation of the reformer Tsarphati's call to move the Jewish Sabbath to Sunday to accommodate workers. After the death of his traditionalist father, however, Godchaux would go on to advocate many of the reforms he had denounced as a teenager, becoming one of the leading contributors to the reformist monthly newspaper, *Les Archives Israélites*, from its inception in 1840.

Though he never attempted to live by his pen, Godchaux Weil was the author of a dozen short stories and over forty witty social commentaries published in *Les Archives Israélites* during the 1840s (including the two stories included in the present volume). He would also publish a pious and patriotic manual for Jewish schoolchildren, *Les matinées du samedi* (Saturday Mornings, 1842), which was widely used throughout the Francophone world and translated into English. Ben-Lévi's fiction frequently employs humor as a weapon to satirize the foibles of his assimilating Parisian coreligionists. In ""Le décret du 17 mars" (The March 17th Decree), however, he strikes a somber, haunting, even tragic note. His goal here is not to satirize but rather to probe the effects of one of the darker chapters in postrevolutionary French history—a moment that many of his assimilating coreligionists no doubt would have preferred to forget.

A rewriting of Honoré de Balzac's realist novel *Le Colonel Chabert* (1832), "The March 17 Decree" depicts a Jewish solider who returns from the Napoleonic Wars to find himself utterly and completely alone—his family having been destroyed by Napoleon's "infamous" 1808 edict that retroactively nullified loans made by Jews to non-Jews if the lender could not prove that he had given full value for the contracted sum. A clear contradiction of the French Revolution's promise of universal equality, the decree would not be renewed by the Restoration government when it lapsed in 1818, but Ben-Lévi shows how its effects continued to be felt decades later.

In this story, the soldier's desire to merge with the crowd of worshippers assembled to celebrate the return of Napoleon's remains to France in 1840, as well as his stubborn clinging to the text of the emperor's unjust decree, captures the difficulties faced by French Jews caught between a desire for assimilation into the French nation and a loyalty to the Jewish past.

*

> Laws are always tainted by the passions and the prejudices of the legislator.
>
> Montesquieu, *The Spirit of the Laws*

In 1807, Mordecai Blum, his wife Rebecca, and his son David were living in a village in Alsace. As in all Jewish families of the time, the father engaged in trade, the son studied Talmud, and the mother took care of the house. Though not very rich, Mordecai Blum was energetic and industrious enough to earn a living and, thanks to the good credit he enjoyed, he even managed to make a profit from his difficult labors. Like others of his kind, he dealt in everything. He bought goods, sold them, and lent money on occasion. Honest in business, trustworthy and charitable, he was generally liked and esteemed—as much as an Israelite could be in that period in Alsace, where a popular prejudice, too old to be uprooted, had established in principle that all Jews were usurers.

David Blum was a tall and handsome young man of twenty, with a calm and reflective nature. Beneath his reserved and timid surface, however, lay original ideas and noble sentiments. He had not limited himself to the study of rabbinical literature but also could read German and French, and he had gained some notions of history from old books bought cheaply off an aristocrat fleeing the revolution. He had thus come to be regarded in the area as a scholar. All the local girls envied Sarah, his fiancée, a young Jewish girl with black hair and bright eyes, who brought him a nice dowry.

Awaiting the time appointed for the union of the young couple, the Blum family lived peacefully and contented until the promulgation of an imperial decree caused the seemingly solid edifice of their happiness to crumble. This decree, which tarnishes the reign of Napoleon with its intolerance, injustice, and disregard for rights, ordained that from March 17, 1808, all French Jews would be forced into military service, without the right to hire a replacement. It contained other draconian measures as well, including the suspension of all obligations, promises, and loans made by a Jew to a non-Israelite unless the lender could prove that he had furnished the full amount of the loan. It's easy to see what havoc such exceptional laws wreaked in Alsace, where nearly all commerce — especially that of money — was in the hands of Israelites.

Among the numerous victims of this iniquitous decree, none was so violently affected as the Blum family. The time to join the army had come for David; his number drawn, he was obliged to leave his parents. As he was leaving, his face burning beneath the tears that his desperate mother spilled on him under the pretext of giving him a goodbye kiss, he received a visit from the father of his fiancée, who informed him — coldly and not without embarrassment — that Sarah couldn't wait for his return and would look for another husband. When poor David had joined his regiment and had begun to adapt to military life, he received terrible news from his family: Mordecai Blum's debtors, immorally profiting from the tyrannical decree against the Jews, were refusing to pay what they owed him unless he could prove he had given them the full sum of the loan. And since such proofs were impossible to give, Mordecai found himself completely ruined overnight. Moreover, since his credit was lost, his lenders, who didn't have to prove anything because they weren't Jews, called in their loans. Because he couldn't pay immediately, he panicked and was declared insolvent. And since of course he didn't keep records, he was condemned to two years in prison for bankruptcy.

As he didn't complain, no one will ever know what Mordecai suffered. A mournful sadness, dull eyes, and hair turned suddenly white were the only signs of his despair until the morning that he was found dead on the foul mattress of his prison. His wife Rebecca had faced everything with a religious resignation, and had even managed to stifle her tears during the hour every day that it was permitted for her to spend at the prison. But once she lost her husband, she gave way to cries of sadness, as well as to threatening curses and fits of rage, which were soon recognized as the symptoms of madness. She became so violently deranged that she had to be locked up in a mental institution, from which God, out of pity, quickly called her to Him.

It would be impossible to describe David Blum's stupor when he received this fatal news in Spain, where he was stationed with his regiment. Constrained by military discipline, he couldn't give full reign to his righteous suffering. He would have surrendered his life to go and defend his father or console his mother, but imprisoned by his uniform, he was not even allowed the sad consolation of crying on their tomb. He cursed the emperor, exhaling his rage in vain threats and his hatred in useless oaths, while his eyes burned with the dark fire of despair and his heart boiled over with the fiery lava of vengeance. Soon he seemed dead to the world. He did his duty with exactitude, but mechanically. He shot and marched with the same inert indifference. A cruel memory had taken over his very being and life became for him a series of lethargic intervals. One day, however, at an inspection, General Guilleminot, struck by the wasted appearance of the young soldier, asked a fellow officer the cause. The latter responded with disdain: "He's an Alsatian Jew and a rather bad soldier. He lacks nerve and courage." At these words, blood rushed to David's head. He stood up straight and grabbed for the handle of his sword. But that flash of animation soon calmed and the pale face of the orphan once again returned to its habitual blankness.

From this time forward, nothing managed to trouble the leaden sleep that weighed down David Blum's senses. When, four years later, he witnessed the burning of Moscow and the sacking of the Kremlin, his calm and indifference did not give away even for an instant amid the dangers that surrounded him. A few days later—it was October 24, 1812—he found himself on the banks of the Luga River with a division of the French army beating a retreat, hotly pursued by the Russians under the command of Kutusoff. The French general, seeing his division getting crushed by the Russian artillery, stationed a hundred of his grenadiers in a church overlooking the road. David was among the hundred brave men who, using the church as cover, fought with such valor that they managed to break the enemy columns five times with their well timed and well aimed fire. They provided the French division the opportunity to regroup in the bottom of a ravine, where, though only eighteen thousand strong, they held out against, and ultimately defeated, fifty thousand Russians.[1] After this brilliant battle, General Guilleminot, the French commander, received the survivors among

---

1. Historical fact. [Author's note.]

those valiant grenadiers who had saved the day. David was designated as having been especially intrepid.

"What is your name?" the general asked him.

"David Blum, Alsatian Jew, whom you designated four years ago in Spain as a bad soldier."

"You are a brave man, David Blum, and I am making you an officer."

"Thank you, general, but I want nothing. I fought in order to defend the lives of my comrades and not for your emperor who ruined, dishonored, and caused the death of my family . . ."

A few weeks later, the French army, in total chaos, was attempting its disastrous retreat across the Beresina. Cold and hunger had strewn the countryside with the dead and dying. Stopping to warm himself at a bivouac, Napoleon was astonished at the morale that one group of soldiers had managed to maintain amid the terrifying disorder of the rest of the army.

"We owe our lives to our comrade David Blum," they told him. "His energy has sustained ours. His courage has saved us from skirmishes with the Cossacks. And his prudence has always provided us with food and fire."

"David Blum," the emperor said in the voice that made all the thrones of Europe tremble, and that, when he wanted to, he could make so sweet and appealing. "You are a good soldier and I offer you a place in my Old Guard." Removing a silver cross that adorned his uniform, he gave it to the Jewish soldier. Overcome by the old hatred that was fermenting in him, but at the same time fascinated by the respectful fear that everyone else felt in the presence of the emperor, David responded with firmness, although his face betrayed the emotions that agitated his soul:

"Sire! I am an Alsatian Jew and cannot accept either advancement or decoration, because to do so would be to accept blood money for my family who were dishonored by the odious decree of March 17th . . ."

"Ah!" responded the displeased emperor, "I have been told of that." He added in a curt tone: "They deceived me yet again in this matter, but we will take it under consideration." A cloud passed over his features, a deep ridge crossed his large brow. Then, as if he wanted to shake off an unpleasant thought, he jumped onto his horse and galloped away, followed by his silent general staff.

David Blum remained standing, one hand giving the military salute while the other held the Cross of the Legion of Honor that the emperor had given him. He stayed frozen, his head buzzing with confused thoughts, his heart beating violently. When his comrades revived him, he felt like he had awoken from a dream. But more serious problems soon distracted his agitated soul. A band of Cossacks appeared in the distance, and after a desperate fight in which an entire French detachment perished, David was wounded and taken prisoner. Since he was in command of his small squadron, they mistook him for an officer. It was to this error that he owed his life and the horror of being brought back to Moscow. After prolonged torture, he was sent to Siberia.

It was to a mine beyond the Ural Mountains, nine hundred leagues from Petersburg, that the unfortunate prisoner was conducted in the most barbarous manner. Descending into what he assumed would be his tomb, he had to relinquish his name, his homeland, and his individuality. His existence was divided between work and the lash. In this desert, peopled by several hundred living beings, all dead to the world, one lived only to suffer. There the miner had no family or friends, only tears and grimaces of rage. There the exile remained tied to the world only by the tender reed of memory that diminished from day to day. There executioners and victims, suffering the same fate, lying side by side, fell into eternal sleep, and the desert that saw so many generations of exiles pass never awaited their return. David Blum spent twenty-eight years in this underground labor. Twenty-eight years during which he had neither regrets, nor worries, nor despair, for his soul had become too hardened to suffering and his heart too inured to blows to experience any new pain.

One morning they told him he was free. At first he didn't understand this word that had been banished from his memory. Then human instinct took over and he began to walk straight in front of him. He had no idea where he was headed, but he was so surprised to be able to walk alone, to be able to stop when he wanted, and to see the sky above him at all times, that his heart was overcome with ineffable joy. He blessed the rain, the wind, and the cold for they made him realize he had come back to life . . . Alas! Along with his reason he soon recovered the awareness of all his sorrows! A poor link detached from the social chain, he despaired at feeling all alone on earth and considered for a moment returning to that alternation of work and the lash that he had called existence for twenty-eight years. But the word France magically awakened his slumbering soul. His courage never wavering for an instant, he crossed all of Europe with only his walking stick to lean on, generous souls to depend on, and the pole star called home to lead the way.

Finally, one morning in December of 1840, he arrived in his native village. So handsome when he had left Alsace many years before, so proud to fill his lungs with the fresh promise of life that his youth offered him, he returned a broken man—frail of body, dull of eye, and slow of step. First he looked about him aghast, for he was told he had arrived and yet he recognized nothing, neither his father's house, nor the walnut tree that had given him shelter during storms. Where was the pretty stream whose capricious course he had followed as a child? What had become of those green shutters that made the building across the way so pretty? And the garden that witnessed his childish games, and the flowers that he used to pick for Sarah, his fiancée? . . . Alas, all this had disappeared. The village had become a little town; there were factory buildings; everything looked different. For the first time in twenty-eight years, David felt a tear wet his eye, a tear of regret for that golden past that the wind of adversity had carried away. The population of the area had also changed. The old folks were dead and the young people were strangers to him. The name of Blum was completely forgotten and unknown. David didn't find a single hand to clasp, only worried looks and suspicious faces.

So, after praying on the tomb of his parents, he set off for Paris. Preparations were underway for the ceremony of the emperor's funeral and the old soldier hoped he would meet some old comrade-in-arms. He arrived in the capital on December 14, worn down with fatigue, suffering from cold and hunger, without papers, without money and not knowing what would become of him. He wandered for a long while in the streets of the big city, often rubbing elbows with people who were talking about the glories of the empire but who didn't care that one of the old instruments of that national glory was suffering beside them. Night came, and since he didn't have a place to lay his head, he stretched out on the icy stone alongside the entry to a theater. Since he was barely clothed, he suffered more from the cold than he had in Siberia. He couldn't sleep and dark thoughts agitated his restless mind. What was he still doing on earth? Why had his entire life been dedicated to suffering? Why did he outlive his father, his mother, his fiancée, his fellow soldiers, his superior officers? Why did he have no friend on earth, no fortune, no work, nothing that could succor his soul or support his body? All this because it had one day pleased a lucky soldier to deprive the Alsatian Jews of their rights. Because, substituting arbitrariness for justice, he had deprived the Jews at once of their fortune and their children. Because this parricidal son of liberty had taken it upon himself to monopolize the heritage of his mother for his own profit...

At this moment, numerous cries of "Long live the emperor!" struck David's ear and made him start like a traveler who accidentally steps on a snake, which recoils and hisses at him. It was the morning crowd heading toward the Invalides to pay their final respects to the hero who was their idol. The old soldier followed them and was struck with admiration at the sight of the imposing spectacle of the Champs-Elysées. Summoned to the funeral party, the Parisian populace soon formed a black mass that engulfed every point with new phalanxes spilling out of each avenue until a single line of heads united the Tuileries with the Arc-de l'Étoile. It was like a raging sea into which spilled twenty overflowing rivers. Every class and profession was represented at this lugubrious occasion. All recriminations, all hatreds against the great man appear forgotten and the great voice of history alone has the right to speak at the tomb of this giant whom humanity could not measure until he was stretched out lifeless.

This sublime spectacle caused a revolution in David's thoughts, which until then had nourished only resentment. Suddenly illuminated, his heart opened itself to pity like a ray of sun violently slashing through a horizon of dark clouds. He remembered with what emotion the emperor had spoken these words to him: "They deceived me yet again!" And bowing before the great misfortune of the French hero, he offered up the forgetting of his hatred as a holocaust along with the forgiveness of the wrongs that had been caused him. He cried, seized with a holy enthusiasm: "How did you fall from the heavens, imperial star shining with so much divine light! How did you die in exile, you who gave orders to kings and drove men into bondage! Colossal giant who wanted to cover the earth with his shadow, how did you end up fighting over a few feet of arid rock on Saint-Helena! No, I don't dare complain about my life of pains and misfortunes when your sufferings have surpassed what the heart of a human being can withstand. Like me, they robbed you of those who were dear to you. Like me, they enchained you in a distant land. Like me, your name was covered with the slime of passion. Like me, you return with a frozen heart and a stiffened arm. And the great Emperor and the humble Jew met for the last time on a soil consecrated once again by liberty, tolerance, and justice, for bad laws last but for a day, while liberty, tolerance, and justice are eternal . . ."[2]

At this moment, the bells of the city rang as if suddenly awakened by the sound of the cannon. Drums sounded their funereal pounding, bugles blew their airy moans, and a distant voice, composed of a hundred thousand voices, cried: "Here he is!" Under the Arc-de-l'Étoile, that stone giant erected so that the emperor's great shadow could be cast upon it in all its glory, appeared the triumphal coffin, ringed by wounded generals, surrounded by tricolored banners covered in crepe and spread-winged eagles that seemed to be flying off toward eternity. It would be impossible to depict what David Blum felt at this sight. He fell to his knees and prayed. Prayer calmed his soul. His mind relaxed its hallucination. And no longer sustained by the second life that thought provides, his body collapsed with fatigue and deprivation. When the crowd parted to watch the convoy pass, an old soldier could be seen leaning lifeless against one of the triumphant columns near the Arc-de-l'Étoile.

The next day, the following newspaper article appeared:

> Among the accidents that took place yesterday, a pitiable man of foreign appearance was found lying unconscious on the Champs-Elysées. It is not known whether he collapsed due to starvation or cold, or whether he was crushed by the crowd. All attempts to revive him were in vain. Taken to Beaujon Hospital, he died during the night after a prolonged struggle. The unknown man will be on view today at the morgue. No money or papers were found on him. However, during his final moments of struggle, his rigid hand violently clutched a package to his chest containing a cross of the Legion of Honor with an effigy of Napoleon on it and an old, folded scrap of paper on which was printed, in barely decipherable letters, the following words: *Imperial Decree Concerning the Jews.—March 17, 1808* . . .

---

2. There is no end-of-quotation mark in the original text.

Salomon Formstecher, "The Stolen Son: A Contemporary Tale" (1859)

Translated from the German by Jonathan M. Hess

Like Ludwig Philippson, Salomon Formstecher (1808–89) was among the first generation of Jews to become university-trained rabbis in the German lands. Born and raised in the central German town of Offenbach, Formstecher received both a traditional-Jewish and a secular education in his native city. He originally planned to learn a trade but when he proved unable to find a master craftsman who would train a Jew, his father decided he should study to become a teacher instead. Formstecher enrolled at the University of Giessen, where he studied philosophy, theology, and philology. After earning his doctorate in 1831, he returned to Offenbach and became a rabbi, serving his local Jewish community for more than five decades. During his lifetime, Formstecher was widely known as a leader of the reform movement in Judaism. He played an important role in the rabbinical conferences of the 1840s that gave reform Judaism prominence in the German-speaking world. In 1833 he began his career as a writer publishing a set of sermons, and today he is largely remembered for his magnum opus, *Die Religion des Geistes* (The Religion of the Spirit, 1841), a treatise that sought to mediate between Judaism and the work of contemporary German philosophers such as Friedrich Schelling and Georg Wilhelm Friedrich Hegel.

Formstecher wrote widely on theological matters. As a rabbi, however, he was also a committed writer of fiction and promoter of Jewish belles lettres. Along with fellow reform rabbi Leopold Stein, he edited *Der Freitagabend: Eine Familienschrift* (Friday Evening: A Family Journal), a weekly magazine launched in 1859 that sought to give Jewish readers "popular literature" written in an "attractive and stimulating manner," and he was involved with numerous other Jewish journals as well. In addition to an ambitious full-length novel *Buchenstein und Cohnberg* (Buchenstein and Cohnberg, 1863), he published any number of short stories, including "Der geraubte Sohn: Ein Sittenbild der Gegenwart" (The Stolen Son: A Contemporary Tale), which appeared in serialized form in Ludwig Philippson's *Jüdisches Volksblatt* (Popular Jewish Paper) in the first half of 1859.

A classic example of a Jewish adaptation of Dickensian melodrama, "The Stolen Son" is a fast-paced novella full of the requisite evil villains and virtuous heroes, filled with intrigue, mystery surrounding circumstances of origins, and a happy end, where the good find redemption and the evil are punished. Indeed, readers of nineteenth-century fiction (and fans of twentieth-century popular melodrama and television miniseries) will find much that is familiar in "The Stolen Son." In his preface to *Buchenstein und Cohnberg*, Formstecher complained explicitly about the caricatures of Jews populating contemporary realist fiction. In many ways, *Buchenstein und Cohnberg* sought to issue a corrective to the best-selling German novel of its era, Gustav Freytag's *Soll und Haben* (Debit and Credit, 1855), a novel famously structured around the opposition of upstanding German bourgeois virtues to Jewish vices and financial wheeling and dealing. In its explicit concerns with anti-Semitism and its positive portrayals of both individual Jews and their relations to the broader Jewish community, "The Stolen Son" undertakes an analogous project, creating an exemplar of sentimental melodrama that celebrates virtuous Jews who come to triumph over anti-Semitism and assume their rightful place in a thriving network of Jewish life.

The subtitle that Formstecher gives this tale sets the story in the present time, like so much nineteenth-century realist fiction. But it also invokes two specific events that sparked international controversies in the mid-nineteenth century. The plot of "The Stolen Son" reworks numerous details of the Damascus affair of 1840, an accusation of ritual murder against the Jewish community in Syria that spawned an international media spectacle. A major event in the Jewish world, the Damascus affair gave a boost to the development of the Jewish press across Europe and in the United States and encouraged Jews to create new venues for international Jewish solidarity such as the Alliance Israélite Universelle in France. If the staging of a blood libel in "The Stolen Son" is reminiscent of the Damascus affair, the life story of the text's protagonist recalls even more recent events, namely, the controversy surrounding the sensational Edgardo Mortara case in 1858, which started unfolding less than a year before installments of "The Stolen Son" began to be published in the *Jüdisches Volksblatt*. Mortara, a Jewish boy in Bologna, was secretly baptized by a Catholic servant girl during a serious childhood illness. Several years later, at the age of six, authorities of the Papal States forcibly took him from his parents to raise him as a Catholic. Eventually, he grew up to become a priest. "The Stolen Son" thus does not just challenge dominant representations of Jews in contemporary realist fiction. This novella also builds on international media spectacles of the nineteenth-century world, imagining a happy Jewish ending for a controversy that was very much unresolved.

I. The Office

In the vast empire of the czar there lies a major port city where Russians, Greeks, and Jews all live together, competing with each other for possessions and wealth. Set off from the hustle and bustle on the northeastern side of town, in a street shaded by old trees, there is a

Greek orthodox monastery. Within the monastery walls, the colorful life of the dynamic city—with its desires and struggles, its light and dark sides—plays itself out much as it does in the world outside; only the forms are different. One stormy evening toward the end of March, when winter was revealing itself once again in all its unfriendly severity, a wealthy Greek merchant walked toward this microcosm of the outside world. He was dressed for the weather, and his powerful gait betrayed courage and resolve. When the gatekeeper heard the monastery bell ring, he opened the heavy door halfway, and once the merchant quickly gave him his name, he whispered to him that the Reverend had been expecting him. The merchant knew his way around the various rooms and the complex passageways of the rather spacious monastery, and he stepped into the main office without being announced. Once there, he was received with a cozy handshake by the abbot of the monastery, who carried the title *higumenos* and who had the right to demand the strictest obedience from all honorable brothers.

"I have been waiting for you for a long time," the higumenos said in a friendly voice, stroking his white beard. "What news do you bring from our mutual friends?"

"Everything is in good shape, Reverend Father," the merchant responded as he sat down and made himself comfortable. "The saints are supporting our undertaking, and allow me to prove this to you by placing this small offering at the altar of the church." With these words he respectfully placed a rather large money bag filled with sparkling gold coins in front of the higumenos.

The Reverend Father smiled with satisfaction as he weighed the golden offering in his hands. He unctuously blessed the good work that had been undertaken and then asked with a devious glance, "Who else, my son, has joined in our enterprise?"

"Important and wealthy men, Reverend Father. The merchant Kriona and the banker Maxmarino have now joined our ranks. They are all faithful devotees of the Holy Church and thus bitter and lethal enemies of those abominable Jews whom the Lord has cursed. Nowadays, the Jews are doing all they can to shake of the yoke of this curse, and indeed, to the dismay of many of the faithful, they act to a large extent as if they've already shaken it off. These execrated Jews, once they were banned, but now they're everywhere: in our markets, at the stock exchange, in our ships, and on our streets! They're buying and selling, making contracts and changing money, acting as if they were in possession of all their rights. In their homes they maintain a flashy lifestyle amid the most splendiferous furnishings. They show up in our theaters and at our balls with their wealthy bejeweled women. They accumulate treasures and property and forget that the Lord cast them off, cursed them to be despised beggars, and damned them to live in misery now and for all eternity! How can the Church assert itself when its enemies are bathing in good fortune in this way?"

"You must calm down, my son," the higumenos responded to the passionate and excited merchant. "My white hair has already experienced many a triumph of the Church over its enemies. It will also come to see the revenge which we are carrying out to glorify the Lord. When we celebrate Holy Easter, the Church will unfold all its power, and the faithful will lend us their powerful arms. The magistrates have all been won over for our pious work and their superior, the chief of police, is already a faithful member of the holy flock. He will give his subordinates firm orders that the faithful are not be disturbed in their work for the Church. We've also inspired several ship captains for our pious work, and their courageous sailors know how to use their knives capably. Our plan is well thought through—it's fail-safe."

The higumenos was an old man of seventy-five, but as he spoke, his radiant eyes revealed that the fire of fanaticism was still burning passionately in his breast. He was anxious as he listened to the merchant Kfidy, who was no less excited himself as he described the different places from which he and his allies were going to work in concert to ransack the city's Jewish quarter.

These two men—the incarnation of blind fanaticism, supersilious arrogance, and sordid avarice—were suddenly interrupted in their conversation by a quiet knocking at the door. The higumenos responded, and the friar Eucharios came in, leading a ragged beggar boy by the hand. Initially caught off guard by the visitors, the merchant Kfidy was about to cover himself with his coat, but then the monk threw back his hood and greeted Kfidy with a familiar voice.

"It's you, dear father," the Greek merchant responded, "and this is likely the boy whom we'll now raise here? Do you know his parents? Who are they?"

"His parents," the monk answered, "live at the entrance to the large Jewish quarter. His father works in the harbor, his mother is a washerwoman. This boy now wants to remain with us, where he'll get nice clothes and good food. Right, Alexis, you like it here?"

Dim-witted and apathetic, the boy agreed, adding that he was very hungry. After discussing some further particulars regarding their plans, the merchant left. The monk Eucharios then took the boy Alexis and went into a small room off to the side. After a half hour, he returned to the office holding his little companion by the hand. The boy hardly looked the same; he had been cleaned up and given a new set of clothes.

"Do you like it here, my child?" the higumenos asked, reaching out his hand to the boy.

"I've eaten so much that I couldn't eat another bite!" was the shy boy's dim-witted answer.

"Good, why don't you put him to bed, then, dear brother? We can hand him over to the brother doctor tomorrow morning. You must come right back, though, and don't forget the pigeon."

While the monk was gone, the higumenos spoke to himself, mulling over his agitated thoughts in a language no one could understand. Soon enough, the trusted monk returned to the office, looking around cautiously as he brought in a small bundle of clothes and a live pigeon. Together, the two men silently left the office, both of them listening carefully to make sure no one was eavesdropping. They passed through a concealed door and then entered a hidden chamber off to the side where Brother Eucharios slaughtered the pigeon, carefully making sure that its blood fell on the ragged clothes the boy had been wearing. While performing this task, his hands trembled, and he looked around anxiously, as if he were committing murder. As soon as he was done, he packed up the clothes and removed the pigeon, and then both men returned to the office without saying a word. Finally, they began to breathe easily again. The higumenos was the first to regain his composure, and he asked the trusted brother in a muted voice whether he could trust the cobbler's wife completely, whether he would be able to count on her silence.

"She is as solid as a rock," Brother Eucharios answered reassuringly. "I have known this woman for a very long time," he added, "her heart and soul are devoted to our church, and she detests the German heretics no less than she hates the damned Jews. She has often asked me whether it is not a sin that she performs so many services for the Jews on Saturday, their Sabbath. She lights their lights, heats their rooms, cooks for them, and much more. I put her mind at rest and told her forebodingly of the hope that the good Lord would someday select her to perform a great service for our holy church. That is why she was so delighted recently when I told her that the merciful hour had arrived and that she was now going to become the instrument through which the Lord would perform the most holy sacrifice for our church. I then told her about the plan for our pious work, and she assured me with holy zeal that the Lord could have placed the execution of this sacred undertaking in no better hands than hers. For years, she told me, she has been the Sabbath woman in the old Jewish cantor's home, and she thus knows every little corner of this house, from cellar to roof. She can walk through and around this house as and when she likes, and she is particularly familiar with the cellar, as that is the place where the coal is kept. That is where she plans to hide the bloody clothes, behind a barrel where they will only be found by the individual whom she will tell about their whereabouts. She is waiting for me this evening in the Church of Saint Stephanos. I should be on my way so that I can give her the bundle."

"May the Lord be with you in your pious work!" the old higumenos said to the friar as he departed.

II. The Laboratory

The friar Dr. Basilides was staring at the ethyl alcohol flame over which a brown alloy of different substances was boiling and bubbling away in a glass retort. Bent glass tubes were carrying the vapors rising up from this mixture through cold water, where they passed into another glass vessel, where they turned into a light and clear liquid. The boy Alexis stood attentively with his mouth open at the doctor's side, passing him this and that object while he supplied curt and simple-minded answers to the questions the doctor was asking him. For even though this boy showed very few traces of genuine intelligence, he knew how to follow the strict orders that Brother Eucharios had given him the evening before. Brother Eucharios had convinced him that only the names of saints could be spoken in the monastery, and more than anything else, he was terrified of desecrating these holy rooms by uttering the unhallowed name by which he and his parents were known in the sinful world outside. That is why, he was told, he would only be called Alexis here, and why his parents' names too would have to be changed to saints' names. Every time Dr. Basilides asked about the boy's name and his parents' names, therefore, his new little helper gave him the same answer. The boy was astute enough to regard these repeated questions as a test of his obedience to Brother Eucharios. More concerned with his scientific experiment than with this simple-minded, taciturn boy's past, Dr. Basilides abandoned this line of questioning, assuming he would have ample opportunity to learn about the this boy's parentage at a later point. Brother Eucharios had told him that the boy's education had been neglected but that he was the son of good and pious parents who were destitute and thus delighted that their son would have the chance to grow up and become a pious friar. For a long time, the doctor had been longing for a capable pupil whom he might teach and train in his science and his art. So, when the young Alexis was presented to him as such a pupil early that morning, he was honestly pleased. To be sure, the boy seemed conspicuously simple-minded and dense, and in just a few hours he had managed to break several glass tubes and evaporating dishes. The good-natured doctor, however, ascribed all this clumsiness to his new pupil's timidity and nervousness. In several weeks, he was convinced, the boy would feel more at home in this new and foreign environment, and he would begin to develop intellectually more rapidly then as well.

Dr. Basilides seldom left his cell, and he rarely had reason to. The lay brothers in the city supplied him with all the instruments and materials that he needed for both his laboratory and the monastery's pharmacy. Yet despite this isolation, there was little in the great world of scientific discovery with which he was not familiar. The best bookshop in the city regularly sent him all the latest scientific literature, and he was well acquainted with all the books and journals which published the results of the most eminent research in natural history and medicine. From his isolated cell, Dr. Basilides maintained correspondence with the greatest scholars of Europe. His extensive knowledge of languages proved particularly helpful in studying these foreign writings. He did not just read the Latin and Greek classics. He was very much at home in modern European languages. He read German, French, English, and Italian books just as easily as his Russian ones. Remarkably, he even knew Hebrew. As a child, he once happened to find a copy of the Hebrew Bible on a table among the books of his teacher and second father, and he held onto this book as a sacred treasure.

The learned doctor was lost in thought producing his chemical compounds when an elderly friar stepped into his laboratory. Exhausted, the friar sat down in an armchair. As Dr. Basilides affectionately walked toward him, the friar said to him, "Yes, my good son, I am not going to be able to get up these stairs much longer with these seventy-year-old legs of mine."

"But Reverend Father," the doctor responded sympathetically, "isn't it time to think about giving up your lay practice? The city has doctors enough to take care of those who are ailing. You have spent the greater part of your life performing your duties so conscientiously. Don't you think you deserve to live out your remaining years in peace, without worries? We follow the rules of our holy order so strictly, performing acts of penance that few brothers subject themselves to. You have taxed your vital forces so much. Don't you think it makes sense at your age to conserve your energy and seek out some rest?"

"I have told you many times," the aged doctor responded, "of my firm resolution that, as long as I am breathing and can manage to get around, I will not deny my assistance to human beings who are suffering. I will seek out the grief-stricken hovels that our noble colleagues intentionally neglect and forget—either because poor people are not good for business or because these suffering people practice a religion which they condemn as heresy. These poor sick people whom our colleagues brand as accursed heretics expect me to provide them with help and assistance. I cannot refuse them my services, even though our reverend higumenos often takes me to task for this."

"Such selflessness!" the younger doctor responded with a gentle reproach.

"This is what my practice is all about," the learned old man responded. "These were the vows that I made when I became a monk, and only death can release me from these duties. And I have still not freed myself of the guilt that is recorded for me in God's book! There is much more that I must do before I will be able to enjoy his grace."

"Father, am I still not permitted to know the dark secret that plagues your spirit and tortures your soul so tyrannically?" the younger doctor asked sympathetically, sitting down across from him. "I am thirty-five years old now. I am no longer a boy. Tell me what oppresses your soul so terribly. The burden will be easier for you if I can share it."

"My son," responded Dr. Apollonios, the older doctor, "let me continue to bear this burden alone. You are no longer too young to share this secret with me. I am just not yet old enough to tell you about it. But know that I shall tell you my secret before I close this mouth of mine for the last time. If for some reason I fail to do so, you must go into my secret cabinet, the one whose door only you know about, and there you will find everything written down that I have been carefully concealing all these years. But let us not talk any further now of this topic—we have spoken about it enough before, I should think."

Dr. Apollonios grew silent and closed his eyes deep in thought. Dr. Basilides, his appreciative former pupil, the adoptive son who loved him like a father, did not dare to disturb him while he thought and reflected. After a solemn period of silence, the old doctor finally looked around and asked, "Who is this boy who is sitting so quietly in the corner?"

"He is my new pupil," answered Dr. Basilides. "Brother Eucharios brought him to me this morning."

"May you give your good teacher someday the same type of pleasure that my pupil here gives me in my old age," the old man called out to the boy in a good-natured tone of voice. He then turned to his son and said, "This boy is probably about ten years old now. You were not half that old when you moved into your little cell here."

"I must have been very young indeed," Dr. Basilides added, "when I was brought to the monastery. For all that I recall from my parental home is faint, confused, and dreamlike visions which are barely distinguishable from real dreams. My memory cannot reach that far back. And none of our honorable brothers will give me even the smallest bit of insight into the enigma of my ancestry. Even the old gatekeeper refuses, when I ask him, saying that only the reverend higumenos has the power to grant my request. I have tried to knock at the iron doors of his callous heart, but he has been unsympathetic to my wishes."

Dr. Apollonios gestured at the boy so as to remind the bold Dr. Basilides that they were not alone in the laboratory. In order to deflect attention away from what Dr. Basilides had just dared to say about the strict abbot, the elderly doctor changed the topic of conversation to talk about the chemical experiment to which his former pupil had just started to return. Soon their conversation took on an entirely scientific character, as the men talked about the influence electricity had on the various chemical corrosions and compounds. They soon forgot about the past, suppressing all thoughts about the secrets that inhabit the walls of all monasteries.

III. The Evening of the Seder[1]

It was the following day, and the evening had quietly and peacefully spread its starry veil over the spring sky. A solemn tranquility had come over the Jewish quarter, which was otherwise constantly in motion. All the shops and grocery stalls were closed, the itinerant peddlers and secondhand dealers were nowhere to be seen, and the streets and alleys were empty and desolate. But friendly lights were shining through the curtains of the homes, announcing clearly that families had gathered around the ceremonial Sabbath lamp to celebrate a holiday that would fortify them, raise their spirits, and enable them to forget the troubles and bitterness of everyday life. "Taste this bread of affliction and this bitter herb," the father of the family said to his table companions that festive evening, "and remember that our forefathers, too, had to suffer hardships and taste the bitterness of life on earth. But the good Lord always stood by their side and held his protective hands over Israel's endangered leaders."

In the festively lit dining room of the community's cantor, Jacob Poskowitzer, the Passover festival songs were also being sung with joy, and Poskowitzer's sons and daughters were carefree as they accompanied their aged parents in singing the melodies. Suddenly, though, while reciting the Song of Songs, Poskowitzer grew silent, and he listened carefully as he shot a questioning glance at his wife. She too found herself

---

1. *Seder*, which means order or sequence in Hebrew, is a term used to designate the festive meal that begins the Jewish holiday of Passover.

unable to speak and then rushed anxiously to the window. The children looked at their parents with shock and fear. Everyone in the room was silent. An abstruse, dull roar could be made out, turning into a thunder as it came closer to the trembling, fearful family. Swearing and cursing were mixed with desperate cries of fear, wailing, and whining. People were throwing heavy stones, shattering people's windows and destroying their shutters. They were breaking down the front doors of homes, and the scuffing waves of a drunk, bellowing throng were rolling through the streets of the Jewish quarter with satanic rage.

"Murderers! You've spilled Christian blood!" was the cry for revenge resounding hundredfold through the frightful night. Driven by brute lust, the predatory, bestial horde attacked the defenseless Jewish families. People who dared to try to protect their belongings or their honor were slaughtered by long sailor's knives or bludgeoned by the angry swinging cudgels that the primitive mob was using to arm itself. Amid all the tumultuous uproar, nevertheless, a clear plan was discernable. The various hordes were all being directed by several ringleaders, who were issuing orders and commanding obedience, and the cursing, screaming mob was moving forward like a wildly roaring mountain stream. Finally, they broke down Jacob Poskowitzer's front door, and sailors and people from the mob violently swarmed into the room, their eyes aglow. They swung their long knives and threatened to kill anyone who dared resist. In a flash they plundered all the silver that was on the table. They broke open cupboards and chests, all the while calling out, "Jew! Where is the Christian boy you slaughtered?" The predatory mob grabbed onto anything that had the least bit of value, clothing and furnishings included. After emptying out the house and smashing the leftover tables and benches with cannibalistic disdain, they moved on with their horrible screaming to plunder and destroy more homes. Dumbfounded and petrified, the members of the Poskowitzer family stared at each other. Unable even to begin lamenting the pain they had just experienced, they were aroused from their numbed state by yet another horrific scene. A police commissioner stepped into the destroyed room, accompanied by several armed policemen. He ordered two men to stand guard at the door and to permit no one to leave; he was going to search the rooms of the house with the other men. Turning to the trembling cantor, he addressed him curtly, "Jew, a Christian boy is missing, and word is that you've butchered him to use his blood to knead your Easter cakes.[2] You're the man who oversees the preparation of these Easter cakes. Spit it out, where is the Christian boy? If you tell the truth you can perhaps hope for mercy. If you deny it, woe is you!"

Faced with this supreme danger, Poskowitzer quickly regained his composure and told the police commissioner everything he could to convince him of his innocence.

"You don't want to confess?" the police officer responded. "Well, then we'll have to search your house. Show us the way!"

With crude blows these guardians of security pushed the trembling cantor around, illuminating all the nooks and crannies of the house. Finally, after a long search, a low-ranking police officer brought forth a bundle of clothes from behind a barrel in the cellar and screamed triumphantly, "Here, here, look! Whose clothes are these?"

The ragged clothes were quickly set out and the police officers shined their lights on them. And then there was a horrific scream: "Those are the clothes of the boy Peter who's missing! Look at all the blood stains! The poor Christian boy! Wait, what just fell on the floor there? Aha! The Jew fainted. Well, the criminal seems to be turning himself in. Tie him up!"

The Jew was promptly tied up. This rough, cannibalistic treatment, however, soon awakened Poskowitzer from his unconscious state. He timidly looked around. Gradually he recalled what had happened, and without resisting, he silently let himself be dragged off by the police's crude henchmen. They carried him, pale as a ghost, to the front door. His wife and daughter desperately fell down on their knees before the police commissioner and tore their hearts out begging for mercy for the innocent man.

"Tie them up too and carry them off along with him!" the barbarian called out to his underlings. They tied up the wife and eighteenth-year-old daughter of the innocent victim, violently tearing them away from the sobbing and crying children who now would be left at home all alone.

Out in the street, the mob was riled up. When the bloody clothes were delivered to them in the torchlight like a captured sign of victory,

---

2. The reference here is to Passover cakes, i.e., matzo, the unleavened bread Jews eat during the festival of Passover.

they kissed them as if they were holy relics. The unfortunate Jews, who were tied up and carried off right behind the clothes, almost succumbed to the rabid pack. The blood-stained evidence for the crime that had been committed was delivered to the court authorities, and the three captives were each put in different jail cells. During this time, the crude mob with its wild lust for destruction went on a rampage in the Jewish quarter. Now that the evidence of the murder had been discovered, they regarded all Jewish homes as fair game, and they looted, plundered, and destroyed everything in sight, pouncing on all those who dared to resist or defend themselves. The Jews had to endure the most outrageous atrocities and blood-curdling acts of cruelty that dreadful night, as the genius of history turned its eyes away from the bestial, rabid mob in disgust.

Soon the rising spring sun ushered in the first morning of Pesach,[3] calling the congregations of Israel to their houses of prayer, where they would thank God for the liberation from Egyptian slavery, for redeeming them from the tyrannical rule of a cruel Pharaoh. The Pesach sun sent its revitalizing rays into the devastated Jewish quarter, but here they exposed a dismal picture of the results of a savage lust for destruction. The mob had broken into storehouses and carried off the most sumptuous pieces of velvet and silk, which they tore to pieces and traipsed through the mud before leaving them to cover the streets. They had broken open barrels of oil and wine and left them on the street, creating huge puddles in which they trampled down on groceries and torn-up pieces of bedding. They had broken mirrors and crystal to smithereens and left them lying about, and piles of broken chairs and tables made it difficult to move. Pale, badly injured men were wandering among these ruins created by organized acts of vandalism, calling out for their women and children who had sought to hide away in remote corners during this abominable night. They were followed by noble-minded doctors guided by sons and daughters hoping to provide aid and assistance to their wounded and unconscious parents. And there were still a few drunken individuals left over from the predatory mob staggering about and making noise as they rampaged through the site of destruction, unwilling to separate themselves from the scene where their

---

3. *Pesach* is the Hebrew term for Passover.

animal brutality had been given free rein. Several of these hoodlums were on the brink of breaking into a Jewish home that had not yet been ransacked when an old man in monk's garb stepped out of the house. Through his words and his gestures, he did everything in his power to deny them entry.

"I am a doctor," he called out in a strained voice to the inebriated men. "A father and a son in this house have suffered mortal injuries. Stay away from this site of misery!"

But the gang seemed not to understand or heed the old man's warning. They cried out, "He's a Jew in disguise, get him out of the way!" and the ones in the back pushed forward into the house. The monk used all his feeble powers to resist and keep the wild horde out of the house, and in all the ensuing commotion he was stabbed by a sailor's knife and fell unconscious.

A police constable jumped into the fray and exclaimed in a powerful voice, "Who stabbed honorable Father Apollonios? Curse the godless murderer!"

As soon as the rioting horde heard the name Father Apollonios, everyone sobered up. Timidly, the crowd dispersed, leaving the unconscious monastery doctor lying in his blood at the threshold of the home.

The police constable called for reinforcements, and the unconscious monk was carefully placed onto a stretcher and brought back to the monastery.

IV. Revelations

That same morning, Higumenos Polycarpos sat in his secluded prayer cell across from the merchant Kfidy and listened carefully to the reports of what had happened. The friars were not permitted to enter this room unannounced, and the trusted Brother Eucharios stood guard at the door to ward off unwanted visitors. On the table in front of the higumenos were a number of tightly stuffed bags of money along with several items that rarely find their way into monasteries: silver pieces that the various synagogues in the city used for the festive decoration of their Torah scrolls. There were a number of silver crowns filled with genuine jewels; artfully decorated little towers from which golden bells were hanging; silver tablets, also decorated with golden bells and Hebrew inscriptions; and several silver scepters whose tips were adorned with a pointing hand.

The head of the monastery grabbed these piled up pieces of silver in his playful hands and said in an unctuous voice, "Yes, up until now these earthly treasures have been glistening in the synagogue dedicated to Satan. Now they shall finally be used for a holy purpose. We'll melt them down to create a great ornament for our church, an offering of thanksgiving to the Lord for crowning our plan with such glorious success! We have exacted revenge on those sinners who put their cursed hand on the son of the Lord. We have glorified God, and the Lord has blessed our pious work."

"Listen to that noise!" said Brother Eucharios, who was listening in. Surprised, he asked, "What kind of turmoil is that out in front of our gate?" The higumenos and his friend Kfidy pricked up their ears and made out an indistinct turmoil in the monastery garden. The former sent out the gatekeeper to see what was causing the commotion. He was away longer than the curiosity of the men remaining behind would have liked. When he finally returned to the room, his face showed nothing, and he answered his boss's impetuous question in an indifferent tone: "Nothing of importance, Reverend, just our old, foolish Brother Apollonios. He visited the Jewish quarter this morning, as he always does, and much to his surprise he found more work there than he had expected. He got into a fight with some drunken sailors, who dealt him such a blow that he fell unconscious. The police officers helped out and carried him back here, and they were followed by a huge crowd of people who are now waiting out in the garden for the Reverend's blessing."

"Then that's what they'll get!" the higumenos said. He went out to the monastery gate and extended his hands in blessing over the crowd outside on their knees. He then visited Brother Apollonios in his cell, where he found several other friars attending to him, Dr. Basilides foremost among them. Brother Apollonios was beginning to come to and to start to speak. When the higumenos asked Brother Basilides how he was doing, he was told that Brother Apollonios had lost a significant amount of blood and was thus feeling very weak; for the time being, undisturbed rest would be the best remedy for his condition. The higumenos nodded, signaling to the attentive friars to leave, and after expressing his earnest sympathy to the patient and entrusting him to the care of his student Basilides, he returned to his prayer cell and to his friend Kfidy, who was waiting for him.

"Are we alone, my son?" the old wounded doctor asked in a weak voice after the higumenos had left.

"Yes, indeed, my father," the faithful student answered anxiously. "Oh no, little Alexis is here. Shall I send him away?"

"Let him first come over to me here in my bed," the old doctor responded. He grabbed the boy's hand and asked him, "My child, isn't it true that you were called Peter Stephen in the sinful world outside?"

Instead of answering, the boy looked around anxiously, nodding yes with his head.

"Your father works in the harbor, and your mother is a washerwoman?"

Once again the boy answered the question by nodding his head, this time adding the words, "I'm not allowed to speak about this here!"

"Never mind," Dr. Apollonios added, "send the boy away now."

Once the boy had left, the ill doctor said to Dr. Basilides in a feeble voice, "My son, come very close to me, I have an appalling discovery to make to you."

The young doctor, reminding him that he was weak and needed to save his energy, asked him to wait until he had had the chance to get some sleep and regain his strength.

Dr. Apollonios, however, responded: "I shall not be sleeping again in this life. One of my most vital organs has been wounded. I can feel it in my breathing that I only have a few minutes left, and I want to use this time to lay bare my secrets at your breast so that you can prevent innocent people from falling prey to heinous deceitfulness." Speaking in a feeble voice and in broken sentences, he then spoke of what he had experienced that morning. He described the atrocious scene of destruction, bestiality, and fanaticism to his astonished young friend, who knew nothing about the bloody drama that had played out in the Jewish quarter. And he also told him of the various feelings that this abominable event had awakened in his breast.

"I was most outraged," he added, summoning up his quickly fading powers, "outraged and petrified by the inhumane madness that vilifies the Jews as cannibals. I thus stood at the doorstep of an old Jewish friend of mine wavering, doubting whether the fatuous barbarians who had attacked the Jews were even worthy of my assistance. Finally, I managed to fight back this doubt. I prescribed something that would help the attackers and went myself to the kitchen so that the maid would know exactly how to prepare the potion I was ordering to cool off their overexcited blood. When I entered the kitchen, however, I did not find the maid there; she had suffered abuse and was lying motionless in her room. Instead, I found the wife of a cobbler I know, a Christian woman who looks after the Jews' household and performs duties for them on the Sabbath. Talking to myself in the presence of this woman, I bemoaned the fate of these unfortunate men, even though they deserved to be punished for the nefarious murder they had committed. The woman looked at me in astonishment, asking, "Are we permitted to feel compassion for Jews? Isn't it a work pleasing to God to go after those who are enemies of our Savior? Just this morning Brother Eucharios was praising me for the good work I did, promising me an entire year's worth of indulgences for my future sins."

"Which work do you mean?" I asked, paying close attention.

"You know, for the work I did with little Peter's bloody clothes," she responded in a muted voice. Suspecting a disgraceful secret, I immediately took on a different tone, praised her for hating the Jews and for the good work she had done. Finally, thanks to my monk's clothes and my reputation for saintliness, the chatty woman finally confessed to me in secret that the missing Christian boy whom the Jews allegedly murdered was your Alexis. Brother Eucharios took his clothes and artificially covered them in blood, handing them over to the cobbler's wife to hide in the Jew's cellar so that they could be found by a police officer whom they had bribed."

The dying man had to exert himself to give this report, speaking in broken sentences as he exhausted nearly all of his diminishing powers. As soon as he was done, he sank down, pale as a ghost, and lost consciousness. The young doctor, who admired him so, used all the stimulants he could find to bring the old man's energy back. And finally, his efforts were crowned with success. The feeble old man opened his eyes again, regaining a little spark of consciousness and memory. Taking the hand of Dr. Basilides, who was deeply moved, into his own, he said, "Farewell, my son! Save the Jews who have been arrested! I owe them this, save them for me. Here is the key to my secret cabinet; the door is behind the altarpiece. For the Jews, my death is atonement for the crime that was committed against them. I shall die in peace, and when you open the cabinet, you'll find . . . "

Too weak to speak, he had just given the younger doctor the small key he was wearing on a silken string around his neck, and all he could do now was to gesture gently with this hand. His head fell back, and his noble soul floated away from its mortal shell.

Powerfully shaken up, the young doctor sat next to the lifeless body of his paternal friend, covering his face with his hands. He had lost so much—he had lost everything! He felt dark and dismal in his soul. He had been so close to the soul who had just departed that he felt as if his own spirit were now extinguished. This paternal friend had not only ushered him into the corridors of science. He had also ignited in his soul the fire of supreme and true religious knowledge, and it was the heavenly glow of this religiosity that helped save him from the demonic shadows of madness, superstition, and persecution that dominated his environment and surrounded him from all sides. The man who had just passed away was the only friend he had in the entire world, the only person with whom he could openly and candidly share his thoughts and feelings. He was the only one who could understand what went on inside his head, because this inner world was itself the product of his intellectual father. Shaken to the core, he now felt cut off from the rest of humanity, which appeared foreign and forbidding to him. More than anything else, it was the monastery, that bastion of deception, that filled him with dislike and repugnance. With contempt and disgust he thought about the higumenos, that devil in human form.

"Yes, I will save them in your name!" he exclaimed, lifting himself up quickly. Suddenly, there was a knocking at the door, and in walked the higumenos, accompanied by Brother Eucharios. He had come to inquire how the dear old brother was doing.

Basilides, pulling himself together quickly, responded quietly, gesturing at the dead body, "His soul is now in a better place." Finally, tears came to alleviate his burning pain. The higumenos, surprised by the doctor's quick death, exclaimed almost instinctively, "We have lost a pious, God-fearing brother!"

"What a shame," Eucharios added, "what a shame that helping such undeserving people cost him his life!"

"What instructions, dear brother, did he pass on to you before entering into eternity?"

"There was very little that he was able to tell me," Basilides responded. "His lung was wounded, and it was difficult for him to speak. He gave me the names of some severely wounded patients whom he had promised to visit once again this evening, and he begged me desperately to look after them."

"My dear son," the higumenos replied, "you're not seriously thinking of carrying on with our departed friend's lay practice? You must consider that this is what caused our blessed brother to lose his life!"

"Reverend Father," Basilides responded, "I promised this to my blessed father with an oath, and I cannot release myself from an oath made to a man on his deathbed."

For several minutes the dismal cell was filled with a deep silence. Finally, the higumenos began to speak. "You must keep your oath, of course, but because of this I must release you from another part of your holy vows: as long as you maintain the lay practice, you must not appear in our noble monastic robes. That which is holy must not be desecrated in the homes of heretics and Jews. When performing these profane duties, you must appear in profane dress. The mortal shell of this blessed brother should be carried into the church and watched over by brothers." The higumenos was outraged. He did not even say goodbye to the young doctor as he proudly left the cell with his companion.

Dr. Basilides once again sat at the side of the dead body of the man who had been so dear to him, surrendering himself to the tides and ebbs of his thoughts and feelings. He recognized clearly that the punishment that the higumenos had imposed on him was going to be extremely conducive to his plans. He was unclear, however, as to which of his various schemes he should pursue first. Deep in thought, he found himself interrupted by the sound of footsteps, and he turned his gaze toward the door. He saw the friars with a catafalque, carrying the body of the deceased brother into the minster amid all sorts of ceremonies. The death knell had summoned all the monks there. The doctor was still in the deceased's cell, from which a side door led into his laboratory. "Now is the moment to act," he thought quickly, "I may not have a second chance." Briskly, he took the altarpiece off the wall. He quickly located the hidden door to the secret closet and discovered there a little black box with silver inlay. He took out the book and hurriedly locked it up in the large closet in his laboratory, replaced the altarpiece, and walked quickly to join the brothers in the minster.

After the funeral was over, Dr. Basilides returned to his cell, where he found the boy Alexis busy cleaning the glass retorts and test tubes. Seeing the boy was a powerful reminder of the sacred task that his dying friend had entrusted to him, and he impatiently waited for the hour when he would return as a doctor to the Jewish quarter. Dr. Basilides had seldom accompanied his old friend while he was caring for lay patients. It was only in the case of highly unusual medical phenomena that he ever visited patients outside the monastery, and for this reason he was completely unknown in the city. Doctor Apollonios's faithful devotees expressed their heartfelt sympathy when Basilides told them that their worthy friend had been taken away from them. They mourned his loss but were happy to entrust themselves to the adept care of his genial successor, the young monastery doctor.

As soon as the sun rose, and again as soon as dusk approached, Dr. Basilides hurried from house to house in the horribly devastated Jewish quarter, giving relief to physical suffering and bringing consolation to depressed spirits. The innocent silent sufferers opened up their hearts to him. Without having to ask many questions, he soon learned everything about the atrocities that had happened and all about the measures that the Jews had since taken with the city authorities. They had pleaded with the authorities for the brute villains to stand trial; they had asked for proper compensation for the victims of the looting; and more than anything else, they had petitioned for Jacob Poskowitzer to be saved from the death sentence that was awaiting him in jail. They had secretly arranged for large amounts of money to be handed over to the relevant judicial authorities in the hopes of securing a lesser sentence, but all they could accomplish was for the trial to be continued. They were unable in any way to influence the judges, who would not waver in their conviction that the cantor had murdered the missing Christian boy. The great majority of the inhabitants of the city felt the same way, and it was only because of the interventions of the Prussian consul residing in the city that the bloodcurdling atrocities of the first night of Passover were not repeated. He had convinced the mayor to use military battalions to prevent any subsequent outbreaks of mob violence.

Dr. Basilides was worn out from visiting all his patients, and he sat in his carefully locked cell, avidly reading the manuscripts that his deceased paternal friend had left in the little black box. His face betrayed the supreme agitation of his soul, which was full of the most diverse and contradictory feelings. His dark eye would fire up with the flames of anger, then a smile would be discernible on his halfway-open mouth, and then emotional tears would stream down his glowing cheeks. He read attentively for a long time. Finally, his lamp began to burn out, and he realized that it was long past midnight. This was the third night in a row that he had stayed up so late reading this thick book packed full of writing. He kissed the book and placed it back in its ebony box, which he hid carefully in his laboratory cabinet. Excitedly, he paced back and forth in his cell. He had too much inner turbulence to be able to rest or sleep. It was difficult to discern his train of thoughts as he muttered isolated sentences out of context. Finally, he sat down. Supporting himself with the decisive spirit of his paternal educator, he spoke, "Yes, my dear father, you had to endure and suffer so much on my account. Oh, if I had only known this, I would have been able to thank you more properly! But your great spirit encompasses me. I vow to you that I shall dedicate my entire life to your memory. Your last wish will be my first deed. Satan himself has spun a huge web of deception, and tomorrow I shall tear it apart!"

V. The Rescue

It was very late when Dr. Basilides finally fell asleep, and the sun was already high in the heavens when its rays passed through the round window panes into his silent cell and woke him up from his deep slumber. Immediately he remembered the resolution he had made the night before, and before long, he found himself outside the dull walls of the monastery, dressed in clothes that would make no one suspect he was a monk. He walked carefully, taking a series of detours, hurrying off to the private residence of the Prussian consul, an elderly man who was a youthfully spry representative of the court of tolerance and intelligence. The consul took in Dr. Basilides with good will and good faith. He lent him an attentive ear, listening to his accounts of what had transpired. With riveting eloquence, the young doctor told him about the evil machinations to kill the Jews and the gruesome manner in which they were carried out. In the name of these poor victims of fanaticism, he thanked the consul for all that he had done to bring the violence to an end. Finally, he asked him, as an ambassador of providence, to help save the innocent Jewish cantor who had been condemned to death. The doctor's animated presentation of what had happened appalled the consul, who was horrified by the black depths into which human passions could be goaded. He promised to do everything in his power to unmask the wickedness and save the innocent. But he also stressed the numerous great difficulties standing in his way. He reminded the doctor how easy it was to bribe civil servants, and many had probably been so blinded by the gold of Greek merchants that they would neither want nor be able to distinguish truth from falsehood in this situation. He reminded him that since the monastery was not subject to the secular authorities, any complaint filed against it would have to be brought before the church patriarch, and this supreme power would do everything in his power to suppress any scandal in his fiefdom. If an investigation were to be initiated, the boy locked up in the monastery would certainly disappear suddenly, and the doctor himself, as a renegade to the Church, would be accused of such things that would result in him spending his life in prison. The Church would also stop at nothing to ensure that the sole witness in the case, the cobbler's wife, would remain eternally silent.

"I do not misjudge the difficulties to be overcome here," Dr. Basilides responded. "I'm also aware of the dangerous position into which these revelations might put both the boy and that woman. But can we sit back on account of such apprehensions and let an innocent man be executed as a criminal? Can we suppress the truth and abandon an entire religious community to persecution and the hatred of their enemies for the future? I can figure out how to skirt the dangers that threaten me. Indeed, as soon as I have managed to save the innocent Jew, I shall be leaving both the monastery and Russia. You, my lord, have been summoned by providence to act as the redeemer of the innocent here. In the name of God almighty, I beg you not to cast off this high calling."

The consul also felt inspired by the idea that it was his holy calling to intervene here as the saving and protecting messenger of providence. He told the doctor that he stood ready to carry out the rescue plan they had hatched, stressing that they would have to proceed with the utmost caution if they were to be successful. The two men thus carefully considered the plan for their undertakings from all possible perspectives, agreeing on fall-back plans if anything should go wrong at any point. After a long discussion, they shook each other's hands and said to each other, looking up at the heavens, "God will crown our efforts with success."

The consul retreated into his office, and much to his private secretary's surprise, he spent several hours at his desk that day all alone, reflecting and writing in his own hand. Finally, the long report was complete, and a packet was sent off to the post office, addressed to the Royal Prussian Embassy in Saint Petersburg. And providence did indeed crown their efforts with success. On the very same day that the Prussian ambassador received the letter from the consul he happened to have an audience with the prime minister of the Russian court, and by the day after that the emperor knew all about the sad events in his distant seaside city and their heinous connection to the horrific acts of vandalism. He was so enraged that he ordered a swift and thorough investigation to ensure that the guilty parties would be punished. A reliable and experienced minister of his was given unlimited imperial power of attorney, and he set out immediately and secretly to the scene where the atrocities had been committed. Only the highest members of the government knew about this mission.

As soon as the Prussian consul was made aware of the minister's arrival in town, he arranged for Dr. Basilides to be informed as well. That very same evening, holding the boy Alexis by the hand and carefully carrying the late Dr. Apollonios's black box under his coat, Dr. Basilides escaped from the monastery through an outlying garden gate, never to enter again. In the Prussian consul's spacious house there were two secluded rooms reserved for him and the boy. The next morning, the emperor's minister issued a dispatch that led to the cobbler's wife being arrested, and the investigation began. At first she was stubborn and tried to deny all the charges being brought against her. When the boy was brought out and joyfully united with his parents, however, her story clearly no longer held up. She confessed her guilt to the examining magistrate and gave a detailed account of the horrific events. She was given fifteen years in jail to reflect on the pious work she had done, and the ringleaders of the murderous rioting were sentenced to pay compensation for damages and loss suffered and given an appropriate punishment. For a long time Higumenos Polycarpos and his trusted accomplice Brother Eucharios refused to appear before the secular court of justice, claiming that only the patriarch of the church could hold them accountable. When the minister wrote to the patriarch, reminding him that the emperor was the supreme patriarch of the Greek orthodox church and that the emperor had given him his power of attorney, the head of the church gave the minister full authority to move forward with an arraignment and sentencing. The higumenos lived out his few remaining years in a penitentiary cell in a monastery in the extreme northern regions of Russia, and Brother Eucharios was sent to the ice fields of Siberia. The general public read about the entire investigation and the sentencing in all the major papers. There was nothing at all in print, however, about the fact that it was Dr. Basilides's revelations that began to unravel this hellish web or that it was the Prussian consul that had brought the entire affair to the emperor's attention. Those in the know shared this information confidentially. And Dr. Basilides was nowhere to be found.

It was on the second of May, the thirty-third day of the Omer, and the Jewish quarter of the large seaside town was a wistful sight to see.[4] That year this half holiday was declared a full holiday in all its glory as a means of expressing gratitude to God for saving the Jews. Early in the morning on that day, all sorts of people—the young and the old, men and women—streamed into the synagogue, where the sorrowful signs of the devastation were now difficult to find. In their place, only joy and gratitude were to be seen. Many people were still suffering and in pain from their wounds, but they were carried or driven to the house of prayer so that they could spend that morning saying their prayers of thanks together with those who had been rescued. The Psalms had never before been recited with such inspiration and such heartfelt devotion in those halls as on that morning, as the congregants expressed

---

4. The holiday referenced here is Lag BaOmer (the thirty-third day of the Omer). Following Leviticus 23:15–16, traditional Jews count the forty-nine days that separate Passover from the Feast of the Tabernacles (Shavuot). This period is a time of partial mourning known as the counting of the Omer, the Omer being an ancient Hebrew measure of grain, and marks the transition from the physical exodus from Egypt to the giving of the law at Mount Sinai. The thirty-third day of the counting of the Omer marks a break in this period, a day when all the restrictions of mourning are lifted and joyful celebrations occur.

their deeply felt gratitude, at times in sonorous joy, at other times in soundless ceremonial silence. When the holy Torah was rolled out and the pale cantor approached to sing the prayers of thanks to the almighty for liberating him from the dark dungeon and saving him from imminent death, he was so moved in prayer that he was unable to speak. Not an eye in the synagogue was dry, and all the men and women were sobbing. After it was read, the Torah was rolled up again and handed back to the rabbi. Carrying the holy book in his arms, the rabbi uttered a prayer of thanksgiving that had been written especially for this occasion. Speaking first in Hebrew and then in the local vernacular, he asked God to bless all those who had dedicated themselves so nobly to saving the innocent. There were many people whom he blessed, but he paid particular attention to the sublime name of the just and benevolent emperor, his high-level civil servants, the Prussian consul, and finally the soul of the late Dr. Apollonios and the noble Dr. Basilides. After the service was over, the congregants organized a collection of funds, pulling together a significant sum to ease the pain and suffering of the Jews who had been the victims of the violent attacks.

VI. The Confession

The Israelites spent the rest of the day celebrating this festival of thanksgiving in their homes as a second Purim,[5] with tears of sadness and joy, and by the time the sun set, the Jewish quarter was permeated by this mood of bliss. That evening the rabbi and his wife were entertaining several friends in their home, and here too the atmosphere was one of religious elation. Outside, the weather was harsh and a storm was raging, with the mix of rain and snow showers that was typical for April. Inside the rabbi's well-heated home, however, the conversation was cozy and warm. Someone had just told an amusing anecdote when the maid came in and announced to the rabbi's wife that an unknown man had come to speak to the rabbi. The hospitable old man did not like to

---

5. Jewish communities often celebrated their own escape from destruction with a second Purim. The festival of Purim commemorates the deliverance of Jews in the Persian empire from the wrath of Haman, the minister who sought their annihilation, as is reported in the book of Esther. Celebrations of a second Purim would often be used to celebrate more local instances of deliverance from destruction.

leave his cheerful surroundings. Just a moment later he returned to his company, however, reassuring them that he would be back as soon as he had the chance to have a brief conversation with the stranger who had come by. He then made his way to his study, a room that was dimly lit by a covered lamp; once there, he started to help his guest take off his wet coat. Suddenly he exclaimed, "Dr. Basilides! What brings you, Reverend Father, to my home, so late and in such stormy weather? To what do I owe this great honor?"

"The reason why I'm coming to you so late and hidden in my coat like this, venerable rabbi, is that I am no longer a 'reverend father.' The monastery officials have excommunicated me. They have publicly declared me a renegade son of the holy order and a traitor. That's why I have to remain in hiding. I creep through secluded streets at night so as not to incite the mob's anger. And why am I being so impertinent as to take you away from your family now? There's a request I would like to make of you. I would like you to tell me, namely, under what conditions I can enter the covenant of the Israelite religion."

Aghast at this statement, the rabbi quickly rose up from his armchair and exclaimed, "Are you trying to create even more hardship for us, when the wounds of the calamity we've just escaped from haven't even yet scared over? Think of all the people who hate us. Once they decide that we caused a friar to convert to our religion, they will only persecute us with renewed anger. Yes, the state authorities themselves would punish us, perhaps even drive us out of the country. You've probably not thought through this decision of yours thoroughly. Perhaps you're just trying to convince us how much you care about what has happened to us. Remain true to your paternal faith, for according to the teachings of our sages the pious of all nations have a share in the world to come. You can find the grace of God and eternal bliss through your own faith."

"No, honored rabbi, I have no choice. I owe the world a public declaration of the religion that I carry in my heart."

"This isn't necessary," the rabbi pointed out once again. "You are only accountable to the eternal one for what you believe and feel. And why would you want to submit yourself to all those difficult religious laws? You're not obligated to follow them by birth."

"Well, now you must learn my secret," the doctor responded. "I was born a Jew, thus according to my ancestry I am your coreligionist."

Once again the rabbi got up from his chair in shock. He entreated the doctor to share with him all the details of his life secret.

"Certainly, but that will have to wait for another occasion," the doctor responded. "I've already kept you longer that I should today, and you should return to your family."

"I shall hurry back to them," the rabbi responded, "but only to tell them that our conversation will go on for longer than I originally anticipated. Then you shall unfold your entire life's story for me. And don't think about giving me anything less than a full report, I'm always in this room well past midnight."

Soon the elderly man returned from his adoring family and sat back down with youthful swiftness, eager to listen to Dr. Basilides, who told him the following: "You know that Dr. Apollonios, of blessed memory, raised me with all the care of a loving father. It was in my arms that his soul passed away into the hereafter. Before he left this earth, he entrusted me with a holy relic, a hidden black box in which much to my surprise I found an incredibly detailed diary he had kept. This life chronicle of that noble man did not only paint a picture of *his* existence on this earth. It also shed light on mine. Yes, I could see that this work was written especially for me. For at many times there would be several pages in a row that addressed me affectionately, speaking of the supreme truths to be known and felt. When I now read these speeches directed at me, I hear the voice of the spirit of my departed friend speaking to me from the peaceful world of the heavenly hereafter.

"As for my life story, I learned that it is much richer than I could have imagined. But I'll skip over all the unessential events to sketch out for you just its general contours. In M——, the important Russian commercial town, there was a man named Samuel Rabbinowicz who enjoyed domestic bliss alongside his faithful and dearly beloved wife, Rachel. This honest couple—my parents—worked hard and managed secure a fine livelihood for themselves, and there was no other wish in their hearts than to be able to enjoy the joys of parenthood. It was I who was supposed to bring them this joy in the sixth year of their marriage, for this is when I was born, their little son, Raphael. I remained the only child of these joyful parents, and I had all the paternal care and tender maternal love in the world to show for it. They hired a nurse for me, to look after me, and they compensated her well. They intentionally hired a Christian woman so that someone could prepare food for me on the Sabbath. To the joy and delight of my happy parents, I grew big and strong. When I was three years old, however, a treacherous case of scarlet fever confined me to bed. My parents' family doctor, Dr. Leander, did everything in his power to strengthen the little flame of life that was quivering weakly at the wick. But to no avail. My fearful parents donated significant alms to the most needy to buy my young life, but this too was in vain. The weak little spark of life in me was glowing more feebly every day. My mother was worn out and she took to desperate measures. She made a vow to fast for two days straight, and she fulfilled her sacred oath with steadfast resolve. On the second evening, lo and behold, she had just said a devout prayer to end her solemn fasting and was about to eat some bread and drink some water when my burning fever finally broke. At last, I broke out in a sweat, as they had been hoping for for so long. I recovered my childlike vitality, and my health improved from day to day. My dear mother was comforted by her conviction that her pious fasting had stolen me out of the arms of the angel of death. As rapidly as children's health can deteriorate, children often recover just as quickly, and after several months I was once again able truly to enjoy life. Once again, my father happily placed his hands in blessing on my head with its black locks of hair on the Sabbath. My mother's gaze was even more drunk with bliss than before when she would stare at me, saying, 'This is the boy I prayed for.' But alas, the higher mortals climb up the mountain of happiness, the more easily this bliss can break into smithereens when nefarious hands conspire to hurl it into shallow waters. It was the evening of the Day of Atonement, and after a long day of fasting and praying, my parents were returning home from synagogue. They expected to come home to find their chipper Raphael, holding his nurse's hand, jumping out to meet them with joy, as he always did. Much to their surprise, they saw that there were no lights burning in their home, and the front door of the house was locked. They knocked, they called out, they screamed, and they ran around in desperation. None of the neighbors could provide them with any information about the whereabouts of their son and his nurse. Finally, the postman joined the crowd in front of their house. This man, who was well known in my parent's house, told them that that afternoon he had seen Ursula traveling off in a mail coach with little Raphael and a suitcase. In the meantime, my parents had managed to get a locksmith to open the door. On the table they found a note that Ursula had written. Its content was as follows:

"'By the time you return home this evening, I will be far away from you, and I will have taken Raphael, the son who was yours, with me. From now on, his name will be Christopher, and it is my intent that be brought up in a monastery as a pious Christian. When your son was sick, I was concerned for his good soul. Worried that he would die and enter into eternal damnation, I sat at his bedside crying. But then I convinced a pious Christian man, who happened to be sitting alone with me, to baptize the child quickly so that his soul could be saved for heaven; it had already been lost for earth. This God-fearing man—I am bound by an oath not to reveal his name—completed the holy baptism according to protocol, and with this act your son was taken into the fold of the Holy Church. The good Lord soon brought him back to health, for he wanted your son to live and act on this earth as a Christian, and it was thus for me a sacred duty to have him raised as a Christian. Do not bother looking for me or for the dear Christopher, for other than that man who baptized him there is no one on earth who knows where I am going with the child. But do not be worried, you should know that the young Christian boy will be raised conscientiously and will be made to fear God. One day he will pray for you. Your servant, Ursula.'

"A day of fasting had already rendered my mother's nervous system fragile, and this news threw her for a loop. She kept losing consciousness for most of the night and was not able to eat anything at all. In the aftermath of this horrendous emotional shock, my mother developed a severe inflammation of the brain. She fell into a state of dementia, from which she emerged only occasionally to enjoy a few minutes of clarity. After an awful, nine-day long battle, the gentle hand of death finally brought an end to her suffering. These blows, coming suddenly one after the next, gave my father considerably agony, and he was so disoriented that he could not even begin to think about trying to find out where Ursula had gone with his child. His friends, however, were committed to rescuing the stolen child for Judaism, and they set out to track her down. Thanks to the postal administration, they were able to figure out where Ursula had traveled for the first forty miles of her journey, but nothing could be discovered about where she had gone from there.

Everyone assumed that after taking the mail coach, Ursula had traveled by foot for several miles and then continued her journey with me under a different name. Eventually she brought me to the monastery here, where I was taken in and given an education.

"After all this happened, my father fell into a depression and had little desire to continue on living. He spoke very little, avoided his friends, and neglected his business affairs, allowing an old bookkeeper to run his business for him. He would be seen spending hours at the Jewish cemetery sitting silently at the grave of his departed wife and staring up toward heaven, paying no attention to the harsh northern wind playing wildly with his hair or the dense cloak of snow piling up on his coat. Spring came bringing its mild sunny days, enticing blossoms out of the earth, and luring the birds back to the thawed homeland. But no mild rays made their way into my melancholy father's frozen heart; the sheet of ice covering it seemed as if it would never melt.

"My father stopped speaking to his friends and acquaintances. The only person to whom he opened up his constricted heart was his family doctor, Dr. Leander. He complained to Dr. Leander of his physical and intellectual pain, asking him why providence, which had otherwise been so kind-hearted, had dealt him such painful suffering. The doctor was the only person he felt the urge to communicate with, and it was only in his breast that he felt he could find honest compassion. This was in part because he observed that Dr. Leander himself also seemed depressed, cheerless, and distracted in the aftermath of my mother's death. The doctor spoke of her with the most profound pain whenever he saw my father, and he would spend hours with him trying to do whatever he could to console him, to cheer him up, and to make him stronger. During one of these conversations, my father handed Dr. Leander a copy of the Hebrew Bible, saying to him: 'If you should ever manage to discover where my son is, please give him this Bible. Once, I, the happy father, wrote his birthday and his and my own name in it, on the first page. This book is the spiritual bond that connects him to me. I myself shall probably never see him again in this life, for I cannot remain any longer in this land. I am suffocating under these skies.' Several weeks later my father disappeared without a trace.

"Unable to sleep or find peace of mind, my father's tortured soul could no longer remain in that city. But he was not the only man who had to flee for these reasons. Dr. Leander was also very much at odds with the world and himself. For he was the one whom Ursula had convinced to baptize me when I was at death's door, and his conscience called out to him constantly and tumultuously: 'The woman is dead, and the man is on the brink of going mad, and this is all your fault! You have inflicted pain and suffering on a family that had shown you nothing but good will and friendship.' This hellish voice of Dr. Leander's conscience tortured him to no end, chasing him from one place to the next. Only extreme religious fanaticism would have been in a position to drown out this horrific voice, and this man was anything but a fanatic. Indeed, when Ursula had asked him to perform the baptism when I was ill, he did so without much forethought, convinced as he was that I was not going to survive another day. After Ursula told a priest the secret of what had happened and then escaped with me, however, he realized the terrible consequences of this act that he had done without great reflection. He blamed himself for everything, and remorse quickly turned into despair, as his conscience reproached him, 'You are the one who murdered these parents!' Dr. Leander had concluded that my father had thrown himself into the river in his efforts to find a release from his torturous existence.

"Like Cain, Dr. Leander escaped from the site of despair without knowing where he was fleeing. His first night in flight he spent lying on the mossy forest floor. He lay there, unable to sleep, but the warm summer night fanned off his smoldering brow, bringing the first, cooling peace to his burning heart. Then and there, in the sublime cathedral of the starry heavens, he made a vow to lead the life of a strictly penitent monk until he died. He would sacrifice his entire being to help human suffering—particularly that of the Jews—and, most importantly, he would do everything in his power to replace my lost father and love me like a son. Fortified by this sacred vow, he made his way on foot to the monastery here, where Ursula had already told the higumenos of my fate. Dr. Leander told the higumenos of his vow. And as you know, as Father Apollonios, he fulfilled this sacred vow in a holy manner.

"And as for Ursula, she suffered from poverty and eventually fell into a life of debauchery. She went to church regularly, but this did not prevent her from sinking deeper and deeper into the mire of vice. She died a miserable death in the poorhouse.

"This, rabbi," Dr. Basilides continued after a short break, "is the story of my life as I was able to piece it together from the extensive entries I found in my teacher's diary. And here," he added, handing the rabbi a thick book, "is the Hebrew Bible, this spiritual bond that connects me eternally with my unfortunate father. Now you will be able to recognize why it is my sacred duty to live as a Jew and dedicate my being to all of humanity but particularly to my coreligionists."

The old rabbi remained silent for a long time. The doctor's story had made a powerful impression on him, touching him in the depths of his soul, and he was struggling to recall indistinct figures buried deep in his memory. "It's you," he finally began to speak. "You are the man who as a boy was stolen from his unfortunate parents, the boy who filled all Israel with sorrow! My ears too heard tell of this awful news at the time. O, Eternal One! Our thoughts are not your thoughts, and your paths are not our paths. Praised be the name of God from now to eternity! Amen. Yes, you shall belong to the divine covenant and return to the fold where you belong by birth. But it is impossible for you to convert back to Judaism in this country. Hurry and travel to Holland; there you can publicly profess the God of your forefathers. The chief rabbi of Holland and I have corresponded with each other for a long time. I will give you a detailed letter of recommendation and send you to him. With the help of God, you'll soon be sending me news that you have safely arrived in Amsterdam."

The two men spoke for a long time about the paths God takes and those that humans take, about the past and the future. Finally, the clock announced, barely audibly, that it was already an hour past midnight. It was late and time for the two men to go their separate ways for the night.

The next day Dr. Basilides again appeared in the rabbi's study, again hidden in his coat. He had come to pick up the letter of recommendation that the rabbi had promised him and then to take leave of the spiritual guide who had become so dear to him.

"If it is God's will," the doctor said, "tomorrow before sunrise I shall be sailing away from here on a Dutch ship as a Prussian subject with a Prussian passport. With God's assistance, I shall arrive safely in Amsterdam. Once I'm there I will write you to express my gratitude once again. Before I leave, though, I must thank you in person from the bottom of my heart."

"May God protect you on your travels," the rabbi responded. "Here is the letter of recommendation, along with a small amount of travel money, which the Israelite community here wants to give you as a token of its gratitude."

The doctor tried to refuse the purse filled with gold that the rabbi gave him, commenting that he did not know what he had done to earn this generous gift. But the rabbi was able to convince him that that community owed him in fact much more, and not just for the medical assistance he had given the sick. He was the one who had saved Cantor Poskowitzer and helped give the community as a whole safety and security. The rabbi placed both of his hands on Dr. Basilides's head and blessed him. The farewell was affectionate and heartwarming.

Even though Amsterdam has a large Israelite community, the news that a Christian doctor from abroad had converted to Judaism managed to travel fast. Soon, all sorts of adventurous tales were circulating about his secret past, with such legends creating out of fact and fiction an outlandish picture of his life. Every Sabbath, the foreign doctor came to the synagogue carrying under his arm his Bible bound in Russian leather, and he participated in the public services there in silent devotion. The synagogue was inevitably full of curious people coming to catch a glimpse of the convert.

On the Sabbath of consolation after the fast day on the ninth of the month of Av,[6] however, there was one individual who came for different reasons. This silent old man was usually indifferent to the objects of curiosity that fascinated common people. He had come to see the new Israelite only because he had heard that he was from Russia, that country that he himself always remembered with sadness and melancholy. At the end of the service the old man went up to the foreign doctor and addressed him in Russian. When the doctor answered him, also in Russian, he happened to notice the new coreligionist's Bible, which was closed tight with silver clasps. Quivering, he grabbed the Bible, opened it up and read the inscription on the first page.

---

6. The ninth day of Av (Tisha b'Av in Hebrew) is a solemn fast day commemorating the destruction of the first and the second temple in Jerusalem. The first Sabbath after Tisha b'Av is called the Sabbath of comfort, named after the opening line of the day's reading from the prophets, Isaiah 40:1.

Pale as a ghost, he stuttered, "Sir, from whom did you get this book?"

"It was my father's Bible," Basilides responded.

"Did a doctor give it to you?" the old man asked in a hurry.

"Surprised and in a deep state of shock, Basilides took a look at the old man and responded, "Yes, indeed, it was Dr. Leander."

"God almighty, my son Raphael!" exclaimed the old man, shaken to the core.

Father and son held each other in an affectionate embrace for a long time, crying tears of melancholy and joy.

Amy Levy, "Cohen of Trinity" (1889)

Amy Levy (1861–89) was born in Clapham, a suburb of London, and lived in the middle-class neighborhood of Bloomsbury, near the British Museum. Her father was a stockbroker; although not religiously observant her parents were members of the West London Synagogue of British Jews (the London reform congregation) and retained social contacts among London Jews. The family ethos was liberal and intellectual, and Levy was educated in Brighton at one of the new progressive girls' schools. She continued her education at Cambridge University, being part of the first generation of British Jews to study there (and the first Jewish woman to do so). She moved among a circle of intellectuals, social campaigners, and writers and traveled extensively in Europe. She read widely, including in contemporary European literature and thought.

Aiming to support herself as a professional writer, Levy published a broad range of writings, supplementing her experimental poetry with more commercially oriented work including middlebrow novels and light satirical articles. In her more serious fiction and criticism she was an early participant in the feminist movement of the 1880s, addressing the social, economic, and intellectual restriction of women with an often despairing rage. She also utilized her knowledge of the Jewish community to write articles for the *Jewish Chronicle* and, in 1888, the novel *Reuben Sachs*, a major attack on the materialism and spiritual poverty of London Jewry. While the narrative included a conventional sneer at the vulgarity of socially ambitious Jews, Levy's central target was the marriage system—especially exemplified by Jews, she thought, but by no means confined to them—that promoted a coldly pragmatic approach to human relations and thus stifled authentic feeling and creativity. The novel was a critical success and spawned several imitations equally scathing about London Jewry, as well as a strong defensive backlash in the Jewish press. This response points to the discomfort generated by satirical literature on Jewish life that addressed both a Jewish and a non-Jewish readership.

"Cohen of Trinity," one of Levy's most powerful stories, was published the following year in the mainstream periodical the *Gentleman's Magazine*, a few months before Levy's own death by suicide at the age of twenty-seven. Although it is tempting to read her story of a talented, misunderstood, and depressive writer in simply autobiographical terms, the text in fact speaks to a number of broader fin de siècle preoccupations. In "Cohen of Trinity" Levy distilled several of the themes and strategies first evident in *Reuben Sachs*. In that novel, Jewish figures are often represented in highly derogatory terms: the narrative emphasizes their ugly, unhealthy bodies and lack of social poise. In the later story too, the awkward physique and vulgar behavior of Cohen is striking, but it is pointedly seen through the cool perspective of the narrator, who, while somewhat fascinated, has no understanding of and little sympathy with what he observes. While Cohen and the narrator's shared belief that Jews have a tendency toward suicide partakes of contemporary degenerationist theory—which regarded Jews as a race in physical and psychological decline—the story also tells us something of Cohen's uncomfortable *social* experience at the elite university. As the narrator's own attitude reveals, Jews remain unwelcome and uncomprehended in upper-class society even if there is no legal barrier to their entry. In some sense, however, Cohen's troubled psyche contributes to his intellectual brilliance. Further, beyond social documentary, lies the influence of philosophical pessimism, a strong current among many writers and thinkers of Levy's time and a key theme in her other writings.

The news of poor Cohen's death came to me both as a shock and a surprise.

It is true that, in his melodramatic, self-conscious fashion, he had often declared a taste for suicide to be among the characteristics of his versatile race. And indeed in the Cambridge days, or in that obscure interval which elapsed between the termination of his unfortunate University career and the publication of *Gubernator*[1] there would have been nothing astonishing in such an act on his part. But now, when his book was in everyone's hands, his name on everyone's lips; when that recognition for which he had longed was so completely his; that success for which he had thirsted was poured out for him in so generous a draught—to turn away, to vanish without a word of explanation (he was so fond of explaining himself) is the very last thing one would have expected of him.

---

1. Steersman (Latin).

I.

He came across the meadows towards the sunset, his upturned face pushed forwards catching the light, and glowing also with another radiance than the rich, reflected glory of the heavens.

A curious figure: slight, ungainly; shoulders in the ears; an awkward, rapid gait, half slouch, half hobble. One arm with its coarse hand swung like a bell-rope as he went; the other pressed a book close against his side, while the hand belonging to it held a few bulrushes and marsh marigolds.

Behind him streamed his shabby gown—it was a glorious afternoon of May—and his dusty trencher-cap pushed to the back of his head revealed clearly the oval contour of the face, the full, prominent lips, full, prominent eyes, and the curved beak of the nose with its restless nostrils.

"Who is he?" I asked my companion, one of the younger dons.

"Cohen of Trinity."[2]

He shook his head. The man had come up on a scholarship, but had entirely failed to follow up this preliminary distinction. He was no good, no good at all. He was idle, he was incompetent, he led a bad life in a bad set.

We passed on to other subjects, and out of sight passed the uncouth figure with the glowing face, the evil reputation, and that strange suggestion of latent force which clung to him.

The next time I saw Cohen was a few days later in Trinity quad.[3] There were three or four men with him—little Cleaver of Sidney,[4] and others of the same pattern. He was yelling and shrieking with laughter—at some joke of his own, apparently—and his companions were joining in the merriment.

Something in his attitude suggested that he was the ruling spirit of the group, that he was indeed enjoying the delights of addressing an audience, and appreciated to the full the advantages of the situation.

---

2. Trinity College is one of the colleges of the University of Cambridge. The continuing Christian ethos of the university is suggested by the name of this particular college, and its juxtaposition with the Jewish name *Cohen* is intended to suggest a jarring incongruity.

3. Quadrangle.

4. Sidney Sussex College.

I came across him next morning, hanging moodily over King's Bridge, a striking contrast to the exuberant figure of yesterday.

He looked yellow and flaccid as a sucked lemon, and eyed the water flowing between the bridges with a suicidal air that its notorious shallowness made ridiculous.

Little Cleaver came up to him and threw out a suggestion of lecture.

Cohen turned round with a self-conscious, sham-tragedy air, gave a great guffaw, and roared out by way of answer the quotation from *Tom Cobb*:

"The world's a beast, and I hate it!"[5]

II.

By degrees I scraped acquaintance with Cohen, who had interested me from the first.

I cannot quite explain my interest on so slight a knowledge; his manners were a distressing mixture of the *bourgeois* and the *canaille*,[6] and a most unattractive lack of simplicity marked his whole personality. There never indeed existed between us anything that could bear the name of friendship. Our relations are easily stated: he liked to talk about himself, and I liked to listen.

I have sometimes reproached myself that I never grew fond of him; but a little reciprocity is necessary in these matters, and poor Cohen had not the art of being fond of people.

I soon discovered that he was desperately lonely and desperately unapproachable.

Once he quoted to me, with reference to himself, the lines from Browning:

> . . . hath spied an icy fish
> That longed to 'scape the rock-stream where she lived,
> And thaw herself within the lukewarm waves,
> O' the lazy sea. . . .
> Only she ever sickened, found repulse
> At the other kind of water not her life,

---

5. *Tom Cobb; or, Fortune's Toy* (1875), a farce by W. S. Gilbert.
6. Common (French).

Flounced back from bliss she was not born to breathe,
And in her old bonds buried her despair,
Hating and loving warmth alike.[7]

Of the men with whom I occasionally saw him—men who would have been willing enough to be his friends—he spoke with an open contempt that did him little credit, considering how unscrupulously he made use of them when his loneliness grew intolerable. There were others, too, besides Cleaver and his set, men of a coarser stamp—boon companions, as the story-books say—with whom, when the fit was on, he consented to herd.

But as friends, as permanent companions even, he rejected them, one and all, with a magnificence, an arrogant and bitter scorn that had in it a distinctly comic element.

I saw him once, to my astonishment, with Norwood, and it came out that he had the greatest admiration for Norwood and his set.

What connection there could be between those young puritans, aristocrats and scholars, the flower of the University—if prigs, a little, and *bornés*[8]—and a man of Cohen's way of life, it would be hard to say.

In aspiring to their acquaintance one scarcely knew if to accuse the man of an insane vanity or a pathetic hankering after better things.

Little Leuniger, who played the fiddle, a Jew, was the fashion at that time among them; but he resolutely turned the cold shoulder to poor Cohen, who, I believe, deeply resented this in his heart, and never lost an opportunity of hurling a bitterness at his compatriot.

A desire to stand well in one another's eyes, to make a brave show before one another, is, I have observed, a marked characteristic of the Jewish people.

As for little Leuniger, he went his way, and contented himself with saying that Cohen's family were not people that one "knew."

On the subject of his family, Cohen himself, at times savagely reserved, at others appallingly frank, volunteered little information, though on one occasion he had touched in with a few vivid strokes the background of his life.

---

7. A slight misquotation of Robert Browning, "Caliban upon Setebos; or, Natural Theology in the Island" (1864), ll. 33–43.

8. Narrow-minded (French).

I seemed to see it all before me: the little new house in Maida Vale;[9] a crowd of children, clamorous, unkempt; a sallow shrew in a torn dressing-gown, who alternately scolded, bewailed herself, and sank into moody silence; a fitful paternal figure coming and going, depressed, exhilarated according to the fluctuations of his mysterious financial affairs; and over everything the fumes of smoke, the glare of gas, the smell of food in preparation.

But, naturally enough, it was as an individual, not as the member of a family, that Cohen cared to discuss himself.

There was, indeed, a force, an exuberance, a robustness about his individuality that atoned—to the curious observer at least—for the presence of certain of the elements which helped to compose it. His unbounded arrogance, his enormous pretensions, alternating with and tempered by a bitter self-depreciation, overflowing at times into self-reviling, impressed me, even while amusing and disgusting me.

It seemed that a frustrated sense of power, a disturbing consciousness of some blind force which sought an outlet, lurked within him and allowed him no rest.

Of his failure at his work he spoke often enough, scoffing at academic standards, yet writhing at his own inability to come up to them.

"On my honour," he said to me once, "I can't do better, and that's the truth. Of course you don't believe it; no one believes it. It's all a talk of wasted opportunities, squandered talents—but, before God, that part of my brain which won the scholarship has clean gone."

I pointed out to him that his way of life was not exactly calculated to encourage the working mood.

"Mood!" he shouted with a loud, exasperated laugh. "Mood! I tell you there's a devil in my brain and in my blood, and Heaven knows where it is leading me."

It led him this way and that at all hours of the day and night.

The end of the matter was not difficult to foresee, and I told him so plainly.

This sobered him a little, and he was quiet for three days, lying out on the grass with a lexicon and a pile of Oxford classics.

On the fourth the old mood was upon him and he rushed about like

---

9. A London suburb where many lower middle-class Jews lived.

a hunted thing from dawn to sunset winding up with an entertainment which threatened his position as a member of the University.

He got off this time, however, but I shall never forget his face the next morning as he blustered loudly past Norwood and Blount in Trinity Street.

If he neglected his own work, he did, as far as could be seen, no other, unless fits of voracious and promiscuous reading may be allowed to count as such. I suspected him of writing verses, but on this matter of writing he always maintained, curiously enough, a profound reserve.

What I had for some time foreseen as inevitable at length came to pass. Cohen disappeared at a short notice from the University, no choice being given him in the matter.

I went off to his lodgings directly the news of his sentence reached me, but the bird had already flown, leaving no trace behind of its whereabouts.

As I stood in the dismantled little room, always untidy, but now littered from end to end with torn and dusty papers, there rose before my mind the vision of Cohen as I had first seen him in the meadows, with the bulrushes in his hand, the book beneath his arm, and on his face, which reflected the sunset, the radiance of a secret joy.

III.

I did not see *Gubernator* till it was in its fourth edition, some three months after its publication and five years after the expulsion of Cohen from Trinity.

The name, Alfred Lazarus Cohen, printed in full on the title-page, revealed what had never before occurred to me, the identity of the author of that much-talked-of book with my unfortunate college acquaintance. I turned over the leaves with a new curiosity, and, it must be added, a new distrust. By-and-bye I ceased from this cursory, tentative inspection, I began at the beginning and finished the book at a sitting.

Everyone knows *Gubernator* by now, and I have no intention of describing it. Half poem, half essay, wholly unclassifiable, with a force, a fire, a vision, a vigour and felicity of phrase that carries you through its most glaring inequalities, its most appalling lapses of taste, the book fairly took the reader by storm.

Here was a clear case of figs from thistles.

I grew anxious to know how Cohen was bearing himself under his success, which must surely have satisfied, for the time being at least, even his enormous claims.

Was that ludicrous, pathetic gap between his dues and his pretensions at last bridged over?

I asked myself this and many more questions, but a natural hesitation to hunt up the successful man where the obscure one had entirely escaped my memory prevented me from taking any steps to the renewal of our acquaintance.

But Cohen, as may be supposed, was beginning to be talked about, heard of and occasionally met, and I had no doubt that chance would soon give me the opportunity I did not feel justified in seeking.

There was growing up, naturally enough, among some of us Cambridge men a sense that Cohen had been hardly used, that (I do not think this was the case) he had been unjustly treated at the University. Lord Norwood, whom I came across one day at the club, remarked that no doubt his widespread popularity would more than atone to Cohen for the flouting he had met with at the hands of Alma Mater. He had read *Gubernator*; it was clever, but the book repelled him, just as the man, poor fellow, had always repelled him. The subject did not seem to interest him, and he went off shortly afterwards with Blount and Leuniger.

A week later I met Cohen at a club dinner, given by a distinguished man of letters. There were present notabilities of every sort—literary, dramatic, artistic—but the author of *Gubernator* was the lion of the evening. He rose undeniably to the situation, and roared as much as was demanded of him. His shrill, uncertain voice, pitched in a loud excited key, shot this way and that across the table. His strange, flexible face, with the full, prominent lips, glowed and quivered with animation. Surely this was his hour of triumph.

He had recognised me at once, and after dinner came round to me, his shoulders in his ears as usual, holding out his hand with a beaming smile. He talked of Cambridge, of one or two mutual acquaintances, without embarrassment. He could not have been less abashed if he had wound up his career at the University amid the cheers of an enthusiastic Senate House.[10]

When the party broke up he came over to me again and suggested that I should go back with him to his rooms. He had never had much opinion of me, as he had been at no pains to conceal, and I concluded that he was in a mood for unbosoming himself. But it seemed that I was wrong, and we walked back to Great Russell Street,[11] where he had two large, untidy rooms, almost in silence. He told me that he was living away from his family, an unexpected legacy from an uncle having given him independence.

"So the Fates aren't doing it by halves?" I remarked, in answer to this communication.

"Oh, no," he replied, with a certain moody irony, staring hard at me over his cigar.

"Do you know what success means?" he asked suddenly, and in the question I seemed to hear Cohen the *poseur*, always at the elbow of, and not always to be distinguished from, Cohen stark-nakedly revealed.

"Ah, no, indeed."

"It means—inundation by the second-rate."

"What does the fellow want?" I cried, uncertain as to the extent of his seriousness.

"I never," he said, "was a believer in the half-loaf theory."

"It strikes me, Cohen, that your loaf looks uncommonly like a whole one, as loaves go on this unsatisfactory planet."

He burst into a laugh.

"Nothing," he said presently, "can alter the relations of things—their permanent, essential relations . . . 'They *shall* know, they *shall* understand, they *shall* feel what I am.' That is what I used to say to myself in the old days. I suppose, now, 'they' do know, more or less, and what of that?"

"I should say the difference from your point of view was a very great one. But you always chose to cry for the moon."

---

10. The governing body of Cambridge University.
11. In the Bloomsbury neighbourhood of central London.

"Well," he said, quietly looking up, "it's the only thing worth having."

I was struck afresh by the man's insatiable demands, which looked at times like a passionate striving after perfection, yet went side by side with the crudest vanity, the most vulgar desire for recognition.

I rose soon after his last remark, which was delivered with a simplicity and an air of conviction which made one cease to suspect the mountebank; we shook hands and bade one another good-night.

* * * * *

I never saw Cohen again.

Ten days after our renewal of acquaintance he sent a bullet through his brain, which, it was believed, must have caused instantaneous death. That small section of the public which interests itself in books discussed the matter for three days, and the jury returned the usual verdict. I have confessed that I was astonished, that I was wholly unprepared by my knowledge of Cohen for the catastrophe. Yet now and then an inkling of his motive, a dim fleeting sense of what may have prompted him to the deed, has stolen in upon me.

In his hour of victory the sense of defeat had been strongest. Is it, then, possible that, amid the warring elements of that discordant nature, the battling forces of that ill-starred, ill-compounded entity, there lurked, clear-eyed and ever-watchful, a baffled idealist?

Israel Zangwill, "Anglicization" (1902)

A maverick figure in Anglo-Jewry, Israel Zangwill (1864–1926) was a novelist, dramatist, poet, and political activist. He was born in Whitechapel in the East End of London to eastern European immigrants. His father was an itinerant peddler, odd-job man, and pious scholar; his mother was more freethinking. Zangwill was educated at the Jews' Free School in the East End, where he excelled; he later worked there as a pupil-teacher, and went on to gain a degree at the University of London in French, English, and Mental and Moral Science.

Zangwill began writing for both the Jewish and non-Jewish press in the late 1880s: as a columnist for a new weekly newspaper, the *Jewish Standard*, as editor of *Ariel; or, The London Puck*, a satirical journal, and as a writer for Jerome K. Jerome's periodical *The Idler*. He associated with "The Wanderers," a self-styled group of acculturated London Jewish intellectuals, who later founded the Maccabeans, an elite association of Jewish professionals. Zangwill also numbered some of the leading lights of contemporary literature and theater among his acquaintances.

With the publication of his novel *Children of the Ghetto: A Study of a Peculiar People* (1892), commissioned by the Jewish Publication Society of America, Zangwill became a literary sensation. The JPS had hoped that Zangwill would produce a work of cultural uplift that, in a period of increasing hostility to Jewish immigration, would offer a positive representation of Anglo-Jewry. Instead Zangwill wrote a detailed, often satirical, series of vignettes displaying the internal fractures and dissensions among London Jews and a moving and ultimately unresolved account of the spiritual malaise of the younger, British-born generation.

The novel was the first Anglo-Jewish bestseller and was translated into many other European languages. In Britain it brought Jewish immigrant life to a mainstream readership and Zangwill became a celebrity Jew. He went on to publish many short stories on Jewish themes in the popular periodical press; these were later collected in *Ghetto Tragedies* (1893) and *Ghetto Comedies* (1907). He also published a picaresque novel about a Jewish beggar set in eighteenth-century London, *The King of Schnorrers* (1894), and a series of fictionalized biographies of Jewish idealists and heretics, *Dreamers of the Ghetto* (1898), while all the while continuing also to publish work without Jewish content.

Zangwill was an energetic political activist. During the mid-1890s he became an ardent supporter of Zionism, representing Britain at several Zionist conferences. In 1905 he split with the mainstream Zionist movement, which remained committed to Palestine, and founded the Jewish Territorial Organization (known as the ITO), which sought to establish an autonomous homeland for the Jews anywhere that unsettled land could be obtained. Later, Zangwill was also a vocal campaigner for women's suffrage and pacifism.

"Anglicization" reflects all these political commitments, implicitly critiquing wartime jingoism as well as the domineering patriarchalism of the Cohn family. Above all it evokes the devastating sense of betrayal experienced by the assimilated Simon Cohn when he realizes that his belief in his Englishness is not shared by all. The story, entitled "S. Cohn & Son; or, 'Anglicization,'" was first published in the London evening newspaper the *Pall Mall Gazette* in February 1902 and in *Cosmopolitan* in the United States, and reprinted with the title "Anglicization" in Zangwill's collection *Ghetto Comedies*. It unfolds against the background of the South African War (1899–1902), also known as the Boer War, a conflict provoked by British immigration to the Boer republics in southern Africa and British imperial ambitions to gain wider control of the region. Through the epigraph, taken from the imperialist Cecil Rhodes, Zangwill draws on resonances between bringing Africa under "English" rule and the shifting terms under which Jews are considered "English." The narrative accurately records the fraught significances attached to Jewishness at this time: the ostentatious patriotism of British Jews at the time of the war (exemplified by the Chanukah service for Jewish soldiers); the contemporary argument that the war had been engineered by Jewish capitalists with interests in South Africa; and the growth of a popular anti-alien movement led by members of the British social elite.

Like Zangwill's other writing, "Anglicization" grapples with the paradoxes and confusions of modern Jewish identity as felt especially acutely by the generation for whom religion seemed archaic and assimilation an obvious and desirable choice. There are echoes here of Zangwill's famous meditation "Chad Gadya," from *Dreamers of the Ghetto*, in which he rewrites the familiar European Jewish narrative of an assimilated intellectual returning to his ghetto home. In Zangwill's version the protagonist, tormented by longing for the stability of a faith in which he can no longer believe, despairs, and commits suicide. Simon Cohn, also beyond the point of return (nor even desiring it) represents a similarly pessimistic image of the Jewish future.

*

"English, all English, that's my dream."

Cecil Rhodes[1]

1. Cecil Rhodes, British financier, mining magnate, and politician in South Africa, where he advanced British imperial interests alongside those of British mine owners. Rhodes believed in the superiority of the British as a governing race and reputedly uttered these words in 1883 while drawing a line across a map of Africa. His support of an attempt in 1895 to

I.

Even in his provincial days at Sudminster Solomon Cohen had distinguished himself by his Anglican mispronunciation of Hebrew and his insistence on a minister who spoke English and looked like a Christian clergyman;[2] and he had set a precedent in the congregation by docking the *e* of his patronymic. There are many ways of concealing from the Briton your shame in being related through a pedigree of three thousand years to Aaron, the High Priest of Israel, and Cohn is one of the simplest and most effective. Once, taken to task by a pietist, Solomon defended himself by the quibble that Hebrew has no vowels. But even this would not account for the whittling away of his "Solomon." "S. Cohn" was the insignium over his clothing establishment. Not that he was anxious to deny his Jewishness—was not the shop closed on Saturdays?—he was merely anxious not to obtrude it. "When we are in England, we are in England," he would say, with his Talmudic sing-song.

S. Cohn was indeed a personage in the seaport of Sudminster, and his name had been printed on voting papers, and, what is more, he had at last become a Town Councillor. Really the citizens liked his staunch adherence to his ancient faith, evidenced so tangibly by his Sabbath shutters: even the Christian clothiers bore him goodwill, not suspecting that S. Cohn's Saturday losses were more than counterbalanced by the general impression that a man who sacrificed business to religion would deal more fairly by you than his fellows. And his person, too, had the rotundity which the ratepayer demands.

But twin with his Town Councillor's pride was his pride in being *Gabbai* (treasurer) of the little synagogue tucked away in a back street: in which for four generations prayer had ebbed and flowed as regularly as the tides of the sea, with whose careless rovers the worshippers did such lucrative business. The synagogue, not the sea, was the poetry of these eager traffickers: here they wore phylacteries and waved palm-branches and did other picturesque things, which in their utter ignorance of Catholic or other ritual they deemed unintelligible to the heathen and a

---

overthrow the Boer government in the Transvaal republic on behalf of the British led to the South African War, which forms the backdrop for "Anglicization." Rhodes had just died when "Anglicization" was published in 1902.

2. Sudminster is a fictional provincial naval port modeled on Portsmouth or Plymouth, where Jewish communities had prospered in the eighteenth century.

barrier from mankind. Very imposing was Solomon Cohn in his official pew under the reading platform, for there is nothing which so enhances a man's dignity in the synagogue as the consideration of his Christian townsmen. That is one of the earliest stages of Anglicization.

II.

Mrs. Cohn was a pale image of Mr. Cohn, seeing things through his gold spectacles, and walking humbly in the shadow of his greatness. She had dutifully borne him many children, and sat on the ground for such as died.[3] Her figure refused the Jewess's tradition of opulency, and remained slender as though repressed. Her work was manifold and unceasing, for besides her domestic and shop-womanly duties she was necessarily a philanthropist, fettered with Jewish charities as the *Gabbai*'s wife, tangled with Christian charities as the consort of the Town Councillor. In speech she was literally his echo, catching up his mistakes, indeed, admonished by him of her slips in speaking the Councillor's English. He had had the start of her by five years, for she had been brought from Poland to marry him, through the good offices of a friend of hers who saw in her little dowry the nucleus of a thriving shop in a thriving port.

And from this initial inferiority she never recovered—five milestones behind on the road of Anglicization! It was enough to keep down a more assertive personality than poor Hannah's. The mere danger of slipping back unconsciously to the banned Yiddish put a curb upon her tongue. Her large, dark eyes had a dog-like look, and they were set pathetically in a sallow face that suggested ill-health, yet immense staying power.

That S. Cohn was a bit of a bully can scarcely be denied. It is difficult to combine the offices of *Gabbai* and Town Councillor without a self-satisfaction that may easily degenerate into dissatisfaction with others. Least endurable was S. Cohn in his religious rigidity, and he could never understand that pietistic exercises in which he found pleasure did not inevitably produce ecstasy in his son and heir. And when Simon was discovered reading "The Pirates of Pechili,"[4] dexterously concealed in his prayer-book, the boy received a strapping that made his mother wince.

---

3. Part of the mourning ritual for an immediate relative.
4. A fictional popular adventure novel.

Simon's breakfast lay only at the end of a long volume of prayers; and, having ascertained by careful experiment the minimum of time his father would accept for the gabbling of these empty Oriental sounds, he had fallen back on penny numbers to while away the hungry minutes. The quartering and burning of these tales in an avenging fireplace was not the least of the reasons why the whipped youth wept, and it needed several pieces of cake, maternally smuggled into his maw while the father's back was turned, to choke his sobs.

III.

With the daughters—and there were three before the son and heir—there was less of religious friction, since women have not the pious privileges and burdens of the sterner sex. When the eldest, Deborah, was married, her husband received, by way of compensation, the goodwill of the Sudminster business, while S. Cohn migrated to the metropolis, in the ambition of making "S. Cohn's trouserings" a household word. He did, indeed, achieve considerable fame in the Holloway Road.[5]

Gradually he came to live away from his business, and in the most fashionable street of Highbury.[6] But he was never to recover his exalted posts. The London parish had older inhabitants, the local synagogue richer members. The cry for Anglicization was common property. From pioneer, S. Cohn found himself outmoded. The minister, indeed, was only too English—and especially his wife. One would almost have thought from their deportment that they considered themselves the superiors instead of the slaves of the congregation. S. Cohn had been accustomed to a series of clergymen, who must needs be taught painfully to parrot "Our Sovereign Lady Queen Victoria, the Prince of Wales, the Princess of Wales, and all the Royal Family"[7]—the indispensable atom of English in the service—so that he, the expert, had held his breath while they groped and stumbled along the precipitous pass. Now the whilom *Gabbai* and Town Councillor found himself almost patron-

---

5. A large shopping street in a suburb north of central London, especially known for high-quality clothing establishments.

6. A wealthy suburb north of central London with a large Jewish population.

7. The prayer for the royal family, added to the synagogue service in the early nineteenth century.

ized—as a poor provincial—by this mincing, genteel clerical couple. He retorted by animadverting upon the preacher's heterodoxy.

An urban unconcern met the profound views so often impressed on Simon with a strap. "We are not in Poland now," said the preacher, shrugging his shoulders.

"In Poland!" S. Cohn's blood boiled. To be twitted with Poland, after decades of Anglicization! He, who employed a host of Anglo-Saxon clerks, counter-jumpers,[8] and packers! "And where did *your* father come from?" he retorted hotly.

He had almost a mind to change his synagogue, but there was no other within such easy walking distance—an important Sabbatic consideration[9]—and besides, the others were reported to be even worse. Dread rumours came of a younger generation that craved almost openly for organs in the synagogue and women's voices in the choir, nay, of even more flagitious spirits—devotional dynamitards—whose dream was a service all English, that could be understood instead of chanted! Dark mutterings against the ancient Rabbis were in the very air of these wealthier quarters of London.

"Oh, shameless ignorance of the new age," S. Cohn was wont to complain, "that does not know the limits of Anglicization!"

IV.

That Simon should enter his father's business was as inevitable as that the business should prosper in spite of Simon.

His career had been settled ere his father became aware that Highbury aspired even to law and medicine, and the idea that Simon's education was finished was not lightly to be dislodged. Simon's education consisted of the knowledge conveyed in seaport schools for the sons of tradesmen, while a long course of penny dreadfuls had given him a peculiar and extensive acquaintance with the ways of the world. Carefully curtained away in a secret compartment, lay his elementary Hebrew lore. It did not enter into his conception of the perfect Englishman. Ah, how he rejoiced in this wider horizon of London, so thickly starred

---

8. Sales assistants.
9. In orthodox observance, travel by vehicles is forbidden on the Sabbath.

with music-halls, billiard-rooms, and restaurants! "We are emancipated now," was his cry: "we have too much intellect to keep all those old laws;" and he swallowed the forbidden oyster in a fine spiritual glow, which somehow or other would not extend to bacon. That stuck more in his throat, and so was only taken in self-defence, to avoid the suspicions of a convivial company.

As he sat at his father's side in the synagogue—a demure son of the Covenant—this young Englishman lurked beneath his praying-shawl, even as beneath his prayer-book had lurked "The Pirates of Pechili."

In this hidden life Mrs. S. Cohn was not an aider or abettor, except in so far as frequent gifts from her own pocket-money might be considered the equivalent of the surreptitious cake of childhood. She would have shared in her husband's horror had she seen Simon banqueting on unrighteousness, and her apoplexy would have been original, not derivative. For her, indeed, London had proved narrowing rather than widening. She became part of a parish instead of part of a town, and of a Ghetto in a parish at that! The vast background of London was practically a mirage—the London suburb was farther from London than the provincial town. No longer did the currents of civic life tingle through her; she sank entirely to family affairs, excluded even from the ladies' committee. Her lord's life, too, shrank, though his business extended—the which, uneasily suspected, did but increase his irritability. He had now the pomp and pose of his late offices minus any visible reason: a Sir Oracle without a shrine, an abdomen without authority.

Even the two new sons-in-law whom his ability to clothe them had soon procured in London, listened impatiently, once they had safely passed under the Canopy and were ensconced in plush parlours of their own.[10] Home and shop became his only realm, and his autocratic tendencies grew the stronger by compression. He read "the largest circulation," and his wife became an echo of its opinions. These opinions, never nebulous, became sharp as illuminated sky-signs when the Boer War began.[11]

---

10. The Jewish marriage ceremony takes place under a canopy.

11. The South African War, also known as the Boer War (1899–1902) was a long and bitter conflict with many British losses and brutal treatment of civilians, ending with the British annexation of the former Boer republics in southern Africa. It initially inspired great public support though enthusiasm waned as the war became protracted.

"The impertinent rascals!" cried S. Cohn furiously. "They have invaded our territory."

"Is it possible?" ejaculated Mrs. Cohn. "This comes of our kindness to them after Majuba!"[12]

V.

A darkness began to overhang the destinies of Britain. Three defeats in one week!

"It is humiliating," said S. Cohn, clenching his fist.

"It makes a miserable Christmas," said Mrs. Cohn gloomily. Although her spouse still set his face against the Christmas pudding which had invaded so many Anglo-Jewish homes, the festival, with its shop-window flamboyance, entered far more vividly into his consciousness than the Jewish holidays, which produced no impression on the life of the streets.

The darkness grew denser. Young men began to enlist for the front: the City formed a new regiment of Imperial Volunteers. S. Cohn gave his foreign houses large orders for khaki trouserings. He sent out several parcels of clothing to the seat of war, and had the same duly recorded in his favourite Christian newspaper, whence it was copied into his favourite Jewish weekly, which was, if possible, still more chauvinist, and had a full-page portrait of Sir Asher Aaronsberg, M.P. for Middleton, who was equipping a local corps at his own expense. Gradually S. Cohn became aware that the military fever of which he read in both his organs was infecting his clothing emporium—that his own counter-jumpers were in heats of adventurous resolve. The military microbes must have lain thick in the khaki they handled. At any rate, S. Cohn, always quick to catch the contagion of the correct thing, announced that he would present a bonus to all who went out to fight for their country, and that he would keep their places open for their return. The Saturday this patriotic offer was recorded in his newspaper—"On inquiry at S. Cohn's, the great clothing purveyor of the Holloway Road,

---

12. The Battle of Majuba Hill (1881) was the decisive battle of the First Boer War (1880–81). The British fled the battlefield with heavy casualties and agreed on a peace treaty with the South African Republic.

our representative was informed that no less than five of the young men were taking advantage of their employer's enthusiasm for England and the Empire"—the already puffed-up Solomon had the honour of being called to read in the Law, and first as befitted the sons of Aaron. It was a man restored almost to his provincial pride who recited the ancient benediction; "Blessed art Thou, O Lord our God, who hast chosen us from among all peoples and given to us His law."

But there was a drop of vinegar in the cup.

"And why wasn't Simon in synagogue?" he inquired of his wife, as she came down the gallery stairs to meet her lord in the lobby, where the congregants loitered to chat.

"Do I know?" murmured Mrs. Cohn, flushing beneath her veil.

"When I left the house he said he was coming on."

"He didn't know you were to be 'called up.'"[13]

"It isn't that, Hannah," he grumbled. "Think of the beautiful war-sermon he missed. In these dark days we should be thinking of our country, not of our pleasures." And he drew her angrily without, where the brightly-dressed worshippers, lingeringly exchanging eulogiums on the "Rule Britannia" sermon, made an Oriental splotch of colour on the wintry pavement.

VI.

At lunch the reprobate appeared, looking downcast.

"Where have you been?" thundered S. Cohn, who, never growing older, imagined Simon likewise stationary.

"I went out for a walk—it was a fine morning."

"And where did you go?"

"Oh, don't bother!"

"But I shall bother. Where did you go?"

He grew sullen. "It doesn't matter—they won't have me."

"Who won't have you?"

"The War Office."

"Thank God!" broke from Mrs. Cohn.

---

13. Being "called up" to read the blessing before the reading of the Torah in the synagogue is a way of honoring individual congregants.

"Eh?" Mr. Cohn looked blankly from one to the other.

"It is nothing—he went to see the enlisting and all that. Your soup is getting cold."

But S. Cohn had taken off his gold spectacles and was polishing them with his serviette—always a sign of a stormy meal.

"It seems to me something has been going on behind my back," he said, looking from mother to son.

"Well, I didn't want to annoy you with Simon's madcap ideas," Hannah murmured. "But it's all over now, thank God!"

"Oh, he'd better know," said Simon sulkily, "especially as I am not going to be choked off. It's all stuff what the doctor says. I'm as strong as a horse. And, what's more, I'm one of the few applicants who can ride one."

"Hannah, will you explain to me what this *Meshuggas* (madness) is?" cried S. Cohn, lapsing into a non-Anglicism.

"I've got to go to the front, just like other young men!"

"What! shrieked S. Cohn. "Enlist! You, that I brought up as a gentleman!"

"It's gentlemen that's going—the City Imperial Volunteers!"

"The volunteers! But that's my own clerks."

"No; there are gentlemen among them. Read your paper."

"But not rich Jews."

"Oh, yes. I saw several chaps from Bayswater."

"We Jews of this favoured country," put in Hannah eagerly, "grateful to the noble people who have given us every right, every liberty, must—"

S. Cohn was taken aback by this half-unconscious quotation from the war-sermon of the morning. "Yes, we must subscribe and all that," he interrupted.

"We must fight," said Simon.

"You fight!" His father laughed half-hysterically. "Why, you'd shoot yourself with your own gun!" He had not been so upset since the day the minister had disregarded his erudition.

"Oh, would I, though?" And Simon pursed his lips and nodded meaningfully.

"As sure as to-day is the Holy Sabbath. And you'd be stuck on your own bayonet, like an obstinate pig."

Simon got up and left the table and the room.

Hannah kept back her tears before the servant. "There!" she said. "And now he's turned sulky and won't eat."

"Didn't I say an obstinate pig? He's always been like that from a baby. But his stomach always surrenders." He resumed his meal with a wronged air, keeping his spectacles on the table, for frequent nervous polishing.

Of a sudden the door reopened and a soldier presented himself—gun on shoulder. For a moment S. Cohn, devoid of his glasses, stared without recognition. Wild hereditary tremors ran through him, born of the Russian persecution, and he had a vague nightmare sense of the *Chappers*, the Jewish man-gatherers who collected the tribute of young Jews for the Little Father.[14] But as Simon began to loom through the red fog, "A gun on the Sabbath!" he cried. It was as if the bullet had gone through all his conceptions of life and of Simon.

Hannah snatched at the side-issue. "I read in Josephus—Simon's prize for Hebrew, you know—that the Jews fought against the Romans on Sabbath."

"Yes; but they fought for themselves—for our Holy Temple."

"But it's for ourselves now," said Simon. "Didn't you always say we are English?"

S. Cohn opened his mouth in angry retort. Then he discovered he had no retort, only anger. And this made him angrier, and his mouth remained open, quite terrifyingly for poor Mrs. Cohn.

"What is the use of arguing with him?" she said imploringly. "The War Office has been sensible enough to refuse him."

"We shall see," said Simon. "I am going to peg away at 'em again, and if I don't get into the Mounted Infantry, I'm a Dutchman—and of the Boer variety."

He seemed any kind of man save a Jew to the puzzled father. "Hannah, you must have known of this—these clothes," S. Cohn spluttered.

"They don't cost anything," she murmured. "The child amuses himself. He will never really be called out."

"If he is, I'll stop his supplies."

"Oh," said Simon airily, "the Government will attend to that."

---

14. Under special regulations designed to remove large numbers of Jewish men from Jewish communities, local Jewish committees in mid-nineteenth-century Russia were required to deliver a high percentage of conscripts for twenty-five-year service in the Russian army.

"Indeed!" And S. Cohn's face grew black. "But remember—you may go, but you shall never come back."

"Oh, Solomon! How can you utter such an awful omen?"

Simon laughed. "Don't bother, mother. He's bound to take me back. Isn't it in the papers that he promised?"

S. Cohn went from black to green.

VII.

Simon got his way. The authorities reconsidered their decision. But the father would not reconsider his. Ignorant of his boy's graceless existence, he fumed at the first fine thing in the boy's life. 'Tis a wise father that knows his own child.

Mere emulation of his Christian comrades, and the fun of the thing, had long ago induced the lad to add volunteering to his other dissipations. But, once in it, the love of arms seized him, and when the call for serious fighters came, some new passion that surprised even himself leapt to his breast—the first call upon an idealism, choked, rather than fed, by a misunderstood Judaism. Anglicization had done its work; from his schooldays he had felt himself a descendant, not of Judas Maccabæus, but of Nelson and Wellington; and now that his brethren were being mowed down by a kopje-guarded foe, his whole soul rose in venomous sympathy. And, mixed with this genuine instinct of devotion to the great cause of country, were stirrings of anticipated adventure, gorgeous visions of charges, forlorn hopes, picked-up shells, redoubts stormed; heritages of "The Pirates of Pechili," and all the military romances that his prayer-book had masked.

He looked every inch an Anglo-Saxon, in his khaki uniform and his great slouch hat, with his bayonet and his bandolier.

The night before he sailed for South Africa there was a service in St. Paul's Cathedral, for which each volunteer had two tickets. Simon sent his to his father. "The Lord Mayor will attend in state. I dare say you'll like to see the show," he wrote flippantly.

"He'll become a Christian next," said S. Cohn, tearing the cards in twain.

Later, Mrs. Cohn pieced them together. It was the last chance of seeing her boy.

VIII.

Unfortunately the Cathedral service fell on a Friday night, when S. Cohn, the Emporium closed, was wont to absorb the Sabbath peace. He would sit, after high tea, of which cold fried fish was the prime ingredient, dozing over the Jewish weekly. He still approved platonically of its bellicose sentiments. This January night, the Sabbath arriving early in the afternoon, he was snoring before seven, and Mrs. Cohn slipped out, risking his wrath. Her religion forced her to make the long journey on foot; but, hurrying, she arrived at St. Paul's before the doors were opened. And throughout the long walk was a morbid sense of one wasted ticket. She almost stopped at a friend's house to offer the exciting spectacle, but dread of a religious rebuff carried her past. With Christians she was not intimate enough to invite companionship. Besides, would not everybody ask why she was going without her husband?

She inquired for the door mentioned on her ticket, and soon found herself one of a crowd of parents on the steps. A very genteel crowd, she noted with pleasure. Her boy would be in good company. The scraps of conversation she caught dealt with a world of alien things—how little she was Anglicized, she thought, after all those years! And when she was borne forward into the Cathedral, her heart beat with a sense of dim, remote glories. To have lived so long in London and never to have entered here! She was awed and soothed by the solemn vistas, the perspectives of pillars and arches, the great nave, the white robes of the choir vaguely stirring a sense of angels, the overarching dome, defined by a fiery rim, but otherwise suggesting dim, skyey space.

Suddenly she realized that she was sitting among the men.[15] But it did not seem to matter. The building kept one's thoughts religious. Around the waiting congregation, the human sea outside the Cathedral rumoured, and whenever the door was opened to admit some dignitary the roar of cheering was heard like a salvo saluting his entry. The Lord Mayor and the Aldermen passed along the aisle, preceded by mace-bearers; and mingled with this dazzle of gilded grandeur and robes, was a regretful memory of the days when, as a Town Councillor's consort,

---

15. In contrast to an orthodox synagogue, where there is separate seating for men and women.

she had at least touched the hem of this unknown historic English life. The skirl of bagpipes shrilled from without—that exotic, half-barbarous sound now coming intimately into her life. And then, a little later, the wild cheers swept into the Cathedral like a furious wind, and the thrill of the marching soldiers passed into the air, and the congregation jumped up on the chairs and craned towards the right aisle to stare at the khaki couples. How she looked for Simon!

The volunteers filed on, filed on—beardless youths mostly, a few with a touch of thought in the face, many with the honest nullity of the clerk and the shopman, some with the prizefighter's jaw, but every face set and serious. Ah! at last, there was her Simon—manlier, handsomer than them all! But he did not see her: he marched on stiffly; he was already sucked up into this strange life. Her heart grew heavy. But it lightened again when the organ pealed out. The newspapers the next day found fault with the plain music, with the responses all in monotone, but to her it was divine. Only the words of the opening hymn, which she read in the "Form of Prayer," discomforted her:

Fight the good fight with all thy might,
Christ is thy Strength and Christ thy Right.

But the bulk of the liturgy surprised her, so strangely like was it to the Jewish. The ninety-first Psalm! Did they, then, pray the Jewish prayers in Christian churches? "For He shall give His angels charge over thee: to keep thee in all thy ways." Ah! how she prayed that for Simon!

As the ecclesiastical voice droned on, unintelligibly, inaudibly, in echoing, vaulted space, she studied the hymns and verses, with their insistent Old Testament savour, culminating in the farewell blessing:

"The Lord bless you and keep you. The Lord make His face to shine upon you and be gracious unto you. The Lord lift up the light of His countenance upon you and give you peace."

How often she had heard it in Hebrew from the priests as they blessed the other tribes! Her husband himself had chanted it, with uplifted palms and curiously grouped fingers. But never before had she felt its beauty: she had never even understood its words till she read the English of them in the gilt-edged Prayer-Book that marked rising wealth. Surely there had been some monstrous mistake in conceiving the two creeds as at daggers drawn, and though she only pretended to kneel with the others, she felt her knees sinking in surrender to the larger life around her.

As the volunteers filed out and the cheers came in, she wormed her way nearer to the aisle, scrambling even over backs of chairs in the general mellay. This time Simon saw her. He stretched out his martial arm and blew her a kiss. Oh, delicious tears, full of heartbreak and exaltation! This was their farewell.

She passed out into the roaring crowd, with a fantastic dream-sense of a night-sky and a great stone building, dark with age and solemnity, and unreal figures perched on railings and points of vantage, and hurrahing hordes that fused themselves with the procession and became part of its marching. She yearned forwards to vague glories, aware of a poor past. She ran with the crowd. How they cheered her boy! *Her* boy! She saw him carried off on the shoulders of Christian citizens. Yes; he was a hero. She was the mother of a hero.

IX.

The first news she got from him was posted at St. Vincent. He wrote to her alone, with a jocose hope that his father would be satisfied with his sufferings on the voyage. Not only had the sea been rough, but he had suffered diabolically from the inoculation against enteric fever, which, even after he had got his sea-legs, kept him to his berth and gave him a "Day of Atonement" thirst.

"Ah!" growled S. Cohn; "he sees what a fool he's been, and he'll take the next boat back."

"But that would be desertion."

"Well, he didn't mind deserting the business."

Mr. Cohn's bewilderment increased with every letter. The boy was sleeping in sodden trenches, sometimes without blankets; and instead of grumbling at that, his one grievance was that the regiment was not getting to the front. Heat and frost, hurricane and dust-storm—nothing came amiss. And he described himself as stronger than ever, and poured scorn on the medical wiseacre who had tried to refuse him.

"All the same," sighed Hannah, "I do hope they will just be used to guard the lines of communication." She was full of war-knowledge acquired with painful eagerness, prattled of Basuto ponies and Mauser bullets, pontoons and pom-poms, knew the exact position of the armies, and marked her war-map with coloured pins.

Simon, too, had developed quite a literary talent under the pressure of so much vivid new life, and from his cheery letters she learned much that was not in the papers, especially in those tense days when the C.I.V.'s did at last get to the front—and remained there: tales of horses mercifully shot, and sheep mercilessly poisoned, and oxen dropping dead as they dragged the convoys; tales of muddle and accident, tales of British soldiers slain by their own protective cannon as they lay behind ant-heaps facing the enemy, and British officers culled under the very eyes of the polo-match; tales of hospital and camp, of shirts turned sable and putties worn to rags, and all the hidden miseries of uncleanliness and insanitation that underlie the glories of war. There were tales, too, of quarter-rations; but these she did not read to her husband, lest the mention of "bully-beef" should remind him of how his son must be eating forbidden food.[16] Once, even, two fat pigs were captured at a hungry moment for the battalion. But there came a day when S. Cohn seized those letters and read them first. He began to speak of his boy at the war—nay, to read the letters to enthralled groups in the synagogue lobby—groups that swallowed without reproach the *tripha* meat cooked in Simon's mess-tin.[17]

It was like being *Gabbai* over again.

Moreover, Simon's view of the Boer was so strictly orthodox as to give almost religious satisfaction to the proud parent. "A canting hypocrite, a psalm-singer and devil-dodger, he has no civilization worth the name, and his customs are filthy. Since the great trek he has acquired, from long intercourse with his Kaffir slaves, many of the native's savage traits. In short, a born liar, credulous and barbarous, crassly ignorant and inconceivably stubborn."

"Crassly ignorant and inconceivably stubborn," repeated S. Cohn, pausing impressively. "Haven't I always said that? The boy only bears out what I knew without going there. But hear further! 'Is it to be wondered at that the Boer farmer, hidden in the vast undulations of the

---

16. Bully-beef is canned salt beef.
17. *Tripha* meat is nonkosher.

endless veldt, with his wife, his children and his slaves, should lose all sense of proportion, ignorant of the outside world, his sole knowledge filtering through Jo-burgh?'"

As S. Cohn made another dramatic pause, it was suddenly borne in on his wife with a stab of insight that he was reading a description of himself—nay, of herself, of her whole race, hidden in the great world, awaiting some vague future of glory that never came. The important voice of her husband broke again upon her reflections:

"'He has held many nights of supplication to his fetish, and is still unconvinced that his God of Battles is asleep.'" The reader chuckled, and a broad smile overspread the synagogue lobby. "'They are brave—oh, yes, but it is not what we mean by it—they are good fighters, because they have Dutch blood at the back of them, and a profound contempt for us. Their whole life has been spent on the open veldt (we are always fighting them on somebody's farm, who knows every inch of the ground), and they never risk anything except in the trap sort of manœuvres. The brave rush of our Tommies is unknown to them, and their slim nature would only see the idiocy of walking into a death-trap, cool as in a play. Were there ever two races less alike?'" wound up the youthful philosopher in his tent. "'I really do not see how they are to live together after the war.'"

"That's easy enough," S. Cohn had already commented to his wife as oracularly as if she did not read the same morning paper. "Intermarriage! In a generation or two there will be one fine Anglo-African race.[18] That's the solution—mark my words. And you can tell the boy as much—only don't say I told you to write to him."

"Father says I'm to tell you intermarriage is the solution," Mrs. Cohn wrote obediently. "He really is getting much softer towards you."

"Tell father that's nonsense," Simon wrote back. "The worst individuals we have to deal with come from a Boer mother and an English father, deposited here by the first Transvaal war."

S. Cohn snorted angrily at the message. "That was because there were two Governments—he forgets there will be only one United Empire now."

He was not appeased till Private Cohn was promoted, and sent

---

18. I.e. Anglo-Afrikaner.

home a thrilling adventure, which the proud reader was persuaded by the lobby to forward to the communal organ. The organ asked for a photograph to boot. Then S. Cohn felt not only *Gabbai*, but town councillor again.

This wonderful letter, of which S. Cohn distributed printed copies to the staff of the Emporium with a bean-feast air,[19] ran:

> "We go out every day—I am speaking of my own squadron—each officer taking his turn with twenty to fifty men, and sweep round the farms a few miles out; and we seldom come back without seeing Boers hanging round on the chance of a snipe at our flanks, or waiting to put up a trap if we go too far. The local commando fell on our cattle-guard the other day—a hundred and fifty to our twenty-five—and we suffered; it was a horrible bit of country. There was a young chap, Winstay—rather a pal of mine—he had a narrow squeak, knocked over by a shot in his breast. I managed to get him safe back to camp—Heaven knows how!—and they made me a lance-corporal, and the beggar says I saved his life; but it was really through carrying a fat letter from his sister—not even his sweetheart. We chaff him at missing such a romantic chance. He got off with a flesh wound, but there is a great blot of red ink on the letter. You may imagine we were not anxious to let our comrades go unavenged. My superiors being sick or otherwise occupied, I was allowed to make a night-march with thirty-five men on a farm nine miles away—just to get square. It was a nasty piece of work, as we were within a few miles of the Boer laager,[20] three hundred strong. There was moonlight, too—it was like a dream, that strange, silent ride, with only the stumble of a horse breaking the regular thud of the hoofs. We surrounded the farm in absolute silence, dismounting some thousand yards away, and fixing bayonets. I told the men I wanted no shots—that would have brought down the commando—but cold steel and silence. We crept up and swept the farm—it was weird, but, alas! they were out on the loot. The men were furious, but we live in hopes."

The end was a trifle disappointing, but S. Cohn, too, lived in hopes—of some monstrous and memorable butchery. Even his wife had got used to the firing-line, now that neither shot nor shell could harm her

---

19. Festive meal given by an employer to employees.
20. Camp.

boy. "For He shall give His angels charge over thee." She had come to think her secret daily repetition of the ninety-first Psalm talismanic.

When Simon sent home the box which had held the chocolates presented by the Queen, a Boer bullet, and other curios, S. Cohn displayed them in his window, and the crowd and the business they brought him put him more and more in sympathy with Simon and the Empire. In conversation he deprecated the non-militarism of the Jew: "If I were only a younger man myself, sir . . . "

The night Mafeking was relieved,[21] the Emporium was decorated with bunting from roof to basement, and a great illuminated window revealed nothing but stacks of khaki trouserings.

So that, although the good man still sulked over Simon to his wife, she was not deceived; and, the time drawing nigh for Simon's return, she began to look happily forward to a truly reunited family.

In her wildest anxiety it never occurred to her that it was her husband who would die. Yet this is what the irony of fate brought to pass. In the unending campaign which death wages with life, S. Cohn was slain, and Simon returned unscratched from the war to recite the *Kaddish*[22] in his memory.

X.

Simon came back bronzed and a man. The shock of finding his father buried had supplied the last transforming touch; and, somewhat to his mother's surprise, he settled down contentedly to the business he had inherited. And now that he had practically unlimited money to spend, he did not seem to be spending it, but to be keeping better hours than when dodging his father's eye. His only absences from home he accounted for as visits to Winstay, his pal of the campaign, with whom he had got chummier than ever since the affair of the cattle-guard. Winstay, he said, was of good English family, with an old house in Harrow[23]—fortunately on the London and North Western Railway, so that he could easily get a breath of country air on Saturday and Sunday

---

21. The lifting of the siege of Mafeking in May 1900 was a decisive victory for the British, prompting extravagant celebrations in Britain.

22. Memorial prayer.

23. A picturesque town north of London.

afternoons. He seemed to have forgotten (although the Emporium was still closed on Saturdays) that riding was forbidden, and his mother did not remind him of it. The life that had been risked for the larger cause, she vaguely felt as enfranchised from the limitations of the smaller.

Nearly two months after Simon's return, a special military service was held at the Great Synagogue on the feast of *Chanukah*—the commemoration of the heroic days of Judas Maccabæus—and the Jewish C.I.V.'s were among the soldiers invited.[24] Mrs. Cohn, too, got a ticket for the imposing ceremony which was fixed for a Sunday afternoon.

As they sat at the midday meal on the exciting day, Mrs. Cohn said suddenly: "Guess who paid me a visit yesterday."

"Goodness knows," said Simon.

"Mr. Sugarman." And she smiled nervously.

"Sugarman?" repeated Simon blankly.

"The—the—er—the matrimonial agent."

"What impudence! Before your year of mourning is up!"

Mrs. Cohn's sallow face became one flame. "Not me! You!" she blurted.

"Me! Well, of all the cheek!" And Simon's flush matched his mother's.

"Oh, it's not so unreasonable," she murmured deprecatingly. "I suppose he thought you would be looking for a wife before long; and naturally," she added, her voice growing bolder, "I should like to see you settled before I follow your father. After all, you are no ordinary match. Sugarman says there isn't a girl in Bayswater, even, who would refuse you."

"The very reason for refusing them," cried Simon hotly. "What a ghastly idea, that your wife would just as soon have married any other fellow with the same income!"

Mrs. Cohn cowered under his scorn, yet felt vaguely exalted by it, as by the organ in St. Paul's, and strange tears of shame came to complicate her emotions further. She remembered how she had been exported from Poland to marry the unseen S. Cohn. Ah! how this new young generation was snapping asunder the ancient coils! how the new and diviner sap ran in its veins!

---

24. Spectacular military Chanukah services took place annually at the Central Synagogue in London from the early 1890s.

"I shall only marry a girl I love, mother. And it's not likely to be one of these Jewish girls, I tell you frankly."

She trembled. "One of which Jewish girls?" she faltered.

"Oh, any sort. They don't appeal to me."

Her face grew sallower. "I am glad your father isn't alive to hear that," she breathed.

"But father said intermarriage is the solution," retorted Simon.

Mrs. Cohn was struck dumb. "He was thinking how to make the Boers English," she said at last.

"And didn't he say the Jews must be English, too?"

"Aren't there plenty of Jewish girls who are English?" she murmured miserably.

"You mean, who don't care a pin about the old customs? Then where's the difference?" retorted Simon.

The meal finished in uncomfortable silence, and Simon went off to don his khaki regimentals and join in the synagogue parade.

Mrs. Cohn's heart was heavy as she dressed for the same spectacle. Her brain was busy piecing it all together. Yes, she understood it all now—those sedulous Saturday and Sunday afternoons at Harrow. She lived at Harrow, then, this Christian, this grateful sister of the rescued Winstay: it was she who had steadied his life; hers were those "fat letters," faintly aromatic. It must be very wonderful, this strange passion, luring her son from his people with its forbidden glamour. How Highbury would be scandalized, robbed of so eligible a bridegroom! The sons-in-law she had enriched would reproach her for the shame imported into the family—they who had cleaved to the Faith! And—more formidable than all the rest—she heard the tongue of her cast-off seaport, to whose reverence or disesteem she still instinctively referred all her triumphs and failures.

Yet, on the other hand, surged her hero-son's scorn at the union by contract consecrated by the generations! But surely a compromise could be found. He should have love—this strange English thing—but could he not find a Jewess? Ah, happy inspiration! he should marry a quite poor Jewess—he had money enough, thank Heaven! That would show him he was not making a match, that he was truly in love.

But this strange girl at Harrow—he would never be happy with her! No, no; there were limits to Anglicization.

XI.

It was not till she was seated in the ancient synagogue, relieved from the squeeze of entry in the wake of soldiers and the exhilaration of hearing "See the Conquering Hero Comes" pealing, she knew not whence, that she woke to the full strangeness of it all, and to the consciousness that she was actually sitting among the men—just as in St. Paul's. And what men! Everywhere the scarlet and grey of uniforms, the glister of gold lace—the familiar decorous lines of devout top-hats broken by glittering helmets, bear-skins, white nodding plumes, busbies, red caps a-cock, glengarries, all the colour of the British army, mixed with the feathered jauntiness of the Colonies and the khaki sombreros of the C.I.V.'s! Coldstream Guards, Scots Guards, Dragoon Guards, Lancers, Hussars, Artillery, Engineers, King's Royal Rifles, all the corps that had for the first time come clearly into her consciousness in her tardy absorption into English realities, Jews seemed to be among them all. And without conscription—oh, what would poor Solomon have thought of that?

The Great Synagogue itself struck a note of modern English gaiety, as of an hotel dining-room, freshly gilded, divested of its historic mellowness, the electric light replacing the ancient candles and flooding the winter afternoon with white resplendence. The pulpit—yes, the pulpit—was swathed in the Union Jack; and looking towards the box of the *Parnass* and *Gabbai*,[25] she saw it was occupied by officers with gold sashes. Somebody whispered that he with the medalled breast was a Christian Knight and Commander of the Bath—"a great honour for the synagogue!" What! were Christians coming to Jewish services, even as she had gone to Christian? Why, here was actually a white cross on an officer's sleeve.

And before these alien eyes, the cantor, intoning his Hebrew chant on the steps of the Ark, lit the great many-branched *Chanukah* candlestick. Truly, the world was changing under her eyes.[26]

And when the Chief Rabbi went toward the Ark in his turn, she saw that he wore a strange scarlet and white gown (military, too, she imagined in her ignorance), and—oh, even rarer sight!—he was followed by

---

25. The *parnass* is the president of the congregation.
26. The festival of Chanukah commemorates the rededication of the Temple in Jerusalem following the successful Maccabean revolt against the Selucid Empire of Syria in the second century B.C.E.

a helmeted soldier, who drew the curtain revealing the ornate Scrolls of the Law.

And amid it all a sound broke forth that sent a sweetness through her blood. An organ! An organ in the Synagogue! Ah! here indeed was Anglicization.

It was thin and reedy even to *her* ears, compared with that divine resonance in St. Paul's: a tinkling apology, timidly disconnected from the congregational singing, and hovering meekly on the borders of the service—she read afterwards that it was only a harmonium—yet it brought a strange exaltation, and there was an uplifting even to tears in the glittering uniforms and nodding plumes. Simon's eyes met his mother's, and a flash of the old childish love passed between them.

There was a sermon—the text taken with dual appropriateness from the Book of Maccabees. Fully one in ten of the Jewish volunteers, said the preacher, had gone forth to drive out the bold invader of the Queen's dominions. Their beloved country had no more devoted citizens than the children of Israel who had settled under her flag. They had been gratified, but not surprised, to see in the Jewish press the names of more than seven hundred Jews serving Queen and country. Many more had gone unrecorded, so that they had proportionally contributed more soldiers—from Colonel to bugler-boy—than their mere numbers would warrant. So at one in spirit and ideals were the Englishman and the Jew whose Scriptures he had imbibed, that it was no accident that the Anglophobes of Europe were also Anti-Semites.

And then the congregation rose, while the preacher behind the folds of the Union Jack read out the names of the Jews who had died for England in the far-off veldt. Every head was bent as the names rose on the hushed air of the synagogue. It went on and on, this list, reeking with each bloody historic field, recalling every regiment, British or colonial; on and on in the reverent silence, till a black pall seemed to descend, inch by inch, overspreading the synagogue. She had never dreamed so many of her brethren had died out there. Ah! surely they were knit now, these races: their friendship sealed in blood!

As the soldiers filed out of synagogue, she squeezed towards Simon and seized his hand for an instant, whispering passionately: "My lamb, marry her—we are all English alike."

Nor did she ever know that she had said these words in Yiddish!

XII.

Now came an enchanting season of confidences; the mother, caught up in the glow of this strange love, learning to see the girl through the boy's eyes, though the only aid to his eloquence was the photograph of a plump little blonde with bewitching dimples. The time was not ripe yet for bringing Lucy and her together, he explained. In fact, he hadn't actually proposed. His mother understood he was waiting for the year of mourning to be up.

"But how will you be married?" she once asked.

"Oh, there's the registrar," he said carelessly.

"But can't you make her a proselyte?" she ventured timidly.

He coloured. "It would be absurd to suddenly start talking religion to her."

"But she knows you're a Jew."

"Oh, I dare say. I never hid it from her brother, so why shouldn't she know? But her father's a bit of a crank, so I rather avoid the subject."

"A crank? About Jews?"

"Well, old Winstay has got it into his noddle that the Jews are responsible for the war—and that they leave the fighting to the English. It's rather sickening: even in South Africa we are not treated as we should be, considering—"

Her dark eye lost its pathetic humility. "But how can he say that, when you yourself—when you saved his—"

"Well, I suppose just because he knows I *was* fighting, he doesn't think of me as a Jew. It's a bit illogical, I know." And he smiled ruefully. "But, then, logic is not the old boy's strong point."

"He seemed such a nice old man," said Mrs. Cohn, as she recalled the photograph of the white-haired cherub writing with a quill at a property desk.

"Oh, off his hobby-horse he's a dear old boy. That's why I don't help him into the saddle."

"But how can he be ignorant that we've sent seven hundred at least to the war?" she persisted. "Why, the paper had all their photographs!"

"What paper?" said Simon, laughing. "Do you suppose he reads the Jewish what's-a-name, like you? Why, he's never heard of it!"

"Then you ought to show him a copy."

"Oh, mother!" and he laughed again. "That would only prove to him there are too many Jews everywhere."

A cloud began to spread over Mrs. Cohn's hard-won content. But apparently it only shadowed her own horizon. Simon was as happily full of his Lucy as ever.

Nevertheless, there came a Sunday evening when Simon returned from Harrow earlier than his wont, and Hannah's dog-like eye noted that the cloud had at last reached his brow.

"You have had a quarrel?" she cried.

"Only with the old boy."

"But what about?"

"The old driveller has just joined some League of Londoners for the suppression of the immigrant alien."[27]

"But you should have told him we all agree there should be decentralization," said Mrs. Cohn, quoting her favourite Jewish organ.

"It isn't that—it's the old fellow's vanity that's hurt. You see, he composed the "Appeal to the Briton," and gloated over it so conceitedly that I couldn't help pointing out the horrible contradictions."

"But Lucy—" his mother began anxiously.

"Lucy's a brick. I don't know what my life would have been without the little darling. But listen, mother." And he drew out a portentous prospectus. "They say aliens should not be admitted unless they produce a certificate of industrial capacity, and in the same breath they accuse them of taking the work away from the British workman. Now this isn't a Jewish question, and I didn't raise it as such—just a piece of muddle—and even as an Englishman I can't see how we can exclude Outlanders here after fighting for the Outland—"

"But Lucy—" his mother interrupted.

His vehement self-assertion passed into an affectionate smile.

"Lucy was dimpling all over her face. She knows the old boy's vanity. Of course she couldn't side with me openly."

---

27. The British Brothers' League, established in February 1901 after the end of the war, was led by members of the British social elite and recruited among the working class. It claimed thousands of members, and campaigned for the restriction of alien immigration. In response, the government appointed a Royal Commission on Alien Immigration in February 1902, the same month that "Anglicization" was published (the following year the Commission recommended restriction).

"But what will happen? Will you go there again?"

The cloud returned to his brow. "Oh, well, we'll see."

A letter from Lucy saved him the trouble of deciding the point.

"Dear silly old Sim," it ran,

"Father has been going on dreadfully, so you had better wait a few Sundays till he has cooled down. After all, you yourself admit there is a grievance of congestion and high rents in the East End. And it is only natural—isn't it?—that after shedding our blood and treasure for the Empire we should not be in a mood to see our country overrun by dirty aliens."

"Dirty!" muttered Simon, as he read. "Has she seen the Christian slums—Flower and Dean Street?"[28] And his handsome Oriental brow grew duskier with anger. It did not clear till he came to:

"Let us meet at the Crystal Palace next Saturday, dear quarrelsome person. Three o'clock, in the Pompeian Room. I *have* got an aunt at Sydenham, and I *can* go in to tea after the concert and hear all about the missionary work in the South Sea Islands."

XIII.

Ensued a new phase in the relation of Simon and Lucy. Once they had met in freedom, neither felt inclined to revert to the restricted courtship of the drawing-room. Even though their chat was merely of books and music and pictures, it was delicious to make their own atmosphere, untroubled by the flippancy of the brother or the earnestness of the father. In the presence of Lucy's artistic knowledge Simon was at once abashed and stimulated. She moved in a delicate world of symphonies and silver-point drawings of whose very existence he had been unaware, and reverence quickened the sense of romance which their secret meetings had already enhanced.

Once or twice he spoke of resuming his visits to Harrow, but the longer he delayed the more difficult the conciliatory visit grew.

"Father is now deeper in the League than ever," she told him. "He has joined the committee, and the prospectus has gone forth in all its glorious self-contradiction."

---

28. A notorious slum street in London's East End.

"But, considering I am the son of an alien, and I have fought for—"

"There, there! quarrelsome person," she interrupted laughingly. "No, no, no, you had better not come till you can forget your remote genealogy. You see, even now father doesn't quite realize you are a Jew. He thinks you have a strain of Jewish blood, but are in every other respect a decent Christian body."

"Christian!" cried Simon in horror.

"Why not? You fought side by side with my brother; you ate ham with us."

Simon blushed hotly. "But, Lucy, you don't think religion is ham?"

"What, then? Merely Shem?" she laughed.

Simon laughed too. How clever she was! "But you know I never could believe in the Trinity and all that. And, what's more, I don't believe you do yourself."

"It isn't exactly what one believes. I was baptized into the Church of England—I feel myself a member. Really, Sim, you are a dreadfully argumentative and quarrelsome person."

"I'll never quarrel with you, Lucy," he said half entreatingly; for somehow he felt a shiver of cold at the word "baptized," as though himself plunged into the font.

In this wise did both glide away from any deep issue or decision till the summer itself glided away. Mrs. Cohn, anxiously following the courtship through Sim's love-smitten eyes, her suggestion that the girl be brought to see her received with equal postponement, began to fret for the great thing to come to pass. One cannot be always heroically stiffened to receive the cavalry of communal criticism. Waiting weakens the backbone. But she concealed from her boy these flaccid relapses.

"You said you'd bring her to see me when she returned from the seaside," she ventured to remind him.

"So I did; but now her father is dragging her away to Scotland."

"You ought to get married the moment she gets back."

"I can't expect her to rush things—with her father to square. Still, you are not wrong, mother. It's high time we came to a definite understanding between ourselves at least."

"What!" gasped Mrs. Cohn. "Aren't you engaged?"

"Oh, in a way, of course. But we've never said so in so many words."

For fear this should be the "English" way, Mrs. Cohn forbore to remark that the definiteness of the Sugarman method was not without compensations. She merely applauded Simon's more sensible mood.

But Mrs. Cohn was fated to a further season of fret. Day after day the "fat letters" arrived with the Scottish postmark and the faint perfume that always stirred her own wistful sense of lost romance—something far-off and delicious, with the sweetness of roses and the salt of tears. And still the lover, floating in his golden mist, vouchsafed her no definite news.

One night she found him restive beyond his wont. She knew the reason. For two days there had been no scented letter, and she saw how he started at every creak of the garden-gate, as he waited for the last post. When at length a step was heard crunching on the gravel, he rushed from the room, and Mrs. Cohn heard the hall-door open. Her ear, disappointed of the rat-tat, morbidly followed every sound; but it seemed a long time before her boy's returning footstep reached her. The strange, slow drag of it worked upon her nerves, and her heart grew sick with premonition.

He held out the letter towards her. His face was white. "She cannot marry me, because I am a Jew," he said tonelessly.

"Cannot marry you!" she whispered huskily. "Oh, but this must not be! I will go to the father; I will explain! You saved his son—he owes you his daughter."

He waved her hopelessly back to her seat—for she had started up. "It isn't the father, it's herself. Now that I won't let her drift any longer, she can't bring herself to it. She's honest, anyway, my little Lucy. She won't fall back on the old Jew-baiter."

"But how dare she—how dare she think herself above you!" Her dog-like eyes were blazing yet once again.

"Why are you Jews surprised?" he said bitterly. "You've held yourself aloof from the others long enough, God knows. Yet you wonder they've got their prejudices, too."

And, suddenly laying his head on the table, he broke into sobs—sobs that tore at his mother's heart, that were charged with memories of his ancient tears, of the days of paternal wrath and the rending of "The Pirates of Pechili." And, again, as in the days when his boyish treasures were changed to ashes, she stole towards him, with an involuntary furtive look to see if S. Cohn's back was turned, and laid her hands upon his heaving shoulders. But he shook her off! "Why didn't a Boer bullet strike me down?" Then with a swift pang of remorse he raised his contorted face and drew hers close against it—their love the one thing saved from Anglicization.

Section 4 *Fictions of Religious Renewal*

Ben Baruch, "The Preacher and the Bellows" (1844)

Translated from the French by Maurice Samuels

Alexandre Créhange (1791–1872), who wrote under the pen name Ben Baruch, was born in Étain, a small town in the province of Lorraine, the very year that the Jews of the region became French citizens. His writing reflects the abrupt changes that French Jews faced as a result of their early emancipation. The son of a cantor, he would attempt throughout his life to plead the cause of religious orthodoxy, but would do so using modern literary forms.

Créhange became a traveling salesman and a bookkeeper, first in Germany and then in Saint-Étienne, near Lyon. Upon his arrival in Paris in the early 1830s, he served as the spokesman for the poor, orthodox workers of the capital in their battles against the Consistory, the state-controlled governing body of French Judaism, which tightly controlled religious practice. Elected by a College of Notables, the Consistory reflected the values of the wealthy bourgeoisie, whom Créhange held to be elitist, irreligious, and totally out of touch with the majority of the Jews of France. Créhange's other bête noire was religious reform, which came to France from Germany in the 1820s. Although the Consistory kept French Judaism officially unified, its openness to moderate reforms further signified its elitism to a religiously conservative but politically radical renegade like Créhange.

The literary persona of Ben Baruch first appeared in the pages of the monthly newspaper *L'Univers Israélite* with the story "Le prédicateur et le soufflet" (The Preacher and the Bellows), translated below. Founded in 1844 by Simon Bloch, *L'Univers Israélite* was closely modeled on *Les Archives Israélites*, but substituted a strict form of neo-orthodoxy for that journal's reformist stance. It seems clear that Créhange saw Ben Baruch as an orthodox counterpart to Ben-Lévi, who published reform-minded fiction in *Les Archives Israélites* (some of which is collected here). In addition to translating and editing a number of liturgical volumes, he eventually found success as the publisher of a Jewish almanac, which appeared from 1850 until his death in 1872.

"The Preacher and the Bellows" reflects Créhange's lifelong crusade on behalf of the orthodox poor. The noble yet victimized valet, Jedidiah, whose outspoken criticism of those in power ensures he plays no role in community affairs, is clearly a portrait of the author. The story, however, also reflects the unorthodox nature of some of Ben Baruch's literary influences: subtitled a tale imitated from the Polish, it contains an epigraph from the seventeenth-century Catholic theologian Jean-Baptiste Massillon. The story itself combines the style of French Enlightenment satire with Talmudic parable. Although the metaphysical ending contains a reference to Jewish mysticism, the story remains focused on the practical morality of the material world and shows how the answers to modern social questions can be found in the Jewish religious tradition.

A Tale Imitated from the Polish

> If we consider the great talents that render men illustrious, we see that when they are given to the impious it is always to the greater unhappiness of their country and of their age. Great knowledge poisoned by pride has also given birth to those leaders and those celebrated teachers of falsehood, who in every age have raised the standard of schism and error.
>
> Massillon[1]

In a neighboring country, a great city has just given birth to a petty reform, a new religion. Its partisans held a meeting to reorganize the religion of their fathers and make it harmonize, as they put it, with civilization, which is to say with *their* civilization. Preaching plays a big role in a new religion and the reformed were searching for a good preacher when they learned of the arrival in their city of Mr. Freyredner,[2] whose reputation had crossed mountains and seas. The sacred orator received a deputation of religious dignitaries, and in response to their repeated entreaties, promised to preach in their temple.

On the appointed day, the preacher rose to the tribune and said: "My dear listeners:

"'Vanity of vanities, all is vanity.'

"'There is nothing new under the sun.'

"'Is there a thing of which it is said, "See, this is new"?'[3]

---

1. "Sermon pour le dimanche de la passion: Sur la fausseté de la gloire humaine" (On the Deceitfulness of Human Glory), sermon delivered on 3 April 1718, in Jean-Baptiste Massillon, *Oeuvres complètes de Massillon, évêque de Clermont* (Paris: Raymond, 1821), 140–41.

2. German for "free speaker."

3. Eccles. 1:2, 9, 10. [Author's note.]

"These words of a great king perfectly characterize the situation. They proclaim that everything we do here is only vanity and they warn me that everything that I might say has already been said, for *there is nothing new under the sun*. Given these two truths, I will not abuse your patience or waste my time but will limit myself to telling you a simple story.

"In the city of N——, on the Vistula, there lived two men.[4] One was named Godfried and the other Jedidiah. Godfried was rich and so ignorant that his stupidity was legendary in the land. As a result, he was a notable, a member of the community council, and one of the heads of the synagogue. He occupied, without paying for it, one of the finest pews, ate game and other meats that weren't subject to the communal tax,[5] and had all the honors at the temple. In this country honors are auctioned to the highest bidder and he who pays for them thinks he has deserved them.

"Possessed by the demon of vanity, Godfried wanted to be decorated. When all his intrigues had failed and all his solicitations had been rebuffed, he declared he could live without the imperial decree, and one fine day the almanacs of N—— proclaimed: 'Godfried, notable, knight of the order of the White Eagle.'[6] Such was Godfried.

"His fellow citizen Jedidiah was poor, but he had good sense and the principles that are taught by our sacred books were deeply engraved upon his soul. לא תקלל חרש.[7] *He did not curse the deaf* like cowards do, but when he wanted to call out foolishness or evil, he did it in a manner to be understood. לפני עור לא תתן מכשול.[8] Not only *did he not put a stumbling block before the blind* like flatterers do, but at the risk of his own safety, he prevented, when he could, the blind from hurling themselves over the cliff. לא תהדר פני גדול.[9] *He did not defer to the great* when it was a matter of

---

4. The Vistula is a river in Poland.

5. Of course, game is not kosher and hence not subject to the Jewish community's tax on kosher meat.

6. This innocent ruse is not unknown among us. [Author's note.]

7. Moses, book 3, 19:14. [Author's note; "Moses, book 3" refers to the third book of the Old Testament, Leviticus. Subsequent references will be in the standard format. English translations of biblical passages from Herbert G. May and Bruce M. Metzger, eds., *The New Oxford Annotated Bible with the Apocrypha, Revised Standard Version* (New York: Oxford University Press, 1977).]

8. Lev. 19:14.

9. Lev. 19:15.

making the truth known. לא תשנא את אחיך בלבבך.[10] Thus *he did not hate his brother in his heart* when he said what needed to be said.

"With such principles, you can well imagine that Jedidiah allowed himself to signal abuses, to indicate improvements, to unmask hypocrites, and what is more, to expose the conduct of the reformers who put their *stock* in religion in order to divide up the dividends among themselves. Of course, Jedidiah was excluded from the affairs of the community: the wise men who ran things did not recognize his capacities.

"Godfried, on the other hand, had a seat on the council. One day, tired of sleeping on his curule chair and bored of making mountains out of molehills, and most of all jealous that his colleague Loewe always spoke and made every decision without asking his opinion, he submitted his resignation and decided to travel.

"He called Jedidiah, whom he held in great esteem because he knew how to read books *in which they had forgotten the vowels*,[11] and said to him, 'Jedidiah, I want to travel. I want to go to the fair in Leipzig. I want to see the countryside, like my friend Blinder,[12] and experience for myself all the pleasures he's always talking about. I will need a valet. If you want, I'll let you have the job. Our preacher said not long ago: וכי ימוך אחיך.[13] *If your brother becomes poor beside you, and sells himself to you, you shall not make him serve as a slave.* You will serve me. Your time will belong to me. You will obey my every command, fulfill my every wish. Isn't that what our pastor means?'

"Poor Jedidiah, who had long dreamed of such a voyage because it would offer him the chance to augment his knowledge, felt no joy at Godfried's proposal. But understanding just how humiliating the position would be for him, he accepted it, saying to htimself: But I also heard our preacher say, לא תאמץ את לבבך ולא תקפץ את ידך מאחיך האביון,[14] *you shall not harden your heart or shut your hand against your poor brother.* And Mr. Godfried is poor, very poor: he is totally lacking in intelligence and good sense. I must help him. I will guard him, if I can, against the

---

10. Lev. 19:17.

11. This really happened. [Author's note; Ben Baruch is mocking the stupidity of a synagogue leader (clearly modeled on a real person) who did not know that Hebrew is customarily written without vowels.]

12. German for "blind man."

13. Lev. 25:39.

14. Deut. 15:8.

poison of flatterers. I will caution him against the fires of passion. This is my duty and I must not shirk it. What do I care if people call me a servant! The true slave is he who is controlled by his vices. Isn't the valet whom nature has endowed with a good heart worth more than the master who lacks one? Isn't the valet who knows the difference between right and wrong esteemed more by the Creator than the master who cannot decide between them? Mr. Godfried has not been favored by nature. I must *open my hand to him and lend him sufficient for his need*. העבט תעביטנו די מחסרו אשר יחסר לו.[15]

"The day of their departure arrived and Godfried made the most ridiculous preparations to travel in comfort. Jedidiah fervently prayed to God to bless their journey and to guard them against any kind of unfortunate accident. When it comes to prayers, the difference between the religious man and the irreligious man is that the latter prays only when he is stricken with some great affliction. Defeated by suffering, weakened by pain, the irreligious man returns to God first when he is low, then from on high. My God, my God, how I suffer! cries the impious man. If he is rich, he will give alms and a few thousand franc bills will rain down with pride into the coffers of a charitable institution. The opulent man won't stop there. He will have prayers said at the synagogue and he will kneel down before a rabbi whom he had scorned the day before! Such are free thinkers, those men without religion! They are a mixture of ostentation and superstition.

"The religious man, on the other hand, does not wait until the time of sadness has arrived to recommend himself to God, to unburden his heart in the bosom of the Creator. He speaks to Him at all times, אברכה את ה' בכל עת,[16] not with prideful alms or with vain words but with a pure charity, a contrite heart. It's the religious man whom the prophet-king spoke of when he said: אשרי שאל יעקב בעזרו שברו על ה' אלהיו,[17] *Happy is he whose help is the God of Jacob, whose hope is in the Lord his God*."

These citations appeared to provoke some murmuring in a part of the assembly. The preacher saw it and said: "Dear listeners, please excuse these citations, I beg you. It's old-fashioned, I know, but I am a

15. Deut. 15:8.
16. Ps. 34:2.
17. Ps. 146:5.

creature of habit. Some of us still go on looking for our religious and moral principles in these books that common people have the weakness to call *holy*. The first four precepts that I quoted signify for the Israelite, FRANKNESS, LOYALTY, COURAGE, and SINCERITY. The three that follow exhort us to PATIENCE, CHARITY, and GOOD WORKS. Finally, the last symbolize for us GRATITUDE and CONFIDENCE in God. But I repeat, all this is old-fashioned, and *your* civilization has no use for such silliness. Let us hope that thanks to your reforms and to the education that will be their necessary complement, soon it will no longer be a question either of Moses or the prophets.

"But I digress.

"Once they had completed the preparations for their journey, they set off. Right from the start of the journey, Godfried displayed his ignorance and the blackness of his soul. He had heard his friend Blinder say that to travel at a brisk pace it was necessary to pay the coachman like a horse and he didn't understand why the coachman, whom he paid like a horse, didn't work as hard as one. He had also always heard Mr. Halseisen,[18] his colleague on the council, say that laborers should work like horses and that Moses, who recommended treating workers gently, לא תרדה בפרך,[19] didn't understand anything about domestic economy. This Mr. Halseisen was known for his immense philanthropy. A regular abolitionist, he treated his valets like slaves. What is more, he was a member of the charitable bureau and was decorated.

"Later, after they had gone a hundred leagues, our Godfried was completely astonished to see a moon just like the one they had at home. Jedidiah could never make him understand that it was the same star. The more the modest valet wore himself out in explanations, the more the imbecilic master got angry, and he would always return to the same line of reasoning: I am rich and a notable, I shall not be contradicted. That argument allowed for no answer. Thus the good Jedidiah remained silent, leaving to Phoebe the responsibility of defending her identity, if she so pleased.[20]

18. German for "iron collar."
19. Lev. 25:43. "You shall not rule over him with harshness, but shall fear your God."
20. In Greek mythology, Phoebe was one of the original Titans, a daughter of Uranus and Gaia, and was associated with the moon.

"Finally, they arrived at the gates of Leipzig.

"They found a man who had been working there for sixty years and who, in his long career, had only ever pronounced the following words: *Your name, Sir? Your profession?* This is Thorschreiber Luchs, the gatekeeper. Three generations had successively passed before his eyes, and had come to daguerreotype themselves in the book of this dean of toll keepers. This book was extremely curious, and the notes that our Argus appended to the names of the travelers were very instructive. For example, there one could read: 'WOLFF, father, banker. —Arrived with four post horses. Some time ago he arrived pushing his own cart.'

"And ten years later: 'WOLFF, son, peddler. —Arrived with a pack. Some time ago he arrived in his own carriage.'

"Next to the name of the father, the philosophical gatekeeper had written: Grew rich off of widows and orphans, and this verse of the Psalmist: *Unless the Lord builds the house, those who build it labor in vain.*[21] Next to the name of the son, he had written: *Unrecht Gut, gedeihet nicht,* 'Crime doesn't pay,' and these words of Moses: פקד עון אבות על בנים,[22] *he visited iniquity of the fathers upon the children.* A terrible warning that those who stir up trouble and sow discord in Israel should ponder."

The preacher had strongly accentuated that last sentence, but he started again in a softer voice: "Please excuse me, dear listeners, a thousand pardons . . . I once again quoted *my Moses* to you. MY MOSES, do you understand? I won't even pretend that he is yours as well. You do not recognize him, that much is clear. But let us return to our voyagers.

"At the gatekeeper's first question, *Your name, sir?* our hero hastened to respond, *Godfried, notable from N——.* But to the second question, *Your profession?* he didn't know what to say and looked entreatingly to Jedidiah, who responded: *He is a gentleman of independent means.*

"'Ah, I see, the gentleman is traveling for pleasure.'

"'And for my education,' added the valet to himself.

"Saxon coachmen are like coachmen the world over: when they have the choice, they don't take you to the best hotels, but rather to the hotels that pay them the most. The charming tunes that these

---

21. Ps., 127:1.
22. Exod. 20:5.

coachmen know how to blow on their little hunting horns warn the hotelkeeper if the voyager has deep pockets. Hans had the choice. The best hotel was the Hôtel de France. He headed toward the Hôtel de l'Angleterre, which was horrible, and taking up his horn, he belted out the tune of:

'Hurtig Knabe nicht gesdumt
Bring den Propfenzieher her!'[23]

"Upon hearing this urgent invitation, Mr. Knoblauch and his entire staff of valets appeared in front of the door of the hotel.[24] The notable was very flattered by all this attention addressed . . . to his wallet.

"Mr. Godfried was taken to his rooms. They were magnificent: thick carpets, sumptuous sofas, chandeliers, golden candelabras, all in exquisite taste. Our voyager was in seventh heaven. As for Jedidiah, they gave him a little room in the attic of the hotel. He brought up a few books and a desk lamp. In most houses, valets are housed above their masters. This is wrong: it could lead servants to think that if they are materially above their masters, they are often morally above them as well. In the case of our voyagers, the distribution of rooms was perfect. The philosophical valet was up above on a high level, near heaven, the land of genius and of intelligence. His noble face cast an admirable shadow against the white walls of his little room. Jedidiah was a man. The prideful master was down below, close to the ground, the dwelling place of brutes, of gold and mud. His sitting room was decorated with pictures of great men among whom the notable was infinitely small. To tell the truth, great men are often ill-advised to hang in their salons pictures of men beside whom they are mere pygmies.

"The time passed quite agreeably in Leipzig. Godfried frequented gambling houses and theaters, sipped champagne at the Hôtel de Pologne, made his horse prance about, ordered around the waiters, and eyed the pretty girls in the Rosenthal.[25] Jedidiah paid visits to scholars, frequented the libraries, meditated in anatomy collections, and attended when he could divine services in all kinds of temples, for Jedidiah loved all religious men indiscriminately. In this respect, he merely followed the

---

23. German for "Come on, lad, hurry and bring the corkscrew!"
24. *Knoblauch* is German for "garlic."
25. The Rosenthal is a park in Leipzig.

word of God Himself, who said בכל המקום אשר אזכיר את שמי אבוא אליך וברכתיך,[26] *In every place where I cause my name to be remembered I will come to you and bless you.* Our voyagers thus did not waste their time. But every night Godfried came home a little wearier and Jedidiah a little better educated.

"One quickly tires of pleasure when one's heart isn't in it. One morning, Godfried rang for his valet and said: 'Jedidiah, I have traveled enough. I want to go home. I long to show my former colleagues that I am a *traveled gentleman*,[27] as the Italians say.'

"'You mean the English, sir.'

"'Fine, so be it, the English. You are always so contrary. Isn't it the same thing? But tell me, Jedidiah, are there notables in England?'

"'Why yes, sir. The Montefiores and the Goldsmiths pass for such. But there are citizens everywhere who can perform the duties of notables, while there are not everywhere notables able to perform the duties of citizens.'

"'I have no idea what you're talking about, but I don't care. Speaking of which,' Godfried continued, 'before I leave, I want to make some purchases, a lot of purchases. You see, my boy, I am a philanthropist, a great philanthropist. I take pleasure in putting laborers to work and in allowing shopkeepers to earn a little money. Those people take such pains to provide bread for their children! But you will accompany me, Jedidiah, because you see, between us, all those laborers and shopkeepers are so many rascals and thieves. When they see a well-dressed man like me, they fleece him, they horribly overcharge for their merchandise. You will therefore pretend you are buying for yourself. They won't overcharge you since you appear to belong to their caste and wolves don't devour each other. Heh, heh, heh!'

"Jedidiah kept silent, bowing his head before that stupidity as he would have before a compliment, and they set off for the fair.

"Taking advantage of the philanthropy and of the insulting distrustfulness of his master, Jedidiah made a pile of purchases. He reasoned that it was just that the superfluity of the rich man should contribute to the well-being of workers. But he made sure only to buy useful things—

---

26. Exod. 20:24.
27. In English in the original.

good books, geographic maps, globes, mathematical instruments, and so on. All of a sudden, however, Mr. Godfried spied a bellows.

"'What is this?'

"'A bellows.'

"'What does a bellows do?'

"'It lights fires.'

"'I want a bellows.'

"'Nothing could be easier, sir.'

"Jedidiah buys a bellows, pays for it. But as soon as he has done so, Godfried takes it away and runs off as fast as his legs will carry him.

"If the notable had been a man to get carried away, Jedidiah would have thought he had gone crazy. But he knew him well and guessed that there was some stupidity at the root of his actions. He thus did not grow worried and returned tranquilly to the hotel, where he was sure to find his master.

"Indeed, he found him there, sitting in front of a richly ornate fireplace, well stocked with wood, blowing, blowing, and blowing the bellows with all his strength.

"'You have deceived me, Jedidiah,' he cried as soon as he saw him enter. 'It's outrageous! I'm getting rid of you . . . You told me that with a bellows I could light a fire. I've been blowing with this bellows for a half hour now and look, traitor, there is no more fire there than in my hand. You have deceived me. It's outrageous! You don't mock a notable and I—'

"'Restrain yourself, sir.' said Jedidiah with the calmness and dignity that only reason can procure. 'In no way did I deceive you. A bellows is truly used to light fires, to bring a flame back to life, to make it burst forth. But you must have a bit of fire to begin with. You must first have a spark. If that spark is lacking, the bellows becomes perfectly useless.'

"My dear listeners, I leave it up to you to judge the conduct and the character of these two men, the master and the valet. But I call your attention to the end of this story.

"You saw a fool sitting before a fireplace full of wood attempting, with the aid of a bellows, to make a fire where there wasn't even a spark. Allow me to explain to you that the fireplace is your temple. The outside is superb. The inside is dark. There is no air, it is stifling, and all that comes out is a useless bit of smoke. The wood, I beg you to forgive me, is you, worm-eaten *logs*,[28] lacking real light, the light that maintains peace and harmony. I am the fool. At your invitation, I came here to flow the sacred fire of religion. But blow and blow and blow as I might, the divine flame will not burst forth: THE SPARK IS LACKING."[29]

---

28. "Des *bûches* vermoulues," emphasis in the original. In colloquial French, a *bûche* is a stupid person.

29. In the Jewish mystical tradition, the spark (*nitzotz* in Hebrew) signifies divinity.

Ben-Lévi, "The Fish and the Breadcrumbs" (1846)
Translated from the French by Maurice Samuels

"Les poissons et les miettes de pain" (The Fish and the Breadcrumbs) was one of a dozen short stories published by Ben-Lévi (pseudonym of Godchaux Baruch Weil) in *Les Archives Israélites* during the 1840s.[1] Founded in 1840 by Samuel Cahen, *Les Archives Israélites* served as the principal organ of the reform movement in France that advocated the modification of Jewish ritual and tradition. The goal of the reformers was to modernize the religion in order to make it more acceptable to the increasingly acculturated Jewish bourgeoisie and thereby to help staunch the flood of religious indifference and disaffection that observers across the religious spectrum saw as the gravest danger facing the French Jewish community in the nineteenth century. The reformers were vigorously opposed by a rival journal, *L'Univers Israélite*, which featured articles by Ben-Lévi's rival, Ben Baruch. Although the Consistory system, which tightly controlled Jewish practice in France, prevented the kind of schism between Orthodox and Reform that divided the Jewish community in German-speaking lands, French reformers did succeed in introducing modest changes into the liturgy.

In "The Fish and Breadcrumbs," Ben-Lévi mocks the pretentious cynicism of an assimilated Jewish lawyer named Gustave, who eats at fashionable cafés and scorns all forms of religion as superstition. Then Gustave and the narrator witness a touching scene in which a widow comforts her young son by performing Tashlich, casting their sins in the guise of breadcrumbs into the water on the afternoon of Rosh Hashanah. By the end of the story, Gustave comes to understand the value that religious ritual can play even in a disenchanted world. In its celebration of the power of a traditional ritual, the story would thus seem to contradict the reformist impulse to modernize the religion by banishing superstition. However, Ben-Lévi refrains from explaining the meaning that the participants attach to the performance of ritual, which is free to take on a new, modern relevance.

Ben-Lévi's Jewish characters are thoroughly at home in France and more readily quote French literary models—such as the fables of La Fontaine—than the texts of

---

1. See the introduction to "The March 17th Decree," in Section 3 of this volume, for biographical information on Godchaux Weil.

the Jewish tradition. Ben-Lévi is very much a French writer, writing for a highly acculturated readership. Like "The March 17th Decree," this story reveals an affinity with Balzac's studies of contemporary Parisian morals that critics at the time were beginning to label "realist." Like Balzac, who very often uses Jewish characters to typify the dangers of modern life, Ben-Lévi's Jewish characters are paragons of social change. But unlike his Christian contemporary, Ben-Lévi seeks a solution for the dilemmas of modernity within Judaism itself, searching for ways to reinvent the religion and reinvigorate Jewish tradition for the modern world.

※

Do you like fishing? Nor do I. And yet I allowed myself to be dragged along this week, by a friend and the current of the Seine, on a nautical exercise near one of those little islands that border Notre Dame Cathedral. It was one of the last days of September—that sad month, epilogue of summer, preface to winter. We were using a net, despite the fact that line fishing is far more virtuous. Don't let such a frank confession give you a bad opinion of my character. I'm a peaceful chap. I wouldn't kill a carp, even in self-defense . . . Moreover, I affirm (and this is strictly between us) that I'm not an inveterate fisherman,[2] and I'm more at home with a boatload of paper than with a rower's oar.[3] But we allow ourselves to copy others, to play the sailor, our best resolutions fall overboard, and one day we find ourselves in a small boat, as M. Florian would have said, engaging in an occupation unworthy of a Frenchman, since the French are the most intellectual people in the world . . . according to us. A great many observations could be made about that weakness that leads us so often to submit to the desires of others, but I will not make them here, and will content myself instead with telling you why I found myself almost against my will fishing these past few days. Have mercy on a poor fisherman.[4]

There was another extenuating circumstance in my case: that circumstance was named Gustave. Gustave has a large mustache, long

---

2. "Je ne suis pas un pêcheur endurci." This is a pun on the near equivalence of *pêcheur* (fisherman) and *pécheur* (sinner).

3. "Je ferais mieux mon affaire d'une rame de papier que d'un aviron de canotier." This is a pun on *rame*, which means both "ream" and "oar."

4. "A tout pêcheur miséricorde." This is another pun on fisherman/sinner.

sideburns, hands with slender fingers. He buys his clothes at Renard's; he dines at the Café Anglais; he's a master at keeping his monocle in place by flexing the muscle of his right eyebrow. And he has studied law, which gives him the legal right to do nothing at all during the day and to spend a part of his nights playing lansquenet.[5] Actually I'm mistaken when I say he does nothing during the day: in winter he hunts, in summer he's a *boater*. I don't know if this national aquatic term can be found in the dictionary, but I'm sure that Parisians will understand it, and that is all that I require for the moment. Moreover, Gustave is already of a certain age (and we know that nothing is more uncertain than that particular age), he is brusque, a skeptic, capricious, headstrong, and his youth has not glowed bright with promise. The portrait I'm painting of him should indicate that he's one of my closest friends. What is more, Gustave is totally indifferent to matters of religion: he was born of Israelite parents, don't ask him for anything more. As for our religion and our history, don't question him about them. *Nescio vos*.[6] Just don't attack the *Jews* in front of him, because then his face grows red, his eyes inflame, and the boater and skeptic give way to the man, whose fists daguerreotype themselves onto the shoulder blades of the poor adversary of Judaism. Gustave calls this shedding light on the question.

Here, then, is the man who acted as a host on the little boat on which I was sailing while pretending to fish. We were both wearing jackets not terribly well suited to the occasion, and pearls of water hung from the tips of each thread of our maritime costumes such that, in celebrating the pleasures of the water, Gustave was literally full of his subject.

As our little boat slowly drifted leeway within sight of the Hôtel-de-Ville, Gustave suddenly cried: "Look at all those good people grouped on the riverbank at the Place de Grève emptying their pockets into the water! Let the devil take me, and you too, if they aren't crazy. And yet there's a policeman next to them allowing them do it with nary a word! ... Let's get closer to get a better look, it's most curious ... " And two

---

5. "Enfin il a fait son droit, et tout cela lui donne celui de ne rien faire le jour et de passer une partie de ses nuits au lansquenet." This is a pun on the double meaning of *droit* as both law and right.

6. This quote from the New Testament, meaning, "I do not know you" (Matt. 25:12), is the Lord's response to the maidens who come late to the wedding and is often used jokingly to refuse some favor or comment.

vigorous rows of the oars having brushed us up against the bottom of the parapet, breadcrumbs rained down on our craft. "What is this?!" exclaimed Gustave. Do these people take us for the swans in the pond of the Tuileries? Or are they in charge of feeding those dwellers of the great deep whom the ancients so stupidly called amphitrites?"

"Those people," I responded gently, "are performing an old religious custom: they are casting their sins into the water. We call it Tashlich in Hebrew."

"You're pulling my leg!"

"Not in the slightest. The prophet Micah said: 'The Lord will have compassion upon us, he will tread our iniquities under foot. The Lord will cast all our sins into the depths of the sea into a place where they shall be no more remembered or ever again come to mind.' And since, like all Oriental peoples, our ancestors were given to materializing ideas that had power over them, they thought it would be a good idea to throw some breadcrumbs from their pockets into the water as Yom Kippur approached, as proof of the lightness that fasting, charity, prayer, and expiation had brought to their conscience, henceforth free of sin!"

"Are you telling the truth? That story out of the *Thousand and One Nights* seems to me quite a tale."

"I assure you that I am most serious."

"So sailor, you want me to swallow that hook, line, and sinker?"

"I do indeed. My story is the historical truth."

"If I were fortunate enough to belong to the boring Antiquarian Society, I would use that custom to prove something quite important."

"What is that?"

"That the ancients had pockets . . ."

"So you will always be a cynic and a skeptic?"

"No, but I'm the declared enemy of the ridiculous."

"That's an elastic word and everyone uses it to mean something different. How do you know that those good people, who are staring at our comic fresh-water sailing gear, don't find us just as profoundly ridiculous?"

"Let them; that would make us equals."

"Look here, Gustave. Fanaticism and superstition are certainly to be feared, but incredulity and ignorance of religion can also be dangerous. At root, all religions are right and reasonable, and if sometimes superstition and fanaticism surround them, it's in the way that brambles and thorns encircle a precious plant, to shield it from the teeth of the flock. In times of struggle, it's good to guard against those parasitical weeds of religion's land, but in times of peace and calm, there is no harm in letting grow alongside us some old anodyne superstition that links some to ancient memories and offers others hope or consolation, and that for all of us is a historical landmark that we cannot but consider with respect."

"But there are so many prejudices in the world . . . and out of it! Are you going to prove to me now that we need to keep them all? Do you believe that time has inscribed on a pile of old ideas: *Leased in perpetuity*? Isn't it wiser and more reasonable to chase the superstitions from the temple and to inscribe on it: *Store for rent*?"

"Certainly, when a custom is dangerous or uncivilized, men should band together to root it out; but, when it is innocent or carries within it some nice moral lesson, what harm is there in keeping it?"

"So now you're going to tell me that we should readopt the usages and customs of ancient Poland, and to reprint this Decalogue in which we find the following commandment, all perfumed with Oriental poetry:

Put on both clothes and underwear
On Holidays and Saturday;
And in the evening take care
To fold them neatly away.[7]

"Jokes aren't reasons. I know that lovers of the new would like to tailor to their own liking a religion bearing the stamp, as we say, of the up-to-date. But if that is possible in the way we worship, it isn't possible for the religion itself, which is unchanging."

"But the religion is old."

"True, but so is God. And, as far as I know, he's nowhere near retirement. That reminds me of how, after the legislator Romme had made the republican calendar that was used in France during the revolutionary era, he bragged to the Abbé Grégoire to have done it specifically to

---

7. "Les samedis et fêtes sortiras, / Habits et culottes pareillement; / Et le soir tu les quitteras / Pour les enfermer proprement."

destroy Sunday. But the former vicar of Embermènil responded slyly: 'Sunday existed before you, it will continue to exist after you.'"

"So, you're telling me that we have to religiously and preciously preserve all those gothic customs, which are as numerous as they are silly?"

"No, of course not. But the rabbis will make an intelligent choice about which ones to keep, or else time will spread its mantle of oblivion over everything equally. You know, this very week our coreligionists are performing a ceremony that might also lend itself to jest: they hold their hands over the head of a chicken or a rooster, then they make the creature flap its wings over their heads, after which they kill it and eat it. There's another religious custom for you."

"And do they buy these chickens at the Valley Butcher, to remind themselves of Jehosephat?"[8]

"Laugh if you like. But admit that what we have there is an innocent commemoration of animal sacrifice that your classical studies must have revealed in all ancient theogonies. 'The man who makes a sacrifice,' said one of the greatest historians of antiquity,[9] 'places his hand on the head of his victim. This is a sign of the purity of life, for God demands of the man who comes to Him a spirit sanctified by good thoughts and a life adorned by noble actions such that he can say in good conscience: these outstretched hands have never been corrupted by bribes, they have never been a source of quarrels, of insult, of injury, or of violence to any other being. They have never committed a shameful deed, but have always lent themselves to actions considered honest, useful, and worthy of approbation by just and wise men.'"

"Those are certainly fine thoughts and they are perfectly expressed. But what do they prove?"

"They prove that religion, when it is properly understood, is a fertile and immortal source of enlightenment and truth, and that everything that is truly linked to it, when it is rightly appreciated, protects and guides the efforts of man toward perfection. They prove that the man who has faith is a hundred times happier than the man who doubts and

---

8. "Et achète-t-on ces poulets à la *Vallée*, pour rappeler celle de Josaphat?" A valley in the Bible, Jehosephat is referred to as a place where the tribes of Israel will gather for the final judgment (Joel 3:2).

9. Philo, *De offerentibus victimas*. [Author's note; see Philo Judaeus, *The Works of Philo Judaeus*, vol. 3, trans. Charles Duke Yonge (London: G. Bell and Sons, 1855–94), 216.]

denies. They prove that in thinking of God one can only do right by his creatures. They prove that there is no torpor of the senses and of matter so profound that religious reflections cannot rouse them, and that Malebranche was not so far from the truth when he said: 'I feel myself inclined to believe that my substance is eternal, that I am part of the Divine Being, and that all my thoughts are but individual modes of the universal reason.'"

Our conversation, having thus turned serious, quieted all of a sudden. Gustave seemed to be reflecting. As for me, I allowed myself, while floating leisurely down the Seine toward Saint-Cloud, to gaze at the blue and white clouds that stood out against the sky like capricious bits of fluff, to listen to the mysterious melodies that the setting sun awakens on the riverbank, and to breathe in the warm evening breeze that was caressing us so sweetly.

My meditations were interrupted by a strident burst of laughter from Gustave.

"I will give you a thousand francs if you can guess the cause of my hilarity. Imagine that I just witnessed a curious dialogue between the different fish wriggling about in our net."

"Well then, here we are back in the time of La Fontaine, *when animals used to speak*. My God! Didn't representative government put an end to that?"

"No, on the contrary. But as Bilboquet says, if politics is besides the point, let's dispense with it. Listen to what I have to say. A moment ago, a kind of revolution took place among the oviparous innocents yielded by our fishing.[10] A young flounder, taking on princely airs, scorned the bigger fish. A sole made very blatant advances to a pike who, taking advantage of her relative strength, smacked her weaker neighbors about with her tail. A bream tried to sing a cavatina by Rossini, and puffed up with pride at the bravos she believed she had merited. A simpering crayfish complained that our boat wasn't moving fast enough, and an eel roundly chastized the assembly for acting all jumpy and agitated rather than being calm and composed like those who are well brought up. As for me, I listened to all these speeches with a profound aston-

---

10. *Oviparous* means egg laying.

ishment, and I was shocked to see the sudden change that had taken place in the distinctive characters of these members of the great family of fish, when suddenly a respectable carp, whitened with age, began to speak with a paternal air: 'My children, I warned you to beware of those breadcrumbs thrown from the quay of the Hôtel-de-Ville that fell into our boat. You took them for manna from heaven and you didn't listen when I told you that those crumbs raining down were really passions. I knew from past experience that every year, between Rosh Hashanah and Kippur, the Israelites throw the residue of their pockets into the water, believing they have rid themselves of sin. This caused them problems for centuries when they were accused of poisoning the rivers. The absurdity of the charge of course didn't stop it from gaining currency. But this custom contained a different danger, no less serious and real, which nobody ever bothered to heed: that the crumbs thrown into our liquid domain arrived there imprinted with the sins of their proprietors, and that, when we mindlessly gobbled up this unexpected food, we were swallowing the germ of the vices and faults from which those people wanted to be free.'"

"'Thus it is that your characters have abruptly changed, that laziness, avarice, coquetry, arrogance and meanness (all vices that are all the more tenacious and dangerous for being feminine) have overtaken you. What will become of you, my children, now that you have been spoiled by the evil gifts of the human race?' At these words, the fish let out the plaintive howls normally reserved for the boiling oil of the frying pan. But a young sturgeon, with a crafty and insouciant air about him, cried in a falsetto voice: 'What does it matter whether we have this or that fault if we are destined to be cooked in a stew? Men have poisoned our environment in making us swallow their vices, but we will return their deadly gifts to them on the day we are served up on their tables!' A great cry of Hurrah! greeted this observation . . . And I," added Gustave with a reflective air, "I began to wonder if there existed between heaven and the deepest entrails of the seas something like a sympathetic ladder on which generations of vices passed up and down."

I stared at Gustave with my mouth agape. Was he speaking truthfully? Was he mocking me? Or was his mind the victim of a hallucination? His physiognomy had not changed and the tone of his voice betrayed no irony. Only his head had fallen pensive onto his hand, which had abandoned the oar. We had arrived at the foot of Meudon. The leafy shrubs and the long water grasses were shielding our boat, when right next to us but without seeing us, a woman appeared on the shore, calling a young boy who bounded over to her playfully. The mother seemed to be consumed with sadness. It was obvious that she was bemoaning the recent loss of her husband. The young boy, with blue eyes and rosy cheeks, let his blond curls blow in the wind. This little group approached the water's edge and the child cried: "Mama! This is where we will do Tashlich." The mother smiled sadly and the child threw into the water the big pieces of bread that were stuffing his pockets. "Kiss me, Mama," said the boy, "now that I am free of sin." And the poor widow held him tenderly in her arms and covered his brow with kisses mixed with tears. Remembering that it was at sea that a recent catastrophe had robbed her of her husband, she said in a sad voice, her hands joined together and her eyes raised to heaven, "Oh! My God, let the sacrifice of this innocent angel calm the fury of the abyss and may it claim no new victim!"

The unfortunate woman wandered away stifling her sobs on the pink lips of her child while Gustave, whose face was illuminated as with a celestial flash, shook my hand with emotion while saying to me in a broken voice, "Yes, there is at the root of every religious custom something holy that only touches the heart when one can understand it." And, bounding onto the bank, he left me as if he needed to be alone with the new thoughts that were stirring him. I heard him murmur to himself: "Chateaubriand was right, *religion is the only power before which one can bow down without disgrace!*"[11]

---

11. François-René de Chateaubriand, *The Congress of Verona*, vol. 2 (London: Richard Bentley, 1838), 424.

Sara Hirsch Guggenheim, "Aurelie Werner" (1863–64)

Translated from the German by Jonathan M. Hess

Sara Hirsch Guggenheim was the eldest daughter of Rabbi Samson Raphael Hirsch, the Frankfurt am Main rabbi who was the towering figure of the modern orthodox movement in the nineteenth century. Unlike her famous father, Guggenheim, the wife of an orthodox rabbi in Moravia, enjoyed no name recognition whatsoever in the nineteenth-century Jewish world. Indeed, like many women writers of her day, she published her work anonymously. When the burgeoning German-language orthodox press began to disseminate large amounts of Jewish fiction in the early 1860s, it was Hirsch's *Jeschurun: Ein Monatsblatt zur Förderung jüdischen Geistes und jüdischen Lebens in Haus, Gemeinde, und Schule* (Jeshurun: A Monthly Journal for the Promotion of Jewish Spirit and Jewish Life in the Home, Congregation, and School) that led the way. As soon as her father committed himself to publishing specifically orthodox forms of literature in serialized form, Guggenheim quickly came out of the woodwork and published prolifically. By the late 1860s, the fiction that she published under the pseudonym "S." often took up a quarter of the entire year's pages of *Jeschurun*. Once *Jeschurun* was superseded by Rabbi Marcus Lehmann's long-running newspaper *Der Israelit: Ein Centralorgan für das orthodoxe Judenthum* (The Israelite: A Central Organ for Orthodox Judaism, 1860–1938), Guggenheim published her work regularly there as well, typically using the pen name Friedrich Rott.

Guggenheim delivered an entire generation of readers Dickensian melodrama with a distinctly orthodox twist, publishing serialized novels, novellas, and short stories that offered multigenerational family sagas charting the struggles of pious Jewish men and women to square away their commitments to orthodox Judaism with the demands of modern life. "Aurelie Werner," originally published in four installments in *Jeschurun* in 1863–1864 under the title "Aus der Gegenwart II: Novelle von S." (A Novella of Contemporary Times II, by S.), was Guggenheim's second major piece of fiction about the contemporary Jewish world. Guggenheim here shows her deep familiarity with eighteenth- and nineteenth-century European literature, primarily the traditions of the bourgeois tragedy, the sentimental novel, and the romance novel, reworking these genres to create a novella about a young Jewish woman who finds her way in the world.

The four chapters of this novella as it is published here correspond with the four installments of "Aurelie Werner" in Hirsch's monthly journal. The town of "B——," where Aurelie Werner first meets Count H—— in the novella, likely refers to the upscale Austrian spa town Baden near Vienna. Baden's location just seventeen miles from Vienna (which the narrator refers to as V——) encouraged many members of the Austrian nobility to build summer palaces there.

I.

Who does not know the charming town of B—— with its neat Swiss country cottages and its magnificent mansions and parks? Adorned with the most magnificent splendor of nature and art, it lies in a wonderfully graceful mountain region. Set in a valley surrounded by mountains covered with carefully cultivated farmland and dense woodlands, B—— itself seems like an immense park. Ever since iron rails have enveloped the world and snorting steam engines travel around with maddening speed, B—— has become so close to the city that it practically seems to be part of it. Many businessmen whose families spend the summer months in this popular resort town work in the city during the day and take the last train to return to their families in B——. Others manage at least to spend Sundays and holidays together with their families.

It was a carefree evening in June, and the cool evening air had driven out the mugginess of the day and lured everyone into the beautiful outdoors. The innkeepers were busy looking after the guests streaming into their establishments. Up at the chalet it was also a busy night, and almost all the tables on the patio in front of this pretty little lodge were taken. One party in particular commanded the attention of everyone there. This group consisted of a lady and a gentleman, both advanced in years, sitting across from three conspicuously beautiful girls. At first glance it was impossible to tell which girl was the most beautiful, but on closer examination it was without a doubt the middle one. Her features bore the imprint of a truly classical beauty. Her tender, translucent complexion and her big blue eyes were befitting of a blond. The hair that streamed forth in rich locks out from under her round straw hat, however, was the most brilliant black. Whenever this towering, Juno-like figure sat up straight, it became easy to excuse the mother for giving her the nickname "my princess." The young girl, however, seemed unconcerned with her own beauty. She had no idea that she was the object of everyone's gaze as she sat there unselfconsciously, chatting with her girlfriends.

"Isn't this a wonderful place to go, Amalie?" she turned to one of the girls, "and don't you find it remarkable that my mother always wants to come here on her daily promenades?"

"It is nice here, to be sure, but where is there in B—— that's not nice? I don't find the chalet particularly appealing, I must say."

"There seem to be any number of people who don't share your view," Aurelie responded. "Many people, I've noticed, come to the chalet on a daily basis."

"Really? Well, there might be all sorts of reasons for that," Amalie replied, with a peculiar and playful smile. The old gentleman across from her seemed to respond to her smile with displeasure. "You are right, indeed, Miss Amalie, I don't particularly like it here either."

"Really, you don't, father?" Aurelie exclaimed, jumping up. "But you haven't even seen the most beautiful thing here. Come, let me show it to you." And without waiting for his reply, she took her father's arm and led him to a secluded area off to the side. She showed him a pool, in the middle of which a sphinx was shooting jets of water that went high up in the air before rippling back down. "Now, dear father, isn't it wonderful here? Look at the reflections of the trees in the water, with Venus peeking through. And the moon is already out, bobbing up and down in the pool."

"That's enough," the father exclaimed, "this is getting too romantic for me. You know, of course, that I have no feeling for natural beauty."

"You're doing yourself a disservice, father, you . . ."

"Miss, won't you allow me to give you these flowers? I believe you've dropped them," said a gentle male voice. Aurelie swiftly turned around. A young man who appeared to be of noble status stood in front of her, presenting her with the bouquet she had lost. He had had been sitting at the table next to her. Aurelie swiftly bowed down in gratitude, yet her cheeks turned a deep red when she noticed the passion with which his glance met her own. The young man politely excused himself. The old man grew even more uncomfortable. "My dear child, it's time for us to make our way back home. Your mother and girlfriends are all ready to go." He gave the elderly lady his arm. The young girls went ahead and soon were deep in lively conversation. The parents followed in silence. "What was Count H—— saying to our daughter, Werner?" his wife finally began.

"I don't think he actually said anything," Werner responded, annoyed. "I believe she lost her flowers, and he found them. But how do you know his name?"

"Well, I've asked around after him. He's a wealthy noble gentleman. People say he's the illegitimate son of the King of ——," she continued, "and I've long since noticed that he's completely smitten with our Aurelie. I know for a fact that it's because of her that he comes here every day."

"You know this?" Werner exclaimed, on the brink of raising his voice. He stopped walking. "You're aware of this, and you still bring her here every day? For heaven's sake, what are you trying to accomplish? Are you trying to make your daughter unhappy?"

"Unhappy? Why should the fact that a noble gentleman is admiring her have to make her unhappy? And shouldn't I as her mother be pleased that a prince likes my daughter? You know that I've always called her 'my princess.'"

"To heck with your prince," Werner exclaimed, losing his temper. "I am just a simple banker, but my name commands respect in all sorts of circles. Even a king doesn't have the right to look at my daughter the way that dandy dared to!"

"But my God, Werner . . ."

"And that you can be happy about this, that you . . . When all's said and done you'd be proud to have your daughter become a prince's mistress," he added, grinding his teeth.

"Werner!" his wife exclaimed, sitting up proudly. "Do I deserve this? How can you think such things of me and your daughter?"

"I'm sorry," he answered, regaining his composure. "I went too far. But shouldn't I get agitated when a vile creature looks at my daughter with his saucy eyes, and my wife, rather than removing her from the situation, puts her in a position where this person sees her every day. Oh, heavens, if I had the blood of a fish it would boil over!"

"But how do you know that Count H—— is such a vile creature, that he . . ."

"How do I know this? . . . But enough, let's not indulge in any further conversation on this subject. I don't have much time. I have to take the first train back to the city tomorrow. And you will have to come back with me unless you can promise me—unless you can give me your most solemn vow—that you will never again go up to the chalet with Aurelie and that you will avoid taking any excursions whatsoever where you might run into the count."

"What? You expect us to spend the most beautiful time of the year in the humid, unhealthy city? How could you demand such a thing of us?"

"Did I demand this? If you promise me what I'm asking, you may remain here."

"Well, I don't really see the point . . . "

"Will you promise me, or not?"

"Of course, yes, I promise. But I ask you, Werner, how do you come to think such awful things? Don't you trust me and Aurelie?" He was about to utter an impolite response, but he controlled himself, and they continued on their way in silence.

Werner left the next morning after his wife reassured him repeatedly and in no uncertain terms that she would keep her promise as conscientiously as possible. Still, he was ill at ease and resolved that he would return to his family as soon as he could. As it turned out, he found occasion to do so earlier than expected, for promptly upon his arrival in the office he received some news that forced him to schedule a business trip that would last several weeks. It was thus a complete surprise when he walked into his family's quarters in B— the very next day, wanting to see his family one last time before his journey. Mrs. Werner was taken aback and expressed her concern that her husband had to travel in such hot weather. Werner himself did not find the heat so excessive, but his attentive wife insisted that he seemed overheated, and she asked her daughter to close the blinds so as to keep the rays of the sun from streaming into the room. As soon as her daughter left the room, she was overjoyed to be able to reassure her husband in good conscience that she had kept her word to the letter. Of course, she had only kept it to the letter. It was not her fault, after all, that Count H— had moved into the residence across from theirs the day before. Whenever Aurelie was at home, he did not budge from his window. And given that Mrs. Werner had not been bothered by the sun, she had thought it unnecessary—until now—to darken her residence with those unfriendly blinds.

It was thus with complete peace of mind that Werner left B—— that evening to set off on his long business trip the following morning. He had no idea that on that very same evening, Count H——, annoyed by the blinds that had removed the beautiful Aurelie from his sight, had arranged for one of his acquaintances to invite him to a gathering held by a family that knew Mrs. Werner well and was staying in the same house as she. It was only natural that he was soon formally introduced to Aurelie and her mother. From then on, Count H—— became Aurelie's daily companion in the garden that both families shared. Initially attracted to her physical beauty, the count soon became captivated by her lively, well-formed spirit, the enthusiasm she had for beautiful things, and her sweet demeanor. Soon he had become her declared admirer. Following the promise she had made to her husband, Mrs. Werner avoided taking any excursions with the count, but the love affair between Count H—— and the beautiful Werner girl was already the talk of the town. It would be difficult to say what Mrs. Werner was thinking in promoting this relationship so explicitly. Did she imagine she would become the count's mother-in-law? But even if she had doubted his true intentions, she knew her husband far too well to think that he would ever give his permission to a union between his daughter and a non-Jew. And it flattered her maternal vanity ever so much to see her daughter being admired by a count—by a prince, as she liked to call him. Someone of his station had access to the highest circles of society, yet he preferred Aurelie above all the others! The relationship between the young people became more and more intimate; they lived only for one another and seemed oblivious to the outside world. Count H—— counted the hours that he had to spend apart from Aurelie, and Aurelie returned his deep love with all the passion of a heart that has just been awoken. What would become of all this? This was not Aurelie's concern. For her there was neither past nor future. She knew only the present and lived only in her love.

Several weeks went by in this way when Werner, done with his business trip, was traveling home. His train had just pulled up to a station, and the conductors announced a twenty-minute break before the journey would continue. All the passengers hurried into the nearby restaurant. Werner too sat down at one of the tables there and ordered some refreshments. Not far from his table sat a group of officers caught up in a lively conversation. "So you've been in B—— for a while?" one of them turned to a nobly dressed gentleman nearby. "Well, you must tell us about our friends there. What is Baron B—— doing, and Count K——, Lieutenant J——, Count H—— and all the rest?"

"They're all well, couldn't be better," the gentleman responded, "and they would all certainly have sent you their best if they had known that I would be so fortunate as to meet you here. But apropos the last fellow you mentioned, I'm not quite sure. He seems to have forgotten the entire world of late. Indeed, he's recently become practically invisible."

"Invisible?"

"Indeed, that is, no one sees him anymore. The only way to do that would be to pay a visit to the pretty Jewish girl whom he's with from morning until night."

"Aha! An interesting liaison?"

"A very interesting one indeed. The girl is really supposed to be *admirablement belle* and just as intelligent and loveable as she is beautiful. K—— tells me that H—— is really quite crazy for her, and he's the one that introduced H—— to her at Madame von J——'s home; she and her beautiful daughter are staying in the same house as the girl."

Werner had heard enough. He was stunned, and he felt as if the room were spinning. He jumped out of his seat, and stood there, white as a ghost. The glass he was about to drink from fell out of his trembling hands onto the floor with a crash, and everyone present looked up at him. "Excuse me, sir," he spluttered to the gentleman who had just been speaking, "might you be able to tell me the name of Count H——'s belle?" "Aurelie Werner," was the answer, and everyone looked at the strange man with surprise.

The bell rang, and the passengers hurried back to the rail cars. Werner followed them mechanically back to the train. He sat leaning into a corner, his hat pressed deep into his face as he frantically stared off into the distance. "Aurelie Werner," his pale lips muttered, "Aurelie Werner," and he clenched his fists in desperation. His traveling companions noticed this strange behavior. At the next stop they all left the rail car, one by one, whispering to the conductor as they gestured at Werner, who was oblivious to all this. He was now alone, all alone with the bitter pain in his anger-filled breast. The train was forging ahead with lighting speed, yet he felt if it were not moving at all. He had to wait twenty hours more before they reached B——, twenty hours more—and then what? "The name of Count H——'s belle . . . Aurelie Werner!" And he had just this one daughter, she was his only child. Night fell, which he did not notice, and he did not sleep a wink. Day broke, but what did he care if the sun were shining? Inside he felt only night, gloomy, dark night. Time passed slowly, as if it were weighed down with lead. He did not feel the midday heat, even though the sweat was pouring down his forehead. Finally it was four o'clock in the afternoon, and several minutes later the train pulled up in B——.

Like a fanatic, Werner jumped out of the train and made a beeline to his wife's residence. Dripping in sweat and covered with dust, he soon arrived. The servants gave him a strange look, and since he was not asking them any questions, they did not dare to address him. He ran up the staircase, opened the door to the parlor, and there he saw with his own eyes what he had been imagining in his mind since yesterday. His daughter sat on the sofa, her beautiful head leaning on the count's shoulders as she listened to the burning words of love he was whispering into her ear. Mrs. Werner sat at a desk by the window, lost in a pile of fashion magazines. A loud groan escaped from his breast.

All three looked up. "Father!" exclaimed Aurelie, who ran over to her father with joy, forgetting the compromising position in which he had discovered her. Werner did not extend his arms to embrace her. Instead, his angry gaze looked right passed her at his wife, and then at the count. The count had a good sense what the father must be feeling, and his cheeks became a bright red. To be sure, the count's original intentions vis-à-vis Aurelie had been less than honorable, but over time he had grown to care for her. She had become much too dear to him that he would ever seek to obtain his pleasure through her disgrace. He felt he could not live without her, and yet there were so many barriers to a union with her, and he had still not been able to overcome the prejudices of class and nation that he had inherited from his childhood and upbringing. But seeing Aurelie's father offended in this manner prompted him to make a resolution that had been germinating in him for some time. With a completely calm voice he asked Mrs. Werner to introduce him to her husband. Stuttering, she could barely fulfill this task.

A painful silence filled the room. Werner had sat down in an armchair, and after many vain attempts to initiate a conversation, the count prepared to leave, in order, as he said, not to disturb the family reunion. When he asked Werner whether he might have a discussion with him the following day, Werner started talking. "I am at your disposal, Count, but it will have to be now, this very minute. I shall not be able to receive you tomorrow. If you please . . . " He opened a door, and they both went into the next room. "I am at your disposal, Count," Werner repeated, "but first I must ask you to listen to me. Four weeks ago I set off on a trip, and I left my daughter with a pure and spotless reputation. Now I return, and yesterday in a restaurant in K——, I heard Aurelie Werner being called Count H——'s belle, my daughter! . . . " He had become pale as a ghost, and his voice was trembling from pain and anger.

"Please accept my apologies, Mr. Werner," the count said in a serious tone of voice, "it pains me terribly to see how this has all upset you, but let's get to the heart of the issue. If you will let Aurelie Werner call herself the bride of Count H——, her reputation will be as pure and spotless as before, and you will make me the happiest of all mortal men." Werner took a deep breath. "I thank you, Count, I thank you warmly for this honorable proposal, and I ask you to forgive me for doubting the purity of your intentions. But how could I have suspected that you would be planning on the impossible?"

"The impossible? Why should it be impossible for Aurelie to become my bride?"

Werner looked at him in bewilderment. "Are you completely unaware, Count, that Aurelie is a Jewess?"

II.

"All it takes is a few drops of water, and she can become a Christian," the count responded, with a smile.

"Never," Werner exclaimed, "as much as your proposal honors me, I shall never be in a position to accept it." The count turned pale; he was not prepared for this. He knew, of course, that he would be making a sacrifice in giving Aurelie his hand in marriage. He had expected that her father would admire him for this and accept his proposal with delight. Yet these new challenges only awakened his desire to conquer them, and possessing Aurelie seemed to him more indispensable than ever before. "You haven't thought the matter through, Mr. Werner. I don't need your decision today or tomorrow, if it's inconvenient for you. Conduct inquiries into my character and into my circumstances, talk with your daughter, with your wife, take time to consider . . . "

"Count," Werner interrupted him, "there is nothing to consider. Aurelie can never become yours. Judaism is not a religion that can be accepted or washed off with a few drops of water. God created my daughter as a Jewess, and this is not something that human beings can change."

"But isn't God the one who brought our hearts together? Why should human beings be able to tear our hearts apart?" the count exclaimed with passion. A sympathetic smile crossed Werner's lips, yet he remained silent. "Mr. Werner," the count continued, "I love your daughter sincerely; I cannot live without her. Yet this doesn't seem to concern you. I know that my passion is reciprocated, that Aurelie loves me as fervently and deeply as I love her. Do you want to make your daughter unhappy?"

"God will help her," Werner responded firmly.

"Oh, such superstition, appealing to God in this manner while denying love, that which is the most divine of all! I swear to you, Mr. Werner, take back your word, and for the sake of everything that is sacred, don't play so carelessly with two people's happiness, with your daughter's happiness! Am I asking anything so terrible from you? We all believe in one God, and the God of the Jews is the same as the God of the Christians. Why does he care in which manner people pray to him?"

"'Why does he care in which manner people pray to him?' If we go this route, we'd have to conclude that he may not care if we pray to him at all. But let's not indulge in dogmatic discussions now, you're much too excited. You just told me that my daughter loves you. For the sake of my daughter's reputation and her tranquility, I thus beseech you urgently to cease your visits and never to speak to Aurelie again."

"And there is nothing that might motivate you to change this decision?"

"Nothing."

"There is also nothing that will make me change my mind. I have pledged to make Aurelie my own, and I will do this or I'm not a nobleman."

"Those are the words of a nobleman, but not of a gentleman," Werner exclaimed, "but thank God there are still laws that protect the authority of fathers and . . . "

"Regardless, Aurelie will be mine," the count interrupted him, beside himself.

"Count, do not forget that I also have the sanctity of the home on my side. Please excuse yourself immediately, and never dare again to set foot in my home."

"But I'm determined to make your daughter my wife!" the count said angrily, barging off in anger.

Werner returned to his family. In a state of supreme agitation, he paced the room with hurried steps. "Have you already dined, Werner?" his wife asked timidly.

"The day before yesterday, in W." he answered dryly.

"Go and tell the servants, Aurelie, to prepare something for your father."

"Don't bother, child, I'm full with joy." Aurelie rushed off as quickly as she could. As soon as she had closed the door, Werner abandoned his self-control and lashed out at his wife in anger. "Have you had enough, woman? Is your maternal vanity satisfied now? You have undermined the pure reputation of your daughter. You've also created a situation in which she will be unhappy now for a very long time, for she will never again see the man whom she loves."

"But she's pure and innocent, I swear to you."

"Thank heaven for that, but who will believe this? The entire world calls her Count H——'s belle." The conversation was interrupted by the servants coming in to set the table for dinner. Aurelie did not return. She had escaped to her room where, overwhelmed by all sorts of different feelings, she had thrown herself onto the sofa. She had never before seen her father like this. She had not been able to make out exactly what her father had said to the count, but she had been able to hear their conversation, and she began to become aware of her situation. She covered her face with her hands and sobbed loudly. She did not know herself how long she remained in this state, but it must have been several hours, for the sun had long since set when a quiet knocking at her door woke her out of the dull numbness into which she had fallen. A young girl from the neighborhood stood at the door and, timidly looking around, clandestinely handed her a sweet-smelling envelope. "From

Count H——," she whispered. Aurelie's cheeks glowed; and she handed the girl a piece of money. The girl thanked her by kissing her hand and then quietly set off in a hurry. As soon as she saw that she was alone, Aurelie hurried to the window to read the letter she had received by the bright moonlight. Her heat beat like a tempest and her hand trembled. She pressed it to her lips and then she finally read the following lines: "Aurelie, my love! This is the first letter that I write to you, and the first letter should be something sacred and full of bliss. But is this possible, since I see in you in tears? Is this possible after the words I heard? I can see into your room from my own. I see your sweet figure trembling with sobs. Oh, Aurelie, do not cry. Every one of your tears falls like a burning drop onto my heart, and I need to speak with you calmly. I harbored such high hopes for your father's return, for it was only with his blessing that I wanted to take you as my bride. This is why I have not told you of these plans until now. And to be received and rejected in this manner! But have courage, my dear. It would be easier to tear away cubs from a lioness than to tear me away from you. And does your father have a right to refuse me your hand? If he, in his ill-fated blindness, commands you to thrust a dagger into your heart, do you have to obey? And is it anything less than a dagger that he's handing you by tearing you away from my heart? For Aurelie, I can read in your heart—as you can in mine—that you love me as passionately and fervently as I love you. I know that you cannot live without me just as I cannot live without you. You would be committing suicide and murder at once by following your father's commands. And why all this? Why? Because you are a Jewess and I am a Christian? Oh, Aurelie, believe me, in your heart you are more a Christian than a Jewess. 'God is love,' our religion teaches, and love is your religion as well. Look around at nature. Nothing is in vain, every atom has its purpose, and could you believe that He planted the most powerful of all human feelings in our heart without a greater purpose? And do human beings have the right to destroy what the Creator has planted with his own hands? And now, beloved, listen to me, I have pleaded with your father, pleaded with him as I have never pleaded with anyone before. Alas, it has all been in vain. Yet before we resort to drastic measures, why don't you have a try with him? Perhaps his daughter's words, perhaps her tears might bend his stubborn spirit. If this fails as well, then, Aurelie, you are no longer bound by filial piety; no father has the right to ask for his child's life. You must declare to him freely and openly that you intend to make my faith your own. Do this freely and openly, for the law will protect you. As soon as the holy water has touched your locks, the priest can unite our hands at the altar. Farewell now, my beloved or, from this hour on, my bride! My little messenger girl will await your response tomorrow afternoon. Adieu once again! In faithful love, I remain yours, Ferdinand von H——."

Aurelie spent a long time staring at the letter in her hands. Dark clouds had long since deprived her of the moonlight and made the words illegible, but in her mind she read them over and over again. Thoughts and feelings that she had never been aware of surged through her breast. Everything that the count had written about their love rang true in the deepest recesses of her heart, and she cried with joy at the thought of following him to the altar. Baptism in and of itself was a simple matter for her. But could she really take this step without her father's consent? Up until now she had loved and idolized her father more than anyone else in the world. Would she be able to go against his will so flagrantly? She did agree with the count that no father had a right to ask for his child's life. She felt she could not live without her beloved—didn't this new sense of duty release her from childlike obedience? Yet her heart was still full of far too much filial love and piety. She wanted to plead with her father, to throw herself at his feet and beg for his permission. How could he possibly refuse her? She knew, of course, how dear she was to him, and he certainly did not want her to be unhappy. With this hope in her heart, she finally regained her equilibrium.

Werner had a keen sense that seeing him would be distressing for his daughter. When he heard that she was in her room, he did not ask further about her that evening.

The family reunited at breakfast. Aurelie entered the room timidly, but her father approached her in a friendly manner, kissing her on the forehead. She took his hand and pressed it to her lips. His gaze rested on her lovingly, and he finally found it possible to start up a neutral conversation. When the meal was over, however, he communicated to his wife and daughter that they would be leaving B—— that very same day, news that was heartbreaking for Aurelie. Trembling, she asked to speak to her father. "Of course, of course, dear child," he answered her in a friendly tone, "nothing could be more enjoyable than conversing with my daughter. For all too long I've had to do without this pleasure." He gave her his arm, and they went together to his room. Werner sat down in an armchair. Amelia leaned up against the backrest.

"Well, child, I thought you wanted to speak with me? What do you have on your mind?"

"My love," Aurelie whispered, blushing heavily as she bent down toward her father, letting her hair touch his. "Poor child," Werner said, wrapping his arm around her waist, "you must be in great pain. If only I could have spared you this suffering, God knows, I'd give my heart and soul to do so."

"But Ferdinand . . . "

"Believe me," her father interrupted her, "it is better for both of you not to see each other again. Just wait until we're back in the city. You'll be able to bear it easier there. Here everything reminds you of what has just happened. In several weeks I hope I'll be able to take you to Italy, and there . . . "

"So this journey is supposed to compensate me for the loss of Ferdinand's love?" Aurelie spoke with a contemptuous smile. "You can't be serious, father. What am I, a child to be bribed with sweets?"

"You're agitated, child, and you're misjudging my intentions completely. Why would I want to bribe you? I'm not asking anything of you. The trip isn't supposed to compensate you for anything. I just want to distract you. Italy would offer such rich pleasures for your sense of art and beauty, and occupying the spirit and the imagination does wonders to heal the heart."

"But I cannot live without Ferdinand, neither here nor in Italy!" Aurelie exclaimed, breaking out into sobs. With a compassionate smile Werner held her even more tightly. "You must learn, child," he spoke gently. "At the beginning it will certainly be difficult, for this is the first major misfortune you've experienced in your life. Up until now your life has been a bed of roses. But you were always my courageous little girl. You won't be frightened if life throws some thorns in your path."

"But why should we be creating thorns where there aren't any? Fortune has been smiling at me now more than ever. Ferdinand has offered me his hand in marriage. Why should I refuse?"

"Why?" Werner exclaimed, full of surprise. "You dare ask why? . . . Because he's a Christian," he added slowly, looking at her head on.

"But I wouldn't be the first Jewess to embrace Christianity," Aurelie said in a barely audible voice.

"Aurelie," her father screamed, aghast, "did I hear you right? The faith of your forefathers, you wanted to . . . "

"Yes, to swap it for my husband's faith," Aurelie interrupted him, with determination. Werner's face turned as pale as a ghost. "You do not know what you are saying. You are speaking in a fever, child, your love has made you sick."

"What did I say that was so horrible?" his daughter continued, becoming bolder and bolder. "That I want to pluck the roses when they bloom? That I'm not looking for thorns? See, father, I am young and have my finest years ahead of me. I can live in happiness. Oh, let me be happy, father! Let me live!"

Bent over in pain, Werner sat with his head resting in his hand. He hardly seemed to hear his daughter. "Live, live, you shall live," he said, barely making a sound. "For living according to the will of the supreme being, that is what life is all about."

"So you give your permission?" Aurelie cried out in joy. "I knew it, my father would never want to make his child unhappy."

Werner seemed to awaken from a dream. "No, I do not want to make you unhappy," he said firmly. "That's why I shall never permit you to disavow our sacred faith."

Aurelie turned pale, but her courage grew. "What would I be disavowing in becoming a Christian? What is the great difference between Judaism and Christianity? The Jewish catechism seems to be a copy of the Christian one, and long before my confirmation, I managed to learn from my schoolmates' Christian catechism everything high and noble that's in the Jewish one."

Werner was overwhelmed with powerful emotions, but he wanted to let his daughter finish speaking entirely.

"And our Hebrew prayers," she continued, "can these really be called prayers? I've used them in prayer, father, because that's what you wished. But is it really praying to pronounce words whose meaning one can't begin to understand? Can this be pleasing to God? The only real prayer book I have—the German one I received at confirmation—also contains prayers that resemble the Christian ones. And is the minister in the temple really saying anything distinctive?[1] So what would I be giving up in renouncing Judaism? Perhaps the Sabbath and dietary laws?" she added with a mocking smile. "My late grandmother observed these laws, and we do too. But how often do I see mother smirking while she violates a law that grandmother would have counted among the most sacred. Indeed, father, you may be the only educated person for whom these superstitious . . . "

"Stop right now!" exclaimed Werner, who could not hold back any further. "Stop this blasphemy. The fact that you're not more familiar with our sacred religion is a serious reproach for me and a heavy burden for me to bear. But this is not the time to complain. Listen to me, Aurelie, just as I have listened to you. Christianity's doctrines of humanity and morality are indeed very similar to those of Judaism. After all, Christianity derives from Judaism. Everything sublime and noble in Christianity is taken from Judaism. The psalms that they sing in church were first sung by the Jewish poets. Every awe-inspiring thought . . . "

"So what does it matter, then," Aurelie chimed in with a smile, "whether I buy these goods first-hand or second-hand?"

A painful tremor came across Werner's lips. "I asked you to listen to me, and you're interrupting me. Yet to stay with this metaphor—which I never expected to hear coming out of my daughter's mouth—you must know that goods that one buys second-hand are never as pure as those one buys first-hand. And do you know the price you have to pay when you buy these goods second-hand? It is the eternal salvation of your soul." Hearing the profound sincerity with which he spoke these final words put Aurelie in a state of shock. "You can become an apostate to Judaism, but you will always be a Jewess. You will never become a Christian."

"But how many hundreds before me have gotten baptized!"

"And they remained Jews, even after baptism."

"You're saying that it is impossible to change religions. But Judaism recognizes those who convert to Judaism as Jews."

---

1. The terms Aurelie is using here, speaking of a "minister" in a "temple," are typical for the nineteenth-century reform movement. Some reform synagogues also introduced organ music, which plays a role in the plot of this novella as well.

"There are good reasons for this. Human beings may certainly elect to take on more duties than those which God imposes on them. But they are never permitted to divest themselves of the primary obligations that God has assigned them. All pure doctrines of the divinity are borrowed from Judaism, and thus those who convert to Judaism are not seeking to divest themselves of a single one of the duties that God imposed on them. They are merely taking on the duties that are particular to Judaism. And do you honestly believe that the priest's baptismal waters have the power to divest you of those duties that God has imparted to you?"

"But God himself put love in my heart, and love is my religion!" Aurelie exclaimed fervidly.

"Love is your religion?" Werner scoffed. "So love is your religion? Why get baptized, then? Why not dedicate yourself to the cult of the goddess of love, become the count's . . . "

"I'd rather die," Aurelie exclaimed, her cheeks glowing.

"You'd rather die?" Werner repeated seriously, gently placing his hand on her shoulders, "This is what I'm hearing from my daughter. Yet you wanted to be his after baptism?"

"Yes, as his wife."

"As his wife? This will never happen, whether you are baptized or not! You are a Jewess, and there is no power on earth that can make a Jewess the wife of a Christian man. Even if this is what you are in the eyes of the world, in the eyes of your father, in the eyes of all Jews who think properly, and in the eyes of your God you would not just be just an apostate: you'd also be a fallen woman . . . "

III.

Aurelie reeled back, her knees shook, and without her father's support she would have not been able to hold herself up. She finally broke out into loud sobbing and cried long and hard. Werner did not say anything, but he held her in an embrace, his fingers gliding quietly through her lustrous locks. When she had calmed down, he silently led her to her room and, using a friendly tone of voice, suggested that she rest for a while. Aurelie threw herself onto the sofa, and Werner left her alone. Still agitated in the highest degree, she paid no attention to the time.

She was thus startled to hear quiet knocking at the door at the noon hour. "Come in," she said, and seeing the young girl who had delivered the count's letter the day before, she remembered that he had asked for a reply. She grabbed her quill and swiftly wrote the following words: "My beloved, my father is unrelenting, but I shall love you forever. Aurelie."

That very same evening the Werner family left B—— and returned to the city.

When Aurelie awoke the next morning, she felt frail and exhausted. The emotional upheaval had been too much for the tender constitution of a young girl who had only been familiar with joy and good cheer. It took her considerable effort to complete her morning routine and join her parents in the parlor. Her mother, noticing Aurelie's lackluster demeanor and pale cheeks with anxious concern, shot a reproachful gaze at Werner. He returned her glance with such bitter severity that she cast her eyes toward the floor. Aurelie herself did not dare look at her father, who was getting ready to leave for the office. When he suggested that she lie down on the sofa, a tear fell down her long dark lashes, and she felt herself unable to respond. Her father's words from yesterday had not failed to make a deep impression on her, and she felt she would not be able to do what the count was asking of her. Yet she also could not imagine renouncing him.

After Werner had left home, his wife sat down with her daughter. She had had a long discussion with her husband the day before, and he had forbidden her in no uncertain terms from receiving the count in her home in the event that he should dare search for Aurelie. Yet as soon as she had heard that Count H—— had actually asked for Aurelie's hand in marriage, she cried and frantically begged her husband not to stand so frivolously in the way of her daughter's happiness. There were no limits to the thousands and thousands of reasons and examples she gave him. Yet Werner was as resolute as he could be in his determination never to give his permission to such a union. "But what about Mendelssohn, the greatest Jewish philosopher?" she finally exclaimed. "The heroes of his age bowed down to him, as does all posterity. Didn't his daughter convert to Christianity? And you want to condemn what Mendelssohn tolerated?"

"What he tolerated?" Werner exclaimed. "Did his children get baptized during his lifetime? We know that Mendelssohn led a Jewish life.

But let's look at how he brought up his children, how he conducted his domestic and social life. Did he manage to give an example of a Jewish life that inspired his children to value Judaism the same way he did? There are remarks he once let slip in a letter to Lessing that would seem to suggest the opposite; he complained that the days of the sacred festival of Passover were 'useless days in which one wants to do nothing but be of ill humor.' In fact, Mendelssohn's thinking neither derived from Jewish sources nor dealt with Jewish ideas. That is why his responses to his Christian friends' attempts to convert him were so lackluster and weak. Read them, and you'll see why his children broke away from a tradition that their otherwise so eloquent father chose to defend with such little enthusiasm." Finally, Werner threatened that if his wife abetted Aurelie's passion in any way at all, he would remove Aurelie from her care and send her far away to live with a female relative whose character he could rely on more than that of his wife. Mrs. Werner appeared to give in to his demands. But inwardly she had firmly resolved to do everything in her power to secure her daughter's happiness. Aurelie could be a countess! The boldest dreams of her maternal vanity were on the brink of being realized, and she was supposed to let her husband's superstitious prejudices reduce them to castles in the air? She swore to make Aurelie a countess—with or without her father's permission.

Mrs. Werner took Aurelie's feverishly hot hands in her own and caressed them. "You are so pale, my dear child, yet so beautiful, so marvelously beautiful," she said, looking at her with tender amazement. "And this almost translucent pallor only accentuates the purity of your features. I believe I've never seen you as beautiful as you are today. I wonder what Count Ferdinand would say if he saw you like this." Aurelie's breast heaved with a deep sigh. "Don't sigh like this, my dear child," her mother begged her, "and don't look so sad. To be sure, this suits you well, and it makes you look charming. Languishing away like this lends your beauty an entirely new type of appeal, and Count Ferdinand would be enraptured. But it pains me to see you suffer like this. And indeed, you have no reason to suffer. Count Ferdinand has offered you his hand in marriage, and I believe you don't think it would be such a great misfortune to become Countess H——."

"But my father has rejected him, he's even forbidden him from our home."

"And don't I matter at all? I'm your mother," Mrs. Werner responded with a smile. "Have I ever denied you a wish? And you know that it's only because of me that you got to know the count. You know how much I have supported your love. How could you think that I would stop halfway? So cheer up and be happy. Everything will turn out well. Believe me, you will become Countess H— and if . . ."

"I shall never become his wife," Aurelie involuntarily repeated her father's words, tears streaming down her face. "Count H— is here," announced a servant entering the room. Aurelie shook her head and motioned to send him away. Her mother looked at her in surprise and then ordered the servant to escort the count in. "This is your doing, mother," Aurelie exclaimed. Smiling, the mother was full of pride as she said, "Count, can you believe that Aurelie was ready to turn you away?"

"Aurelie, could this be possible?"

"My father," she muttered.

"And I, your mother, don't have I have the right to receive the count in my home?"

"I was counting on this extraordinarily good nature of yours, Madame, when I resolved to cross this threshold despite your husband's insults."

"Oh, do not let yourself deterred by him. My husband will have to deal with the situation. I, for my part, don't believe that we'll be successful in conquering his superstitious aversion to a union between you, Count, and Aurelie, but if Aurelie has made up her mind . . ."

"You're making me very happy, Madame. I explained my plan to Aurelie the day before yesterday, and . . ."

"No, Ferdinand, no!" Aurelie exclaimed, crying loudly. "I shall love you forever and ever, and I shall die because I cannot be yours, but . . ." She was sobbing so much that she could not continue talking.

Surprised, Mrs. Werner and the count looked at each other. They had not expected Aurelie to have second thoughts. Acting heartbroken, the count fell down at Aurelie's feet and spoke of his love for her in the most glowing terms. With captivating eloquence, he begged her not to force him to commit suicide; he painted her a picture of the blessings of the Christian religion with the most dazzling colors imaginable; and he spoke, finally, of the good fortune that would await her as soon as she would become his. They would dedicate the first period of their marriage to traveling and seeing great works of art. After that they would go back and forth between spending time in the city traveling in the circles of the highest aristocracy and visiting his extensive country estates, where she would be a beneficent mistress to her numerous servants and a benefactress to any number of small little hamlets.

Aurelie had still not made up her mind when she heard the powerful sounds of the organ coming from the nearby cathedral. "Listen, Aurelie," the count exclaimed, full of enthusiasm, "do you hear those sacred sounds? They are meant for us. They're calling us. The priest is waiting for us. Come, follow me now and receive holy baptism. And then both of us together can receive the priest's blessing so that I can take you home as my wife."

The sounds of the organ became louder and louder, and Aurelie could not help listening to the powerful music. The organ is the most beautiful and the most powerful of all musical instruments, and its sounds exercise a force of their own over the human mind. Pope Vitalian knew the power of this instrument well when he introduced it into worship services. Organ music elevates the mind and prepares it for pious prayer, lulling the spirit into a sweet and gentle slumber in which no doubts can be awakened. The powerfully intoxicating sounds of the organ coerce the conscience into silence, making the human heart feel happy and pure.

Aurelie too felt exalted and happy. Her cheeks and eyes glowed, and her conscience too had been silenced. She had forgotten the words of her father. She heard only the organ and saw herself in her mind's eye at her beloved's side at the altar. She cried out in joy, "Ferdinand, I am yours!" and she sank into his arms. The count held the charming girl in a tight embrace and covered her face with passionate kisses.

Suddenly, however, she found herself being ripped out of his arms by a gargantuan force. "Scoundrel, my daughter is not your harlot yet!"

"Aurelie," the count exclaimed, "I shall leave, but only to make the necessary arrangements!" The count hurried off without even dignifying Werner with a glance. But the person to whom Werner had addressed his words had not heard him. Aurelie lay unconscious in her mother's arms. "Woman," Werner gnashed, "you've become a procuress for your own daughter! By God I shall prevent you from doing this. I shall take her away from you immediately and ensure that you do not see her for years." Full of anxious concern over her daughter's state, Mrs. Werner barely even heard her husband. When she could not get Aurelie even to open her eyes, she became overwhelmed with anxiety and horror. "Werner," she screamed, "this is no usual fainting spell, she's dying! My child is dying. You've murdered your own daughter!"

"I'm her murderer?" exclaimed Werner with a wild laugh. "Did I arrange for her to get to know this count? Did I set up the rendezvous with the vile creature?" Yet as soon as he gazed at his unconscious daughter, he began to share his wife's terror, and he ran off to send for a doctor.

Aurelie's illness was severe and long-lasting. Weeks went by, and the doctors continued to find little reason to be hopeful. Finally they declared a recovery impossible unless the barriers to her love were lifted as soon as possible. Mrs. Werner was beside herself seeing her daughter, her only child, the idol of her maternal vanity, fade away. Throwing herself at her husband's feet, she pleaded with him on her knees to keep her child alive. "How can you dare sacrifice your daughter like this? Do you want to bear the responsibility for her death?" But Werner remained steadfast: "To prevent less, a pagan father once thrust a dagger through his daughter's heart.[2] Should a Jewish father prefer his daughter to lead a life of disgrace?"

Count H—— implored Mrs. Werner to let him see Aurelie. Yet she too refused him decisively. "You cannot see your bride in her father's house," she wrote back to him. "My husband is reckless, and if he were to find you here, a scene might ensue that would endanger Aurelie's life."

Soon, however, the count used his influence to arrange for a court order that forbade the Jewish banker Werner in the most stringent terms possible from interfering with his daughter's conversion or her marital union with Count H——. Full of despair, Werner ran from one official agency to the next, but in vain. His daughter had reached the age of legal maturity and she was free to choose her own faith.

Aurelie was furnished with a copy of the court order, and this joyful news made her feel as if she had been born again. Her condition improved visibly, and after several days she felt strong enough for the

---

2. The reference here is to the Roman centurion Lucius Virginius, who murdered his daughter Virginia. Gotthold Ephraim Lessing's celebrated bourgeois tragedy *Emilia Galotti* (1772) invokes this same story in its concluding scenes.

doctors to permit her to be carried to the church and complete the ceremonies there.

The night before the day that had been set for the ceremonies the unhappy father could not sleep. Restlessly he walked through the desolate rooms in his house. A storm raged outside, and rain pattered on the roof. Inside, however, there was peace and quiet. Involuntarily, Werner walked toward Aurelie's room. Opening the door quietly, he stepped in and looked at his daughter sleeping gently. For weeks she had done without the boon of such rest. The happy hope of seeing her beloved and of belonging to him forever had done wonders to heal her.

Seeing the youthfully graceful countenance of his daughter caused Werner to have painful thoughts. "Oh, if she would but sleep on and on," he mumbled quietly. "If she would just sleep and never awaken again on earth! God in heaven, come take her to you before she commits this horrible act. You are all-merciful. Send your guardian angel to save her before the morning breaks." He threw himself down on the floor and prayed long and hard. Here he was, a father standing at the beside of his child—the child who had barely just recovered, the child on whom all his hopes once rested—praying to God passionately and zealously for her death.

Aurelie woke up at daybreak with a blissful smile on her lips, and as pale as her face was, it did not betray a trace of suffering. Joy had healed her completely. With tears of elation in her eyes, her mother stood at her side and could not stop praising her daughter's good fortune and her charming appearance. "Mother, don't you think that Ferdinand will think I've changed?" "Of course, he'll find you've changed," she responded, "of course, you've become infinitely more beautiful." A rosy luster spread over the cheeks that just days before had been so close to death.

Mrs. Werner did not want to miss helping her daughter get dressed. Once Aurelie was finished getting ready, she handed her mother the myrtle wreath, asking her to attach it to her locks. Her mother promptly responded, "Not yet child, not yet. It might offend the count if you were to appear with the bridal wreath in your hair while you're still a Jewess. I'll help you put it on in the cathedral, right before the wedding ceremony."

Aurelie's facial expression grew more somber. A servant announced that Count H—— was waiting outside the entrance to the house with a sedan chair. Propped up on her mother's arm, Aurelie left the room, turning her back forever on the home in which she had spent the happy years of her childhood and youth. Her gaze swept down the long corridor and landed on the half-open room of her father. She could not resist looking in as she walked by. But was the man whom she saw sunken down in the arm chair really her father? He seemed to have aged decades since she had last seen him. And why was he staring at the wall so absently? There was nothing there. But the wall had not always been bare. In the spring, before his daughter left the city with her mother to go to B——, Werner had commissioned a magnificent oil painting of Aurelie so that, even in her absence, he might have his darling in front of his eyes. Werner was staring at the place on the wall, above his desk, where he had hung the portrait. The picture itself had been removed.

Aurelie could not suppress a sigh. Werner looked up and saw his daughter in her wedding dress. He stepped toward her, lifted his arms, and Aurelie felt his horrible gaze, full of pain and anger. Aurelie felt he was cursing her and cried out in horror.

"The count awaits, child, let's not keep Ferdinand waiting any longer," Mrs. Werner whispered as she whisked her away . . .

IV.

Four years had gone by, and Count H—— was in B—— with his family. Aurelie had been able to convince him to take the same apartment in which they first made each other's acquaintance. He rarely gave in to her wishes, and he smiled mockingly at her when he granted her this one request. "What a fool," he muttered to himself after she had left, "she thinks that by remembering the first days of our love she'll be able to bring this love back. As if one could love a woman forever! Of course, I thought I would. Otherwise I never would have been so mad as to sacrifice everything in the world to marry a simple Jewish banker's daughter! Heaven knows what I was thinking. If the old Jew hadn't put up such a desperate fight, there never would have been a marriage. Even at the last minute I was about to retreat, but then he provoked me. At least she could deign to recognize what I've given up. But no, my Jewish banker's daughter only speaks of what she had to sacrifice for me, how she had to stoop down to become Countess

H——. I'd find this hilarious if it weren't about me and my situation. But the world will laugh at Aurelie for me, for she shows her jealously much too openly. 'Poor count,' Countess B—— said yesterday, acting as if she pitied me because I wasn't able to take my wife to the court ball. And it is horrible even to appear pitiful. I know, of course, that Countess B—— only said this to annoy me because she can't forgive me for not marrying her ugly, pockmarked daughter, and to be honest, it might have been more prudent to have picked her. The B—— family is among the eldest in the empire, and women's faces are a curious thing. As each day goes by, the beautiful ones appear increasingly common, insipid, and boring. In downright ugly faces, on the other hand, we often discover certain charms over time, and after a while we no longer see the ugliness. My little Pauline is not half as beautiful as Aurelie. But for now I'd prefer her a thousand times over. Aurelie is still beautiful—one has to concede her this—but she's also awfully boring. And such monstrous sentimentality! I can't spend more than a quarter hour with her without being driven away!"

Aurelie sat alone in the gazebo where four years earlier her beloved had sworn the most passionate vows to her. Every tree, every shrub reawakened her longing for the happiness she had lost. She sat there reflecting blearily in her mind's eye on the past four years. Oh, how happy she had been at the count's side during the first years, when he seemed to be concerned only with her happiness. Yet even during this period of blissful delight, she was often haunted by the vision of her father as she had last seen him, and in her dreams she would hear him pronounce a curse on her. She would wake up full of fear, causing the count to inquire with tender concern what had frightened her so. When she would tell him, her lips trembling with fear, he would respond with restrained anger rather than caring sympathy. The arrogant count found his pride rankled by the fact that the Countess H—— should care about a Jewish banker's curse!

The relationship between the lovers had already lost much of its intimacy when the couple was blessed with a thriving son. This event reawakened the count's feelings of tenderness for the mother of his child, and once again several months of pure and unadulterated happiness went by. But then Aurelie caught a cold at a masquerade ball and had to spend a great deal of time confined to her room. She thus had to forsake for some time all the distractions and pleasures that had been the couple's main activities. Given that her illness was not serious, the count saw no reason not to go out in society himself, and he soon discovered the allures of going out alone. Unhampered, he could now travel in circles that for the sake of propriety he had had to avoid while in the company of the woman he called his wife. He also had access to many of the houses of the very highest nobility, people who had refused outright to receive the Jewish banker's daughter into their homes but who now greeted the likeable young aristocrat with the utmost politeness. As many pleasantries as the latter offered him, he found himself attracted far more to the former.

Ravenously, he enjoyed the freedom that Aurelie's absence afforded him. He threw himself into the maelstrom of the wildest pleasures and started up an affair with a beautiful ballerina. This relationship became more and more passionate as each day went by, sinking deeper and deeper into debauchery of the most wanton type.

When Aurelie recovered and was ready to partake of the pleasures of the world again, the count made up all sorts of excuses either to keep her at home or to leave her alone at social gatherings. Aurelie keenly perceived this change in their lifestyle, and it gave her great pain. But this was just the beginning. Soon, entire days went by when she would not even see the count, and it was only a matter of time before she learned about his relationship with the dancer. When she first got wind of the count's infidelity, she erupted like an enraged lioness. She had sacrificed so much for this man. He was the reason she had brought her father's curse on herself. She burst into his room and found him staring at the dancer's picture. They couple soon entered into a dreadful fight in which they each harkened back to the sacrifices they had each made for the other. To be sure, they both had made many sacrifices, for they had loved each other passionately. But it had not been true love, but merely a form of selfishness: they made sacrifices in order to be happy, not to make each other happy.

Once the count had been found out, maintaining appearances for the sake of propriety came to an end. He freely and openly gave in to his debauchery. The dancer gave way to another lover, and then to another, and he paid no consideration at all to his child or his mother.

Aurelie found herself completely alone in her grandiose rooms, her breast full of the pain and desperation of an abandoned woman. She had lost touch with all her earlier friends, whether because of the count's pride or her own, and she only had acquaintances in the circles in which she now traveled. She had not made any real friends. And when she saw the count's indifference toward his own child, she remembered all the love that her father always showed her. How had she repaid all this? Her heart was full of bitterest remorse. And the more she felt neglected, the more she heard the words of her father: "There is no power on the earth that can make a Jewess the wife of a Christian man."

"And I'm thus no different than those vile creatures that stole him away from me," she would then cry out, "and I have no right to complain." Full of despair, she would throw herself onto the sumptuous divan and find comfort only in her tears.

The one person who could have kept her company was her mother, for immediately following his daughter's baptism Werner had separated from his wife. Her mother would have loved to have spent time with her daughter the countess. After the wedding, however, the courtesies that the count had shown Mrs. Werner came to an abrupt halt, and he began treating her with condescension and arrogance. Mrs. Werner was hurt deeply by this, and as a result, she seldom visited her daughter in her palace. But her daughter hardly missed her, and she would have been the last person to whom she would have turned now for consolation. She recognized the difference between the tenderness of her mother and that of her father much too late.

As it turned out, Mrs. Werner was also in B—— at the time, and one morning she came to pay her daughter a visit. "Good morning, Countess," she exclaimed with a smile. Aurelie slowly rose to greet her mother, who easily recognized that her daughter had been crying. "Child, child, your eternal mourning and crying will sap away at your beauty," she warned, shaking her head. "Oh, if I only had never possessed this unfortunate beauty which has stolen everything from me," Aurelie sighed.

Her mother looked at her in wonder. "Your beauty stole everything from you? Wasn't it your beauty that made you a countess?"

"And that's precisely what has made me so unhappy, being a countess!"

"A countess cannot be unhappy," her mother smiled.

Just then the count came in. "Good morning, Aurelie," he called out happily to her, "we've not seen each other for so long, my dear. But

I'm coming now to tell you that we won't be seeing each other again for quite some time. I've got to take the next train to V——. If letters should come for me here, won't you be so kind as to forward them to me?" Aurelie responded merely by nodding her head. "Au revoir, ma belle," the count said, humming an aria to himself as he went off.

"Do you know," Aurelie asked her mother in a monotone, "why he has to set off for V—— so suddenly?" Her mother gave her a questioning look. "It's because his mistress, the singer Pauline H——, is going to be performing there."

"And he has the audacity to ask you to forward his mail, that's outrageous!" exclaimed Mrs. Werner.

"Oh, but a countess can't be unhappy," Aurelie responded bitterly.

"But it's your own fault that you're unhappy," her mother continued impetuously, "why do you let him get away with all this?"

"What am I supposed to do?"

"Pay him back in kind, tit for tat. Why don't you have some affairs, or at least pretend to, to make him jealous?"

"I should make Ferdinand jealous?" Aurelie exclaimed with a raucous laugh. "That would be difficult! After all, he's told me himself that I should love whomever I like. As long as I don't create a public scandal, he's fine with whatever I do." She covered her trembling, pain-stricken face with her hands and groaned loudly. "This is what he tells me, the mother of his child, his wife . . . " She could not finish. Again she was hearing those words of her father in her ears. "Oh, my father, oh, my father," she sighed.

Mrs. Werner got up, insulted. "Why are you calling out for your father? Didn't he leave me just the way Ferdinand is leaving you?"

"Mother," Aurelie exclaimed, "do not compare my noble father with the vile creature that has betrayed me."

"Then why not go to your noble father and ask him for help and consolation?" Mrs. Werner responded angrily, leaving her daughter's garden in haste.

Aurelie was once again all alone in her magnificent garden. "Consolation, help," she lamented in a barely audible voice, "Oh, I am not to be helped, there is no one who can help me. God, help me, and let me die!" She stood still, looking up to the heavens, and then suddenly she shuddered and collapsed. "Whom am I praying to, to God? Oh, he will not help me, I've offended him far too deeply, far too horribly. What was I praying for?" she continued, trembling, and a horrible fear gripped her heart. "For death, for death? No, no, I do not want to die, no, no! Life is horrible, but death would be much more ghastly. My father told me that the step I took would cost me the eternal salvation of my soul." Her face turned ashen pale, and her teeth chattered as if she were in a deep freeze. "Oh, oh!" she exclaimed, wringing her hands in unspeakable agony, "where can I turn now? Whom shall I pray to? My father has cursed me, and God has cast me off!" Her anguish grew more and more terrifying, and her despair grew more and more extreme.

In the dreadful, agitated state that she was in she did not notice that the sky was covered with dark clouds and that it was raining heavily. All at once a blazing bolt of lightning twitched through the sky, followed almost immediately by the crashing sound of thunder. For a moment, the constantly growing agonies of her conscience overpowered her, and she thought she was hearing the voice of the punitive judge of the world. She believed her time had come, and with a loud shriek of fear she collapsed.

It was in this state that she was discovered by her chamber maid, who realized she did not know where her mistress was when the weather broke out and, remembering that she had seen her in the garden, went to look for her there. Half-unconscious, Aurelie let the girl escort her back to her room. It was as if she were numb, but this numbness served her well; it allowed her to forget herself.

The servant girl helped her lie down on the sofa, and when she saw that the countess's eyes were shut, she assumed that she was asleep and crept quietly into the sitting room. Aurelie was not sleeping. On the contrary, she had regained consciousness and was contemplating her miserable state. As exhausted as she was, she could not rest. Her eyes kept opening up. Impetuously, she got up and paced the room, with hurried, staggering steps. Suddenly she noticed a small, glittering object on the floor. She mechanically bent down to pick it up, and she could not suppress a gasp of surprise. It was a small, elegantly produced medallion containing a meager little lock of silver white hair. Aurelie had worn this piece of jewelry for many years, and it was only when she became Countess H—— that she began to wear a locket with the count's picture in its place. She had lost track of it, and she did not know how it appeared so suddenly or where it had come from. She did not even think of such questions now. She just stood there and stared at it as dark, dormant memories came back to her. The hair belonged to her grandmother, and a few days before she died, her grandmother had given her this medallion and placed it around her neck. Aurelie had always worn it with childlike piety, and the longer she looked at the medallion now, the more vividly she felt transported back to her childhood. She saw herself as a small girl, barely eight years old, sitting at the feet of an old, eighty-year-old woman. But this woman was so kind and friendly; she was always cheerful, even though she was suffering physically; never once did the little girl see her leave the high armchair to which her paralysis had confined her in the eight years the girl knew her. She, Werner's mother, had died on Yom Kippur, the Day of Atonement. Aurelie remembered this day distinctly. Her grandmother had not felt worse than usual. Her father had left for the synagogue after his mother gave him her maternal blessing for the holiday. After he left, she placed her hands in blessing on her granddaughter's head. Complaining in pain that she was not able to celebrate this sacred day in the house of worship, she attempted to explain to the eagerly listening little girl the lofty and somber meaning of this, the most sacred of all days. Aurelie felt she could still hear the words of the pious old lady who had disappeared from her memory for so long. She spoke about the all-merciful nature of God, who pardons the repentant sinner, and stressed that no human being can ever sink so low that God would refuse his or her true remorse and true repentance. The more vividly these memories came back to her, the more peaceful she felt in her heart, and yet she felt her heart was throbbing louder and louder and more and more violently. "Oh," she exclaimed, "perhaps I am not yet lost, perhaps even I might return. Oh, God, if I might be permitted to call you my God once again." She lifted her hands up toward heaven, sank down on the floor, and cried for a long time.

She was at peace when she finally got up again, for she had made up her mind what to do. She called her servant girl and told her that the count should expect her in the city, as she and her child would be accompanying him to V——. She ordered the child's attendant to get herself ready to leave B—— that very same evening.

The servants shook their head, whispering among themselves that the jealous countess was now going after the count. But her commands were followed to the letter.

It was already dark when Aurelie left B——, accompanied by her child and his attendant. She traveled incognito, wearing dense veils and dark robes. Oh, how anxiously her breast heaved, full of fear and hope. She held the medallion with the white hair in her hand, almost unconsciously holding it up to her lips. "Mine, mine!" her child yelled, reaching out his hands for it. "The little one found it some time ago in the Countess's room and he's been playing with it ever since—until he lost it this morning," the attendant explained. Aurelie took off her locket with the count's picture and gave it to the little one, who was happy to play with it. She held the medallion with her grandmother's hair close to her neck.

Soon the train pulled into the city, and they got off. The servant girl was astonished to see her mistress hail a simple hackney coach rather than the usual elegant horse-drawn carriage with liveried footmen. She was equally surprised as well to hear her direct the driver to go to a hotel.

At the hotel Aurelie left her child with his attendant and then set off on her way to her father's apartment, which was just steps away.

Trembling, she rang the bell. A servant opened, and trying in vain to speak with a steadfast voice, she asked whether Mr. Werner might be at home. Her question was answered in the affirmative, and she handed a gold piece to the servant, asking him to take her to his master without announcing her first. Surprised, he obeyed, and Aurelie soon stood in front of her father's room. She was trembling so much that the servant wanted to give her a hand, but she beckoned him off. Quietly she knocked at the door, and when she heard "come in," it was only with great effort that she could open the door. But succeed she did, and for the first time in four years she stood before her father. She felt she was going to sink to the floor, so she held onto the walls. Werner, bewildered, looked at her and politely asked what she wanted. She slowly took off her veil. "Aurelie!" Werner exclaimed with an expression of the most joyful surprise. But this expression then disappeared immediately, and his face took on the color of marble, becoming cold as iron. "What brings Countess H—— to my home?" he asked harshly. "Father!"

Aurelie implored him. "I am not the father of Countess H——!" he shouted out angrily. "And am I Countess H——?" Aurelie asked quietly, trembling as she looked at the floor. "Only the wife of the count is a countess, and you were the one who told me I could never become his wife." Werner pressed his hand to his heart and sighed in pain. "Father," Aurelie begged, in a barely perceptible voice, "I have sinned, I have transgressed, but I am repentant, deeply and truly. Oh, please take me back, father, let me return to you and to my God!" She reached out her arms and edged forward one step. Werner jumped to her and held his daughter in a tight embrace. He could not manage to speak, but Aurelie felt how he pressed her to his heart as he cried out loud.

"Oh, remove the curse you pronounced on me," she asked him in a whisper. Werner shook his head. "I have never cursed you, child, how could I have? I myself feel so burdened with guilt for what happened."

"You blame yourself, father, really?"

"Who else would be to blame, other from myself? Whose fault is it other than my own that you knew so little about our sacred law? In earlier times, in the days of the ghettoes when Jews had little contact with non-Jews, it was enough for our daughters to have the example of the hostile environment we lived in. Like so many others today, I made a fateful mistake, thinking that this would be enough in our day. I failed to recognize that the environment we live in is an entirely different one, and today, unfortunately, girls have the example of their . . . " He stopped, not wanting to accuse his daughter's mother in her presence. "But tell me, child," he continued, tell me, what brought about your resolve to come back?" She handed him the medallion with his mother's hair and told him about all she had been feeling over the course of the past day.

"And am I not right now to blame myself?" Werner said, moved as he looked at the white hair. "The only teaching that you received ultimately led you back. Please forgive me, my child, forgive me, and let me show you now the path to truth. But you are not alone?"

Aurelie's cheeks became a deep red. Anxiously looking at her father with a pleading gaze, she spoke quietly, "My child is with me, and he is a Christian. Yet I cannot abandon him."

"You must not abandon him. I shall be his father and perform all the duties of a Jewish father for him. For even though his father is a

Christian, the son of a Jewess is a born Jew. Baptism cannot make even him into a Christian. Yet Aurelie, we mustn't forget that in the eyes of the world you are still the wife of the count. You've run away from him, and as soon as he gets word of this, he can summon up the authorities against you. It's thus out of the question for you to remain here. Tomorrow at daybreak we shall set out. I'll accompany you to Amsterdam where you'll both be safe. And my first order of business there will be to arrange for my young grandson to be circumcised and enter into our sacred covenant."

Full of gratitude, Aurelie pressed her father's hand to her lips.

"For this too is impossible here," he continued. "Afterward I shall have to leave you for a while, to get my affairs in order here. But soon enough I shall return. And then I shall never again have reason to leave you."

Israel Zangwill, "Transitional" (1899)

Although not religiously observant himself, Zangwill wrote repeatedly about the place of Judaism in the modern world, sometimes critiquing the blind superstitions of eastern European orthodoxy and sometimes eulogizing the unique spiritual intensity of traditional Judaism and the racial bond that united Jews throughout the diaspora. He was not a supporter of reform Judaism but his thought often moved toward a notion of universalism grounded in Jewish ethics. In "Anglicization," in Section 3 of this volume, a Jewish character experiences a moment of spiritual elevation in a cathedral, opening her mind to the common ground between Jewish and Christian worshippers. In contrast, in his most famous play, *The Melting Pot* (1908), Zangwill was to propose American national identity as a kind of universal faith beyond the particularisms of ethnicity and religion.

In an article for the intellectual journal the *Jewish Quarterly Review*, in 1889, Zangwill described English Judaism as "transitional," and the possible future paths it might take furnished the subject of much of his fiction. His story "Transitional" was first published in *Harper's New Monthly Magazine* in 1899 and reprinted in the same year in Zangwill's collection *"They That Walk in Darkness": Ghetto Tragedies*, reissued and expanded from its 1893 first edition. The volume's title daringly utilizes a phrase conventionally applied by Christians to Jews, referring to their refusal to acknowledge the new religion of Christ. Rather than dismissing this idea as simply anti-Judaic, however, Zangwill explores the various ways in which an unquestioning attachment to traditional faith shapes modern Jewish lives.

Zangwill was writing in the context of a long tradition of apologia in Anglo-Jewish writing, in which Jewish writers, like Grace Aguilar, had felt obliged to refute charges that Judaism was unspiritual and legalistic. By the late nineteenth century, Judaism was also often represented in the language of ethnography as a primitive, tribal religion. "Transitional," however, deploys a Dickensian mix of sentimental melodrama and sharp social satire to defend what Zangwill regards as highly refined Jewish ideals while critiquing the hypocrisies of nominal Jews. He does this through the figure of Schnapsie, the young idealist who argues in "Transitional" that Judaism is a religion with values as noble as those of Christianity. In this respect we can see a clear echo of Kompert's *The Peddler* (1849), in which the protagonist returns to Judaism with an altered sense of its spiritual potential. However, the story also imagines religious renewal beyond the level of the individual, looking to what Schnapsie calls the "nobler future" of Judaism itself.

I.

The day came when old Daniel Peyser could no longer withstand his wife's desire for a wider social sphere and a horizon blacker with advancing bachelors. For there were seven daughters, and not a man to the pack. Indeed, there had been only one marriage in the whole Portsmouth congregation during the last five years, and the Christian papers had had reports of the novel ceremony, with the ritual bathing of the bride and the breaking of the glass under the bridegroom's heel. To Mrs. Peyser, brought up amid the facile pairing of the Russian pale, this congestion of celibacy approached immorality.

Portsmouth with its careless soldiers and sailors might be an excellent town for pawnbroking, especially when one was not too punctiliously acceptant of the ethics of the heathen, but as a market for maidens—even with dowries and pretty faces—it was hopeless. But it was not wholly as an emporium for bachelors that London appealed. It was the natural goal of the provincial Jew, the reward of his industry. The best people had all drifted to the mighty magic city, whose fascination survived even cheap excursions to it.

Would father deny that they had now made enough to warrant the migration? No, father would not deny it. Ever since he had left Germany as a boy he had been saving money, and his surplus he had shrewdly invested in the neighbouring soil of Southsea, fast growing into a watering-place. Even allowing three thousand pounds for each daughter's dowry, he would still have a goodly estate.

Was there any social reason why they should not cut as great a dash as the Benjamins or the Rosenweilers? No, father would not deny that his girls were prettier and more polished than the daughters of these pioneers, especially when six of them crowded around the stern granite figure, arguing, imploring, cajoling, kissing.

"But I don't see why we should waste the money," he urged, with the cautious instincts of early poverty.

"Waste!" and the pretty lips made reproachful "Oh's!"

"Yes, waste!" he retorted, "In India one treads on diamonds and gold, but in London the land one treads on costs diamonds and gold."

"But are we never to have a grandson?" cried Mrs. Peyser.

The Indian item was left unquestioned, so that little Schnapsie, whose childish imagination was greatly impressed by these eventful family debates, had for years a vivid picture of picking her way with bare feet over sharp-pointed diamonds and pebbly gold. Indeed, long after she had learned to wonder at her father's naïve geography the word *India* always shone for her with barbaric splendour.

Environed by so much persistent femininity, the rugged elderly toiler was at last nagged into accepting a leisured life in London.

II.

And so the family spread its wings joyfully and migrated to the wonder-town. Only its head and tail—old Daniel and little Schnapsie—felt the least sentiment for the things left behind. Old Daniel left the dingy synagogue to whose presidency he had mounted with the fattening of his purse, and in which he bought for himself, or those he delighted to honour, the choicest privileges of ark-opening or scroll-bearing;[1] left the cronies who dropped in to play "Klabberjagd" on Sunday afternoons;[2] left the bustling lucrative Saturday nights in the shop when the heathen housewives came to redeem their Sabbath finery.

And little Schnapsie—who was only eleven, and not keen about husbands—left the twinkling tarry harbour, with its heroic hulks and modern men-of-war amid which the halfpenny steamer plied; left the great waves that smashed on the pebbly beach, and the friendly moon that threw shimmering paths across their tranquillity; left the narrow lively streets in which she had played, and the school in which she had always headed her class, and the salt wind that blew over all.

Little Schnapsie was only Schnapsie to her father. Her real name was Florence. The four younger girls all bore pagan names—Sylvia, Lily, Daisy, Florence—symbolic of the influence upon the family councils of

---

1 Opening the ark and carrying the scrolls of the Torah during the synagogue service are considered great privileges; in recognition of this the congregant so honoured is expected to make a monetary donation to the synagogue.

2. Klabberjass, a card game particularly popular among Jewish communities.

the three elder girls, grown to years of discretion and disgust with their own Leah, Rachael, and Rebecca. Between these two strata of girls—Jewish and pagan—two boys had intervened, but their stay was brief and pitiful, so that all this plethora of progeny had not provided the father with a male mourner to say the *Kaddish*.[3] But it seemed likely a grandson would not long be a-wanting, for the eldest girl was twenty-five, and all were good-looking. As if in irony, the Jewish group was blond, almost Christian, in colouring (for they took after the Teuton father), while the pagan group had characteristically Oriental traits. In little Schnapsie these Eastern charms—a whit heavy in her sisters—were repeated in a key of exquisite refinement. The thick black eyebrows and hair were soft as silk, dark dreamy eyes suffused her oval face with poetry, and her skin was like dead ivory flushing into life.

III.

The first year at Highbury, that genteel suburb in the north of London, was an enchanted ecstasy for the mother and the Jewish group of girls, taken at once to the bosom of a great German clan, and admitted to a new world of dances and dinners, of "at homes" and theatres and card parties.[4] The eldest of the pagan group, Sylvia—tyrannically kept young in the interests of her sisters—was the only one who grumbled at the change, for Lily and Daisy found sufficient gain in the prospect of replacing the elder group when it should have passed away in an odour of orange blossom.[5] The scent of that was always in the air, and Mrs. Peyser and her three hopefuls sniffed it night and day.

"No, no; Rebecca shall have him."

"Not me! I am not going to marry a man with carroty hair. Leah's the eldest; it's her turn first."

"Thank you, my dear. Don't give away what you haven't got."

Every new young man who showed the faintest signs of liking to drop in, provoked a similar semi-facetious but also semi-serious canvassing—his person, his income, and the girl to whom he should be

---

3. In orthodox tradition the Jewish memorial prayer for the dead can be recited only by male relatives.
4. An "at home" was an informal reception in a private house.
5. Traditionally worn by brides in Europe and America.

allotted supplying the sauce of every meal at which he—or his fellow—was not present.

Thus, whether in the flesh or the spirit, the Young Man—for so many of him appeared on the scene that he hovered in the air rather as a type than an individual—was a permanent guest at the Peyser table.

But all this new domestic excitement did not compensate little Schnapsie for her moonlit waters and the strange ships that came and went with their cargo of mystery.

And poor old Daniel found no cronies to appeal to him like the old, nothing in the roar of London to compensate for the Saturday night bustle of the pawnshop, no dingy little synagogue desirous of his presidential pomp. He sat inconspicuously in a handsome half-empty edifice, and knew himself a superfluous atom in a vast lonely wilderness.

He was not, indeed, an imposing figure, with his ragged graying whiskers and his boyish blue eyes. In the street he had the stoop and shuffle of the Ghetto, and forgot to hide his coarse red hands with gloves; in the house he persisted in wearing a pious skull-cap. At first his more adaptable wife and his English-bred daughters tried to fit him for decent society, and to make him feel at home during their "at homes." But he was soon relegated to the background of these brilliant social tableaux; for he was either too silent or too talkative, with old-fashioned Jewish jokes which disconcerted the smart young men, and with Hebrew quotations which they could not even understand. And sometimes there thrilled through the small-talk the trumpet-note of his nose, as he blew it into a coloured handkerchief. Gradually he was eliminated from the drawing-room altogether.

But for some years longer he reigned supreme in the dining-room—when there was no company. Old habit kept the girls at table when he intoned with noisy unction the Hebrew grace after meals; they even joined in the melodious morceaux that diversified the plain-chant. But little by little their contributions dwindled to silence. And when they had smart company to dinner, the old man himself was hushed by rows of blond and bugle eyebrows; especially after he had once or twice put young men to shame by offering them the honour of reciting the grace they did not know.

Daniel's prayer on such occasions was at length reduced to a pious mumbling, which went unobserved amid the joyous clatter of dessert, even as his pious skull-cap passed as a preventive against cold.

Last stage of all, the mumbling of his company manners passed over into the domestic circle; and this humble whispering to God became symbolic of his suppression.

IV.

"I don't think he means Rachael at all."

"Oh, how can you say so, Leah? It was me he took down to supper."

"Nonsense! it isn't either of you he's after; that's only his politeness to my sisters. Didn't he say the bouquet was for me?"

"Don't be silly, Rebecca. You know you can't have him. The eldest must take precedence."

This changed tone indicated their humbler attitude toward the Young Man as the years went by. For the first young man did not propose, either to the sisterhood *en bloc* or to a particular sister. And his example was followed by his successors. In fact, a procession of young men passed and repassed through the house, or danced with the girls at balls, without a single application for any of these many hands. And the first season passed into the second, and the second into the third, with tantalising mirages of marriage. Balls, dances, dinners, a universe of nebulous matrimonial matter on the whirl, but never the shot-off star of an engagement! Mrs. Peyser's hair began to whiten faster. She even surreptitiously called in the Shadchan,[6] or rather surrendered to his solicitations.

"Pooh! Not find any one suitable?" he declared, rubbing his hands. "I have hundreds of young men on my books, just your sort, real gentlemen."

At first the girls refused to consider applications from such a source. It was not done in their set, they said.

Mrs. Peyser snorted sceptically. "Oh, indeed! and pray how did those Rosenweiler girls find husbands?"

"Oh, yes, the Rosenweilers!" They shrugged their shoulders; they knew they had not that disadvantage of hideousness.

---

6. Professional marriage agent.

Nevertheless they lent an ear to the agent's suggestions as filtered through the mother, though under pretence of deriding them.

But the day came when even that pretence was dropped, and with broken spirit they waited eagerly for each new possibility. And with the passing of the years the Young Man aged. He grew balder, less gentlemanly, poorer.

Once indeed, he turned up as a handsome and wealthy Christian, but this time it was he that was rejected in a unanimous sisterly shudder. Five slow years wore by, then of a sudden the luck changed. A water-proof manufacturer on the sunny side of forty appeared, the long glacial epoch was broken up, and the first orange blossom ripened for the Peyser household.

It was Rebecca, the youngest of the Jewish group, who proved the pioneer to the canopy,[7] but her marriage gave a new lease of youth even to the oldest. And miraculously, mysteriously, within a few months two other girls flew off Mrs. Peyser's shoulders—a Jewish and a pagan—though Sylvia was not yet formally "out."

And though Leah, the first born, still remained unchosen, yet Sylvia's marriage to a Bayswater household had raised the family status, and provided a better field for operations. The Shadchan was frozen off.

But he returned. For despite all these auguries and auspices another arctic winter set in. No orange blossoms, only desolate lichens of fruitless flirtation.

Gradually the pagan group pushed its way into unconcealable womanhood. The problem darkened all the horizon. The Young Man grew middle-aged again. He lost all his money; he wanted old Daniel to set him up in business. Even this seemed better than a barren fine ladyhood, and Leah might have even harked back to the parental pawnshop had not another sudden epidemic of felicity married off all save little Schnapsie within eighteen months. Mrs. Peyser was knocked breathless by all these shocks. First a rich German banker, then a prosperous solicitor (for Leah), then a Cape financier—any one in himself catch enough to "gouge out the eyes" of the neighbours.

"I told you so," she said, her portly bosom swelling portlier with exultation as the sixth bride was whirled off in a rice shower from the

---

7. The Jewish marriage ceremony is conducted under a canopy.

Highbury villa, while the other five sat around in radiant matronhood. "I told you to come to London."

Daniel pressed her hand in gratitude for all the happiness she had given herself and the girls.

"If it were not for Florence," she went on wistfully.

"Ah, little Schnapsie!" sighed Daniel. Somehow he felt he would have preferred her hymeneal felicity to all these marvellous marriages. For there had grown up a strange sympathy between the poor lonely old man, now nearly seventy, and his little girl, now twenty-four. They never conversed except about commonplaces, but somehow he felt that her presence warmed the air. And she—she divined his solitude, albeit dimly; had an intuition of what life had been for him in the days before she was born: the long days behind the counter, the risings in the grey dawn to chant orisons and don phylacteries[8] ere the pawn-shop opened, the lengthy prayer and the swift supper when the shutters were at last put up—all the bare rock on which this floriage of prosperity had been sown. And long after the others had dropped kissing him good-night, she would tender her lips, partly because of the necessary domestic fiction that she was still a baby, but also because she felt instinctively that the kiss counted in his life.

Through all these years of sordid squabbles and canvassings and weary waiting, all those endless scenes of hysteria engendered by the mutual friction of all that close-packed femininity, poor Schnapsie had lived, shuddering. Sometimes a sense of the pathos of it all, of the tragedy of women's lives, swept over her. She regretted every inch she grew, it seemed to shame her celibate sisters so. She clung willingly to short skirts until she was of age, wore her long raven hair in a plait with a red ribbon.

"Well, Florence," said Leah genially, when the last outsider at Daisy's wedding had departed, "it's your turn next. You'd better hurry up."

"Thank you," said Florence coldly. "I shall take my own time; fortunately there is no one behind me."

"Humph!" said Leah, playing with her diamond rings. "It don't do to be too particular. Why don't you come round and see me sometimes?"

---

8. *Tefilin* (phylacteries) are small boxes containing parchments inscribed with writings from the Hebrew scriptures, attached to the forehead and arm during men's daily prayers.

"There are so many of you now," murmured Florence. She was not attracted by the solicitors and traders in whose society and carriages her mother lolled luxuriously, and she resented the matronly airs of her sisters. With Leah, however, she was conscious of a different and more paradoxical provocation. Leah had an incredible air of juvenility. All those unthinkable, innumerable years little Schnapsie had conceived of her eldest sister as an old maid, hopeless, senescent, despite the wonderful belt that had kept her figure dashing; but now that she was married she had become the girlish bride, kittenish, irresistible, while little Schnapsie was the old maid, the sister in peril of being passed by. And indeed she felt herself appallingly ancient, prematurely aged by her long stay at seventeen.

"Yes, you are right, Leah," she said pensively, with a touch of malice. "To-morrow I shall be twenty-four."

"What?" shrieked Leah.

"Yes," Florence said obstinately. "And oh, how glad I shall be!" She raised her arms exultingly and stretched herself, as if shooting up seven years as soon as the pressure of her sisters was removed.

"Do you hear, mother?" whispered Leah. "That fool of a Florence is going to celebrate her twenty-fourth birthday. Not the slightest consideration for *us*!"

"I didn't say I would celebrate it publicly," said Florence. "Besides," she suggested, smiling, "very soon people will forget that I am *not* the eldest."

"Then your folly will recoil on your own head," said Leah.

Little Schnapsie gave a devil-may-care shrug—a Ghetto trait that still clung to all the sisters.

"Yes," added Mrs. Peyser. "Think what it will be in ten years' time!"

"I shall be thirty-four," said Florence imperturbably. Another little smile lit up the dreamy eyes. "Then I *shall* be the eldest."

"Madness!" cried Mrs. Peyser, aloud, forgetting that her daughters' husbands were about. "God forbid I should live to see any girl of mine thirty-four!"

"Hush, mother!" said Florence quietly. "I hope you will; indeed, I am sure you will, for I shall *never* marry. So don't bother to put me on the books—I'm not on the market. Good-night."

She sought out poor Daniel, who, awed by the culture and standing of his five sons-in-law, not to speak of the guests, was hanging about the deserted supper-room, smoking cigar after cigar, much to the disgust of the caterer's men, who were waiting to spirit away the box.

Having duly kissed her father, little Schnapsie retired to bed to read Browning's love-poems. Her mother had to take a glass of champagne to restore her ruffled nerves to the appropriate ecstasy.

V.

Poor portly Mrs. Peyser was not destined to enjoy her harvest of happiness for more than a few years. But these years were an overbrimming cup, with only the bitter drop of Florence's heretical indifference to the Young Man. Environed by the six households which she had begotten, Mrs. Peyser breathed that atmosphere of ebullient babyhood which was the breath of her Jewish nostrils; babies appeared almost every other month. It was a seething well-spring of healthy life. Religious ceremonies connected with these chubby new-comers, or medical recipes for their bodily salvation, absorbed her. But her exuberant grandmotherliness usually received a check in the summer, when the babies were deported to scattered sea-shores; and thus it came to pass that the summer of her death found her still lingering in London with a bad cold, with only Daniel and little Schnapsie at hand. And before the others could be called, Mrs. Peyser passed away in peace, in the old Portsmouth bed, overlooked by the old Hebrew picture exiled from the London dining-room.

It was a curious end. She did not know she was dying, but Daniel was anxious she should not be reft into silence before she had made the immemorial proclamation of the Unity.[9] At the same time he hesitated to appall her with the grim knowledge.

He was blubbering piteously, yet striving to hide his sobs. The early days of his struggle came back, the first weeks of wedded happiness, then the long years of progressive prosperity and godly cheerfulness in Portsmouth ere she had grown fashionable and he unimportant; and a vast self-pity mingled with his pitiful sense of her excellencies—the

---

9. "Shema Yisrael," the deathbed prayer, is an avowal of the divine unity. See Chapter 1, note 8.

children she had borne him in agony, the economy of her house management, the good bargains she had driven with the clod-pated soldiers and sailors, the later splendour of her social achievement.

And little Schnapsie wept with a sense of the vanity of these dual existences to which she owed her own empty life.

Suddenly Mrs. Peyser, over whose black eyes a glaze had been stealing, let the long dark eyelashes fall over them.

"Sarah!" whispered Daniel frantically. "Say the Shemang!"

"Hear, O Israel, the Lord our God, the Lord is one," said the sensuous lips obediently.

Little Schnapsie shrugged her shoulders rebelliously. The dogma seemed so irrelevant.

Mrs. Peyser opened her eyes, and a beautiful mother-light came into them as she saw the weeping girl.

"Ah, Florrie, do not fret," she said reassuringly, in her long-lapsed Yiddish. "I will find thee a bridegroom."

Her eyes closed, and little Schnapsie shuddered with a weird image of a lover fetched from the shrouded dead.

VI.

After his Sarah had been lowered into "The House of Life,"[10] and the excitement of the tombstone recording her virtues had subsided, Daniel would have withered away in an empty world but for little Schnapsie. The two kept house together; the same big house that had reeked with so much feminine life, and about which the odours of perfumes and powders still seemed to linger. But father and daughter only met at meals. He spent hours over the morning paper, with the old quaint delusions about India and other things he read of, and he pottered about the streets, or wandered into the Beth-Hamidrash,[11] which a local fanatic had just instituted in North London, and in which, under the guidance of a Polish sage, Daniel strove to concentrate his aged wits on the ritual problems of Babylon. At long intervals he brushed his old-fashioned high hat carefully, and timidly rang the bell of one

---

10. Cemetery.
11. Institution, often attached to a synagogue, for studying rabbbinic texts.

of his daughters' mansions, and was permitted to caress a loudly remonstrating baby; but they all lived so far from him and one another in this mighty London. From Sylvia's, where there was a boy with buttons, he had always been frightened off, and when the others began to emulate her, his visits ceased altogether. As for the sisters coming to see him, all pleaded overwhelming domestic duty, and the frigidity of Florence's reception of them. "Now if you lived alone—or with one of us!" But somehow Daniel felt the latter alternative would be as desolate as the former. And though he knew some wide vague river flowed between even his present housemate's life and his own, yet he felt far more clearly the bridge of love over which their souls passed to each other.

Figure then the septuagenarian's amaze when, one fine morning, as he was shuffling about in his carpet slippers, the servant brought him word that his six daughters demanded his instantaneous presence in the drawing-room.

The shock drove out all thoughts of toilet; his heart beat quicker with a painful premonition of he knew not what. This simultaneous visit recalled funerals, weddings. He looked out of a window and saw four carriages drawn up, and that completed his sense of something elemental. He tottered into the drawing-room—grown dingy now that it had no more daughters to dispose of—and shrank before the resplendence with which their presence reinvested it. They rustled with silks, shone with gold necklaces, and impregnated the air with its ancient aroma of powders and perfumes. He felt himself dwindling before all this pungent prosperity, like some more creative Frankenstein before a congress of his own monsters.

They did not rise as he entered. The Jewish group and the pagan group were promiscuously seated—marriage had broken down all the ancient landmarks. They all looked about the same agelessness—a standstill buxom matronhood.

Daniel stood at the door, glancing from one to another. Some coughed; others fidgeted with muffs.

"Sit down, sit down, father," said Rachael kindly, though she retained the armchair,—and there was a general air of relief at her voice. But the old embarrassment returned as the silence re-established itself when Daniel had drooped into a stiff chair.

At last Leah took the word: "We have come while Florrie is at her slumming—"[12]

"At her slumming!" repeated Sylvia, with more significance, and a meaning smile spread over the six faces.

"Yes?" Daniel murmured.

"—Because we did not want her to know of our coming."

"It concerns Schnapsie?" he murmured.

"Yes, your little Schnapsie," said Daisy viciously.

"Yes; she has no time to come and see *us*," cried Rebecca. "But she has plenty of time for her—*slumming*."

"Well, she does good," he murmured apologetically.

"A fat lot of good!" sniggered Rachael.

"To herself!" corrected Lily.

"I do not understand," he muttered uneasily.

"Well—" began Lily. "You tell him, Leah; you know more about it."

"You know as much as I do."

He looked appealingly from one to the other.

"I always said the slums were dangerous places for people of our class," said Sylvia. "She doesn't even confine herself to her own people."

The faces began to lighten—evidently they felt the ice broken.

"Dangerous!" he repeated, catching at the ominous word.

"Dreadful!" in a common shudder.

He half rose. "You have bad news?" he cried.

The faces gloomed over, the heads nodded.

"About Schnapsie?" he shrieked, jumping up.

"Sit down, sit down; she's not dead," said Leah contemptuously.

He sat down.

"Well, what is it? What has happened?"

"She's engaged!" In Leah's mouth the word sounded like a death-bell.

"Engaged!" he breathed, with a glimmering foreboding of the horror.

"To a Christian!" said Daisy brutally.

He sank back, pale and trembling. A tense silence fell on the room.

---

12. Contemporary term used somewhat sneeringly of middle-class philanthropists who worked amongst the poor.

"But how? Who?" he murmured at last.

The girls recovered themselves. Now they were all speaking at once.

"Another slummer."

"He's the son of an archdeacon."

"An awful Christian crank."

"And that's your pet Schnapsie."

"If *we* had wanted Christians, we could have been married twenty years ago."

"It's a terrible disgrace for us."

"She doesn't consider us in the least."

"She'll be miserable, anyhow. When they quarrel, he'll always throw it up to her that she's a Jewess."

"And wouldn't join our Daughters of Mercy committee—had no time."

"Wasn't going to marry—turned up her nose at all the Jewish young men!"

"But she would have told me!" he murmured hopelessly. "I don't believe it. My little Schnapsie!"

"Don't believe it?" snorted Leah. "Why, she didn't even deny it."

"Have you spoken to her, then?"

"Have we spoken to her! Why, she says Judaism is all nonsense! She will disgrace us all."

The blind racial instinct spoke through them—the twenty-five centuries of tested separateness. But Daniel felt in super-addition the conscious religious horror.

"But is she to be married in a Christian church?" he breathed.

"Oh, she isn't going to marry—yet."

His poor heart fluttered at the reprieve.

"She doesn't care a pin for *our* feelings," went on Leah. "But of course she won't marry while *you* are alive."

Lily took up the thread. "We all told her if she'd only marry a Jew, we'd all be glad to have you—in turn. But she said it wasn't that. She could have you herself; her Alfred wouldn't mind. It's the shock to your religious feelings that keeps her back. She doesn't want to hurt you."

"God bless her, my good little Schnapsie!" he murmured. His dazed brain did not grasp all the bearings, was only conscious of a vast relief.

Disgust darkened all the faces.

He groped to understand it, putting his hand over the white hairs that straggled from his skull-cap.

"But then—then it's all right."

"Yes, all right," said Leah brutally. "But for how long?"

Her meaning seized him like an icy claw upon his heart. For the first time in his life he realized the certainty of death, and simultaneously with the certainty its imminence.

"We want you to put a stop to it *now*," said Sylvia. "For our sakes make her promise that even when—You're the only one who has any influence over her."

She rose, as if to wind up the painful interview, and the others rose, too, with a multiplex rustling of silken skirts. He shook the six jewelled hands as in a dream, and promised to do his best; and as he watched the little procession of carriages roll off, it seemed to him indeed a funeral, and his own.

VII.

Ah God, that it should have come to this! Little Schnapsie could not be happy till he was dead. Well, why should he keep her waiting? What mattered the few odd years or months? He was already dead. There was his funeral going down the street.

To speak to Schnapsie he had never intended, even while he was promising it. Those years of silent life together had made real conversation impossible. The bridge on which his soul passed over to hers was a bridge over which hung a sacred silence. Under the weight of words, especially of angry parental words, it might break down for ever. And that would be worse than death.

No; little Schnapsie had her own life, and he somehow knew he had not the right to question it, even though it seemed on the verge of deadly sin. He could not have expressed it in logical speech, was not even clearly conscious of it; but his tender relation with her had educated him to a sense of her moral rightness, which now survived and subsisted with his conviction that she was hopelessly astray. No; he had not the right to interfere with her life, with her prospect of happiness in her own way. He must give up living. Little Schnapsie must be nearly thirty; the best of her youth was gone. She should be happy with this strange man.

But if he killed himself, that would bring disgrace on the family—and little Schnapsie. Perhaps, too, Alfred would not marry her. Was there no way of slipping quietly out of existence? But then suicide was another deadly sin. If only that had really been his funeral procession!

"O God, God of Israel, tell me what to do!"

VIII.

A sudden inspiration leapt to his heart. She should not have to wait for his death to be happy; he would *live* to see her happy. He would pretend that her marriage cost him no pang; indeed, would not truly the pang be swallowed up in the thought of her happiness? But *would* she be happy? *Could* she be happy with this alien? Ah, there was the chilling doubt! If a quarrel came, would not the man always throw it in her face that she was a Jewess? Well, that must be left to herself. She was old enough not to rush into misery. Through all these years he had taken her pensive brow as the seat of all wisdom, her tender eyes as the glow of all goodness, and he could not suddenly readjust himself to a contradictory conception. By the time she came in he had composed himself for his task.

"Ah, my dear," he said, with a beaming smile, "I have heard the good news."

The answering smile died out of her eyes. She looked frightened.

"It's all right, little Schnapsie," he said roguishly. "So now I shall have seven sons-in-law. And Alfred the Second, eh?"

"You have heard?"

"Yes," he said, pinching her ear. "Thinks she can keep anything from her old father, does she?"

"But do you know that he is a—a—"

"A Christian? Of course. What's the difference, as long as he's a good man, eh?" He laughed noisily.

Little Schnapsie looked more frightened than ever. Were her father's wits wandering at last?

"But I thought—"

"Thought I would want you to sacrifice yourself! No, no, my dear;

we are not in India, where women are burnt alive to please their dead husbands."

Little Schnapsie had an irrelevant vision of herself treading on diamonds and gold. She murmured, "Who told you?"

"Leah."

"Leah! But Leah is angry about it!"

"So she is. She came to me in a tantrum, but I told her whatever little Schnapsie did was right."

"Father!" With a sudden cry of belief and affection she fell on his neck and kissed him. "But isn't the darling old Jew shocked?" she said, half smiling, half weeping.

Cunning lent him clairvoyance. "How much Judaism is there in your sisters' husbands?" he said. "And without the religion, what is the use of the race?"

"Why, father, that's what I'm always preaching!" she cried, in astonishment. "Think what our Judaism was in the dear old Portsmouth days. What is the Sabbath here? A mockery. Not one of your sons-in-law closes his business. But there, when the Sabbath came in, how beautiful! Gradually it glided, glided; you heard the angel's wings. Then its shining presence was upon you, and a holy peace settled over the house."

"Yes, yes." His eyes filled with tears. He saw the row of innocent girl faces at the white Sabbath table. What had London and prosperity brought him instead?

"And then the Atonement days, when the ram's horn thrilled us with a sense of sin and judgment,[13] when we thought the heavenly scrolls were being signed and sealed. Who feels that here, father? Some of us don't even fast."

"True, true." He forgot his part. "Then you are a good Jewess still?"

She shook her head sadly. "We have outlived our destiny. Our isolation is a meaningless relic."

But she had kindled a new spark of hope.

"Can't you bring him over to us?"

"To what? To our empty synagogues?"

"Then you are going over to him?" He tried to keep his voice steady.

---

13. A ram's horn (Hebrew *shofar*) is blown in the synagogue on the Day of Atonement.

"I must; his father is an archdeacon."

"I know, I know," he said, though she might as well have said an archangel.

"But you do not believe in—in—"

"I believe in self-sacrifice; that is Christianity."

"Is it? I thought it was three Gods."

"That is not the essential."

"Thank God!" he said. Then he added hurriedly: "But will you be happy with him? Such different bringing up! You can't really feel close to him."

She laughed and blushed. "There are deeper things than one's bringing up, father."

"But if after marriage you should have a quarrel, he would always throw up to you that you are a Jewess."

"No, Alfred will never do that."

"Then make haste, little Schnapsie, or your old father won't live to see you under the canopy."

She smiled happily, believing him. "But there won't be any canopy," she said.

"Well, well, whatever it is," he laughed back, with horrid imagining that it might be a Cross.

IX.

It was agreed between them that, to avoid endless family councils, the sisters should not be told, and that the ceremony should be conducted as privately as possible. The archdeacon himself was coming up to town to perform the ceremony in the church of another of his sons in Chalk Farm. After the short honeymoon, Daniel was to come and live with the couple in Whitechapel, for they were to live in the centre of their labours. Poor Daniel tried to find some comfort in the thought that Whitechapel was a more Jewish and a homelier quarter than Highbury.[14] But the unhomely impression produced upon him by his latest son-in-law neutralized everything. All his other sons-in-law had more

---

14. Whitechapel was a working-class district in the East End of London also home to a large Jewish immigrant population.

or less awed him, but beneath the awe ran a tunnel of brotherhood. With this Alfred, however, he was conscious of a glacial current, which not all the young man's cordiality could tepefy.

"Are you sure you will be happy with him, little Schnapsie?" he asked anxiously.

"You dear worrying old thing!"

"But if after marriage you quarrel, he will always throw it up to you that you are—"

"And I'll throw it up to him that he is a Christian, and oughtn't to quarrel."

He was silenced. But his heart thanked God that his dear old wife had been spared the coming ordeal.

"This too was for good," he murmured, in the Hebrew proverb.

And so the tragic day drew nigh.

X.

One short week before, Daniel was wandering about, dazed by the near prospect. An unholy fascination drew him toward Chalk Farm,[15] to gaze on the church in which the profane union would be perpetrated. Perhaps he ought even to go inside; to get over his first horror at being in such a building, so as not to betray himself during the actual ceremony.

As he drew near the heathen edifice he saw a striped awning, carriages, a bustle of people entering, a pressing, peeping crowd. A wedding!

Ah, good! There was no doubt now he must go in; he would see what this unknown ceremony in this unknown building was like. It would be a sort of rehearsal; it would help to steel him at the tragic moment. He was passing through the central doors with some other men, but a policeman motioned them to a side door. He shuffled timidly within.

Full as the church was, the chill stone spaces struck cold to his heart; all the vast alien life they typified froze his soul. The dread word *Meshumad*—apostate—seemed echoing and re-echoing from the cold pillars. He perceived his companions had bared their heads, and he hastily snatched off his rusty beaver. The unaccustomed sensation in his scalp completed his sense of unholiness.

15. A north London suburb.

Nothing seemed going on yet, but as he slipped into a seat in the aisle he became aware of an organ playing joyous preludes, almost jiggish. For a moment he wondered dully what there was to be gay about, and his eyes filled with bitter tears.

A craning forward in the nondescript congregation made the old man peer forward.

He saw, at the far end of the church, a sort of platform upon which four men, in strange, flowing robes, stood under a cross. He hid his eyes from the sight of the symbol that had overshadowed his ancestors' lives. When he opened his eyes again the men were kneeling. Would *he* have to kneel, he wondered? Would his old joints have to assume that pagan posture? Presently four bridesmaids, shielded by great glowing bouquets, appeared on the platform, and descending, passed with measured theatric pace down the farther avenue, too remote for his clear vision. His neighbours stood up to stare at them, and he rose, too. And throughout the organ bubbled out its playful cadenzas.

A stir and a buzz swept through the church. A procession began to file in. At its head was a pale, severe young man, supported by a cheerful young man. Other young men followed; then the bridesmaids reappeared. And finally—target of every glance—there passed a glory of white veil supported by an old military-looking man in a satin waistcoat.

Ah, that would be he and Schnapsie, then. Up that long avenue, beneath all these curious Christian eyes, he, Daniel Peyser, would have to walk. He tried to rehearse it mentally now, so that he might not shame her; he paced pompously and stiffly, with beautiful Schnapsie on his arm, a glory of white veil.

He saw himself slowly reaching the platform, under the chilling cross; then everything swam before him, and he sank shuddering into his seat. His little Schnapsie! She was being sucked up into all this hateful heathendom, to the seductive music of satanic orchestras.

He sat in a strange daze, vaguely conscious that the organ had ceased, and that some preacher's recitative had begun instead. When he looked up again, the bridal party before the altar loomed vague, as through a mist. He passed his hand over his clouded brow. Of a sudden a sentence of the recitative pierced sharply to his brain:—

"Therefore if any man can show any just cause why they may not lawfully be joined together, let him now speak, or else hereafter forever hold his peace."

O God of Israel! Then it was the last chance! He sprang to his feet, and shouted in agony: "No, no, she must not marry him! She must not!"

All heads turned toward the shabby old man. An electric shiver ran through the church. The bride paled; a bridesmaid shrieked; the minister, taken aback, stood silent. A white-gloved usher hurried up.

"Do you forbid the banns?"[16] called the minister.

The old man's mind awoke, and groped mistily.

"Come, what have you to say?" snapped the usher.

"I—I—nothing," he murmured in awed confusion.

"He is drunk," said the usher. "Out with you, my man." He hustled Daniel toward the side door, and let it swing behind him.

But Daniel shrank from facing the cordon of spectators outside. He hung miserably about the vestibule till the Wedding March swelled in ironic triumph, and the human outpour swept him into the street.

XI.

His abstracted look, his ragged talk, troubled Schnapsie at the evening meal, but she could not elicit that anything had happened.

In the evening paper, her eye, avid of marriage items, paused on a big-headed paragraph.

"I FORBID THE BANNS!"
STRANGE SCENE AT A CHALK FARM CHURCH.

When she had finished the paragraph and read another, the first began to come back to her, shadowed with a strange suspicion. Why, this was the very church—? A Jewish-looking old man—! Great heavens! Then all this had been mere pose, self-sacrifice. And his wits were straying under the too heavy burden! Only blind craving for her own happiness could have made her believe that the mental habits of seventy years could be broken off.

---

16. The "banns": a public announcement in a parish church of an intended marriage. Forbidding the banns is raising an objection to the intended marriage (e.g., because of suspected bigamy).

"Well, father," she said brightly, "you will be losing me very soon now."

His lips quivered into a pathetic smile.

"I am very glad." He paused, struggling with himself. "If you are sure you will be happy!"

"But haven't we talked that over enough, father?"

"Yes—but you know—if a quarrel arose, he would always throw it up—that—"

"Nonsense, nonsense," she laughed. But the repetition of the old thought struck her poignantly as a sign of maundering wits.

"And you are sure you will get along together?"

"Quite sure."

"Then I am glad." He drew her to him, and kissed her.

She broke down and wept under the conviction of his lying. He became the comforter in his turn.

"Don't cry, little Schnapsie, don't cry. I didn't mean to frighten you. Alfred is a good man, and I am sure, even if you quarrel, he will never throw it—" The mumbling passed into a kiss on her wet cheek.

XII.

That night, after a long passionate vigil in her bedroom, little Schnapsie wrote a letter:—

"DEAREST ALFRED,—This will be as painful for you to read as for me to write. I find at the eleventh hour I cannot marry you. I owe it to you to state my reason. As you know, I did not consent to our love being crowned by union till my father had given his consent. I now find that this consent was not the free outcome of my father's soul, that it was only to promote my happiness. Try to imagine what it means for an old man of seventy-odd years to wrench himself away from all his life-long prejudices, and you will realise what he has been trying to do for me. But the wrench was beyond his strength. He is breaking his heart over it, and, I fear, even wandering in his mind.

"You will say, let us again consent to wait for a contingency which I am not cold-blooded enough to set down more openly. But I do not think it is fair to you to let you risk your happiness further by keeping it entangled with mine. A new current of thought has been set going in my mind. If a religion that I thought all formalism is capable of producing such types of abnegation as my dear father, then it must, too, somewhere or other, hold in solution all those ennobling ingredients, all those stimuli to self-sacrifice, which the world calls Christian. Perhaps I have always misunderstood. We were so badly taught. Perhaps the prosaic epoch of Judaism into which I was born is only transitional, perhaps it only belongs to the middle classes, for I know I felt more of its poetry in my childhood; perhaps the future will develop (or recultivate) its diviner sides and lay more stress upon the life beautiful, and thus all this blind instinct of isolation may prove only the conservation of the race for its nobler future, when it may still become, in very truth, a witness to the Highest, a chosen people in whom all the families of the earth may be blessed. I do not know; all this is very confused and chaotic to me to-night. I only know I can hold out no certain hope of the earthly fulfilment of our love. I, too, feel in transition, and I know not to what. But, dearest Alfred, shall we not be living the Christian life—the life of abnegation—more truly if we give up the hope of personal happiness? Forgive me, darling, the pain I am causing you, and thus help me to bear my own.

"Your friend till death,

FLORENCE."

It was an hour past midnight ere the letter was finished, and when it was sealed a sense of relief at remaining in the Jewish fold stole over her, though she would scarcely acknowledge it to herself, and impatiently analysed it away as hereditary. And despite it, if she slept on the letter, would it ever be posted?

But the house was sunk in darkness. She was the only creature stirring. And yet she yearned to have the thing over, irrevocable. Perhaps she might venture out herself with her latch-key. There was a letter-box at the street corner. She lit a candle and stole out on the landing, casting a monstrous shadow which frightened her. In her over-wrought mood it almost seemed an uncanny creature grinning at her. Her mother's death-bed rose suddenly before her; her mother's voice cried: "Ah,

Florrie, do not fret. I will find thee a bridegroom." Was this the bridegroom—was this the only one she would ever know?

"Father! father!" she shrieked, with sudden terror.

A door was thrown open; a figure shambled forth in carpet slippers—a dear, homely, reassuring figure—holding the coloured handkerchief which had helped to banish him from the drawing-room. His face was smeared; his eyelids under the pushed-up horn spectacles were red: he, too, had kept vigil.

"What is it? What is it, little Schnapsie?"

"Nothing. I—I—I only wanted to ask you if you would be good enough to post this letter—to-night."

"Good enough? Why, I shall enjoy a breath of air."

He took the letter and essayed a roguish laugh as his eye caught the superscription.

"Ho! ho!" He pinched her cheek. "So we mustn't let a day pass without writing to him, eh?"

She quivered under this unforeseen misconception.

"No," she echoed, with added firmness, "we mustn't let a day pass."

"But go to bed at once, little Schnapsie. You look quite pale. If you stay up so late writing him letters, you won't make him a beautiful bride."

"No," she repeated, "I won't make him a beautiful bride."

She heard the hall door close gently upon his cautious footsteps, and her eyes dimmed with divine tears as she thought of the joy that awaited his return.

Sources

Leopold Kompert, "The Peddler": "Der Dorfgeher," in *Böhmische Juden: Geschichten* (Vienna: Jasper, Hügel und Manz, 1851), 1–81.

Alexandre Weill, "Braendel": "Braendel," in *Histoires de village* (Paris: L. Hachette, 1860), 211–52.

David Schornstein, "The Tithe": "La dîme," *Les Archives Israélites* (1864, serialized).

Samuel Gordon, "Daughters of Shem: A Study in Sisters," in *Daughters of Shem and Other Stories* (London: Greenberg, 1898), 1–78.

Grace Aguilar, "The Escape: A Tale of 1755," in *Home Scenes and Heart Studies* (1852; reprint, London: Groombridge and Sons, 1886), 162–85.

Ludwig Philippson, "The Three Brothers": "Die drei Brüder," *Jüdisches Volksblatt* (1854, serialized).

David Schornstein, "The Marranos: A Spanish Chronicle": "Les Marannos: Chronique espagnole," *La Vérité Israélite* (1861, serialized).

Eugénie Foa, "Rachel; or, The Inheritance": "Rachel; ou, L'héritage," in *Rachel* (Paris: Henri Dupuy, 1833), vii–xxxii.

Ben-Lévi, "The March 17th Decree": "Le décret du 17 mars," *Les Archives Israélites* (1841), 79–88.

Salomon Formstecher, "The Stolen Son": "Der geraubte Sohn: Ein Sittenbild der Gegenwart," *Jüdisches Volksblatt* (1859, serialized).

Amy Levy, "Cohen of Trinity," *Gentleman's Magazine* 266 (May 1889), 412–23.

Israel Zangwill, "Anglicization," in *Ghetto Comedies* (1907; reprint, London: Globe, 1925), 49–86.

Ben Baruch, "The Preacher and the Bellows": "Le prédicateur et le soufflet," *L'Univers Israélite* (1844), 198–208.

Ben-Lévi, "The Fish and the Breadcrumbs": "Les poissons et les miettes de pain," *Les Archives Israélites* (1846), 630–38.

Sara Hirsch Guggenheim, "Aurelie Werner": "Aus der Gegenwart II: Novelle von S.," *Jeschurun: Ein Monatsblatt zur Förderung jüdischen Geistes und jüdischen Lebens in Haus, Gemeinde und Schule* (1863–64, serialized).

Israel Zangwill, "Transitional," in *"They That Walk in Darkness": Ghetto Tragedies* (1899; reprint, London: Globe, 1925), 29–54.

Suggestions for Further Reading

Aschheim, Steven E. *Brothers and Strangers: The East European Jew in German and German Jewish Consciousness, 1800–1923*. Madison: University of Wisconsin Press, 1982.
Baumgarten, Jean. *Introduction to Old Yiddish Literature*. Ed. and trans. Jerold C. Frakes. Oxford: Oxford University Press, 2005.
Berkovitz, Jay R. *Rites and Passages: The Beginnings of Modern Jewish Culture in France, 1650–1860*. Philadelphia: University of Pennsylvania Press, 2004.
Black, Eugene C. *The Social Politics of Anglo-Jewry, 1880–1920*. Oxford: Blackwell, 1988.
Borovaya, Olga. *Modern Ladino Culture: Press, Belles Lettres, and Theater in the Late Ottoman Empire*. Bloomington: Indiana University Press, 2011.
Boyarin, Daniel. "Placing Reading: Ancient Israel and Medieval Europe." In *The Ethnography of Reading*, ed. Jonathan Boyarin, 10–37. Berkeley: University of California Press, 1993.
Cheyette, Bryan. "'From Apology to Revolt': Benjamin Farjeon, Amy Levy, and the Post-Emancipation Anglo-Jewish Novel, 1880–1900." *Transactions of the Jewish Historical Society of England* 24 (1982–86): 253–65.
———, "The Other Self: Anglo-Jewish Fiction and the Representation of Jews in England, 1875–1905." In *The Making of Modern Anglo-Jewry*, ed. David Cesarani, 97–111. Oxford: Blackwell, 1990.
Cohen, Richard I. *Jewish Icons: Art and Society in Modern Europe*. Berkeley: University of California Press, 1998.
Donovan, Josephine. *European Local-Color Literature: National Tales, Dorfgeschichten, Romans Champêtres*. New York: Continuum, 2010.
Endelman, Todd M., *The Jews of Britain 1656 to 2000*. Berkeley: University of California Press, 2002.
Feldman, David. *Englishmen and Jews: Social Relations and Political Culture, 1840–1914*. New Haven, CT: Yale University Press, 1994.
Galchinsky, Michael. *The Origins of the Modern Jewish Woman Writer: Romance and Reform in Victorian England*. Detroit: Wayne State University Press, 1996.
Hess, Jonathan M. *Middlebrow Literature and the Making of German-Jewish Identity*. Stanford, CA: Stanford University Press, 2010.

Hyman, Paula E. *Gender and Assimilation in Modern Jewish History: The Roles and Representations of Women*. Seattle: University of Washington Press, 1995.

Kaplan, Marion A. *The Making of the Jewish Middle Class: Women, Family, and Identity in Imperial Germany*. New York: Oxford University Press, 1991.

Kiron, Arthur. "An Atlantic Jewish Republic of Letters?" *Jewish History* 20 (June 2006): 171–211.

Leff, Lisa Moses. *Sacred Bonds of Solidarity: The Rise of Jewish Internationalism in Nineteenth-Century France*. Stanford, CA: Stanford University Press, 2006.

Lichtenstein, Diane. *Writing Their Nations: The Tradition of Nineteenth-Century American Jewish Women Writers*. Bloomington: Indiana University Press, 1992.

Lowenstein, Stephen. "The Yiddish Written Word in Nineteenth-Century Germany." *Leo Baeck Institute Year Book* 24 (1979): 179–92.

Mendelsohn, Adam. "Tongue Ties: The Emergence of the Anglophone Diaspora in the Mid-Nineteenth Century." *American Jewish History* 93, no. 2 (2007): 177–209.

Meyer, Michael A., and Michael Brenner, eds. *German-Jewish History in Modern Times*. 4 vols. New York: Columbia University Press, 1996–98.

Miron, Dan. *A Traveler Disguised: The Rise of Modern Yiddish Fiction in the Nineteenth Century*. Syracuse, NY: Syracuse University Press, 1996.

Parush, Iris. *Reading Jewish Women: Marginality and Modernization in Nineteenth-Century Eastern European Jewish Society*. Waltham, MA: Brandeis University Press, 2004.

Quint, Alyssa. "'Yiddish Literature for the Masses'? A Reconsideration of Who Read What." *AJS Review* 29, no. 1 (2005): 61–89.

Robertson, Ritchie. *The "Jewish Question" in German Literature, 1749–1939: Emancipation and Its Discontents*. Oxford: Oxford University Press, 1999.

Rochelson, Meri-Jane. *A Jew in the Public Arena: The Career of Israel Zangwill*. Detroit: Wayne State University Press, 2008.

Rodrigue, Aron. *French Jews, Turkish Jews: The Alliance Israélite Universelle and the Politics of Jewish Schooling in Turkey, 1860–1925*. Bloomington: Indiana University Press, 1990.

Safran, Gabriella. *Rewriting the Jew: Assimilation Narratives in the Russian Empire*. Stanford, CA: Stanford University Press, 2000.

Samuels, Maurice. *Inventing the Israelite: Jewish Fiction in Nineteenth-Century France*. Stanford, CA: Stanford University Press, 2010.

Schechter, Ronald. *Obstinate Hebrews: Representations of Jews in France, 1715–1815*. Berkeley: University of California Press, 2003.

Shrayer, Maxim D. *An Anthology of Jewish-Russian Literature: Two Centuries of Dual Identity in Prose and Poetry*. 2 vols. Armonk, NY: Sharpe, 2007.

Skolnik, Jonathan. *Jewish Pasts, German Fictions: History, Memory, and Minority Culture in Germany*. Stanford, CA: Stanford University Press, 2013.

Stein, Sarah Abrevaya. *Making Jews Modern: The Yiddish and Ladino Press in the Russian and Ottoman Empires*. Bloomington: Indiana University Press, 2004.
Valman, Nadia. *The Jewess in Nineteenth-Century British Literary Culture*. Cambridge: Cambridge University Press, 2007.
Veidlinger, Jeffrey. "Reading: From Sacred Duty to Leisure Time." In *Jewish Public Culture in the Late Russian Empire*, 67–113. Bloomington: Indiana University Press, 2009.
Wirth-Nesher, Hana, ed. *What Is Jewish Literature?* Philadelphia: Jewish Publication Society, 1994.
Wisse, Ruth. *The Modern Jewish Canon: A Journey Through Language and Culture*. Chicago: University of Chicago Press, 2001.
Zatlin, Linda Gertner. *The Nineteenth-Century Anglo-Jewish Novel*. Boston: Twayne, 1981.

The authorized representative in the EU for product safety and compliance is:
Mare Nostrum Group
B.V Doelen 72
4831 GR Breda
The Netherlands

www.ingramcontent.com/pod-product-compliance
Lightning Source LLC
Chambersburg PA
CBHW030559230426
43661CB00053B/1781